MUSIC, SCHOLASTICISM AND REFORM

Manchester University Press

Manchester Medieval Studies

SERIES EDITOR   Professor S. H. Rigby

The study of medieval Europe is being transformed as old orthodoxies are challenged, new methods embraced and fresh fields of enquiry opened up. The adoption of interdisciplinary perspectives and the challenge of economic, social and cultural theory are forcing medievalists to ask new questions and to see familiar topics in a fresh light.

The aim of this series is to combine the scholarship traditionally associated with medieval studies with an awareness of more recent issues and approaches in a form accessible to the non-specialist reader.

ALREADY PUBLISHED IN THE SERIES

Reform and the papacy in the eleventh century
Kathleen G. Cushing

Picturing women in late medieval and Renaissance art
Christa Grössinger

The Vikings in England
D. M. Hadley

The politics of carnival
Christopher Humphrey

Holy motherhood
Elizabeth L'Estrange

Medieval law in context
Anthony Musson

Medieval maidens
Kim M. Phillips

Gentry culture in late medieval England
Raluca Radulescu and Alison Truelove (eds)

Chaucer in context
S. H. Rigby

The life cycle in Western Europe, c.1300–c.1500
Deborah Youngs

═══ MANCHESTER MEDIEVAL STUDIES ═══

MUSIC, SCHOLASTICISM AND REFORM
SALIAN GERMANY, 1024–1125

T. J. H. McCarthy

Manchester University Press
Manchester and New York
*distributed in the USA exclusively
by Palgrave Macmillan*

Copyright © T. J. H. McCarthy 2009

The right of T. J. H. McCarthy to be identified as the author of this work has been asserted by him in accordance with the Copyright, Designs and Patents Act 1988.

Published by Manchester University Press
Oxford Road, Manchester M13 9NR, UK
and Room 400, 175 Fifth Avenue, New York, NY 10010, USA
www.manchesteruniversitypress.co.uk

Distributed in the United States exclusively by
Palgrave, 175 Fifth Avenue, New York,
NY 10010, USA

Distributed in Canada exclusively by
UBC Press, University of British Columbia, 2029 West Mall,
Vancouver, BC, Canada V6T 1Z2

British Library Cataloguing-in-Publication Data
A catalogue record for this book is available from the British Library

Library of Congress Cataloging-in-Publication Data applied for

ISBN   978 0 7190 7889 7   *hardback*

First published 2009

18 17 16 15 14 13 12 11 10 09   10 9 8 7 6 5 4 3 2 1

Typeset
by Servis Filmsetting Limited, Stockport, Cheshire
Printed in Great Britain
by the MPG Books Group

I. S. Robinson

modernorum magister magistrorum

CONTENTS

List of maps and figures	*page* xi
List of plates	xiii
Acknowledgements	xv
Abbreviations	xvii
The ancient Greek *systema teleion* and the south-German gamut	xix

INTRODUCTION	1
1 THE SOUTH-GERMAN CIRCLE: AN HISTORICAL INTRODUCTION	11
Eleventh-century monastic reforms	11
Reform and friendship networks	15
Reichenau and the beginnings of the south-German circle	18
Bern of Reichenau	18
Herman of Reichenau	23
St Emmeram and the development of the south-German circle	31
William of Hirsau	31
Theoger of Metz	34
Aribo	37
Frutolf of Michelsberg	40
The wider south-German circle	43
The 'Wolf Anonymous'	44
Master Henry of Augsburg	45
John	47
Quaestiones in musica	50
Other theorists	52
2 ANCIENT DOCTORS AND MODERN MASTERS: THE SOUTH-GERMAN CIRCLE AT WORK	55
Classical sources for music theory	55
Boethius	56
The influence of the Carolingian theorists	60

The influence of Bern of Reichenau upon the south-German circle	62
The impact of Herman of Reichenau upon the reception of *Prologus in tonarium*	62
The interpolated version of *Prologus in tonarium*	72
The influence of Guido of Arezzo	80
Guido and Herman of Reichenau	82
Guido and the wider south-German circle	85
The transmission of ideas within the south-German circle	93
Frutolf of Michelsberg	94

3 DIALECTIC AND THE THEORY OF MUSIC ... 109
Dialectical texts in German libraries ... 110
Attitudes to dialectic in the eleventh century ... 113
The *ars logica* in eleventh-century literature ... 116
Dialectic in the south-German music treatises ... 120
The two sets of tetrachords ... 122
Tetrachords and the 'seats of the modes' ... 125
'Species' theory ... 126
Taxonomy of modes ... 130
The division of music according to Henry of Augsburg ... 132
Anonymous I and the Wolf Anonymous on the species of consonance ... 135
Dialectic in Aribo's *De musica* ... 138
Conclusion ... 145

4 PLATO, HIS INTERPRETERS AND THE SOUTH-GERMAN CIRCLE ... 147
Manuscript sources for Platonic texts in eleventh-century Germany ... 148
Timaeus in Calcidius' translation and commentary ... 148
Macrobius' *Commentarius in Somnium Scipionis* ... 150
Martianus Capella's *De nuptiis Philologiae et Mercurii* ... 151
Platonic influence in the south-German music treatises ... 152
The significance of number ... 152
Platonic metaphor and vocabulary ... 158
Aribo and Platonic language ... 162
God and *natura* ... 168
Conclusion ... 171

5 'TEXTBOOK CODICES': MUSIC THEORY MANUSCRIPTS OF THE
    ELEVENTH AND TWELFTH CENTURIES 175
    The textbook codex tradition 175
    Bernold of St Blasien: a compiler and adapter of texts 176
    Doctrinal handbooks 178
    Hartwic of St Emmeram 179
    Textbooks in the linguistic arts 181
    Music theory compilations and textbooks 182
    Kassel, Landesbibliothek und Murhardsche Bibliothek der
        Stadt Kassel, 4° Mss Math. 1 183
    Music theory textbooks 196
    Guido of Arezzo 200
    Pseudo-Odo of Cluny 203
    Bern of Reichenau 203
    Herman of Reichenau 205
    William of Hirsau 205
    Theoger of Metz 206
    Aribo 207
    Frutolf of Michelsberg 208
    The Wolf Anonymous, Master Henry of Augsburg, John
        and *Quaestiones in musica* 208
    Carolingian works 208
    Classical authors 210
    Tonaries 210
    Notated didactic verses 211
    Measurement texts 211
    Other miscellaneous texts 213
    Conclusions 214

CONCLUSION 217

Bibliography 229
Index 255

ix

MAPS AND FIGURES

Maps

1	Germany in the Salian period, 1024–1125	*page*	xx
2	Southern Germany in the late eleventh century		xxi
3	The direct and indirect spread of the Hirsau reform		14

Figures

	The ancient Greek *systema teleion* and the south-German gamut	xix
2.1	The species according to Bern of Reichenau	65
2.2	The species according to Herman of Reichenau	66
2.3	Diagram from Guido's *Regule rithmice* quoted by William of Hirsau	86
2.4	William of Hirsau's correction of Guido's error	86
3.1	The hierarchical division of the gamut	122
3.2	The tetrachords of the *graves, finales, superiores* and *excellentes*	123
3.3	The two sets of tetrachords	123
3.4	The modal properties of the tetrachords	125
3.5	The seats of the modes	126
3.6	The species of *diatessaron*	127
3.7	The species of *diapente*	128
3.8	The species of *diapason*	129
5.1	Diagram of the seventh and eighth tones from *Musica* by Theoger of Metz	188

LIST OF PLATES

1 The proportions of the gamut. Diagram from Frutolf of Michelsberg's *Breviarium de musica*. Munich, Bayerische Staatsbibliothek, Clm 14965b, fol. 9v   *page* 104
2 The proportions of the gamut. Diagram from Aribo's *De musica*. Rochester, Eastman School of Music, Sibley Music Library, ML 92/1200, fol. 28r   105
3 The division of dialectic into its species. Leipzig, Universitätsbibliothek, Cod. 1493, fol. 78v   135
4 *Figura monochordi* from William of Hirsau's *Musica*. Vienna, Österreichische Nationalbibliothek, Cod. 51, fol. 1v   163
5 The *Quadripartita figura modernorum* criticized by Aribo. Darmstadt, Universitäts- und Hochschulbibliothek, 1988, fol. 171r   163
6 Aribo's *Caprea*. Darmstadt, Universitäts- und Hochschulbibliothek, 1988, fol. 171v   166
7 *Musica* personified and seated at the monochord. Wolfenbüttel, Herzog-August Bibliothek, Gud. Lat. 334 8°, fol. 2v   172
8 Kassel, Landesbibliothek und Murhardsche Bibliothek der Stadt Kassel, 4° Mss Math. 1, fols 28v, 29r   190
9 Kassel, Landesbibliothek und Murhardsche Bibliothek der Stadt Kassel, 4° Mss Math. 1, fol. 33r   193
10 Notated didactic verses on the modes. Munich, Bayerische Staatsbibliothek, Clm 14965a, fol. 5r   212
11 Mnemonic verses from Frutolf of Michelsberg's *Breviarium de musica*. Munich, Bayerische Staatsbibliothek, Clm 14965b, fol. 22v   213

ACKNOWLEDGEMENTS

This book would not have been possible without the assistance of various institutions and people. The final stages of the research for this book were undertaken during research fellowships at Trinity College, Dublin (funded by the Irish Research Council for the Humanities and Social Sciences) and at the Pontifical Institute of Mediaeval Studies, Toronto (funded by the Andrew W. Mellon Foundation). I also wish to acknowledge the generous support of Oriel College and the History Faculty at Oxford: in this regard I am especially indebted to the interest taken in my research by the Revd Professor Ernest Nicholson, sometime Provost of Oriel and by the late Professor Rees Davies, sometime Chichele Professor of Medieval History and Fellow of All Souls, Oxford. I should like to thank the staff of those libraries in which I have been privileged to work: the library of Oriel College, the Bodleian Library, the Taylor Institute, the Radcliffe Science Library, and the History and Music Faculty libraries at Oxford; the Historisches Seminar and Musiklesesaal of the University of Freiburg im Breisgau; the manuscript departments at Bamberg, Basel, Berlin, Darmstadt, Karlsruhe, Kassel, Leiden, Leipzig, Munich, Rochester (New York), St Gallen, Vienna and Wolfenbüttel; the University libraries and the library of the Pontifical Institute in Toronto.

I owe much to the advice of some distinguished scholars: Dr Michael Bernhard (Munich), Dr John Marenbon (Cambridge), Professor Henry Mayr-Harting (Oxford), Professor Constant Mews (Monash University) and Professor Rodney Thomson (Tasmania). I should like to thank Professor S. H. Rigby for his support and helpfulness throughout this project. My friend and teacher Mr Andrew Johnstone (Trinity College, Dublin) read this book in its entirety and suggested many improvements, while Professor Carrie Beneš (New College of Florida) contributed valuable critical observations. Special thanks are due to my friends who aided my studies through their hospitality and generosity: Alexander Täumer (Frankfurt am Main), Dr Tobias Frische (Berlin), David Hughes (Leipzig), Dr Stephen Mossmann and Ben Arnold (Oxford). My friends in Dublin have also been of the greatest encouragement: Dr Kerry Houston, Dr Martin Adams, Dr Helga Robinson-Hammerstein, Revd Dr Alan

McCormack, Dr Jacco Thijssen and Sophie Ross. I wish to express my particular thanks to Dr Jean Dunbabin and Professor John Caldwell, who supervised my doctoral research in Oxford and contributed much to the ideas found in this book. Finally, I must acknowledge my debt of gratitude to Professor I. S. Robinson (Trinity College, Dublin), who has long been a source of inspiration and a generous help to my studies.

T. J. H. McCarthy,
Sarasota, Florida
in dominica prima adventus
Domini, A.S. MMVIII

LIST OF ABBREVIATIONS

The following abbreviations and short titles are used in the footnotes.

DA	*Deutsches Archiv für Erforschung des Mittelalters*
GS	M. Gerbert (ed.), *Scriptores ecclesiastici de musica sacra potissimum. Ex variis codicibus manuscriptiis collecti a M. Gerberto*, 3 vols (St Blasien, 1784)
MBDS	*Mittelalterliche Bibliothekskataloge Deutschlands und der Schweiz*, 4 vols (Munich, 1918–79)
MBÖ	*Mittelalterliche Bibliothekskataloge Österreichs*, 4 vols (Vienna, 1915–66)
MGG	L. Finscher (ed.), *Die Musik in Geschichte und Gegenwart. Allgemeine Enzyklopädie der Musik*
Personenteil	17 vols (Kassel, 1999–2007)
Sachteil	9 vols (Kassel, 1994–9)
MGH	*Monumenta Germaniae Historica*
Briefe	*Die Briefe der deutschen Kaiserzeit*
Libelli	*Libelli de lite imperatorum et pontificum*
NecG	*Necrologiae Germaniae*
Quellen	*Quellen zur Geistesgeschichte des Mittelalters*
SS	*Scriptores* (in Folio)
SSrG	*Scriptores rerum Germanicarum in usum scholarum separatim editi*
SSrG NS	*Scriptores rerum Germanicarum, Nova Series*
NA	*Neues Archiv der Geschichte für ältere deutsche Geschichtskunde*
NG	S. Sadie (ed.), *The New Grove Dictionary of Music and Musicians*, 2nd edn, 29 vols (London, 2001)
PL	J. P. Migne (ed.), *Patrologiae cursus completus. Series latina*, 221 vols (Paris, 1844–55)
RISM B	J. Smits van Waesberghe, P. Ernstbrunner, P. Fischer, C. Mass, M. Huglo, C. Meyer, N. C. Phillips, A. Rausch and C. Ruini (eds), *The Theory of Music from the Carolingian Era up to 1400: Descriptive Catalogue of Manuscripts*

	(Répertoire International des Sources Musicales, Series B 3/1–6; Duisburg and Munich, 1961–2003)
SMGBZ	*Studien und Mitteilungen zur Geschichte des Benediktinerordens und seiner Zweige*
Verfasserlexikon	K. Ruh, G. Keil, W. Schröder, B. Wachinger and F.-J. Worstbrock (eds), *Die deutsche Literatur des Mittelalters. Verfasserlexikon*, 11 vols (Berlin and New York, 1978–2004)

Biblical references are given according to the Vulgate.

THE ANCIENT GREEK *SYSTEMA TELEION* AND THE SOUTH-GERMAN GAMUT

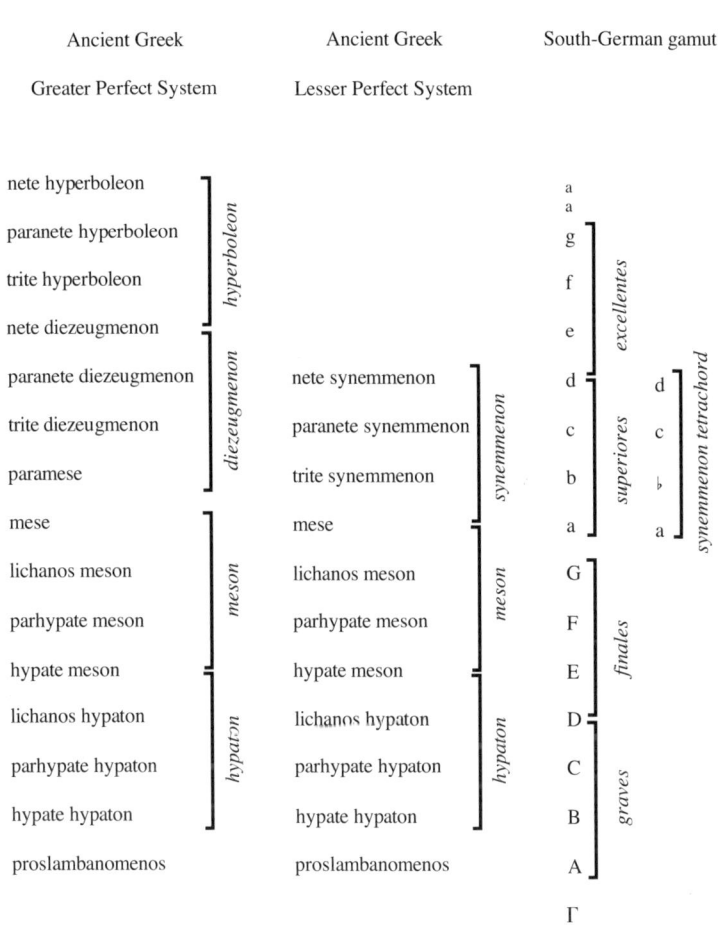

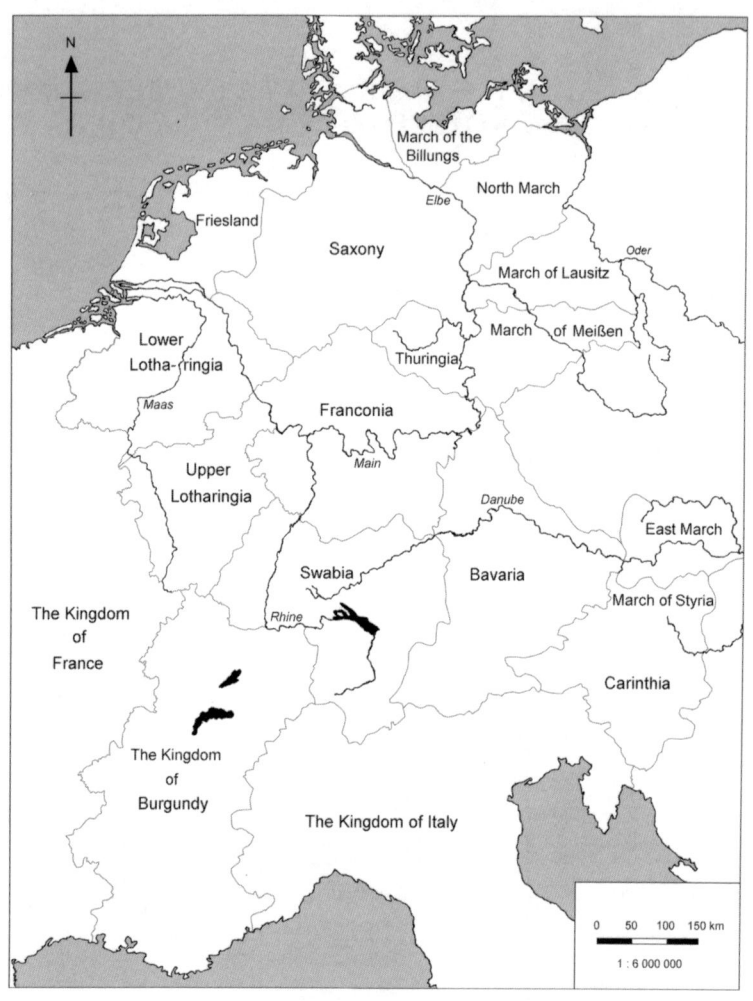

1   Germany in the Salian period, 1024–1125

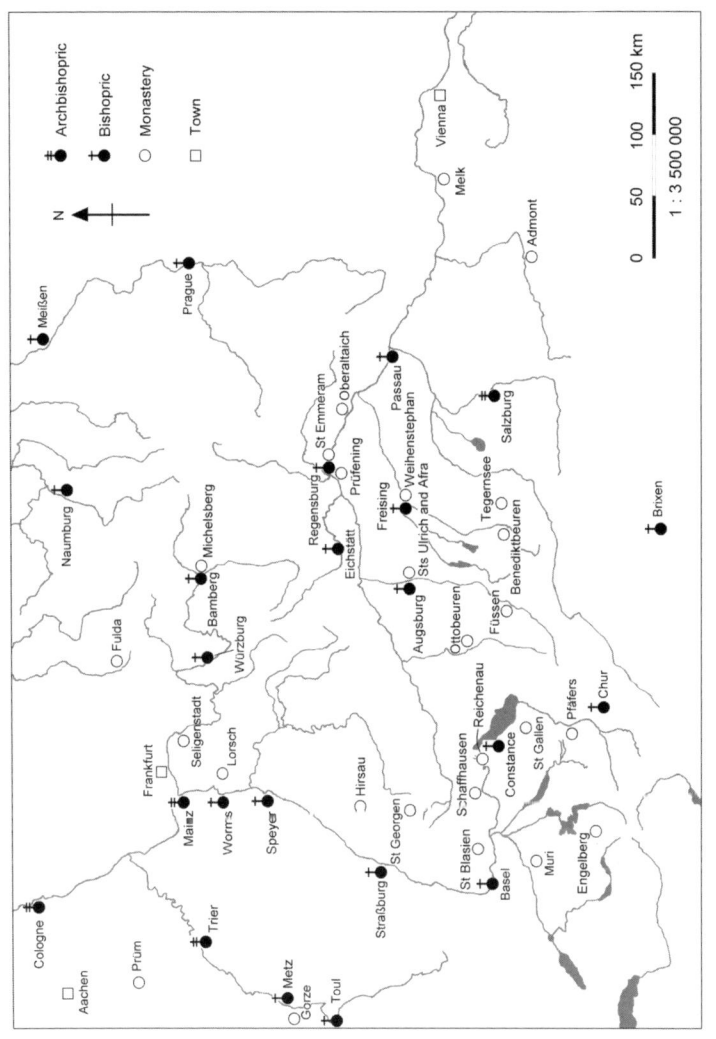

2 Southern Germany in the late eleventh century

Introduction

This book is concerned with the study of music in the monastic and cathedral schools of Salian Germany (1024-1125). In order to compress such a subject into one volume, my approach has necessarily been selective. I must begin, therefore, by explaining precisely which aspects of the history of music are treated in this book. Although music was central to the liturgy that regulated religious life in the Middle Ages, histories of medieval culture rarely take into account either its theory or its practice. While historians have ignored the role of music in intellectual life – perhaps discouraged by its seeming complexity – musicologists have generally focused on technical issues such as the transmission of plainchant or the development of notation. This book studies music as an aspect of intellectual history by treating the works of music theory produced in Salian Germany as early scholastic texts. It is concerned with the textual and conceptual links that exist between these works, with the motivations and preoccupations of their authors, and with the way in which these authors applied to the study of music the techniques they applied also to other disciplines. Although the book contains some detailed discussions of music theory, it is not intended primarily as a musicological account of that theory's development.[1] Rather, is it a discussion of one of the central subjects of the *artes* at a moment of important intellectual developments in the Kingdom of Germany.

The surviving works of music theory from the Salian period illustrate the extent to which music exercised the minds of some of Germany's

---

[1] David Hiley's excellent work *Western plainchant: a handbook* (Oxford, 1993) provides an indispensable guide to the wider musicological background of plainchant in this period.

leading intellectuals, producing what has been described as a 'learned and long-lived theoretical tradition' that distinguised Germany from other European territories.[2] These treatises circulated widely in contemporary manuscripts and the most important examples are available in published editions: *Prologus in tonarium* by Bern of Reichenau (d. 1048),[3] *Musica* by Herman of Reichenau (1013–54),[4] the treatise by the 'Wolf Anonymous' (*fl.* 1060),[5] *Musica* by William of Hirsau (d. 1091),[6] *Musica* by Master Henry of Augsburg (d. 1083),[7] *De musica* by Aribo (*fl.* 1070),[8] *Breviarium de musica* by Frutolf of Michelsberg (d. 1103),[9] *Musica* by Theoger of Metz (*c.* 1050–1120),[10] *De musica* by the otherwise unknown John (early twelfth century),[11] and the anonymous *Quaestiones in musica*, which dates from the early twelfth century.[12] To these may be added a

[2] C. M. Bower, 'The transmission of ancient music theory in the Middle Ages', in T. Christensen (ed.), *The Cambridge history of western music theory* (Cambridge, 2002), p. 161. On the absence of an equivalent theoretical tradition in the French Kingdom see L. Gushee, 'Questions of genre in medieval treatises on music', in W. Arlt, E. Lichtenhahn and H. Oesch (eds), *Gattungen der Musik in Einzeldarstellungen. Gedenkschrift Leo Schrade* (Munich, 1973), p. 410. For an introduction to the Italian theorists pseudo-Odo and Guido of Arezzo, who were widely disseminated in Germany, see Hiley, *Western plainchant*, pp. 463–70.

[3] Bern of Reichenau, *Epistola de tonis, Prologus in tonarium, Tonarius*, ed. A. Rausch, *Die Musiktraktate des Abtes Bern von Reichenau. Edition und Interpretation* (Tutzing, 1999). Still fundamental to the study of the treatises are the three volumes of Dom. Martin Gerbert: *Scriptores ecclesiastici de musica sacra potissimum* (St Blasien, 1784). See also the important revisions by M. Bernhard, *Clavis Gerberti. Eine Revision von Martin Gerberts Scriptores ecclesiastici de musica sacra potissimum (St. Blasien 1784)* (Munich, 1989).

[4] Herman of Reichenau, *Musica*, ed. and trans. L. Ellinwood, *Musica Hermanni Contracti* (Rochester, NY, 1936).

[5] Wolf Anonymous, [*Musica*], ed. J. Wolf, 'Ein anonymer Musiktraktat des elften bis zwölften Jahrhunderts', *Vierteljahrsschrift Musikwissenschaft* 9 (1893), 186–234.

[6] William of Hirsau, *Musica*, ed. D. Harbinson, *Willehelmi Hirsaugensis Musica* (Rome, 1975).

[7] Henry of Augsburg, *Musica*, ed. J. Smits van Waesberghe, *Musica domni Heinrici Augustensis magistri* (Buren, 1977).

[8] Aribo, *De musica*, ed. J. Smits van Waesberghe, *Aribonis De musica* (Rome, 1951).

[9] Frutolf of Michelsberg, *Breviarium de musica, Tonarius*, ed. C. Vivell, 'Frutolfi Breviarium de musica et Tonarius', *Akademie der Wissenschaften in Wien. Philosophische historische Klasse, Sitzungsberichte* 188/2 (1919), 1–188.

[10] Theoger of Metz, *Musica*, ed. and trans. F. C. Lochner, 'Dietger (Theogerus) of Metz and his "Musica"' (Ph.D. dissertation, University of Notre Dame, 1995).

[11] John, *De musica, Tonarius*, ed. J. Smits van Waesberghe, *Johannis Afflighemensis De musica cum tonario* (Rome, 1950).

[12] *Quaestiones in musica*, ed. R. Steglich, *Die Quaestiones in Musica. Ein Choraltraktat des zentralen Mittelalters und ihr mutmaßlicher Verfasser Rudolf von St. Trond (1070–1138)* (Leipzig, 1911; repr. 1971).

number of anonymous works – many of them short or fragmentary – which, for the sake of clarity, will be discussed only in passing. I refer to the authors of the treatises as the 'south-German circle' of music theorists, a label justified by their predominant activity in the religious institutions of southern Germany.

The eleventh- and twelfth-century manuscripts in which these works circulate frequently contain other texts designed to complement the south-German treatises that form their core. To have included a detailed survey of these tonaries, measurement texts and notated examples would have made this book far too long and consequently they are mentioned only when relevant. In any case, some of these have been ably studied by historians.[13] Similarly, I have not discussed the relevance of the south-German treatises to elementary music education in my period.[14] The extent to which they were useful for the instruction of boys in monastic and cathedral schools is a worthy subject for future study. Some historians have drawn false distinctions between the south-German treatises in this regard. One consensus juxtaposes the supposedly sterile theorizing of Bern, Herman or William with the 'practical' theory inspired by Guido of Arezzo (*c.* 991–*c.* 1033) and echoed in German treatises such as John's *De musica*, a manual intended 'like Guido's, to educate the boys of a cathedral or choir school in the singing of plainchant'.[15] This is unlikely. The south-German treatises, on account of their sophistication, could only have been of use to those clerks and monks undertaking advanced curricular studies. They were designed to instruct teachers in the singing of plainchant by setting out in a thorough fashion all the elements of and theory behind singing. My suggestion is that their impact upon schoolboys came indirectly through the teacher for whom they were intended. A contemporary example from another discipline will clarify the point: the school-book *Colores rhetorici*,

---

[13] On tonaries see the magisterial study by M. Huglo, *Les tonaires. Inventaire, analyse, comparaison* (Paris, 1971), as well as the same author's article 'Tonary', *NG* 25, pp. 594–8. Medieval organ-pipe measurements have been carefully studied: K.-J. Sachs (ed.), *Mensura fistularum. Die Mensurierung der Orgelpfeifen im Mittelalter*, 2 vols (Stuttgart, 1970, 1980). Bell measurements have been less thoroughly studied: see J. Smits van Waesberghe (ed.), *Cymbala: bells in the Middle Ages* (Rome, 1951). For studies of monochord measurements see M. Markovits, *Das Tonsystem der abendländischen Musik im frühen Mittelalter* (Bern, 1977), pp. 29–52; C. Meyer, *Mensura monochordi. La division du monochord (IXe–XVe siècles)* (Paris, 1996).

[14] See K.-J. Sachs, 'Musikalische Elementarlehre im Mittelalter', in M. Bernhard and F. Zaminer (eds), *Rezeption des antiken Fachs im Mittelalter* (Darmstadt, 1990), pp. 105–61.

[15] C. V. Palisca in W. Babb (trans.) and C. V. Palisca (ed.), *Hucbald, Guido and John on music: three medieval treatises* (New Haven and London, 1978), p. 87.

3

written by Master Onulf of Speyer in the 1070s, was produced, not for mass dissemination among pupils, but in response to a request from a monk who required it for instructing boys in the linguistic arts.[16]

Music theory in the eleventh and twelfth centuries was thought of within the traditional framework of the curriculum of the seven liberal arts: the three linguistic arts (the trivium) of grammar, rhetoric and dialectic; and the four mathematical arts (the quadrivium) of arithmetic, music, geometry and astronomy. The first descriptions of this framework date from the Latin encyclopaedists of the fifth and sixth centuries, whose works were keenly studied in the Middle Ages. The most explicit of these descriptions is the elaborate allegory by Martianus Capella (*fl.* 410–39) entitled *De nuptiis Philologiae et Mercurii*, in which each of seven sisters presents her academic discipline at the wedding feast of the erudite young lady Philology and the god Mercury.[17] According to certain Carolingian commentators of the ninth and tenth centuries, the marriage symbolized the union of learning (Philology) and eloquence (Mercury), that is, of the mathematical and linguistic arts. The music of the curriculum envisaged by Martianus Capella and his contemporaries was, however, different in character from that of the medieval period. Based upon the ancient Greek model, it theorized about the mathematical proportions that governed the intervals; about the proportions that held the cosmos and all its elements together. It was not a theory of melody. But these mathematical elements were incorporated into a theory of melody by western Europe's earliest post-classical theorists during the Carolingian era. In the Middle Ages music theory was taught to pupils, not that they might probe the fabric of the cosmos, but that they might sing the praise of God correctly. The resulting hybrid used the vocabulary of ancient theory to describe the new liturgical song of the Christian West.

The disparate elements of medieval theory are shown to good effect in a treatise on the seven liberal arts entitled *De animae exsilio et patria* by the widely-read German author Honorius Augustodunensis (*c.*

---

[16] Onulf of Speyer, *Colores rhetorici*, ed. W. Wattenbach, 'Magister Onulf von Speyer', *Sitzungsberichte der königlichen Preußischen Akademie der Wissenschaften zu Berlin* 1 (1894), 361–86. On its dating see C. Erdmann, 'Onulf von Speyer und Amarcius', in C. Erdmann, *Forschungen zur politischen Ideenwelt des Frühmittelalters. Aus dem Nachlass des Verfassers*, ed. F. Baethgen (Berlin, 1951), pp. 126–8. See also J. C. Linde, 'Die "Rhetorici colores" des Magister Onulf von Speyer', *Mittellateinisches Jahrbuch* 40 (2005), 333–81.

[17] Martianus Capella, *De nuptiis Philologiae et Mercurii*, ed. J. Willis, Martianus Capella opera (Leipzig, 1983). See also S. Grebe, *Martianus Capella 'De nuptiis Philologiae et Mercurii'. Darstellung der Sieben Freien Künste und ihrer Beziehungen zueinander* (Stuttgart and Leipzig, 1999).

1080/90–*c.* 1156).[18] In this work, Honorius portrays the student of the arts as a symbolic traveller journeying through seven cities. Each city represents one of the arts and is described in terms appropriate to subject matter of that art: the five gates of the city of dialectic, for example, are called genus, species, difference, property and accidents.[19] The fifth city is music, which, as Honorius says, lies in the country of singing:

> In this city, through the teaching of Boethius, here the low chorus of men and there the high voices of boys praise God; the pipes of organs and the strings of cithara resonate; the ringing of bells sounds; the seven dissonant notes produce the consonance of harmony.[20]

Though Honorius correlates the music of the curriculum with singing, the trappings of Antiquity remain: he considers the teaching of Boethius fundamental and behind the Virgilian metaphor of the *septem discrimina vocum* lies the ancient emphasis on proportion and harmony. Music theory, therefore, is the theory of singing correctly: it is the ability to understand and properly to organize and command all the elements constituting or affecting the performance, composition and criticism of songs.

The south-German theorists considered the gamut of notes to be a series of seven pitches (A–G) repeated at the higher octave (a–g). From the late tenth century it became common to place *gamma* (Γ) at the bottom and $\underset{a}{a}$ at the top. (Later in the Middle Ages the word *scala* – ladder – was used to describe this series of notes: whence scale.)

Γ A B C D E F G a b c d e f g $\underset{a}{a}$

The octave (A–G) was then expressed as a group of two tetrachords, necessarily conjunct around the note D (A–D and D–G), this arrangement being repeated at the higher octave (a–g conjunct around d). Onto this system were mapped the species of fourth (or *diatessaron*), the species of

---

[18] On Honorius Augustodunensis see V. I. J. Flint, 'The career of Honorius Augustodunensis: some fresh evidence', *Revue bénédictine* 82 (1972), 63–86; 'The place and purpose of the works of Honorius Augustodunensis', *Revue bénédictine* 87 (1977), 97–127; 'Heinricus of Augsburg and Honorius Augustodunensis: are they the same person?', *Revue bénédictine* 92 (1982), 148–58; T. J. H. McCarthy, 'The identity of Master Henry of Augsburg (d. 1083)', *Revue bénédictine* 114 (2004), 140–57.

[19] Honorius Augustodunensis, *De animae exsilio et patria, alias de artibus* 4 (*PL* 172.1244AB). Honorius' allegory lists ten cities: the seven cities representing the liberal arts are followed by the eighth, ninth and tenth cities, representing *physica, mechanica* and *oeconomica* respectively (*PL* 172.1245BC).

[20] Ibid. 6 (*PL* 172.1244D): In hac urbe per Boetii doctrinam hinc chorus viris gravibus, inde puerilis acutis vocibus Deo jubilat: organa fistulis, citharae fidibus concrepant, cymbala pulsu tinniunt; septem dissonae voces consonam harmoniae efficiunt.

fifth (or *diapente*) and the species of octave (or *diapason*). (These terms were taken from ancient Greek music theory where they functioned differently as part of the Greater and Lesser Perfect Systems.)[21]

Then there were the modes: four of them, whose finals or keynotes were respectively the notes D, E, F and G or, as they were called, *protus*, *deuterus*, *tritus* and *tetrardus* (terms again taken from ancient theory).[22] Each mode was subdivided with reference to high and low ambit, or range, into two 'tones': the higher version of a given mode occupied the ambit of an octave above its final and was called authentic; the lower version occupied the octave ambit extending from a fourth below the final to a fifth above it and was called plagal. There were, therefore, four modes and eight tones. To give an example: in the mode with the final D (*protus*), the authentic version (or first tone) runs from D to d; the plagal version (or second tone) from the A to a.

The theorists identified the eight tones with different systems of nomenclature, sometimes referring to them ordinally (first to eighth), sometimes descriptively (as authentic *protus*, plagal *tritus* and so forth), and sometimes with the Latinized forms of the old Greek names *dorius*, *frigius*, *lidius* and *mixolidius* to indicate authentic *protus*, *deuterus*, *tritus* and *tetrardus* respectively, adding the prefix *hypo-* to indicate the appropriate plagal versions. The relationship of the modes to the system of notes and tetrachords was paramount, since the repertoire of plainchant was classified according to mode. To sing a chant in the wrong mode could change its character entirely, a thing abhorred by the theorists. The theory of singing, therefore, involved understanding all of this; being mindful of it when singing so as to avoid mistakes; remembering it when arranging chants according to mode so as to avoid false classifications; following it when writing melodies so as to ensure they be correct and regular. Its importance was summed up by Herman of Reichenau:

> We must understand that the whole intent of the method of music bears towards the establishment of the science of composing chants correctly, of judging them by rule and of performing them fittingly.[23]

According to the influential Italian theorist Guido of Arezzo, whose work Herman probably knew, this faculty distinguished the mere *cantor* 'who

---

[21] See T. J. Mathiesen, 'Greece', *NG* 10, pp. 335–48 with bibliography.
[22] See H. S. Power and F. Wiering, 'Mode', *NG* 16, pp. 777–90, 819–21.
[23] Herman of Reichenau, *Musica* 15, p. 47: Oportet autem nos scire, quod omnis musicae rationis ad hoc spectat intentio, ut cantilenae rationabiliter componendae, regulariter iudicandae, decenter modulandae scientia comparetur.

does what he understands not' from the *musicus* 'who knows what comprises music'.[24]

Chapter 1 offers an historical introduction to the south-German circle of music theorists. Although many of the theorists were leading religious and intellectual figures, their contribution to the history of ideas has been all but ignored by English-speaking historians. This reflects a long tradition of English language scholarship, which has written the history of the central Middle Ages with predominant reference to Anglo-French sources, and which has largely overlooked the important religious, political and intellectual developments that took place within the Western Empire during the eleventh and twelfth centuries.[25] There are, however, signs of change: Rodney Thomson, writing in an important collection of essays, has drawn attention to the distorted picture of European history that has resulted from unwillingness or inability to study German sources.[26] Biographies that distil relevant German scholarship and place the theorists in their proper intellectual contexts are, therefore, vital for the reader, who will encounter these theorists throughout this book. This chapter also highlights the connexion between the south-German circle and eleventh-century Church reforms. Church reform was not the monolithic force that has been portrayed by some historians, but in reality a connected series of movements and efforts.[27] As the monastic reforms of Gorze and Hirsau differed, so too did the reforms of the Burgundian-Lotharingian papacy in the third

---

[24] Guido of Arezzo, *Regule rithmice* lines 7–10, ed. D. Pesce, *Guido d'Arezzo's Regule rithmice, Prologus in antiphonarium and Epistola ad Michahelem: a critical text and translation* (Ottawa, 1999), pp. 330–2: Musicorum et cantorum magna est distantia; isti dicunt, illi sciunt, que componit musica.

[25] See, for example, C. H. Haskins, *The renaissance of the twelfth century* (Cambridge, Mass. and London, 1927); R. W. Southern, *Medieval humanism and other studies* (Oxford, 1970); S. R. Packard, *Twelfth century Europe: an interpretative essay* (Amherst, 1973); R. W. Southern, *Scholastic humanism and the unification of Europe*, 2 vols (Oxford, 1995, 2001).

[26] R. Thomson, 'The place of Germany in the twelfth-century Renaissance', in A. I. Beach (ed.), *Manuscripts and monastic culture: reform and renewal in twelfth-century Germany* (Turnhout, 2007), pp. 19–42. See also C. S. Jaeger, *The envy of angels: cathedral schools and social ideas in medieval Europe, 950–1200* (Philadelphia, 1994), p. 15. Studies in English that address this lacuna are beginning to emerge: A. S. Cohen, *The Uta Codex: art, philosophy and reform in eleventh-century Germany* (University Park, Pa., 2000); J. Nightingale, *Monasteries and patrons in the Gorze reform: Lotharingia c. 850–1000* (Oxford, 2001); A. I. Beach, *Women as scribes: book production and monastic reform in twelfth-century Bavaria* (Cambridge, 2004).

[27] See G. Tellenbach, *The church in western Europe from the tenth to the early twelfth century*, trans. T. Reuter (Cambridge, 1993; repr. 1996), pp. 157–84 for an introduction to this topic.

quarter of the eleventh century differ from those of the Gregorian papacy in the 1070s and 1080s. The later reforms, however, built upon the foundations laid by the earlier movements, especially upon the close links between the monasteries of southern Germany that were established by the Gorze movement. This cultural network (which extended to cathedral chapters sympathetic to reform) facilitated communication between scholars over great distances and allowed for the interchange of monks and books. Letter collections show its use by scholars who debated questions of logic and doctrine. For Pope Gregory VII and his supporters in the 1070s and 1080s, the south-German monastic network was an important vehicle for the dissemination of reform ideology in Germany. The extent to which the south-German theorists availed themselves of these networks is shown by the textual correspondences and affinity of ideas in their treatises.

Chapter 2 builds upon this material by examining the main sources that influenced the south-German treatises. These sources fall into different categories. The first includes both classical and Carolingian influences upon the eleventh-century theorists. As Honorius Augustodunensis pointed out, Boethius was central to music theory: he was the conduit through which most of the ancient theory reached the Middle Ages. That theory was assimilated by the Carolingian theorists, who were the first to use it in the analysis and categorization of Western plainchant. The next category is made up of contemporary external influences. Here one important author is paramount: Guido of Arezzo, whose treatises were quickly recognized throughout Europe as the most fundamental works of music theory since Boethius. Guido's *Micrologus*, *Regule rithmice*, *Prologus in antiphonarium* and *Epistola ad Michahelem* were also highly regarded by the south-German circle, though they were not received uncritically by it. The final major influence upon the south-German circle was internal. It started with Abbot Bern of Reichenau, who synthesized Carolingian theory in his *Prologus in tonarium*, and can be regarded as the founding father of the south-German circle. Bern's theory was amplified (and in some aspects modified) by his pupil Herman of Reichenau: together they set the tone of German music theory for the next century.

The members of the south-German circle were above all organizers and codifiers. Their studies in dialectic taught them the importance of definition, discrimination, distinction and division. Chapter 3 studies the connexion between music theory and dialectic. Historians of medieval logic have concentrated their efforts on the French schools of the early twelfth century and largely ignored Germany. This emphasis gives a distorted picture of learning during the central Middle Ages, for in Germany

– the richest and most powerful of the European territories – there existed resources far beyond those available in France. Chapter 3 begins with a survey of dialectical studies in the Empire and argues that the study of dialectic had a profound influence upon music theory. The chapter shows the nature and extent of this influence in a number of case studies.

The regularity that the music theorists sought in plainchant was a response to the universal order of God who 'ordered all things in measure and number and weight'.[28] Almost as important as the biblical precedent for universal harmony was the Platonic one. Plato's *Timaeus* (and the works of the late-classical authors who commented upon it) seemed to provide medieval scholars with the scheme whereby the world was designed. It was, therefore, of considerable interest to the south-German music theorists, who saw music as a reflexion of the natural and perfect order of the universe. Chapter 4 clarifies the process through which this Platonic inheritance reached the eleventh-century theorists and shows how Platonic ideas and metaphors were applied by the south-German theorists to show the natural order of the musical system they proposed.

Chapter 5 studies the manuscript dissemination of the treatises, concentrating in particular upon music-theory textbooks, that is, codices compiled largely from the south-German treatises that appear to have been used as 'handbooks' for studying music theory. The compilation of textbooks was not unique to music theory, but was a characteristic feature of contemporary scholasticism. I begin the chapter by showing the development of the textbook tradition during the eleventh century in disciplines such as canon law, theology, doctrine and the subjects of the trivium. The music textbooks are a further part of this tradition. One of these – Kassel, Landesbibliothek und Murhardsche Bibliothek der Stadt, 4° Mss Math. 1 – is analysed in detail as a case study. The chapter concludes with a survey of twenty similar music textbooks. Many of these manuscripts reveal themselves to have been compiled by scribes who had a clear eye for their form and content. They provide a useful perspective on contemporary attitudes by showing which texts eleventh- and twelfth-century scribes considered useful and necessary for studying music.

Above all, this book is a study of the institutional and intellectual background to music theory. It is concerned with the history of ideas, with the attitudes and motivations of the theorists and their contemporaries. Consequently, I have not been afraid to use the tools of historical and textual reconstruction. My treatment of the interpolated version of

---

[28] Wisdom 11.21.

Prologus in tonarium by Bern of Reichenau in Chapter 2 and my reconstruction of the genesis of the Kassel manuscript in Chapter 5 (which has important implications for the wider body of manuscripts that I survey subsequently) are obvious examples of this. In places, I have deviated from the available printed editions of the treatises, quoting instead the text from manuscript sources: this is the case in my discussion of the *Prologus* interpolations (for the history of which the manuscript Karlsruhe, Badische Landesbibliothek, 504 is crucial) and of Frutolf's *Breviarium de musica* (where the manuscript Munich, Bayerische Staatsbibliothek, Clm 14965b provides a better guide to Frutolf's intentions than does Vivell's edition). Ultimately, these and other textual studies are presented for the light they shed upon the motivations and attitudes of the music theorists and the scribes who copied their work. Similarly, when discussing the music theorists, the treatises and their sources, I have taken every opportunity to draw comparisons with the other *artes*. Hence my discussion of the state of dialectical studies in eleventh-century Germany and of the wider eleventh-century textbook movement at the beginning of Chapter 5. This approach is vital if we are to study the south-German circle in its appropriate intellectual context.

Although the title of this book extends my survey to the early twelfth century, my discussion shows that the most productive period for the south-German circle was the second half of the eleventh century. The timespan indicated by the title merely allows me to mention the later reiteration of the themes common to the music treatises in sources such as John's *De musica* and the anonymous *Quaestiones in musica*, and to include the work of twelfth-century scribes in my discussion of the music textbooks. An examination of these sources reveals how much they owe to the works composed in the eleventh century.

1

The south-German circle: an historical introduction

Eleventh-century monastic reforms

The history of monasticism in eleventh-century Germany is dominated by reform. Hallinger's seminal study of German monastic reform in the tenth and eleventh centuries emphasized in particular the determining influence of the Lotharingian monastery of Gorze (reformed in 933), whose brand of reform was transmitted across Germany: to and by such houses as Reichenau, St Emmeram in Regensburg, Niederaltaich, Lorsch and Einsiedeln.[1] In the light of more recent researches, Hallinger's view sometimes seems too monolithic: the Gorze movement was essentially a series of different but related reforms diffused through networks of German monasteries in which other monasteries – notably St Maximin in Trier – often played a decisive role. Nevertheless, this quintessentially Germanic reform can be contrasted with the Cluniac reform, which was somewhat slow to take hold in Germany. Indeed, chronicles and letters of the period show that German monasteries were often hostile to what they saw as the 'innovations' of Cluny.[2] Though Hallinger has, perhaps, overemphasized this hostility,[3]

---

[1] K. Hallinger, *Gorze-Kluny. Studien zu den monastischen Lebensformen und Gegensätzen im Hochmittelalter*, 2 vols (Rome, 1950, 1951).

[2] The Gorze reform also aroused hostility in some monasteries: see J. Nightingale, *Monasteries and patrons in the Gorze reform: Lotharingia c. 850–1000* (Oxford, 2001), pp. 19–20; for attempts to impose the Gorze reform on St Gallen see A. Hauck, *Kirchengeschichte Deutschlands* 3 (Leipzig, 1906; repr. 1953), pp. 315, 508–10, 867–8.

[3] See T. Schieffer, 'Cluniazensische oder Gorzische Reformbewegung?', *Archiv für mittelrheinische Kirchengeschichte* 4 (1952), 24–44; 'Cluny et la querelle des investitures', *Revue historique* 225 (1961), 47–72; G. Tellenbach, 'Zum Wesen der Cluniacenser', *Saeculum* 9 (1958), 370–9.

11

the fact remains that until the end of the eleventh century 'Cluny and its customs had made little real impact upon the German-speaking lands'.[4]

Unlike Cluny, Gorze possessed no readily ascertainable network of daughter houses: newly reformed monasteries retained much of their own character and were thus not a mere replica of Gorze. Indeed, in many cases the reform of a monastery was undertaken, not from Gorze itself, but from a house that had been reformed by it: such was the case with St Emmeram when in 975 its new abbot, Ramwold, introduced the customs of his own monastery of St Maximin in Trier.[5] For these reasons the intellectual and cultural implications of the Gorze reform are less well understood than those of the later Hirsau reform, which largely overshadowed it and which possessed a more defined structure. Nevertheless, in the first three-quarters of the eleventh century the Gorze movement undoubtedly promoted and strengthened the links that existed between many German monasteries.

The century and a half of dominance enjoyed by the Gorze movement came to an end in the third quarter of the eleventh century. The reasons are not yet apparent, but may own something to a crisis of confidence within the movement, as well as to the emergence of separate reform initiatives that were unrelated to Gorze. These initiatives were largely undertaken by members of the lay nobility or powerful churchmen, and may have been in part a reaction to the imperially dominated Gorze movement. Examples are found in the reform movements emanating from the Lotharingian monastery of Siegburg (founded by Archbishop Anno of Cologne, 1056–75) and the co-operative venture between Rudolf of Rheinfelden, duke of Swabia, and the Empress Agnes in 1072, which introduced to the monastery of St Blasien in the Black Forest the reforms associated with the north-Italian monastery of Fruttuaria.[6] Indeed, the initial reform of Hirsau (carried out under the patronage of Count Adalbert II of Calw) was part of a wave of monastic reform instigated by the south-German aristocracy in the late 1060s and early 1070s.[7] It saw the removal of Abbot Frederick and his replacement with a monk of St Emmeram named William.

---

[4] H. E. J. Cowdrey, *The Cluniacs and the Gregorian reform* (Oxford, 1970), p. 193.

[5] On Ramwold and the introduction of the Gorze reform to St Emmeram see W. Wattenbach and R. Holtzmann, *Deutschlands Geschichtsquellen im Mittelalter. Die Zeit der Sachsen und Salier* 1, ed. F.-J. Schmale (Cologne and Graz, 1967), pp. 266–9.

[6] J. Semmler, *Die Klosterreform von Siegburg. Ihre Ausbreitung und ihr Reformprogramm im 11. und 12. Jahrhundert* (Bonn, 1959), pp. 35–50; J. Vogel, 'Rudolf von Rheinfelden, die Fürstenopposition gegen Heinrich IV. im Jahr 1072 und die Reform des Klosters St. Blasien', *Zeitschrift für die Geschichte des Oberrheins* 132 (1984), 1–30.

[7] K. Schmid, 'Adel und Reform in Schwaben', in J. Fleckenstein (ed.), *Investiturstreit und Reichsverfassung* (Sigmaringen, 1973), pp. 295–319.

William had initially sought to improve monastic discipline at Hirsau through the introduction of the customs of St Emmeram, taken as they originally were from the Gorze model. A portentous meeting between Abbot William and Pope Gregory VII at Rome in 1075, however, resulted in William's persuasion to a zealous Gregorian stance.[8] In 1078 William was persuaded by the Papal Legate, Abbot Bernard of St Victor in Marseilles, to adopt Cluniac customs in Hirsau, and this reform was then extended to a confederation of houses based upon the Hirsau model.[9] The Cluniac reform, therefore, became the Hirsau reform in its German manifestation. It was a movement associated from the beginning with the Gregorian papacy. Much important work has been done by historians in tracing the spread of the Hirsau reform. Hermann Jakobs in particular has identified its different strands.[10] As with Gorze, the picture that emerges is not one of a monolithic reform movement, but rather of reform groups emanating from different centres. In the period from c. 1079 to c. 1121, for example, the monasteries of Schaffhausen, Petershausen, Zwiefalten, Blaubeuren, St Paul in Lavanttal, Weingarten, Pfäfers and Prüfening near Regensburg, among others, were reformed by monks from Hirsau.[11] In addition, new cells of Hirsau were established, of which St Georgen in the Black Forest – founded in 1083 – is the most notable example.[12] Many of these houses in turn became bases for the propagation of reform: in 1106 the imperial abbey of Benediktbeuren was reformed by monks from Schaffhausen,[13] while monks from the newly established priory of St Georgen were responsible for the reform of Ottobeuren (from 1102), Sts Ulrich and Afra in Augsburg (1109) and Admont (1115).[14] This last house continued the process: in 1143 monks of Admont reformed St Emmeram, which many years before had been a noted outlet of the Gorze reform.[15] The example of St Emmeram is not the only one showing that the Hirsau reform often replaced that of

[8] Ibid., pp. 196–200; I. S. Robinson, 'The friendship network of Gregory VII', *History* 63 (1978), 1–6.
[9] Cowdrey, *The Cluniacs and the Gregorian reform*, p. xxi. On the importance of Hirsau and Abbot William to the Gregorian cause see pp. 196–213.
[10] H. Jakobs, *Die Hirsauer. Ihre Ausbreitung und Rechtsstellung im Zeitalter des Investiturstreites* (Cologne and Graz, 1961), pp. 36–71. See also J. Wollasch, 'Muri und St. Blasien. Perspektiven schwäbischen Mönchtums in der Reform', *DA* 17 (1961), 420–46; R. Bauerreiß, 'St. Georgen im Schwarzwald. Ein Reformmittelpunkt Südostdeutschlands im beginnenden 12. Jahrhundert', *SMGBZ* 51 (1933), 196–201; 52 (1934), 47–56.
[11] Jakobs, *Die Hirsauer*, pp. 36–57.
[12] Ibid., p. 41.
[13] Ibid., p. 58.
[14] Ibid., pp. 58–9, 60.
[15] Ibid., p. 71.

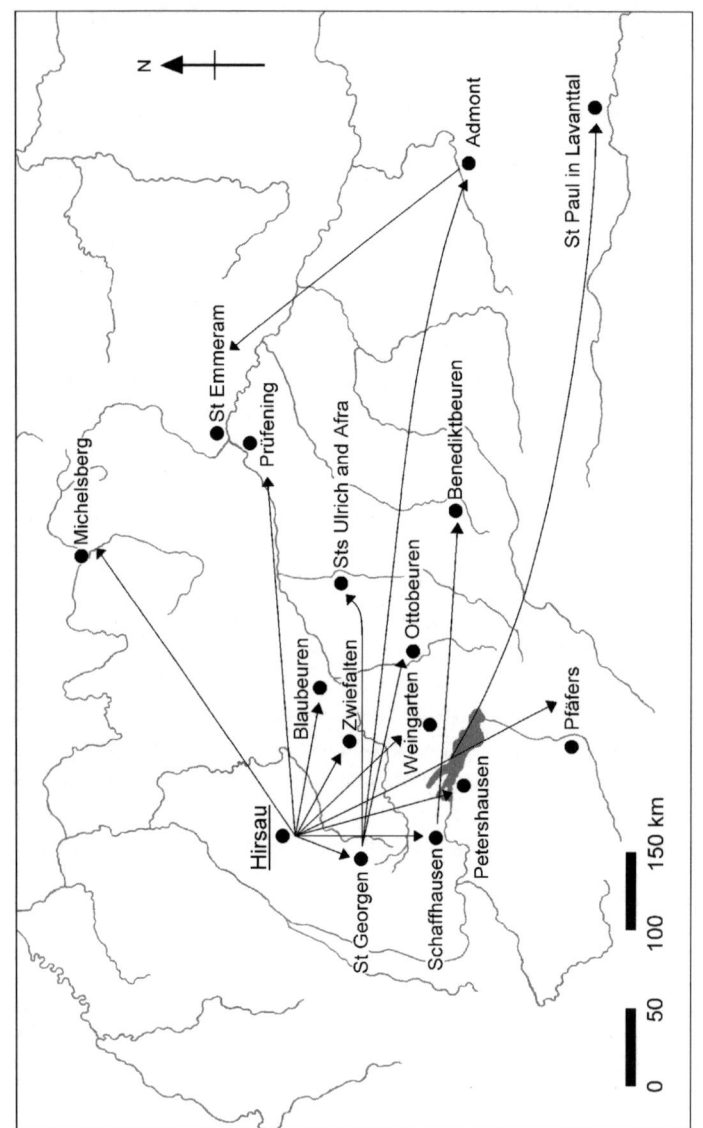

3 The direct and indirect spread of the Hirsau reform

Gorze: the monastery of Michelsberg in Bamberg (founded in 1015) was heavily influenced in its early years by the Gorze-style customs of St Emmeram, but in 1112 was reformed by monks of Hirsau.

Reform and friendship networks

One consequence of the meeting between Gregory VII and William of Hirsau in 1075 – and of the resulting Hirsau reform movement – was that the pope was able to avail himself of a 'friendship network' of German monks and clerks sympathetic to Gregorian ideals. As in the case of eleventh-century monasticism, where it is possible to distinguish different reforms, so too is it possible to speak, not of one 'friendship network', but of 'friendship networks'. The researches of I. S. Robinson have drawn attention to such networks in France (co-ordinated through the efforts of the papal legate, Hugh of Die) and in Italy from the pontificate of Alexander II, 1061–73.[16] In addition, he has identified other networks: among them the circle of biblical scholars and canonists that gathered around Bernard, master of the cathedral school at Constance (and from *c.* 1072 to *c.* 1085 *scholasticus* at Hildesheim). The members of this circle included Master Bernard's pupil Bernold of Constance (later a monk of St Blasien and Schaffhausen respectively), the important Gregorian polemicist Manegold of Lautenbach, Archbishop Gebhard of Salzburg, and writers such as the Hirsau Anonymous and the 'Swabian annalist' (pseudo-Berthold of Reichenau).[17] The writings of this circle demonstrate how its members built upon the researches of their colleagues. Specifically, the codex Sélestat, Bibliothèque Municipale, 13 – which belonged originally to Hirsau – contains sentence collections that the circle used in common and shows traces of Manegold's borrowing from the writings of Bernold of St Blasien, 'a crucial figure in the history of Gregorian ecclesiology and legal thought'.[18]

[16] Robinson, 'The friendship network of Gregory VII', 18–21, 10–14.

[17] I. S. Robinson, 'The Bible in the Investiture Contest: the south-German Gregorian circle', in K. Walsh and D. Wood (eds), *The Bible in the medieval world: essays in memory of Beryl Smalley* (Oxford, 1985), pp. 61–84. On Bernold see I. S. Robinson, 'Zur Arbeitsweise Bernolds von Konstanz und seines Kreises. Untersuchungen zum Schlettstädter Codex 13', *DA* 34 (1978), 51–122. On the importance of Constance as a centre see J. Autenrieth, *Die Domschule von Konstanz zur Zeit des Investiturstreits. Die Wissenschaftliche Arbeitsweise Bernholds von Konstanz und zweier Kleriker dargestellt auf Grund von Handschriftenstudien* (Stuttgart, 1956); 'Bernold von Konstanz und der Codex Sangallensis 676', in *Friedrich Baethgen zu seinem 65. Geburtstag* (Munich: MGH typescript, 1955), pp. 1–17. See Chapter 5, pp. 176–8.

[18] Robinson, 'The Bible in the Investiture Contest', p. 67; 'Zur Arbeitsweise Bernolds von Konstanz', 101–22.

It was not, however, as an exclusive response to the vicissitudes of the struggle between Papacy and Empire that such friendship networks came into being: rather were Gregory VII and others able to exploit an already existing and well established social and intellectual institution. 'Friendship networks', in differing forms, had been common throughout the eleventh century and would continue to be so in the twelfth. The importance of letters in maintaining contact between individuals and groups, and the concomitant 'cult of friendship' that became ever more noticeable during the twelfth century has been realized in recent years by historians.[19] Two important letter collections show friendship networks in operation: the collection originating at the cathedral school in Worms, part of which reflects the educational activities of Wolzo, master of the school under Bishop Azecho, 1025–44; and the Hildesheim collection, dating from the third quarter of the eleventh century, which details the interests of that cathedral school and its pupils.[20] The distinguished teacher Herman of Reichenau received a letter from his former pupil Meinzo, *scholasticus* of Constance, asking his help on a difficult geometrical problem 'on account of the great love you have had for me, which I have not merited'.[21] The scholar Otloh of St Emmeram (*c.* 1010–70), who was educated at Tegernsee and spent time at other monasteries, mentions the theological discussions that resulted from the visit of the monk Henry of Reichenau to St Emmeram, and elsewhere recorded that he had copied and sent books to friends in Bohemia, Padua and Tegernsee.[22]

It was from among such people that the music theorists of Salian Germany were drawn. They form a south-German circle comparable to others from this period. Like other scholars, the music theorists availed themselves of friendship networks that were facilitated by the Gorze and Hirsau movements. The idea that many of the eleventh-century music trea-

---

[19] See B. P. McGuire, *Friendship and community: the monastic experience, 350–1250* (Kalamazoo, 1989) with good bibliography.

[20] *Die ältere Wormser Briefsammlung*, ed. W. Bulst, *MGH Briefe* 3; *Die Jüngere Hildesheimer Briefsammlung*, ed. R. de Kegel, *MGH Briefe* 7. See B. P. McGuire, *Friendship and community*, pp. 185–8.

[21] E. Dümmler (ed.), 'Ein Schreiben Meinzos von Constanz an Hermann den Lahmen', *NA* 5 (1880), 202–6.

[22] Otloh of St Emmeram, *Liber de suis scriptoribus* (*PL* 146.0058). On Otloh see E. Dümmler, 'Über den Mönch Otloh von St. Emmeram', *Sitzungsberichte der königlich Preußischen Akademie der Wissenschaften zu Berlin* 2 (1895), 1071–1102; H. E. Schauwecker, *Otloh von St. Emmeram. Ein Beitrag zur Bildungs- und Frömmigkeitsgeschichte des 11. Jahrhunderts* (Munich, 1964); G. R. Evans, '"Studium discendi": Otloh of St Emmeram and the seven liberal arts', *Recherches de théologie ancienne et médiévale* 44 (1977), 29–54.

tises could be linked in such a way is not new. In 1949 the influential Dutch musicologist Joseph Smits van Waesberghe published an article in *Musica disciplina* stating firmly his belief in the existence of a 'Liège school of music theory' spanning the period from the middle of the eleventh century to James of Liège's monumental *Speculum musicae* in the fourteenth.[23] Examining twelve music treatises, he wrote of an 'evident kinship of medieval treatises and implied purpose of their authors to continue in the line of their predecessors', and elsewhere identified an interdependence that was 'a determining influence in the development of music theory'.[24] He suggested that instruction in *musica* formed an integral part of the curriculum at the cathedral school in Liège, as well as in the monasteries of St Laurence and St James, and interpreted the growth in structure of these two houses in the second half of the eleventh century as we might interpret the development of Parisian Mont Ste Geneviève in the middle years of the twelfth. Much of Smits van Waesberghe's other work on medieval music theory was coloured by this interpretation.[25] This grand theory was perhaps based more upon nationalistic pride than sound scholarship, for it is undermined by forced interpretations and faulty reasoning. His ascriptions of authors and treatises to the 'school of Liège' have steadily been questioned and revised, leaving the supposed school itself little by way of historical foundation.[26]

In its place, modern scholars have favoured a south-German school, though none has offered a study devoted to it and its members. Claude Palisca was one of the first to suggest this when he wrote of countering 'van Waesberghe's Liège school with a south-German school'.[27] David Hiley has also spoken of the south-German theorists as a group, and the implications of this are beginning to be exploited in a number of studies on individual theorists and their works.[28] It is surely more helpful, however, to

[23] J. Smits van Waesberghe, 'Some music treatises and their interrelation: a school of Liége c. 1050–1200?', *Musica disciplina* 3 (1949), 25–31, 95–118.
[24] Ibid., 26.
[25] J. Smits van Waesberghe, *Muziekgeschiedenis der Middeleeuwen 1. De Luiksche muziekschool als centrum van het muziektheoretische onderricht in de middeleeuwen* (Tilburg, 1936); *School en muziek in de middeleeuwen. De muziekdidatiek de vroege middeleeuwen* (Amsterdam, 1949); *Musikerziehung. Lehre und Theorie der Musik im Mittelalter* (Leipzig, 1969).
[26] See below, pp. 37, 44–5, 47–8.
[27] C. V. Palisca in W. Babb (trans.) and C. V. Palisca (ed.), *Hucbald, Guido and John on music: three medieval treatises* (New Haven and London, 1978), p. 94.
[28] D. Hiley, *Western plainchant: a handbook* (Oxford, 1993), pp. 470–7. See also A. Rausch, 'Der Tonar des Bern von Reichenau und die süddeutsche Tradition', *Musicologica austriaca* 14/15 (1996), 157–66; C. Meyer, 'Organistrum et synemmenon grave. Observations

view the theorists as a circle of scholars connected by certain themes and shared concerns rather than as a 'school'. Their connexion was not the rigid one that is suggested by the term school, but a fluid one that relied as much upon the relatively free movement of personnel, texts and ideas between centres, as upon bonds between teacher and pupil. The importance of personal and institutional links will be a recurring theme in the study of the south-German circle of music theorists.

Reichenau and the beginnings of the south-German circle

Bern of Reichenau

Bern of Reichenau, who died in 1048 having been abbot of Reichenau for forty years, can be seen as the originator of the south-German circle of music theorists. Hans Oesch, working on the estimate that Bern was thirty on becoming abbot of Reichenau, has suggested that he was born *c.* 978.[29] Little is known of Bern's life before 1008, the year he was named abbot of the imperial abbey of Reichenau on Lake Constance by King Henry II. Two hypotheses concerning his early life, which were put forward in the older historiography, are no longer accepted: the first sought to identify him with St Gallen, the second with Fleury.[30] The latter interpretation, which was advocated by some distinguished historians, was based upon the belief that the author of the liturgical tract *Ratio generalis de initio adventus Domini* was a monk of Fleury, and the assumption that this person and Bern were identical.[31] It has been shown, however, that Bern was not the author of this treatise, thus undermining the Fleury hypothesis.[32] A more plausible interpretation is offered by Bern's pupil and friend,

---

Footnote 28 (*cont.*)
   sur l'échelle acoustique dans l'espace germanique (XIe–XIIIe siècle)', in W. Pass and A. Rausch (eds), *Mittelalterliche Musiktheorie in Zentraleuropa* (Tutzing, 1998), pp. 87–106; M. Bernhard, 'The *Seligenstadt Tonary*', *Plainsong and medieval music* 13 (2004), 115; G. Ilnitchi, *The play of meanings: Aribo's De musica and the hermeneutics of musical thought* (Lanham, Md., 2005).

[29] H. Oesch, *Berno und Hermann von Reichenau als Musiktheoretiker. Mit einem Überblick über ihr Leben und die handschriftliche Überlieferung ihrer Werke* (Bern, 1961), p. 32 n. 2.

[30] Ibid., pp. 28–9.

[31] *Ratio generalis de initio adventus Domini* (*PL* 142.1088A); M. Manitius, *Geschichte der Lateinischen Literatur des Mittelalters* 2 (Munich, 1923; repr. 1976), p. 62; G. Pietzsch, *Die Klassifikation der Musik von Boethius bis Ugolino von Orvieto* (Halle, 1929), p. 132.

[32] Oesch, *Berno und Hermann*, pp. 29–32. The Fleury myth is unwittingly repeated by A. Wagner, *Gorze au XIe siècle. Contribution à l'histoire du monachisme bénédictine dans l'Empire* (n.p., 1996), p. 48.

Herman of Reichenau, whose *Chronicle* for 1008 identifies him as a monk of the Lotharingian monastery of Prüm.³³ The appointment of Bern in 1008 continued the influence of the Gorze reform upon Reichenau. This had started in the tenth century with the appointment of Abbot Ruodmann, 972–85. In 1006 the pious Henry II, as part of a renewed effort to promote the customs of Gorze in a number of imperial abbeys, imposed Immo – then abbot both of Gorze and of Prüm – on Reichenau. The king's intervention in the affairs of Reichenau, as in the affairs of some other imperial abbeys, was unsuccessful: Immo, although enjoying a favourable reputation as a reformer in Lotharingia and at the Imperial court, was greatly resented by the monks of Reichenau. Herman of Reichenau described him as 'a harsh man' who severely afflicted the monks.³⁴ It was only in 1008 that Henry II, 'learning at last of the cruelty of Immo, removed him and appointed Bern, a learned and pious man and a monk of Prüm'.³⁵ Bern was in fact a pupil of Immo and continued to implement in Reichenau the customs associated with the Gorze reform. Although Bern was in contact with Abbot Odilo of Cluny, 992–1049, whose reforms he admired, the model of reform with which he was most familiar was that of Lotharingia and Gorze: his abbacy was characterized by 'dedication to monastic reform and loyalty to the German king and emperor, the patron and protector of the imperial abbey of Reichenau'.³⁶

Abbot Bern's dedication to monastic reform was reflected in his scholarly activity. The inspiration for his liturgical works, for example, is rooted in the emphasis placed upon monastic observance by the Gorze reform.³⁷ This concern is evident in his *Qualiter adventus Domini celebretur* and *Qualiter quatuor temporum ieiunia par sua sabbata sint observanda*, both of which take the form of letters addressed to Archbishop Aribo of Mainz, as well as in

---

[33] Herman of Reichenau, *Chronicon* 1008, *MGH SS* 5, p. 119.

[34] Ibid. 1006, p. 118.40–2: Sed rex Heinricus eius insolentiam, quamvis ab eo peccunias accepisset, detestatus, fratribusque apud se accusatis infensus, Ymmonem quendam, Gorziensem abbatem, qui et Prumiam ipso tempore tenebat, virum austerum, ipsis invitis praeposuit.

[35] Ibid. 1008, p. 119.8–10: Ipso anno Heinricus rex, cognita tandem post duos annos Ymmonis crudelitate, remoto eo, Bern, virum doctum et pium, Prumiensem monachum, Augiae constituit abbatem.

[36] I. S. Robinson (trans.), *Eleventh-century Germany: the Swabian Chronicles* (Manchester, 2008), p. 1.

[37] On the liturgical implications of the Gorze reform see H. Mayr-Harting, *Ottonian book illumination: an historical study*, 2 vols (London, 1991), 1, pp. 83–8; 2, pp. 126–7; L. Donnat, 'Vie et coutume monastique dans la Vita de Jean de Gorze' and A. Angenendt, 'Die Liturgie in der Vita des Johannes von Gorze', in M. Parisse and O. Oexle (eds), *L'Abbaye de Gorze au Xe siècle* (Nancy, 1993), pp. 159–82, 193–211.

De quibusdam rebus ad missae officium pertinentibus (also called *De officio missae*).³⁸ A fourth liturgical treatise – *De varia psalmorum atque cantuum modulatione* – concerns the textual differences of the Gallican and Roman psalters. Although it survives in an eleventh-century source, doubts have been raised about its authenticity.³⁹ Bern's theological works include a fragmentary treatise on prayer addressed to Henry III, 1039–56 and ten sermons.⁴⁰ His *Vita* of St Ulrich of Augsburg was extremely popular, surviving in some fifty manuscripts from the eleventh century to the fifteenth.⁴¹ His musical compositions comprise three hymns, three sequences, an Epiphany prose and a *Historia* for St Ulrich.⁴² A *Historia* for St Meinrad has also been attributed to Bern, although it survives only in one thirteenth-century source.⁴³ (The *Historia* is a Festal Office for a saint's day where the usual antiphons and responds from First to Second Vespers are replaced by specially composed hagiographical and historical material relating to that saint.) A number of Bern's letters also survive: these provide a useful picture of his life as abbot of an influential monastery in eleventh-century society.⁴⁴

---

³⁸ Bern of Reichenau, *Qualiter adventus Domini celebretur*, ed. F.-J. Schmale, *Die Briefe des Abtes Bern von Reichenau* (Stuttgart, 1961), pp. 39–46 (*PL* 142.1079–1086); *Qualiter quatuor temporum ieiunia par sua sabbata sint observanda* (*PL* 142.1085–1088), *De quibusdam rebus ad missae officium pertinentibus* (*PL* 142.1055–1080). See Oesch, *Berno und Hermann*, pp. 50–4. H. Hüschen, 'Bern von Reichenau', *Verfasserlexikon* 1 (1978), cols 739–40 dates *Qualiter adventus Domini* and *Qualiter quatuor temporum* to before 1027, while dating *De quibusdam rebus* between 1024 and 1032.

³⁹ Heidelberg, Universitätsbibliothek, Cod. IX 20, fols 69r–82r, *GS* 2, pp. 91–114 (*PL* 142.1131–1154). Hüschen, 'Bern von Reichenau', col. 740 dates it to before 1040. See, however, Oesch, *Berno und Hermann*, pp. 54–6; L. Gushee and D. Pesce, 'Berno of Reichenau', *NG* 3, p. 442.

⁴⁰ B. de Vergille, 'Fragment d'un traité de la prière, dédié par Bernon de Reichenau à Henri III, roi de Germanie', *Revue du moyen âge latin* 2 (1946), 264–5; F.-J. Schmale (ed.), *Die Briefe des Abtes Bern von Reichenau*, pp. 68–9. On Bern's sermons see Oesch, *Berno und Hermann*, pp. 61–4. Three have been published: *De Matthia Apostolo*, *GS* 2, pp. 122–4; *De conceptione Mariae* and *De natali Domini*, in A. Sanderus (ed.), *Bibliotheca belgica manuscripta* 1 (Lille, 1641; repr. Brussels 1972), pp. 244–56.

⁴¹ Bern of Reichenau, *Vita sancti Udalrici*, ed. K.-E. Geith, *Das leben des Heiligen Ulrich* (Berlin, 1971), pp. 23–78 (*PL* 142.1183–1204); Oesch, *Berno und Hermann*, p. 58; Hüschen, 'Bern von Reichenau', col. 741.

⁴² *GS* 2, pp. 117–22. Oesch, *Berno und Hermann*, pp. 78–82; M. Klaper, 'Die musikalische Überlieferung aus dem Kloster Reichenau im 11. Jahrhundert und die kompositorische Tätigkeit des Abtes Bern (1008–1048)', in W. Pass and A. Rausch (eds), *Beiträge zur Musik, Musiktheorie und Liturgie der Abtei Reichenau. Bericht über die Tagung Heiligenkreuz 6.–8. Dezember 1999* (Tutzing, 2001), pp. 1–28.

⁴³ Einsiedeln, Stiftsbibliothek, Cod. 611, fols 163v–167v; Oesch, *Berno und Hermann*, p. 82; A. Rausch, 'Bern', *MGG. Personenteil* 2, col. 1357.

⁴⁴ Bern of Reichenau, *Letters*, ed. Schmale, *Die Briefe des Abtes Bern von Reichenau*. See also C. Erdmann, 'Bern von Reichenau und Heinrich III.', in C. Erdmann, *Forschungen zur*

Abbot Bern enjoyed a reputation as a learned musician. This is evident from two twelfth-century sources: Sigebert of Gembloux's *Liber de illustribus viris* and the bibliographic *De scriptoribus ecclesiasticis*. Sigebert – writing about 1112 – devoted much of his entry on Bern to this musical reputation, proclaiming his eminence in music, in the rules of the consonances, in the measurement of the monochord, his advocacy of the usefulness of the *synemmenon* tetrachord and his authorship of a tonary.[45] *De scriptoribus ecclesiasticis* was originally attributed to an anonymous author based in Melk, but Emile Ettlinger has identified it with Prüfening.[46] Heinrich von Fichtenau has attributed it to Wolfger of Prüfening and dated it to shortly after 1165.[47] Like Sigebert, Wolfger emphasized Bern's musical reputation, and mentioned that he wrote a 'most excellent' work on music.[48]

This 'most excellent' work on music is surely *Prologus in tonarium*, Bern's most extensive and most frequently copied work of music theory. *Prologus* and its accompanying tonary were frequently separated in manuscripts, so it is unclear whether Wolfger was referring to a version with or without the tonary. The original was dedicated to Archbishop Pilgrim of Cologne, which implies that it was written between 1021 and 1036.[49]

politischen Ideenwelt des Frühmittelalters. Aus dem Nachlass des Verfassers, ed. F. Baethgen (Berlin, 1951), pp. 112–19; H. Schwarmaier, 'Reichenauer Gedenkbucheinträge aus der Anfangszeit der Regierung König Konrad II.', *Zeitschrift für Württembergische Landesgeschichte* 22 (1963), 19–28.

[45] Sigebert of Gembloux, *Liber de illustribus viris* 157, ed. R. Witte, *Catalogus Sigeberti Gemblacensis monachi de viris illustribus. Kritische Ausgabe* (Bern and Frankfurt am Main, 1974), p. 98: Berno abbas Augiensis in humana et divina scientia claruit. Pretero ea, que de humana scientia scripsit, in quibus eminet hoc, quod in arte musice prepollens de regulis simphoniarum et tonorum scripsit et quod in mensurando monocordo ultra regulam Boetii, sed assensu iunioris Boetio Guidonis supposuit unum tonum tetracordo ypaton et contra usum maiorum in ipso tetracordo ypaton inseruit utiliter sinemenon.

[46] See E. Ettlinger in Wolfger of Prüfening, *De scriptoribus ecclesiasticis*, ed. E. Ettlinger, *Der sogenannte Anonymus Mellicensis De scriptoribus ecclesiasticis* (Straßburg, 1896), pp. 4–23.

[47] H. von Fichtenau, 'Wolfger von Prüfening', *Mitteilungen des Instituts für Österreichische Geschichtsforschung* 51 (1937), 341–51; B. Bischoff, 'Wolfger', in K. Langosch (ed.), *Die deutsche Literatur des Mittelalters. Verfasserlexikon* 4 (Berlin, 1953), cols 1051–6 suggests 1170.

[48] Wolfger of Prüfening, *De scriptoribus ecclesiasticis* 81, pp. 81–2: Bern musicus, pius ac doctus in monasterio Prumensi sub monastica professione deguit, quem postmodum Henricus Pius imperator abbatem Augiae constituit; qui gratanter acceptus a fratribus fratres dispersos recollegit, et a Lamperto Constantiensi episcopo consecratus, magna insignis pietate ac scientia praefuit annis quadraginta. Hic scripsit librum De institutione missarum, et de Musica opus praestantissimum. Vitam quoque sancti Udalrici Augustensis episcopi.

[49] Hauck, *Kirchengeschichte Deutschlands* 3, p. 994.

In writing *Prologus in tonarium*, Bern was influenced by Hucbald of St Amand (c. 840–930),[50] pseudo-Bernelinus,[51] the anonymous *Musica enchiriadis*,[52] and Regino of Prüm (c. 842–915), whose treatise and tonary he had probably studied while a monk of that monastery.[53] *Prologus in tonarium* exerted a considerable influence on subsequent generations of south-German music theorists. It was widely copied during the eleventh and twelfth centuries: today *Prologus* survives in over thirty manuscripts, *Tonarius* in seventeen.[54] To this total must be added the evidence of library catalogues and known lost copies: the treatise was also available in the monasteries of St Blasien, St Georgen, Muri, Tegernsee, Weissenau and Reichenau during the eleventh and twelfth centuries.[55] Not only was *Prologus* copied frequently, but a group of manuscripts exists containing extensive textual interpolations.[56] These interpolations represent the efforts of eleventh-century clerks to explain and understand particular points of Bern's music theory, and stand as testimony to the importance of *Prologus in tonarium* in the eleventh and twelfth centuries.

Abbot Bern's other work of music theory is in the form of a short treatise and tonary that survives in one eleventh-century manuscript devoted to his works: St Gallen, Stiftsbibliothek, Cod. 898.[57] Martin Gerbert edited this treatise under the title *De consona tonorum diversitate*, but Alexander Rausch – the most recent editor of Bern's musical works – has chosen the title *Epistola de tonis*.[58] In so doing Rausch has placed this work firmly within the eleventh-century epistolary genre. Many contemporary treatises (including Bern's liturgical works) were entitled not *tractatus* or *liber*, but *epistola*, a convention upon which the influential papal reformer Peter

---

[50] Hucbald of St Amand, *Musica*, ed. Y. Chartier, *L'Œuvre musicale d'Hucbald de Saint-Amand. Les compositions et le traité de musique* (Montreal, 1995); *GS* 1, pp. 103–25.

[51] Pseudo-Bernelinus, *Cita et vera divisio monochordi*, *GS* 1, pp. 312–30.

[52] Anon., *Musica enchiriadis*, ed. H. Schmid, *Musica et scolica enchiriadis, una cum aliquibus tractatulis adiunctis*. (Munich, 1981).

[53] Regino of Prüm, *Epistola de harmonica institutione et tonarius*, ed. M. P. le Roux, 'The *De harmonica institutione* and *Tonarius* of Regino of Prüm' (Ph.D. dissertation, Catholic University of America, 1965); *Epistola de harmonica institutione*, ed. M. Bernhard, *Clavis Gerberti. Eine Revision von Martin Gerberts Scriptores ecclesiastici de musica sacra potissimum (St. Blasien 1784)* (Munich, 1989), pp. 37–73.

[54] A. Rausch (ed.), *Die Musiktraktate des Abtes Bern von Reichenau. Edition und Interpretation* (Tutzing, 1999), pp. 17–24, 71.

[55] Oesch, *Berno und Hermann*, p. 45.

[56] See Chapter 2, pp. 72–80.

[57] *RISM B* 3/1, pp. 78–9; Klaper, 'Die musikalische Überlieferung aus dem Kloster Reichenau im 11. Jahrhundert', pp. 2–10, 24–5.

[58] *GS* 2, pp. 114–17.

Damian had insisted, and which was copied by many German scholars, among them Master Onulf of Speyer, who characterized his own treatise on the rhetorical figures as 'opusculum seu carta seu epistola'.[59] *Epistola de tonis* was written in response to questions from the monks of Reichenau: Bern addressed it to 'his beloved sons in Christ, Burchard and Kerung, along with the other teachers in the school of Reichenau'.[60] (This Burchard is probably the monk who was also cantor of Reichenau, an active copyist in the Reichenau scriptorium and – from 1030 until his death in 1037 – abbot of St Emmeram in Regensburg.) It probably predates *Prologus in tonarium*, and may have been intended by Bern as a preliminary answer to the questions he would deal with more thoroughly in the later treatise. The protocol indicates that Bern was away from Reichenau at the time of writing, perhaps on one of the extended political trips necessitated by his influential position as abbot of Reichenau. Abbot Bern accompanied Henry II on his Roman expeditions of 1014 and 1022, for example, so it is possible that *Epistola de tonis* was written on such an occasion.[61]

The dedication to the teachers of Reichenau indicates the intended audience, not only of *Epistola de tonis*, but also of the other south-German treatises: like Master Onulf of Speyer's *Colores rhetorici*, it was intended as a resource for teachers.[62] The practicality that underlines each of Bern's music treatises, as well as those of later German theorists, stems from the emphasis that the Gorze reform placed upon the proper regulation of the *vita communis* in general and of the *opus Dei* in particular.

Herman of Reichenau

The legacy of Abbot Bern's musical scholarship passed in the first place to the distinguished scholar Herman of Reichenau. Herman tells us in his *Chronicle* that he was born on 18 July 1013, one of fifteen children of

---

[59] I. S. Robinson, 'The "Colores rhetorici" in the Investiture Contest', *Traditio* 32 (1976), 231; T. J. H. McCarthy, 'Literary practice in eleventh-century music theory: the *colores rhetorici* and Aribo's *De musica*', *Medium Aevum* 71 (2002), 192; Onulf of Speyer, *Colores rhetorici* 1.25, ed. W. Wattenbach, 'Magister Onulf von Speyer', *Sitzungsberichte der königlich Preußischen Akademie der Wissenschaften zu Berlin* 1 (1894), 380. See also F.-J. Schmale, 'Zu den Briefen Berns von Reichenau', *Zeitschrift für Kirchengeschichte* 68 (1957), 73.

[60] Bern of Reichenau, *Epistola de tonis*, p. 12: . . . dilectissimis in Christo filiis Purchardo et Kerungo, una cum caeteris in dominicarum scolarum gymnasio Augiae . . .

[61] See, however, Rausch (ed.), *Die Musiktraktate des Abtes Bern*, pp. 129–30, who suggests *c*. 1008.

[62] See Introduction, pp. 3–4.

Swabian magnate Count Wolferad II of Altshausen (d. 1065).[63] Perhaps the most important and detailed contemporary source for Herman's life – from which most of our information is derived – is the obituary provided by his pupil and close associate Berthold of Reichenau, who continued Herman's *Chronicle* from 1054 to 1080.[64] Berthold recorded that Herman 'was from his earliest years . . . totally lame in all his limbs from a paralytic disease'.[65] On account of this, Herman was entrusted as an oblate to Bern of Reichenau, in an action that reflected a common practice among noble families with handicapped children at the time.[66] The exact date is unknown, but some scholars have taken Herman's autobiographical comment that he began his schooling on 15 September 1020 as the date for his entry to Reichenau.[67] Herman took his solemn vows in 1043.

As with Abbot Bern, there have been several competing hypotheses about Herman's early life. Following the example of the historian Johannes Trithemius (1462–1516), Jodokus Metzler (1574–1639) claimed in his *De viris illustribus monasterii S. Galli* that Herman had spent his early years in St Gallen,[68] while Johannes Egon, in his roughly contemporary *De viris illustribus monasterii Augiae Majoris*, claimed that distinction for Reichenau.[69] In the 1930s Jacques Handschin suggested that Herman was placed in care 'apud Augustam Vindelicam' ('at Augsburg'). The basis for this claim was a miracle story extant in a twelfth-century English manuscript (Cambridge, Corpus Christi College, 111).[70] Neither Berthold's obit-

---

[63] On Herman's family see J. Kerkhoff, 'Die Grafen von Altshausen-Veringen. Die Ausbildung der Familie zum Adelsgeschlecht und der Aufbau ihrer Herrschaft im 11. und 12. Jahrhundert', *Hohenzollerische Jahreshefte* 24 (1964), 1–132; H. Jänichen, 'Zur Genealogie der älteren Grafen von Veringen', *Zeitschrift für Württembergische Landesgeschichte* 27 (1968), 1–30.

[64] Berthold of Reichenau, *Chronicon*, ed. I. S. Robinson, *MGH SSrG NS* 14, pp. 163–74.

[65] Ibid., 1054, p. 163: Herimannus. . .ab ineunte etate in exteriori homine passione paralytica omnibus membris dissolutorie contractus.

[66] For contemporary criticism of this practice see the letter from Ulrich of Zell to William of Hirsau, *Antiquiores consuetudines monasterii Cluniacenses* (*PL* 149.0635A–0636A).

[67] A. Borst, *Mönche am Bodensee, 610–1525* (Sigmaringen, 1978), p. 107.

[68] J. Metzler, *De viris illustribus monasterii S. Galli libri II* 1.47, in B. Pez, *Thesaurus anecdotarum novissimus. Seu veterum monumentorum praecipue ecclesiasticorum, ex Germanicis potissimum bibliothecis adornata collectio recentissima. Omnia cum praefationibus, observationibus [&c] publici juris facta, a B. Pezio* 1.3 (Augsburg, 1721), cols 581–3.

[69] J. Egon, *De viris illustribus monasterii Augiae Majoris, seu Divitis* 28, in B. Pez, *Thesaurus anecdotarum novissimus* 1.3, cols 688–99.

[70] J. Handschin, 'Hermannus Contractus-Legende – nur Legende?', *Zeitschrift für deutsches Altertum und deutsche Literatur* 72 (1932), 1–8. Handschin's theory has been repeated and amplified in N. Hörberg, *Libri sanctae Afrae. St. Ulrich und Afra zu Augsburg im 11. und 12. Jahrhundert nach Zeugnissen der Klosterbibliothek* (Göttingen, 1983), pp. 216–24.

uary nor any of Herman's autobiographical comments in his *Chronicle*, however, suggests anything other than that Herman spent his early years at Reichenau. Berthold of Reichenau was a close friend and colleague of his teacher: his testimony, therefore, casts grave doubt on the putative associations with St Gallen and Augsburg. Indeed, these have been rejected by several authorities.[71]

Berthold's obituary provides the most detailed description of Herman's scholarly activities: he ascribes to Herman works on astronomy, the computus, geometry and music, in addition to historical and poetical works. Berthold also recorded Herman's authorship of *Historia* for 'St George, Sts Gordian and Epymachus, the martyr St Afra, St Magnus the Confessor and the holy bishop Wolfgang [of Regensburg]', emphasizing that Herman was responsible for both the poetry and the music of these festal offices.[72]

Although there has been a tendency in recent years to question some of these attributions, manuscript evidence underlines the general accuracy of Berthold's testimony. Herman's four treatises on astronomy comprise two on the astrolabe, entitled *De mensura astrolabii* and *De utilitatibus astrolabii* respectively;[73] *De mense lunari*, praised by Berthold for offering 'the most reliable rules concerning the illumination of the moon, by means of which it may very clearly be known at what hour of the day or night the moon is illuminated by the sun';[74] and a treatise concerned with the calculation of lunar eclipses – *De defectu solis et lunae* – which alone of the four is yet unedited. Also unedited is Herman's treatise on the computus (*Regulae in computum*) in which, according to Berthold, he 'greatly surpassed all his

[71] I. Herwegen, 'Die hl. Hildegard von Bingen und das Oblateninstitut', *SMGBZ* 33 (1912), 543–52; P. Hofmeister, 'Die Klaustral-Oblaten', *SMGBZ* 72 (1961), 5–45; Oesch, *Berno und Hermann*, pp. 128–31 and Borst, *Mönche am Bodensee*, p. 107; Robinson, *Eleventh-century Germany: the Swabian Chronicles*, p. 5. Robinson tellingly suggests that since Augsburg and Reichenau shared a patron, the twelfth-century author of the miracle story or a scribe copying his work may well have confused the churches of St Mary in *Augia* (Reichenau) and *Augusta* (Augsburg).

[72] Berthold of Reichenau, *Chronicon* 1054, p. 168: Cantus item hystoriales plenarios, utpote quo musicus peritior non erat, de sancto Georgio, sanctis Gordiano et Epimacho, sancta Affra martyre, sancto Magno confessore et de sancto Wolfgango episcopo mira suavitate et elegantia euphonicos preter alia huiusmodi perplura neumatizavit et composuit.

[73] Herman of Reichenau, *De mensura astrolabii*, ed. J. Drecker, 'Hermannus Contractus. Über das Astrolab', *Isis* 16 (1931), 203–12; *De utilitatibus astrolabii*, ed. N. Bubnov, *Gerberti postea Silvestri II papae opera mathematica* 2 (Berlin, 1899; repr. Hildesheim, 1963), pp. 109–47.

[74] Herman of Reichenau, *De mense lunari*, ed. A. Borst, 'Ein Forschungsbericht Hermanns des Lahmen', *DA* 40 (1984), 474–7. Berthold of Reichenau, *Chronicon* 1054, p. 167: . . . et preter cetera de naturali lune incensione regulares experientissimos adinvenit, per quos evidentissime sciatur, in qualibet hora diei sive noctis a sole incendatur.

predecessors'.[75] The work on geometry mentioned by Berthold does not seem to have survived: those geometrical works once ascribed to Herman are now thought not to be by him. Herman's arithmetical writings include a treatise on the abacus – *Regulae qualiter multiplicationes fiant in abaco* – and a treatise on the arithmetical game rythmomachia entitled *De rhythmimachia*.[76] A set of fraction tables that survives in two early twelfth-century English manuscripts has been attributed to Herman, although this is based almost entirely on the fact that the manuscripts name the author of the tables as 'Hermannus'.[77] Herman's sole surviving historical work is his *Chronicle* of the world to 1054, which was continued by Berthold.[78] Herman was probably stimulated to begin work on the chronicle in its present version by the death of Abbot Bern in 1048: the annal for 1008, which records Bern's arrival at Reichenau, states that he was abbot for forty years.[79] The works describing the deeds of the emperors Conrad II and Henry III mentioned by Berthold are no longer extant, although Otto of Freising (*c*. 1114–58) referred to them in his chronicle.[80] A lengthy poem on the eight principal vices, which remained unfinished at Herman's death, as well as his other surviving metrical works, show him to have been a poet of considerable skill.[81] Herman was also responsible for a continuation of the martyrology

---

[75] Berthold of Reichenau, *Chronicon* 1054, p. 167: Compoti igitur rationem regulas et nonnulla argumenta, in quo prioribus cunctis non parum precelluit; A. Cordiolani, 'Le computiste Hermann de Reichenau', *Miscellanea di Storia Ligure* 3 (1961), 167–90.

[76] Herman of Reichenau, *Regulae qualiter multiplicationes fiant in abaco*, ed. M. Hellmann, 'Der Rechenlehrer Herimannus. Mit Edition der *Regulae, qualiter multiplicationes fiant in abaco* und Abdruck der Bruchtabellen', in W. Berschin and M. Hellmann, *Hermann der Lahme. Gelehrter und Dichter (1013–1054)* (Heidelberg, 2005), pp. 33–72.; *De rhythmimachia*, ed. A. Borst, *Das mittelalterliche Zahlenkampfspiel* (Heidelberg, 1986), pp. 335–9. See also E. W. Wappler, 'Bemerkungen zur Rhythmomachie', *Zeitschrift für Mathematik und Physik* 37 (1892), 1–17.

[77] F. A. Yeldham, 'Fraction tables of Hermannus Contractus', *Speculum* 3 (1928), 241–5.

[78] Herman of Reichenau, *Chronicon*, *MGH SS* 5, pp. 67–133. See also F.-J. Schmale, 'Die Reichenauer Weltchronistik', in H. Maurer (ed.), *Die Abtei Reichenau. Neue Beiträge zur Geschichte und Kultur des Inselklosters* (Sigmaringen, 1974), pp. 125–58; A. Borst, 'Hermann der Lahme und die Geschichte', *Hegau* 32–3 (1975–6), 7–18.

[79] Borst, *Mönche am Bodensee*, p. 111 dates this to 1044/45, presumably because the annals become more detailed at this point. Herman may well have been collecting material for the chronicle in the years preceeding 1048.

[80] Otto of Freising, *Chronicon* 6.33, *MGH SS* 20, p. 245.

[81] Herman of Reichenau, *De octo vitiis principalibus*, ed. E. Dümmler, 'Opusculum Herimanni diverso metro compositum', *Zeitschrift für deutsches Altertum* 13 (1867), 385–431. For an assessment of his poetry see P. Dronke, *The medieval lyric*, 3rd edn (Cambridge, 1996), pp. 44–8 and W. Berschin, 'Hermann der Lahme als Sequenzendichter. Mit Diskussion der Antiphonen *Salve regina* und *Alma redemptoris mater*', in Berschin and Hellmann, *Hermann der Lahme*, pp. 73–106.

by Notker of St Gallen (840–912).[82] Bernhard Bischoff's attribution of glosses on the Pauline Epistles to Herman has been disputed.[83]

To this extensive erudition must be added Herman's musical reputation. In Berthold's opinion there was never a 'more learned' musician, an assessment that was corroborated some 100 years later by Wolfger of Prüfening who supposed that hardly a more subtle modern theorist had ever existed.[84] Of the five *historiae* mentioned by Berthold, those for St Wolfgang, St Afra and St Magnus survive today, in addition to some five sequences and two antiphons.[85]

The office for St Wolfgang was commissioned specially for the canonization of Wolfgang, bishop of Regensburg from 972 to 994, which took place at St Emmeram in 1052. The canonization itself was a piece of grand ecclesiastical and political theatre organized by Abbot Reginward of St Emmeram, 1040–c. 1060, as part of on-going attempts to out-manoeuvre Bishop Gebhard of Regensburg, universally perceived by the monks as an implacable enemy of their monastery.[86] It was attended by Emperor Henry III and performed by his kinsman Pope Leo IX, whose recent attempts to enforce papal

---

[82] E. Dümmler (ed.), 'Das Martyrologium Notkers und seiner Verwandten', *Forschung zur deutschen Geschichte* 25 (1885), 209-12.

[83] These marginal and interlinear glosses, extant in St Gallen, Stiftsbibliothek, Cod. 64, pp. 2–269, have been edited by B. Bischoff: 'Glossen Hermanns des Lahmen und Metrische Glossen zu den Paulinischen Briefen (vor 1054)', in B. Bischoff, *Anecdota novissima. Texte des vierten bis sechzehnten Jahrhunderts* (Stuttgart, 1984), pp. 35–48. See, however, W. Berschin, *Eremus und Insula. St. Gallen und die Reichenau im Mittelalter. Modell einer lateinischen Literaturlandschaft* (Wiesbaden, 2005), pp. 67-70, who ascribes them to Herman of St Gallen.

[84] Berthold of Reichenau, *Chronicle* 1054, p. 168.9: Cantus item hystoriales plenarios, utpote quo musicus peritior non erat; p. 169.12: In horologicis et musicis instrumentis et mechanicis nulli par erat componendis; Wolfger of Prüfening, *De scriptoribus ecclesiasticis* 91, p. 85: In musica sane pene modernis omnibus subtilior exstitit, et cantilenas plurimas de musica, cantusque de sanctis satis auctorabiles edidit.

[85] Herman of Reichenau, *Historia sancti Wolfgangi*, ed. D. Hiley, *Historia sancti Wolfgangi episcopi Ratisbonensis. Einführung und Edition* (Ottawa, 2002); *Historia Sanctae Afrae*, ed. D. Hiley and W. Berschin, *Historia Sanctae Afrae martyris Augustensis* (Ottawa, 2004). The office for St Magnus has been cited as forthcoming: see Hiley and Berschin (eds), *Historia Sanctae Afrae*, p. 4 n. 6. Herman's authorship of a number of other liturgical pieces is disputed: Oesch, *Berno und Hermann*, pp. 135-83.

[86] On Gebhard and St Emmeram see F. Mögle-Hofacker and P. Morsbach, 'Bischoff Gebhard III. von Regensburg' and A. Schmid, ' "Auf glühendem Thron in der Hölle." Gebhard III., Otloh von St. Emmeram und die Dionysiusfälschung', in P. Morsbach (ed.), *Ratisbona sacra: das Bistum Regensburg im Mittelalter. Ausstellung anlässlich des 1250jährigen Jubiläums der kanonischen Errichtung des Bistums Regensburg durch Bonifatius 739-1989. Diözesanmuseum Obermünster Regensburg, 2. Juni bis 1. Oktober 1989* (Munich, 1989), pp. 113–18, 119–21.

monopoly on canonization fitted conveniently with Abbot Reginward's plans. Wolfgang, who had begun his schooling at Reichenau, was an apposite figure for canonization: he was simultaneously bishop of Regensburg and abbot of St Emmeram, but separated the two positions when, in 975, he called his friend Ramwold, a monk of St Maximin in Trier, to be abbot of St Emmeram. His career thus signified the emancipation of the monastery from the interference of the local bishop and stood as a public warning to Bishop Gebhard. Although Herman's composition of the *historia* for this occasion owed much to his reputation as a musician, it also reflected the strong links between Reichenau and St Emmeram at this time. In terms of its musical style, the festal office for St Wolfgang is notable for the fact that the way in which the chants are written adheres to the theoretical precepts for composition laid down by Herman in his treatise *Musica*.[87] By practising his dictum that the study of music was concerned with the 'science of composing chants correctly, of judging them by rule and of performing them fittingly', Herman was continuing the emphasis of Abbot Bern – drawn from the Gorze reform – on the necessity for worship to be correct and regular.[88]

Herman's music treatise is built upon the foundations laid by Bern of Reichenau: by reconciling the double octave gamut and system of tetrachords, Herman shaped the theoretical outlook for later generations of German theorists. In doing so he did not unquestioningly follow his teacher: indeed, he disagreed with and criticized Bern's teaching on several points, although he took great care never to mention Bern by name.[89] His refusal to be bound by the authority of earlier writers is also a trait of his arithmetical and astronomical works.[90] Although Hans Oesch could not be certain that Herman knew of Guido of Arezzo, internal evidence from *Musica* shows that Herman was indeed familiar with some of Guido's teaching.[91] As with later German authors, Herman was not slow to criticize the faults he perceived in Guido's work.

The date of *Musica* is uncertain. Although many scholars believe that Herman wrote it after Abbot Bern's death in 1048 (because of its criticisms

---

[87] D. Hiley, 'Das Wolfgang-Offiziums des Hermannus Contractus – Zum Wechselspiel von Modustheorie und Gesangspraxis in der Mitte des XI. Jahrhunderts', in W. Berschin and D. Hiley (eds), *Die Offizien des Mittelalters. Dichtung und Musik* (Tutzing, 1999), 129–42.
[88] Herman of Reichenau, *Musica* 15, p. 47.
[89] See Chapter 2, pp. 65–72.
[90] W. Bergmann, 'Chronographie und Komputistik bei Hermann von Reichenau', in D. Berg and H.-W. Goetz (eds), *Historiographia mediaevalis. Studien zur Geschichtsschreibung und Quellenkunde des Mittelalters. Festschrift für Franz-Joseph Schmale zum 65. Geburtstag* (Darmstadt, 1988), pp. 103–17.
[91] See Chapter 2, pp. 82–5.

of Bern's teaching), Arno Borst perceived a less mature style and suggested it belongs to an earlier part of Herman's career. He described it as possibly Herman's 'first major work' and assigned it to the early 1030s.[92] David Hiley has favoured Borst's theory, which has allowed him to suggest that the monk Burchard, cantor of Reichenau and co-addressee of Bern's *Epistola de tonis* (who probably also taught Herman), may have been responsible for the introduction of Reichenau musical scholarship to St Emmeram after he became abbot there in 1030. In truth, however, the evidence is inconclusive. The suggestion that Herman waited until after Bern's death before voicing his criticisms is entirely plausible: aware of the obligations of monastic obedience, he would probably have been embarrassed to question publicly a master whom he greatly admired. Borst's argument for dating needs the corroboration of a detailed study of Herman's Latin style across all his works before it can be accepted as accurate. Nevertheless, the stylistic evidence of the surviving festal offices indicates that Herman's theoretical outlook must have been formed before their composition.

Only two surviving manuscripts contain a full recension of Herman's *Musica*: the late eleventh-century Rochester, Eastman School of Music, ML 92/1100 and the early twelfth-century Vienna, Österreichische Nationalbibliothek, Cod. 51. Another manuscript – Kassel, Landesbibliothek, 4° Mss Math. 1 – transmits a substantial extract.[93] An assessment of the treatise's influence based solely upon the surviving manuscripts is, however, misleading. Herman's treatise was available at Hirsau,[94] and it is likely that many others copies, now lost, once existed: William of Hirsau, Theoger of Metz, Frutolf of Michelsberg, the Wolf Anonymous and the author of *Quaestiones in musica* all knew Herman's treatise at first hand.[95] Herman also composed a number of mnemonic verses, which explain respectively a notational system that he devised, the musical consonances and the modes. These verses were very influential and enjoyed considerable popularity among subsequent generations of clerks: they survive fully or partly in some thirty manuscripts.[96] Herman's

[92] Borst, 'Ein Forschungsbericht Hermanns des Lahmen', 398.
[93] Kassel, Landesbibliothek und Murhardsche Bibliothek der Stadt Kassel, 4° Mss Math. 1, fols 33v–35r; cf. Herman, *Musica* 19–21, ed. and trans. L. Ellinwood, *Musica Hermanni Contracti* (Rochester, NY, 1936), pp. 57–66.
[94] M. Manitius, 'Geschichtliches aus mittelalterlichen Bibliothekskatalogen', *NA* 32 (1906–07), 692.
[95] See Chapter 2, pp. 71–2.
[96] M. Bernhard, 'Zur Rezeption der musiktheoretischen Werke des Hermannus Contractus', in W. Pass and A. Rausch (eds), *Beiträge zur Musik, Musiktheorie und Liturgie der Abtei Reichenau. Bericht über die Tagung Heiligenkreuz 6.–8. Dezember 1999*

musical works, therefore, were no less widely disseminated than his other works on the quadrivium.

The monastery of St Emmeram in Regensburg was crucial to the dissemination of Herman's works: early copies of the majority of his works survive in St Emmeram manuscripts. This trend is especially noticeable for those works that survive only in a handful of sources: two manuscripts containing *Regulae qualiter multiplicationes fiant in abaco*, for example, are from St Emmeram,[97] while a third was copied during the second half of the eleventh century at Michelsberg, a monastery closely linked to St Emmeram.[98] The sole surviving sources for *De octo vitiis principalibus* and for the verses that Herman wrote on the death of his mother are also St Emmeram manuscripts.[99] Indeed, St Emmeram may also have perpetuated Herman's influence through the later Hirsau reform, for his mnemonic verses, as well as his *historiae* for St Afra and St Magnus, survive in a number of manuscripts connected with the Hirsau movement.[100] Taken together, the appointment of Burchard of Reichenau as abbot of St Emmeram in 1030, Herman's involvement in the canonization of St Wolfgang in 1052, and the transmission of his works in St Emmeram manuscripts, point to significant links between these two monasteries influenced by the Gorze tradition. These links would prove vital for the transmission of the music theory of Bern and Herman of Reichenau.

Footnote 96 (*cont.*)

(Tutzing, 2001), pp. 105–21. The considerable number of recensions of Herman's mnemonic verses contradicts the editorial assertion in *RISM B* 3/3, p. xviii that they had little influence. The third verse – 'Ter terni sunt modi' – is attributed to William of Hirsau in two sources; see Chapter 5, p. 185 n. 43.

[97] Munich, Bayerische Staatsbibliothek, Clm 14689 (early twelfth century) and Clm 14836 (eleventh century). Oesch, *Berno und Hermann*, pp. 157; L. Toneatto, *Codices artis mensoriae. I manoscritto degli antichi opusculi Latini d'agrimensura (v–xix sec.)* 3 (Spoleto, 1995), pp. 1041–2.

[98] Karlsruhe, Badische Landesbibliothek, 504. See T. J. H. McCarthy, 'Biblical scholarship in eleventh-century Michelsberg: the *Glosa in vetus et novum testamentum* of MS Karlsruhe, Badische Landesbibliothek, 504', *Scriptorium* 62 (2008), 6–7.

[99] Munich, Bayerische Staatsbibliothek, Clm 14689 and Clm 14613 (eleventh century). Oesch, *Berno und Hermann*, pp. 177–9.

[100] F. Heinzer, 'Kodifizierung und Vereinheitlichung liturgischer Traditionen. Historisches Phänomen und Interpretationsschlüssel handschriftlicher Überlieferung', in K. Heller, H. Möller and A. Waczkat (eds), *Musik in Mecklenburg. Beiträge eines Kolloquiums zur mecklenburgischen Musikgeschichte veranstaltet vom Institut für Musikwissenschaft der Universität Rostock, 24.–27. September 1997. Mit einer Zeittafel und einer Auswahlbibliographie zur mecklenburgischen Musikgeschichte* (Hildesheim, 2000), pp. 99–103; Hiley and Berschin (eds), *Historia Sanctae Afrae*, pp. 15–16.

St Emmeram and the development of the south-German circle

William of Hirsau

With the deaths of Bern and Herman, attention shifts to the monastery St Emmeram in Regensburg, which was an important centre for the reception and further dissemination of the music theory they pioneered. From the tenth century the monastery – with its richly stocked library – had been a major cultural and intellectual centre.[101] In the eleventh century the names of certain figures, such as Arnold of St Emmeram or the visionary Otloh, stand out.[102] But there is also much evidence of activity in areas such as biblical studies and the quadrivium. In the quadrivium in particular, the monk William, later abbot of Hirsau, was a leading figure.[103] The early-modern historian and Hirsau monk Johannes Trithemius stated that William was born in 1026.[104] In 1069, William was called to become abbot of Hirsau deep in the Black Forest at the behest of Count Adalbert II of Calw, the proprietary overlord of Hirsau. He did not receive abbatial benediction, however, until Ascensiontide 1071. The events of 1069 and 1071 are not entirely clear and reservations about Count Adalbert's high-handed deposition of Abbot Frederick of Hirsau may well have weighed seriously on William's mind. Abbot Frederick seems to have been deposed for being too contemplative rather than for any spiritual or moral unworthiness.[105] Though William's *Vita* declares that the delay in assuming office was caused by a desire to secure liberty from secular proprietorship, such a remark bears the stamp of later controversies and is not surprising in a biography written in the 1090s.[106] Nevertheless, William may have felt some such reservations of a less clearly formulated kind and the truth of the situation may well lie in a combination of these reasons. The distinguished author Bernold of St Blasien, whose writings from 1075 until his death in

---

[101] See J. D. Kyle, 'St Emmeram (Regensburg) as a centre of culture in the late tenth century' (Ph.D. dissertation, Univerity of Pittsburgh, 1976).

[102] See E. Joyce, 'Speaking of spiritual matters: visions and the rhetoric of reform in the *Liber visionum* of Otloh of St Emmeram', in A. I. Beach (ed.), *Manuscripts and monastic culture: reform and renewal in twelfth-century Germany* (Turnhout, 2007), pp. 69–98.

[103] See M. Pfaff, 'Abt Wilhelm von Hirsau', *Erbe und Auftrag* 48 (1972), 83–94.

[104] *MGH SS* 12, p. 211 n. 2.

[105] Jakobs, *Die Hirsauer*, p. 8 n. 21. On Hirsau see K. Schreiner, 'Hirsau und die Hirsauer Reform. Spiritualität, Lebensform und Sozialprofil einer benediktinischen Erneuerungsbewegung im 11. und 12. Jahrhundert', in K. Schreiner (ed.), *Hirsau. St. Peter und Paul 1091–1991* 2 (Stuttgart, 1991), pp. 59–84; H. E. J. Cowdrey, *Pope Gregory VII: 1073–1085* (Oxford, 1998), pp. 253–64.

[106] Haimo of Hirsau, *Vita Willihelmi Abbatis Hirsaugiensis*, *MGH SS* 12, p. 212; see also Cowdrey, *The Cluniacs and the Gregorian reform*, p. 197.

1100 had considerable influence on the papal party in Germany, tells us in his *Chronicle* that William died on 5 July 1091.[107]

William of Hirsau became a leading member of the reform party in southern Germany. The first years of his abbacy saw the introduction of Gorze-style reforms based upon the customs of St Emmeram, and in 1075 he received full exemption for Hirsau from the jurisdiction of the bishop of Speyer, in whose diocese the monastery was located.[108] This charter, concerned with securing the 'liberty' of Hirsau, exhibited considerable similarity to the Cluniac charter of 909. The influence of Cluny on Hirsau increased in the aftermath of Abbot William's visit to Rome in 1075, when he met Pope Gregory VII, whose powerful personality and enthusiasm for Cluniac reform affected William deeply.[109] The conversion of William to a radical Gregorian stance linked Hirsau more closely with the papacy than any previous German monastery. William was 'most fervent in the cause of St Peter' according to Bernold.[110] At the height of the Investiture Contest William acted as Gregory VII's special envoy in southern Germany and Hirsau became an important base for the reformers. The Abbot of Hirsau was named by Paul of Bernried, Gregory VII's biographer, together with Ulrich of Zell, Bishop Altmann of Passau and Abbot Siegfried of Schaffhausen as one of the four pre-eminent Gregorians of Germany.[111]

In addition to being a prominent reformer, William was also remembered as a scholar of exceptional renown. He undertook the studies for which he was noted while still at St Emmeram, before becoming a major figure in south-German Gregorianism. Echoing Berthold's eulogy of Herman, Prior Haimo of Hirsau – the author of William's *Vita* – extolled William's reputation in the monochord, in singing and in time-reckoning, declaring that he 'transcended nearly every master' in the quadrivium.[112]

---

[107] Bernold of St Blasien, *Chronicon* 1091, *MGH SSrG NS* 14, p. 484.10: Willihelmus piae memoriae Hirsaugiensis abbas, in causa sancti Petri ferventissimus et in monastica religione studiosissimus, utpote multorum pater monasteriorum, III. Non. Iulii migravit ad Dominum.

[108] Ibid., p. 484.14: . . . in regularibus disciplinis mirabiliter exaltavit, ipsumque privilegio sedis apostolicae sub Gregorio papa in perpetuum libertavit.

[109] See Robinson, 'The friendship network of Gregory VII', 1–3.

[110] Bernold of St Blasien, *Chronicon* 1091, p. 484.11.

[111] Paul of Bernried, *Vita Gregorii VII papae* 118, ed. J. M. Watterich, *Pontificum Romanorum vitae* 1 (Leipzig, 1862), p. 543; trans. I. S. Robinson, *The papal reform of the eleventh century: lives of Pope Leo IX and Pope Gregory VII* (Manchester, 2004), p. 360.

[112] Haimo of Hirsau, *Vita Willihelmi Abbatis Hirsaugiensis, MGH SS* 12, p. 225.4–10: Struxit et instruxit, quia recto tramite duxit, Collapsam dudum vitam reparans monachorum. Quadruvii priscos transcendit et ipse magistros, Cantibus errorem varium

Similarly, Bernold of St Blasien's *Chronicle* contains valuable information about William's scholarly activities: it records the invention of a natural clock based on the celestial hemisphere, experiments related to the equinox and lucid explanations of computistical problems, 'all of which one of his familiar friends took care to commit to writing'.[113] This is probably a reference to William's treatise *Astronomica*, of which only the prologue survives in the early twelfth-century St Emmeram manuscript Munich, Bayerische Staatsbibliothek, Clm 14689.[114] The prologue, which ends with a reference to the solstices and equinoxes, identifies William's 'familiar friend' as 'O', most likely Otloh of St Emmeram.[115]

William's other work on the quadrivium is his treatise *Musica*, which – like his lost *Astronomica* – is written as a dialogue with his 'familiar friend' Otloh.[116] The treatise survives today in six manuscripts to which others now lost may be added. In addition, extracts from William's *Musica* and other short texts attributed to him were copied as glosses in music-theory manuscripts.[117] As with Bern and Herman of Reichenau, William's text emphasizes the practicality of the subjects of the quadrivium for the monastic author. This trait was also highlighted by Bernold of St Blasien, who declared that William 'was most learned in music . . . elucidated many subtleties of that art unknown to the ancient doctors, and having seized upon the many errors in singing, corrected them very reasonably according to the art'.[118]

    correxit ad artem. Terrarum metas scrutans et temporis horas, Ac numeros abaci vidit tam mente sagaci, Artibus his illi queat ut vix quis similari. See also J. Wiesenbach, 'Wilhelm von Hirsau. Astrolab und Astronomie im 11. Jahrhundert', in Schreiner (ed.), *Hirsau. St. Peter und Paul 2*, pp. 109–56.

[113] Bernold of St Blasien, *Chronicon*, p. 486.1: Nam naturale horologium ad exemplum celestis hemisperii excogitavit, naturalia solsticia sive equinoctia et statum mundi certis experimentis invenire monstravit, quae omnia quidam eius familiaris etiam literis mandare curavit. Multas etiam quaestiones de compoto probatissimis rationibus enodavit. Cf. Wolfger of Prüfening, *De scriptoribus ecclesiasticis* 108, p. 93.

[114] See E. Klemm, *Die romanischen Handschriften der Bayerischen Staatsbibliothek: Teil 1. Die Bistümer Regensburg, Passau und Salzburg* (Wiesbaden, 1980), pp. 23–4; *PL* 150.1639.

[115] Schauwecker, *Otloh von St. Emmeram*, pp. 224–32; M. Manitius, *Geschichte der Lateinischen Literatur des Mittelalters 3* (Munich, 1931; repr. 1976), pp. 220–1 allows that 'O' could refer to another interlocutor whom he identifies as Otoch based upon manuscript annotations.

[116] M. Huglo, *Les tonaires. Inventaire, analyse, comparaison* (Paris, 1971), p. 282 states the date of composition to be before 1068.

[117] Munich, Bayerische Staatsbibliothek, Clm 9921, fol. 22v is such an example.

[118] Bernold of St Blasien, *Chronicon*, p. 486.6: Hic in musica peritissimus fuit, multaque illius artis subtilia, antiquis doctoribus incognita, elucidavit. Multos etiam errores in cantibus deprehensos satis rationabiliter ad artem correxit.

Theoger of Metz

Theoger of Metz (c. 1050–1120), successively monk of Hirsau, prior of Reichenbach, abbot of St Georgen in the Black Forest and bishop of Metz, was a pupil of William of Hirsau. The prominent place that Theoger occupied in ecclesiastical politics and the Hirsau reform movement has resulted in the survival of a good deal of information about his career. Theoger's *Vita* (written by Wolfger of Prüfening sometime between 1138 and 1146) was commissioned by his close friend and colleague Abbot Erbo of Prüfening, 1121–62.[119] This friendship can be traced back to the time when Erbo had been a monk of St Georgen while Theoger had been its abbot: it offers yet another example of the importance to intellectual life of the links established by monastic reform movements, in this case the Hirsau movement. Although the *Vita* survives only in one incomplete manuscript from St Georgen, Johannes Trithemius presented another account of Theoger's life in his *Annales Hirsaugienses*, for which he probably relied on a complete copy.[120] This work provides important information about Theoger's early life and education that is missing from the extant version of the *Vita*.

According to Trithemius, Theoger was born of humble parents in 'east Francia, which by another name was called of old *Teutonica*'.[121] He studied under Manegold of Lautenbach, 'the foremost scholar in the province of Alsace'.[122] Master Manegold (c. 1030–1103) was a learned Augustinian canon and pro-papal polemicist who, on the destruction of the priory at Lautenbach by supporters of Henry IV in 1086, fled to the Bavarian monastery of Raitenbach, before later returning to the Alsatian house of

---

[119] H. von Fichtenau, 'Wolfger von Prüfening', pp. 345–51. D. Andernacht, 'Die Biographen Bischof Ottos von Bamberg' (Dissertation, Johann Wolfgang Goethe University, Frankfurt am Main, 1950) and H. G. Schmitz, *Kloster Prüfening im 12. Jahrhundert* (Munich, 1975), p. 238 disagree. See, however, F.-J. Schmale, *Deutschlands Geschichtsquellen im Mittelalter. Vom Tode Kaiser Heinrichs V. bis zum Ende des Interregnum* (Darmstadt, 1976), pp. 237–9, who reconfirms von Fichtenau's interpretation; also F. C. Lochner in Theoger of Metz, *Musica*, ed. F. C. Lochner, 'Dietger (Theogerus) of Metz and his "Musica"' (Ph.D. dissertation, University of Notre Dame, 1995), pp. 66–9.

[120] Paris, Bibliothèque National, Résidu St Germain 215; J. Trithemius, *Annales Hirsaugienses* (St Gallen, 1690).

[121] Wolfger, *Vita Theogeri*, *MGH SS* 12, p. 450.33: Theogerus oriundus fuit ex Francia orientali, quam alio nomine Teutonicam vocaverunt antiqui. P. Jaffé, who edited the *MGH* edition, has augmented the missing sections of the Paris manuscript with Trithemius' account in *Annales Hirsaugienses*.

[122] Ibid., p. 450.35: ponitur et sub magisterio cuiusdam Manegoldi, praefecti scholarum in Alsatiae provincia.

Marbach as prior.[123] Manegold was, as Trithemius noted, skilled not only in the seven liberal arts, but in the higher studies of Scripture and ethics.[124] Theoger's studies with Manegold probably took place in the late 1060s or early 1070s. He became a canon of the collegiate church at Neuhausen near Worms in 1073; he was later made schoolmaster, which involved the teaching of sacred and secular literature as well as music.[125]

In a step that was taken by many clerks sympathetic to reform, Theoger decided to eschew the secular life for the regular: he entered the monastery of Hirsau in the 1070s, possibly around 1077, after a meeting with Abbot William. Learning was an aspect of monastic life emphasized at Hirsau and Theoger, who was noted for his erudition, must have made a success of his monastic profession, for in 1082 Abbot William sent him to the newly founded daughter house of Reichenbach as prior. In 1088 William appointed Theoger abbot of St Georgen in the Black Forest. This monastery was one of many in the south-German area that looked to Hirsau for its customs after the adoption of Cluniac reforms there from the late 1070s. Theoger was elected bishop of Metz in 1118. His *Vita* gives a sympathetic and pro-papal account of this election. It recounts how the former bishop, Adalbert, had ruined the bishopric of Metz. Strong language is used to describe his injustices and he is accused of having co-operated with the king.[126] According to the biographer Wolfger, the church of Metz had reached a state of destitution.[127] Only the pope's intervention rescued the situation: having consulted with his 'brothers the cardinals', he decided that his legate Conrad, cardinal bishop of Palestrina, should compel the 'pseudo-bishop' Adalbert to abdicate.[128] The ejection of Adalbert took

---

[123] On Manegold see especially W. Hartmann, 'Manegold von Lautenbach und die Anfänge der Frühscholastik', *DA* 26 (1970), 47–150; F. Châtillon, 'Recherches critiques sur les différents personnages nommés Manegold', *Revue du moyen âge latin* 9 (1953), 153–70; J. Gross, 'Die Erbsündenlehre Manegolds von Lautenbach nach seinem Psalmen-Kommentar', *Zeitschrift für Kirchengeschicte* 71 (1960), 252–61.

[124] Wolfger, *Vita Theogeri*, p. 450.

[125] A. Helmsdörfer, *Forschungen zur Geschichte des Abtes Wilhelm von Hirschau* (Göttingen, 1874), p. 41 n. 1; H. J. Wollasch, *Die Anfänge des Klosters St. Georgen im Schwarzwald. Zur Ausbildung der geschichtlichen Eigenart eines Klosters innerhalb der Hirsauer Reform* (Freiburg, 1964), p. 148.

[126] Wolfger, *Vita Theogeri*, p. 466.31: . . .ut quoque modo miserabilibus Mettensis ecclesiae ruinis occurreret: praedictus episcopus tanto eum odio est prosecutus, ut multis affectum iniuriis etiam ex urbe propelleret. Ex eo iam tempore coepit Alberium rex habere suspectum.

[127] Ibid., p. 467.3: Asserit Mettensem ecclesiam episcopali penitus regimine destitutam.

[128] Ibid., p. 467.10: Romanus pontifex autem super tantis ecclesiae miseriis ingemiscens, rem ad fratres cardinales refert, et cum eis communicato consilio, mittit a latere suo

place in 1116.[129] In the resulting election, according to the *Vita*, the influence of the Holy Spirit was manifested in the choice of Theoger. After much protestation on his part (a characteristic contemporary expression of humility), Theoger was named bishop of Metz in 1118 and the following year St Georgen elected a new abbot.[130] Despite the efforts of the reforming party, Theoger was unable to occupy the bishopric of Metz. The *Chronicle of Metz* records that he became a monk of Cluny, while Wolfger of Prüfening states that he died there 'a pauper and an exile . . . passing the time in contemplating the divine and in prayer.'[131]

Theoger's sole surviving work of music theory is his treatise *Musica*. His *Vita* states that it was written after he became a monk of Hirsau, which suggests a date of between *c*. 1077 and 1082 for its composition.[132] It is possible that he was encouraged in this task by Abbot William, whose own studies on the quadrivium had been ended by the pressures of his new position.[133] Theoger's *Musica* is very much a work of the south-German circle: it shares the same concern for the proper regulation of plainchant that is evident in the treatises of Bern, Herman and William. Wolfger of Prüfening described it in the *Vita* as 'not only useful but at the same time exceedingly instructive and elegant',[134] while in *De scriptoribus ecclesiasticis* he characterized it as 'somewhat brief but satisfyingly subtle'.[135] The late evidence of Trithemius corroborates this and emphasizes Theoger's reputation for erudition: Theoger was 'excellently skilled in all disciplines of the liberal arts, consummate in music and outstanding in its

---

Footnote 128 (*cont.*)
   Cunonem Praenestinum episcopum cardinalem . . . quatenus Alberio pseudoepiscopo abdicato dignum pastorem eligerent.
[129] *MGH SS* 24, p. 544 n. 89.
[130] *Annales Sancti Georgii in Nigra Silva* 1119, *MGH SS* 17, p. 296.9: Werinherus abbas eligitur. Theogerus Metensis episcopus et abbas Sancti Georgii.
[131] *Chronica Universalis Mettense* 1104, *MGH SS* 24, p. 514.45: Adalbero IIII, sed postea eiectus, et post eum Theogerus, et ipse depositus factus est Cluniacensis monachus. Wolfger of Prüfening, *Vita Theogeri*, p. 479.42: . . . sanctus praesul Theogerus in eodem loco pauper et exul, Pontio abbate petente, remansit quatuor mensibus, tempus omne in contemplatione divinorum et oratione consumens.
[132] Wolfger of Prüfening, *Vita Theogeri*, p. 450.38: Nam factus postea in Hirsaugia monachus librum scripsit de musica . . .
[133] Lochner, 'Dietger', pp. 81–2.
[134] Wolfger of Prüfening, *Vita Theogeri*, p. 450.38: . . . non solum utilem sed etiam valde instructum et elegantem.
[135] Wolfger of Prüfening, *De scriptoribus ecclesiasticis* 109, pp. 93–4: Et hic quoque tractatum unum de musica scribit, in quo de eius inventione et numeris, ac proportionibus iuxta arithmeticos breviter quidem, sed satis subtiliter agit.

performance'.¹³⁶ So too does a tradition known to the eighteenth-century Benedictine historian Jean Mabillon, which related how William of Hirsau asked Theoger and the learned monk Herino to 'correct whatever in the whole of the Old and New Testament had been distorted by the errors of scribes'.¹³⁷

Aribo

Another figure who can be connected firmly with William of Hirsau is the theorist Aribo. Little precise information about Aribo survives, and he is known virtually only as the author of an erudite treatise entitled *De musica*.¹³⁸ The older historiography on Aribo is dominated by Joseph Smits van Waesberghe, who constructed an elaborate narrative of Aribo's life that sought to link him with Liège and portray him as a leading figure in the supposed Liège school of music theory.¹³⁹ Nevertheless, Smits van Waesberghe's sweeping theories about Aribo have been shown to lack all historical cogency and have rightly been dismissed.¹⁴⁰

The few surviving eleventh- and twelfth-century biographical references to Aribo link him, in the first place, with Freising. Aribo prefaced *De musica* with a letter of dedication to 'his lord the most worthy of bishops Ellenhard'.¹⁴¹ This Ellenhard, who was bishop of Freising from 1052 to 1078, is noted in the contemporary sources as a royalist and a familiar of King Henry IV.¹⁴² The character of Aribo's dedication to Ellenhard and the knowledge it betrays of the singing at the cathedral in Freising imply that he was a member of the cathedral chapter.¹⁴³ Indeed, one of the

---

[136] J. Trithemius, *Annales Hirsaugienses*, quoted in *MGH SS* 12, p. 450.38: In omnibus namque artium liberalium disciplinis egregie fuit peritus et in musica singulari exercitatione consummatus.

[137] J. Mabillon, *Annales ordinis S. Benedicti* 5 (Paris, 1713), p. 277.

[138] Aribo, *De musica*, ed. J. Smits van Waesberghe, *Aribonis De musica* (Rome, 1951). On Aribo's identity see especially T. J. H. McCarthy, 'Aribo's *De musica* and Abbot William of Hirsau', *Revue bénédictine* 116 (2006), 62–82. For a different perspective see Ilnitchi, *The play of meanings: Aribo's De musica and the hermeneutics of musical thought*.

[139] Smits van Waesberghe, *Muziekgeschiedenis der Middeleeuwen* 1, pp. 23–107; 'Some music treatises and their interrelation', 25–31, 95–118.

[140] See L. Schrade, '*De musica*, ed. J. Smits van Waesberghe', *Journal of the American Musicological Society* 9 (1956), 215; J. Kreps, 'Aribon de Liège. Une légende', *Revue belge de musicologie* 2 (1948), 138–43.

[141] Aribo, *De musica*, p. 1.2, J. Smits van Waesberghe, *Aribonis De musica* (Rome, 1951): Domno suo Ellenardo praesulum dignissimo, in universa morum honestate praeclaro, Aribo, quae praeparavit Deus diligentibus se.

[142] McCarthy, 'Aribo's *De musica* and Abbot William of Hirsau', 65–6.

[143] Aribo, *De musica*, p. 1.4: Cum summae capacitatis in musicae monochordique sitis regulis, ut cantilenarum vestrarum observata diligentia affatim vobis perhibent testimonia.

surviving full recensions of *De musica* – a twelfth-century codex from Admont – describes Aribo as *scholasticus*, suggesting that he was also master of the cathedral school.[144] The link with Freising is further corroborated by the testimony of Wolfger of Prüfening.[145] Wolfger had obviously read *De musica* carefully, for he quoted from it in *De scriptoribus ecclesiasticis*.[146] He ended his entry on Aribo by quoting a couplet not found in any surviving manuscript of *De musica*:

> Therefore, he [Aribo] offered this treatise to his bishop, to whom he wrote it, as he says:
>> Aribo the musician has composed this treatise,
>> And gave [it] as a gift to his own bishop.[147]

As the style of this couplet is consistent with other examples from *De musica*, it is entirely possible that Wolfger saw the manuscript presented to Ellenhard, which carried dedicatory verses not present in other copies. An apposite parallel is provided by Donizo of Canossa's *Vita* of Countess Mathilda of Tuscany (1046–1115), the dedicatory copy of which includes panegyrical verses not found in other manuscripts.[148]

A number of seemingly diverse pieces of evidence connect Aribo with Hirsau and the Hirsau reform movement. First, there is the comment from the fourteenth-century music theorist Engelbert of Admont, who called Aribo 'scolasticus aurelianensis'.[149] Although 'aurelianensis' ostensibly means 'of Orléans', neither Aribo nor his treatise can possibly be connected with France. The description, therefore, probably results from a scribal corruption and is far is more likely to refer to St Aurelius, the patron of Hirsau, whose name was frequently used as a synonym for that monastery in eleventh-century sources.[150] Secondly, the eleventh-century

---

[144] Rochester (NY), Eastman School of Music, ML 92/1200, fol. 11r: 'Incipit musica aribonis scolastici'.

[145] Wolfger of Prüfening, *De scriptoribus ecclesiasticis* 106, p. 103: Aribo Cirinus musicus musicam scribit, quam propter eius mensurae celeritatem Capream nuncupavit.

[146] Ibid.

[147] Ibid.: Hunc itaque tractatum pontifici suo obtulit, cui et scribit, sicut ait: Aribo tractatum depinxit musicus istum, Atque dedit dono pontifici proprio.

[148] Donizo of Canossa, *Vita Mathildis*, *MGH SS* 12, pp. 348–409.

[149] Engelbert of Admont, *De musica* 1.2, ed. P. Ernstbrunner, *Der Musiktraktat des Engelbert von Admont (ca. 1250–1331)* (Tutzing, 1998), p. 170.

[150] See Robinson, 'Zur Arbeitsweise Bernolds von Konstanz', 52; Cowdrey, *Pope Gregory VII*, pp. 255–7; *Historia Hirsaugiensis monasterii*, *MGH SS* 6, p. 255.42; K. Schmid, 'Sankt Aurelius in Hirsau 830 (?)–1049/75. Bemerkungen zur Traditionskritik und zur Gründerproblematik' and T. Klüppel, 'Der heilige Aurelius in Hirsau. Ein Beitrag zur Verehrungsgeschichte des Hirsauer Klosterpatrons', in Schreiner (ed.), *Hirsau. St. Peter und Paul* 2, pp. 11–44, 221–58.

necrology from the cathedral in Freising records the death of an 'Aribo pr[es]b[ite]r et fr[ater]', a wording that clearly implies a priest and monk.[151] Since former community members were customarily remembered in necrologies, it is evident that this Aribo had left the cathedral for a monastery. Thirdly, Aribo himself claimed a close friendship with William of Hirsau, describing William in *De musica* as the 'greatest among modern musicians, without doubt an Orpheus and Pythagoras' who 'loved me beyond any worthiness that my poverty may possess'.[152] This remark is characteristic of the close friendships based upon membership of monastic communities that increasingly found expression in the aftermath of monastic reform and revival in the eleventh century, and is a strong indication that Aribo was at one time or another a member of such a community.[153] Finally, three early manuscripts of *De musica* originated in monasteries that were part of the Hirsau reform movement.[154] This evidence provides grounds for suggesting that Aribo left the cathedral at Freising for Hirsau. If this is so, then Aribo was not alone in heeding the call of reform: Theoger of Metz, Henry of Augsburg and Bernold of St Blasien provide contemporary examples of clerks who also renounced the secular world for the reformed cloister.

De musica was written between *c*. 1070 and 1078. Its *terminus post quem* is established by Aribo's comment that 'lord William, formerly a monk of St Emmeram in Regensburg' was 'now venerable abbot elsewhere', a clear reference to William's appointment as abbot of Hirsau in 1069. Its *terminus ante quem* is fixed by the death of Bishop Ellenhard in 1078. Aribo's treatise survives wholly or partly in thirteen manuscripts from the eleventh and twelfth centuries. Only two of these contain the full text, neither of which is the autograph.[155] Four later manuscripts contain material taken directly from the treatise or from intermediate sources.[156]

De musica shows that Aribo was well versed in the music theory of Bern and Herman of Reichenau. William of Hirsau was also a prominent influence: in addition to including William's directions for measuring organ

---

[151] *MGH NecG* 3, p. 83; McCarthy, 'Aribo's *De musica* and Abbot William of Hirsau', 79.

[152] Aribo, *De musica*, p. 42.57: Nam meam dilexit parvitatem ultra parvitatis dignitatem, qui est musicus primus, modernus videlicet Orpheus et Pythagoras.

[153] McGuire, *Friendship and community*, pp. 181–2, 194–5, 196–203, 210–21. For other examples of monastic friendship see the relationship of Otloh of St Emmeram and Henry of Reichenau in Otloh's *Dialogus de tribus quaestionibus* (*PL* 146.0059).

[154] McCarthy, 'Aribo's *De musica* and Abbot William of Hirsau', 80.

[155] Salzburg, Stiftsbibliothek St. Peter, a. V. 2, fols 114v–145r; Rochester (NY), Eastman School of Music, ML 92/1200, fols 11r–42r.

[156] McCarthy, 'Aribo's *De musica* and Abbot William of Hirsau', 63 n. 3.

pipes, Aribo devoted the opening chapters of *De musica* to a lengthy examination and critique of a diagram concerned with the workings of the monochord that originated with William of Hirsau.[157] Aribo was among the first of the south-German theorists to address Guido of Arezzo's teaching: he discussed Guido's melodic theory in detail, and returned to this subject in two *sententiae*, which he appended to *De musica* shortly after he wrote it.

Although *De musica* shares a commonality of approach with the earlier south-German treatises, it is quite different in character. It contains over a hundred chapters, in which Aribo is keen to integrate his learning in grammar, rhetoric, dialectic, theology and the Classics with music.[158] Indeed, the way in which he does this with such delight and felicity contrasts with the more measured monastic approach of Bern or Herman, and is perhaps explained by his initial career as a secular clerk.

Frutolf of Michelsberg

The importance of St Emmeram in Regensburg as a centre for the dissemination of ideas is illustrated by the career of Frutolf of Michelsberg (d. 1103), who was probably an oblate and subsequently a monk of St Emmeram before moving to the monastery of Michelsberg in Bamberg at some point during the eleventh century.[159] Hartmut Hoffmann has suggested, based upon his researches on Frutolf's autograph manuscripts, that Frutolf learned to write from Otloh of St Emmeram.[160] Michelsberg, which was founded in 1015, was heavily influenced during its early years by the Gorze-style reform associated with St Emmeram. Between 1066 and 1112, for example, three of its abbots came from St Emmeram: Ruotpert, 1066–71; Tiemo, 1086–94 and Gumpold, 1094–1112.[161] Claudia Märtl has suggested that Frutolf could have come to Michelsberg with one of these abbots.[162]

---

[157] Ibid., 74–6.
[158] On Aribo's use of the *colores rhetorici* see McCarthy, 'Literary practice in eleventh-century music theory', 195–203; for his use of dialectic see Chapter 3, pp. 138–45.
[159] C. Märtl, 'Die Bamberger Schulen – ein Bildungszentrum des Salierreichs', in S. Weinfurter (ed.), *Die Salier und das Reich 3. Gesellschaftlicher und ideengeschichtlicher Wandel im Reich der Salier* (Sigmaringen, 1991), pp. 342–3. See also see Manitius, *Geschichte der lateinischen Literatur* 3, pp. 350–61; F.-J. Schmale, 'Frutolf von Michelsberg', *Verfasserlexikon* 2, cols 993–8; A. Rausch, 'Frutolf von Michelsberg', *MGG. Personenteil* 7, cols 210–12.
[160] H. Hoffmann, *Buchkunst und Königtum im ottonischen und frühsalischen Reich* (Stuttgart, 1986), p. 440.
[161] Hallinger, *Gorze-Kluny* 1, pp. 344–50, 347 n. 16. See also E. Freise, D. Geuenich and J. Wollasch (eds), *Das Martyrolog-Necrolog von St. Emmeram in Regensburg, MGH Libri memoriales N. S.* 3, pp. 25–6, 105, 178.
[162] Märtl, 'Die Bamberger Schulen', p. 342.

A unique source from Michelsberg contains valuable information about Frutolf's scholarly activities. Sometime during the abbacy of Wolfram I, 1112-23, Prior Burchard of Michelsberg (d. 1147) began compiling the monastery's first library catalogue since its foundation in 1015. The date at which Burchard began the catalogue is unspecified, but he included in his inventory a list of books that belonged to the monks Frutolf and Thiemo. (Thiemo, who died in 1119, was a friend and collaborator of Frutolf and succeeded him as prior.) Two points from Burchard's inventory are noteworthy: his comment that Frutolf copied 'nearly all of these books with his own hand' and the fact that Thiemo possessed many of the same works himself.[163] These works, as Harry Bresslau has suggested, may well have been Thiemo's own copies of the books owned by his teacher Frutolf.[164]

Burchard's list shows that Frutolf was a scholar of wide-ranging interests. Some works, such as Priscian's *De accentibus* or Bede's *De arte metrica*, reflect Frutolf's activities as a teacher of the arts of the trivium. Others reflect his activities as a biblical scholar: the inventory records him as the author of glosses on the Psalter, the Old Testament, the 'Apostle' (by which Burchard meant St Paul), and the Old and New Testament.[165] Two of these works – the glosses on the Psalter and the Old Testament – reappear in the Michelsberg library catalogue of 1483 attributed to Frutolf, thereby confirming the accuracy of Burchard's inventory.[166] The gloss on St Paul has disappeared, but that on the Old and New Testaments has recently been identified as the *Glosa in vetus et novum testamentum* of Karlsruhe, Badische Landesbibliothek, 504, fols 119v–152r.[167] This recension, which belonged to Frutolf's friend and collaborator Thiemo of Michelsberg, was probably copied from Frutolf's original. The 'Liber cronicorum' recorded by Burchard is without doubt Frutolf's detailed *Chronicle* of world history, a distinctive feature of which is its new calculation of the world's beginning.[168] Frutolf's autograph of his chronicle

[163] P. Ruf (ed.), *MBDS* 3/3, p. 360: Subnotatos libros pie memorie Frutolfus, cenobii huius prior, huic loco contulit, quos manu sua pene omnes ipse scripsit.
[164] H. Bresslau, 'Bamberger Studien', *NA* 21 (1896), 216.
[165] Ruf (ed.), *MBDS* 3/3, p. 360: Glose super psalterium. Glose super vetus testamentum. Glose super apostolum. Glosarius super vetus et novum testamentum.
[166] Ibid., p. 373.
[167] McCarthy, 'Biblical scholarship in eleventh-century Michelsberg', 3–45.
[168] Frutolf of Michelsberg, *Chronicon*, *MGH SS* 6, pp. 33–210 (edited as a work of Ekkehard of Aura). The portion from the year 1002 has been published in a Latin-German edition: F.-J. Schmale and I. Schmale-Ott (eds and trans.), *Frutolfs und Ekkehards Chroniken und die Anonyme Kaiserchronik* (Darmstadt, 1972); see also F.-J. Schmale, 'Zur Abfassungszeit von Frutolfs Weltchronik', *Bericht der historischen Veröffentlichung*

survives in Jena, Universitätsbibliothek, Bos. q. 19, along with a continuation by Ekkehard of Aura (d. 1126). A partial recension – giving the annals from 1057 to 1102 – is transmitted in a contemporary hand in Karlsruhe, Badische Landesbibliothek, 504, fols 187r–199v.

Burchard's inventory also shows that Frutolf had a particular interest in the quadrivium: he possessed copies of music treatises by Guido of Arezzo, Bern of Reichenau and William of Hirsau, as well as Herman of Reichenau on the computus and the astrolabe.[169] One of these copies survives: the interpolated version of Bern's *Prologus in tonarium* in Frutolf's own handwriting, extant in Karlruhe, Badische Landesbibliothek, 504, fols 1r–14v. This codex, which is a binding of a number of originally independent manuscripts, is an important witness to the activity of Michelsberg scriptorium in the second half of the eleventh century. It is closely connected with the circle of Frutolf, for it also transmits the *Glosa in vetus et novum testamentum* and the partial recension of his *Chronicle*.[170]

Two other works are not mentioned in Burchard's inventory. A unedited liturgical treatise in two books entitled *De officiis divinis* survives in Frutolf's handwriting in Bamberg, Staatsbibliothek, Msc. Lit. 134,[171] while the twelfth-century manuscript Wrocław, Biblioteka Uniwersytecka, R. 54 contains a treatise on the rhythmomachia game, which ends with the explicit 'Finit opus Fortolfi'.[172] Although the *Rithmimachia* has been edited as a work of Frutolf, F.-J. Schmale has questioned this attribution on the grounds that it possesses no stylistic parallels with Frutolf's known works and that it was not mentioned in Burchard's inventory.[173] Schmale's objections, however, are not definitive: only a more detailed study of the *Rithmimachia* in the context of Frutolf's other known works will resolve the question of its authorship.

Footnote 168 (*cont.*)
    Bamberg 102 (1966), 81–7. On Frutolf's chronology see A.-D. von den Brincken, *Studien zur lateinischen Weltchronistik bis in das Zeitalter Ottos von Freising* (Düsseldorf, 1957), pp. 187–93.

[169] Ruf (ed.), *MBDS* 3/3, p. 360: Musica Gwidonis. Breviarium Frutolfi de musica. Tonarius, musica Bernonis, dialogus Wilhelmi in uno volumine . . . Compotus Hermanni et mensura astrolabii in uno volumine.

[170] On the Michelsberg scriptorium see H. Hoffmann, *Bamberger Handschriften des 10. und des 11. Jahrhunderts* (Hanover, 1995), pp. 70–7.

[171] Bresslau, 'Bamberger Studien', 223–5. V. L. Kennedy, 'The "De officiis divinis" of MS Bamberg Lit. 34', *Ephemerides liturgicae* 52 (1938), 312–26 seeks to diminish its connexion with Frutolf, although unconvincingly.

[172] K. Dengler-Schreiber, *Scriptorium und Bibliothek des Klosters Michelsberg in Bamberg* (Graz, 1979), p. 36.

[173] R. Peiper, 'Fortolfi Rythmimachia', *Zeitschrift für Mathematik und Physik* 25 (1880), 167–97; Schmale (ed.), *Frutolfs und Ekkehards Chroniken*, p. 7.

Frutolf's lengthy and sophisticated *Brevarium de musica* and its accompanying tonary survives complete in one manuscript from the late eleventh century: Munich, Bayerische Staatsbibliothek, Clm 14965b.[174] Its contents reveal the wide variety of sources to which Frutolf had access: Boethius, Guido of Arezzo, Bern and Herman of Reichenau, Anonymous I, William of Hirsau, Aribo and Henry of Augsburg are among the authors used.[175] Its subject matter is typical of the south-German theorists, with heavy emphasis on the monochord, the tetrachords, the species of *diatessaron*, *diapente* and *diapason*, the modes and the conformity of plainchant to the rules and proportions of music. The addition of an extensive tonary at the end of the treatise imitates the influential *Tonarius* by Bern of Reichenau. A recent study has suggested that it was used as a performance guide, a further indication of the practical emphasis of south-German music theory.[176] Parts of Frutolf's *Breviarium* and *Tonarius* were disseminated throughout southern Germany during the twelfth century.[177]

The wider south-German circle

The members of the south-German circle already discussed can be connected through personal friendships or institutional links. For a number of other theorists, however, it is not possible to form so detailed a picture of institutional connexions and friendship networks. Nevertheless, these theorists demonstrate in their work that they too were heirs to the teaching that spread from Reichenau. The familiarity they display with the writings of their eleventh-century antecessors stands in lieu of frequently absent biographical evidence and justifies their inclusion in the south-German circle.

---

[174] The exact origins of this manuscript are unknown. Dengler-Schreiber, *Scriptorium und Bibliothek des Klosters Michelsberg in Bamberg*, p. 212 was unable to attribute either of its two hands to the Michelsberg scriptorium, although she had previously suggested (p. 35) that it may have been Thiemo's copy of Frutolf's *Breviarium*. See also Klemm, *Die romanischen Handschriften der Bayerische Staatsbibliothek* 1, p. 22.

[175] C. Vivell, 'Vom uneditierten Tonarius des Mönches Frutolf', *Sammelbände der Internationalen Musik-Gesellschaft* 14 (1912–13), 463–84. See also M. Huglo, 'Frutolfus of Michelsberg', *NG* 9, p. 302; B. Stäblein, 'Frutolf von Michelsberg als Musiker', 57–60; M. Bernhard, 'Zur Überlieferung des 11. Kapitels in Frutolfs "Breviarium"', M. Bernhard (ed.), *Quellen und Studien zur Musiktheorie des Mittelalters* (Munich, 1990), pp. 37–67.

[176] R. Maloy, 'The roles of notation in Frutolf of Michelsberg's tonary', *Journal of Musicology* 19 (2002), 689.

[177] Rausch, 'Frutolf', cols 211–12.

The 'Wolf Anonymous'

The treatise generally known as the Wolf Anonymous – on account of the fact that it has been edited and published by Johannes Wolf – is extant in only one manuscript: Darmstadt, Universitäts- und Hochschulbibliothek, 1988, fols 182v–189v.[178] This codex of 189 folios is a binding of three separate manuscripts dating from the fourteenth, early twelfth and late eleventh centuries respectively. The second and third manuscripts each contain collections of music treatises, similar to many other contemporary German codices.[179] It is possible that they were bound together well before the first manuscript was added in the early fifteenth century. Although the Darmstadt codex belonged to the abbey of St James in Liège by the fifteenth century, there is nothing to prove that its second and third constituent manuscripts were copied there.

The scope of the Wolf Anonymous is traditional in its character. Its organization and general tone reveals the mind of one concerned primarily with the synthesis and consolidation of well-established thought. Of the ancient authorities, the author has read Boethius, as can be seen from his references to the Greek theorists Ptolemy and Pythagoras.[180] There is little direct evidence of reliance upon other late-Classical authors such as Macrobius or Martianus Capella. The author does, however, exhibit a very marked dependence on modern theorists: he was intimately acquainted with Herman of Reichenau's *Musica*, especially in the later chapters dealing with tetrachords and the species of *diatessaron*, *diapente* and *diapason*.[181] Indeed, passages from the corresponding chapters from Herman's work are quoted almost word for word and carefully assimilated into the anonymous author's text. He paraphrases Bern of Reichenau extensively, appropriating something of the flavour of Bern's *Prologus* by his use of the Greek note names – *lichanos hypaton*, *meson* and so forth – as well as by his similarity of phrase to Abbot Bern on the topic of *intensio* and *remissio*. Elsewhere, he relies extensively on the contemporary treatise known as Anonymous I, particularly when dealing with consonances, intervals and the modes.

These traits help to place the treatise and its author. Although Joseph Smits van Waesberghe sought to assign the work to his 'Liège school', the treatise's close familiarity with Bern and Herman of Reichenau (particularly

---

[178] Wolf Anonymous, [*Musica*], ed. J. Wolf, 'Ein anonymer Musiktraktat des elften bis zwölften Jahrhunderts', *Vierteljahrschrift Musikwissenschaft* 9 (1893), 186–234.

[179] See Chapter 5, pp. 196–214, especially pp. 199–200.

[180] Wolf (ed.), 'Ein anonymer Musiktraktat', 211, 213, for example.

[181] Ibid., 217–24.

with Herman's system of notation) and concern over the explanation of the modes through the constructs of tetrachords and species are indicative of its south-German character.[182] The treatise, however, shows no familiarity with the work of German theorists active in the second half of the eleventh century, or indeed with Guido of Arezzo, who by then was regularly discussed in German sources. These factors militate against Wolf's suggestion of Conrad of Hirsau (c. 1070–c. 1150) as a possible author: had Conrad written this treatise at Hirsau under the immediate successors of Abbot William, it seems likely that he would have been well aware of the teaching of so important a figure associated with his own monastery.[183] The author is essentially conservative and seeks to reconcile the sureness of Abbot Bern's theorizing with the more subtle innovations of Herman of Reichenau. The treatise has been dated to c. 1060, a date that is generally accepted by modern scholars.[184]

Master Henry of Augsburg

Master Henry, who was *scholasticus* of Augsburg and a member of the cathedral chapter until 1077, died in 1083. He has been mistakenly identified with Honorius Augustodunensis (c. 1080/90–c. 1156) and confused with another canon of Augsburg named Henry, who was made Patriarch of Aquileia in 1077.[185] As with most cathedral canons in eleventh-century Germany, it is likely that he had been at the cathedral since his childhood.[186] Henry spent the last six years of his life at the monastery of St Magnus in Füssen. The *Annals of Augsburg* for 1083 record that 'Master Henry, a canon of Augsburg, who had been expelled with the bishop Wigold, died and was buried at the monastery of St Magnus'.[187] The reference by the annalist here is to the disputed episcopal election of 1077, in which Master Henry sided with a member of the local clergy named

---

[182] Smits van Waesberghe, 'Some music treatises and their interrelation', 27.
[183] Wolf (ed.), 'Ein anonymer Musiktraktat', 191–3. Wolf based his suggestion on a passage from Johannes Trithemius, *Chronicon insigne Monasterii Hirsaugiensis* (Basel, 1559), which recorded Conrad as the author of a music treatise.
[184] Hiley, *Western Plainchant*, p. 472.
[185] V. I. J. Flint, 'Heinricus of Augsburg and Honorius Augustodunensis: are they the same person?', *Revue bénédictine* 92 (1982), 148–58; M. L. Colker, 'Heinrici Augustensis Planctus Evae', *Traditio* 12 (1956), 149–53. See, however, T. J. H. McCarthy, 'The identity of Master Henry of Augsburg', *Revue bénédictine* 114 (2004), 140–57 for a discussion of Master Henry's career and the rejection of Flint's and Colker's conclusions. See also M. Huglo, 'Heinrich von Augsburg', *MGG. Personenteil* 8, cols 1212–13.
[186] J. Barrow, 'Education and the recruitment of cathedral canons in England and Germany 1100–1225', *Viator* 20 (1989), 117–38.
[187] *Annals of Augsburg* 1083, *MGH SS* 3, p. 130.47: Magister Heinricus, Augustensis canonicus, cum Wigoldo episcopo expulsus, in coenobio sancti Magni obiit et sepultus est.

Wigold, whose election was set aside by King Henry IV in favour of another member of the chapter and former royal chaplain, Siegfried.[188] Wigold was unable to establish his episcopate and fled the city; it was not until 1084 and the capture of Augsburg by Welf IV, the deposed duke of Bavaria, that the Henrician Bishop Siegfried II was expelled in favour of Wigold.[189] By siding with the choice of the church and people of Augsburg, Master Henry was adhering to the proper canonical procedures for episcopal election and publicly declaring his support for the Gregorian reform movement.

Master Henry's greatest surviving work is a lengthy and sophisticated poem on Genesis entitled *Planctus Evae*. Its elaborate structure presents an exegesis of Genesis through a symbolic interpretation of the text, along with a study of sin through the relationship of Adam and Jesus.[190] It has also been suggested that Master Henry is the author of the 'Proverbia Heinrici' that are found in a twelfth-century manuscript from St Emmeram (Munich, Bayerische Staatsbibliothek, Clm 14506) and a grammatical poem that is extant in a contemporary manuscript from Tegernsee (Munich, Bayerische Staatsbibliothek, Clm 18580).[191]

The only other lengthy work by Henry of Augsburg is a music treatise written as a dialogue between master and pupil. It survives incomplete in one source: the early twelfth-century south-German codex Vienna, Österreichische Nationalbibliothek, Cod. 51, where it is entitled 'Musica Domni Heinrici Augustensis Magistri'.[192] The treatise is the last in an elaborate collection of music treatises written in a few similar and clear early twelfth-century hands: also included are Boethius, Guido of Arezzo's theoretical writings in full, *Dialogus de musica* by pseudo-Odo of Cluny, the treatises by Bern and Herman of Reichenau, William of Hirsau and John, in addition to two tonaries and numerous short texts on the measurement of organ pipes, monochords, bells and specific aspects of music theory. The codex also contains non-musical material: Cicero's *De inventione*, the pseudo-Ciceronian *Rhetorica ad Herennium*, an extensive section of 'chapters' on geometry and Hyginus on astronomy.[193]

---

[188] G. Meyer von Knonau, *Jahrbücher des deutschen Reiches unter Heinrich IV. und Heinrich V.* 3 (Leipzig, 1900), pp. 65–6.

[189] I. S. Robinson, *Henry IV of Germany, 1056–1106* (Cambridge, 1999), pp. 175, 187 n. 76, 239.

[190] M. L. Colker, 'Heinrici Augustensis Planctus Evae', *Traditio* 12 (1956), 157.

[191] Ibid., 152.

[192] Vienna, Österreichische Nationalbibliothek, Cod. 51, fols 90r–91ar. Fol. 91 is a partial folio, empty on the verso.

[193] McCarthy, 'The identity of Master Henry of Augsburg', 140; Toneatto, *Codices artis mensoriae* 3, pp. 985–95; *RISM B* 3/6, p. 61.

Master Henry's *Musica* differs in character from many of the other south-German treatises. It shows no obvious textual dependence upon the Carolingian theorists (as in Bern's *Prologus in tonarium*), or intimate familiarity with contemporary German theorists (as displayed by Herman, William, Theoger, Aribo and Frutolf). The extant portion is not focused on singing without error – which is the guiding dictum of the south-German treatises – and nowhere to be found are the subtleties of Herman's or of William's modal theory. What survives is concerned primarily with the classification of music and its elements, and in that sense, perhaps the inspiration for the topics discussed came from Boethius' *De institutione musica*. It is also heavily influenced by the art of logic, a subject that Henry probably taught at Augsburg.[194] Indeed, Henry's fascination with dialectic is matched only by Aribo, who was also a cathedral clerk for part of his career. It is entirely possible, however, that Henry moved on to deal with music as the 'science of singing' in the portion of his treatise that is unknown to us.

Master Henry's authorship of a set of widely copied mnemonic verses on the modes proves that he was a competent musician who was well-versed in singing plainchant.[195] These verses are clearly attributed to him in the manuscript Bamberg, Staatsbibliothek, Msc. Lit. 10 with the heading 'Henry, *scholasticus* of the city of Augsburg, composed these verses on the modes relating to the Introit'.[196] They circulated widely in contemporary manuscripts, and in most sources survive with notation.[197] To judge the impact of Henry's teaching solely on the basis of the single extant manuscript of his music treatise, therefore, is a mistake. As with Herman of Reichenau, the popularity of his mnemonic verses points to a wider reception of his ideas than might initially be thought.

John

The theorist John, frequently, but mistakenly, known as John Cotton, Johannes Cottonis or John of Affligem, is the author of a music treatise and

---

[194] Henry of Augsburg, *Musica*, ed. J. Smits van Waesberghe, *Musica domni Heinrici Augustensis magistri* (Buren, 1977), p. 35: D[iscipulus]. Estne musica genus an species? M[agister]. Species est, et subalternum genus. See Chapter 3, pp. 132–5.

[195] M. Huglo, 'Un théoricien du XIe siècle: Henri d'Augsburg', *Revue de musicologie* 53 (1967), 57.

[196] Bamberg, Staatsbibliothek, Msc. Lit. 10, fol. 98v: Heinricus auguste urbis scolasticus fecdb hos versiculos tonorum ad introitus pertinentium. See also F. Leitschuh and H. Fischer, *Katalog der Handschriften der königlichen Bibliothek zu Bamberg* 1/1 (Bamberg, 1895; repr. Wiesbaden, 1966), pp. 150–1.

[197] Chapter 5, pp. 184, 208, 211.

tonary that circulated widely in twelfth- and thirteenth-century German manuscripts: today his *De musica* survives in some twenty manuscripts and his tonary in seven.[198] The confusion surrounding John's identity stems largely from the elliptical opening of the dedicatory letter that prefaces *De musica*, in which John identifies himself as the subject of a 'bishop Fulgentius'.[199] The earliest manuscript tradition of *De musica* shows that two competing readings of a crucial phrase were in circulation: the first is 'Domino et patri suo venerabili anglorum antistiti Fulgentio', which describes Fulgentius as 'bishop of the English'; the second is 'Domino et patri suo venerabili angelorum antistiti Fulgentio', which describes him as a 'bishop of angels'. Although twelfth-century scribes had difficulty choosing between the two readings, it seems that, on the whole, they found 'anglorum' more plausible than 'angelorum', and so favoured the former.[200] The usually reliable biographer Wolfger of Prüfening mirrored this trend, for he described John as being 'of the English nation'.[201]

In some medieval sources the epithet 'Cottonis' is applied to John.[202] The earliest instance of this description is in a heading that was added to a twelfth-century copy of *De musica* sometime in the thirteenth century, which reads 'Epistola Johannis Cottonis ad fulgentium episcopum anglorum'.[203] Martin Gerbert's *Scriptores de musica* of 1784, which for over two centuries was the only available edition of John's treatise, is largely responsible for perpetuating this epithet.[204] One twentieth-century musicologist, who continued to treat the name 'Cottonis' as authentic, identified the dedicatee as Archbishop Anselm of Canterbury and postulated a career for John at the monastery of Bec in Normandy.[205] This interpretation,

---

[198] See W. Hirschmann, 'Johannes', *MGG. Personenteil* 9, cols 1077–81, with bibliography.

[199] John, *De musica*, ed. J. Smits van Waesberghe, *Johannis Afflighemensis De musica cum tonario* (Rome, 1950), p. 44: Domino et patri suo venerabili Ang[e]lorum antistiti Fulgentio, viro scilicet ex re nomen habenti, quippe qui et prudentia pollet et sanctitate fulget, Iohannes servus servorum Dei, quicquid patri filius dominoque servus.

[200] Smits van Waesberghe (ed.), *Johannis Afflighemensis De musica*, pp. 22–5.

[201] M. Huglo, 'L'Auteur du traité de musique dédié à Fulgence d'Affligem', *Revue Belge de Musicologie* 31 (1977), 5–8; Wolfger of Prüfening, *De scriptoribus ecclesiasticis* 59: Joannes musicus, natione Anglicus, vir admodum subtilis ingenii fuit, qui et libellum praestantissimum de musica arte composuit.

[202] Many English-speaking scholars render 'Johannes Cottonis' as 'John Cotton'. This confusing innovation is, however, based upon the assumption of John's English origin.

[203] Washington, Library of Congress, ML 171 J56, fol. 1r; Smits van Waesberghe, 'John of Affligem or John Cotton?', 140–1.

[204] *GS* 2, p. 230.

[205] E. F. Flindell, 'Joh[ann]is Cottonis', *Musica disciplina* 20 (1966), 11–30, and 'Joh[ann]is Cottonis, *corrigenda et addenda*', *Musica disciplina* 23 (1969), 7–11.

however, has been rightly dismissed for lacking cogency.[206] More recent speculation has sought to place John at the monastery of St Maximin in Trier while simultaneously explaining 'Cottonis' as 'John wearer of the cotta, the official dress of a cantor, from *cotta*, a tunic or surplice; that is to say, not a monk, but a cantor, a member of a choir'.[207] Finally, the identification of John as 'John of Affligem' is largely due to Joseph Smits van Waesberghe, who argued for this as part of his repeatedly asserted conviction in the existence of a 'Liège school of music theory'.[208] Although the word *antistes* in John's dedication unequivocally means 'bishop', there was no bishop named Fulgentius in Germany, England or France during the eleventh or twelfth centuries.[209] This allowed Smits van Waesberghe to identify Fulgentius as the abbot of the Lotharingian monastery of Affligem between 1089 and 1122. Consequently, John became John of Affligem, and could be easily placed in the purported Liège school.

None of these theories adequately explains the nature and scope of John's treatise, which points unambiguously to southern Germany. Michel Huglo's study of western European tonaries from this period has shown that John's responsory citations come exclusively from the German repertoire.[210] John's knowledge of the practice of using letters with a specific meaning to annotate melodies, such as *c* for *cito* (quickly), also points to southern Germany. This habit – which John rejected because of its ambiguity – was probably inspired by a letter written by Notker of St Gallen (840–912). Only two copies of this letter survive: one from the tenth century in Metz and one from the eleventh in Reichenau.[211] The only other eleventh-century sources to mention these *litterae significativae* are Aribo's *De musica* and the Wolf Anonymous, both of south-German origin. Similarly, John's knowledge of Bern of Reichenau's *Prologus in tonarium*, of Herman of Reichenau's notational system and of diagrams from Aribo's *De musica*, as well as his use of the letters a, e, i, o, u, H, y and Ω to designate the eight tones (a practice that was confined to the area around St

---

[206] Babb (trans.), *Hucbald, Guido and John*, p. 89.
[207] Malcolm, 'Epistola Johannis Cottonis ad Fulgentium episcopum', *Musica disciplina* 47 (1993), 163–8. The theory that *cottonis* means 'wearer of the cotta' is neither correct nor plausible. If *cotta* were a Latin word – as opposed to an Italian one – its genitive would be *cottae* and not *cottonis*, which is the genitive of *cotto*. Additionally, the distinction drawn between monk and cantor is false: they are not mutually exclusive.
[208] See above pp. 17–18; Smits van Waesberghe, 'Some music treatises', pp. 25–31, 95–118.
[209] See P. B. Gams, *Series episcoporum ecclesiae catholicae* (Regensburg, 1873; repr. Graz:, 1957); also Hauck, *Kirchengeschichte Deutschlands* 3 and 4 (Leipzig, 1912; repr 1953).
[210] Huglo, *Les Tonaires*, pp. 299–301.
[211] Babb (trans.), *Hucbald, Guido and John*, pp. 93–4.

Gallen), indicates that he was working within the south-German intellectual milieu.[212] Finally, the manuscript dissemination of John's treatise indicates southern Germany as its most likely origin. The researches of Huglo have arranged the manuscripts into 'western', 'transitional' and 'eastern' groups: the majority of manuscripts belong to the eastern, or German group.[213]

The character and transmission of John's treatise and tonary, therefore, show it to be the product of southern Germany. The identity of its dedicatee must remain, for the moment, ambiguous. It is probable that the Fulgentius of John's dedication is a cognomen, for the rhetorical nature of the opening indicates that John was indulging in a subtle form of word play. The prologue does, however, make clear that there existed a personal relationship between John and his patron. As with Aribo's dedication to Bishop Ellenhard of Freising, it is another example of the 'cult of friendship' so popular in letter writing from the late eleventh century.

Quaestiones in musica

The treatise entitled *Quaestiones in musica* shows how elements of the teaching of individual south-German theorists could be brought together in a critical manner. Its earliest surviving source, dating from the early twelfth century, is the second of the three manuscripts that constitute Darmstadt, Universitäts- und Hochschulbibliothek, 1988.[214] This copy is the work of one scribe with a very neat and clear hand; the care that he took is also evident from the numerous diagrams, which have been drawn with great clarity and precision. Two other manuscripts that transmit the treatise date from the twelfth and fifteenth centuries respectively: Copenhagen, Det Kongelige Bibliothek, S. 73 8°, and Brussels, Bibliothèque Royale, 10162/66.[215]

Quaestiones in musica is divided into two parts. The first is concerned with the usual topics of the south-German theorists: the monochord, the intervals, the species and tetrachords, and the application of these concepts to plainchant; the second focuses largely on the mathematical principles underlying the generation of intervals and proportions. The Darmstadt copy begins with a list of chapters for each of these parts:

---

[212] Ibid.; John, *De musica*, pp. 29–30.
[213] Huglo, 'L'Auteur du traité de musique', pp. 9–10.
[214] *RISM B* 3/3, p. 39.
[215] *RISM B* 3/1, p. 81; E. Jørgensen, *Catalogus codicum Latinorum medii aevi Bibliothecae regiae Hafniensis* (Copenhagen, 1926), p. 426; *RISM B* 3/1, pp. 58–62. The Brussels manuscript is a partial copy of Darmstadt, Universitäts- und Hochschulbibliothek, 1988.

'Incipiunt capitula Questionum in musica'.[216] The chapter headings, in a manner that prefigures the *quaestio* technique associated with the twelfth-century schools of northern France, take the form of propositions to be demonstrated: 'Why it is not possible to have more than seven distinct notes' or 'Why a span of one octave is not sufficient for the monochord', for example.[217] The subject matter that forms the resolution to each of the *quaestiones* in the first part of the treatise is a skilful compilation of quotations and paraphrases from theorists such as Hucbald of St Amand, pseudo-Odo of Cluny, Bern of Reichenau, Aribo and Guido of Arezzo. The work of these theorists is interwoven with material that is presumably the individual contribution of the author himself. The second part, which relies heavily on the Carolingian treatise *Scolica enchiriadis*, contains much less original material. Both parts show the essentially cumulative nature of a good deal of contemporary scholarship: originality was not considered the virtue it is believed to be today.

The identity of the treatise's author is unknown, although two possibilities have been suggested: Cölestin Vivell argued for Franco of Liège (1047–c. 1093) as a possible author, while Rudolf Steglich attributed it to Abbot Rudolf of St Trond (c. 1070–1138), author of the *Deeds of the Abbots of St Trond*.[218] Vivell's attribution to Franco of Liège rests almost completely on the provenance of the Darmstadt codex to the monastery of St James in Liège. Although the individual manuscript containing *Quaestiones in musica* was at Liège by the first half of the fourteenth century – the theorist James of Liège used it as a source for his *Speculum musicae* – it is not certain that it originated there.[219] Steglich's competing suggestion is not in itself implausible. Before becoming abbot, Rudolf had been the schoolmaster at St Trond; the monk who continued the *Deeds of the Abbots of St Trond* after Rudolf's death records that he taught the boys not only *dictamen* and metrics, but 'also music following the principles of Guido of Arezzo'.[220]

---

[216] Darmstadt, Universitäts- und Hochschulbibliothek, 1988, fol. 110v. The table of contents is not printed in the only available edition of the treatise: R. Steglich (ed.), *Die Quaestiones in Musica. Ein Choraltraktat des zentralen Mittelalters und ihr mutmaßlicher Verfasser Rudolf von St. Trond (1070–1138)* (Leipzig, 1911; repr. 1971).
[217] Steglich (ed.), *Die Quaestiones in Musica*, pp. 12, 13.
[218] C. Vivell, 'Die *Quaestiones in musica*, ihre handschriftliche Quelle und ihr mutmaßlicher Verfasser', *Gregoriusblatt* 38 (1913), 70; 'Nachtrag zu den *Quaestiones in musica*', *Gregoriusblatt* 39 (1914), 51; Steglich (ed.), *Die Quaestiones in Musica*, pp. 1–11.
[219] K. Desmond, 'New light on Jacobus, author of *Speculum musicae*', *Plainsong and medieval music* 9 (2000), 22.
[220] *Gesta abbatum Trudonensium* 8 (*Continuatio* 1), *MGH SS* 10, p. 273.28: Scripsit igitur ei eodem primo anno volumen illud utilissimum multum continens scripturae, et pueros

Furthermore, there were close links between the monasteries of St Trond and St James in Liège during the eleventh and twelfth centuries.[221] Nevertheless, Steglich's attribution is ultimately based on the reasoning that since Rudolf taught music at St Trond, and since *Quaestiones in musica* is a contemporary music treatise with links to Lotharingia, he must be its author. In the absence of a stronger connexion between these figures and *Quaestiones in musica*, both suggestions must remain largely speculative.

The date of the Darmstadt manuscript, coupled with the treatise's reliance on Aribo, indicates that *Quaestiones in musica* was written sometime in the late eleventh or early twelfth century. Although its author may have been working in Lotharingia, the contents and textual borrowings in the treatise indicate that he had access to manuscripts containing the works of the south-German circle.

Other theorists

To these authors might be added a number of other anonymous theorists whose works, like those already discussed, address the familiar themes of German music theory. The treatise generally known today as Anonymous I, for example, was probably written shortly after Bern of Reichenau's *Prologus in tonarium*.[222] Sometimes misattributed to Bern of Reichenau in manuscripts, it influenced the interpolated version of *Prologus in tonarium*, and was known to the Wolf Anonymous and Frutolf of Michelsberg.[223] The so-called *Tonarius Augiensis* (extant only in the fifteenth-century manuscript Leipzig, Universitätsbibliothek, Cod. 1492) shows detailed knowledge of the notational system devised by Herman of Reichenau.[224] Perhaps also written in the vicinity of Lake Constance is the

---

Footnote 220 (*cont.*)
    vix musam declinare sciolos non tam dictamen quam metrum quoque componere docuit . . . Instruxit etiam eos arte musica secundum Guidonem.

[221] Steglich (ed.), *Die Quaestiones in Musica*, p. 6.

[222] *GS* 1, pp. 330–8. Anonymous I has been edited more recently by Smits van Waesberghe (who mistakenly attributed it Bern of Reichenau) under the title *De mensurando monochordo*: J. Smits van Waesberghe (ed.), *Bernonis Augiensis Abbatis de arte musica disputationes traditae. Pars A: Bernonis Augiensis De mensurando monochordo* (Buren, 1978). See T. J. H. McCarthy, 'Anonymous I and *Prologus in tonarium*: changing interpretations of music theory in eleventh-century Germany', *Journal of the Society for Musicology in Ireland* 1 (2005), 19–32; Rausch (ed.), *Die Musiktraktate des Abtes Bern von Reichenau*, p. 123, however, dates the treatise to *c.* 1100.

[223] McCarthy, 'Anonymous I and *Prologus in tonarium*', 26–9, 29–31.

[224] *Tonarius Augiensis*, ed. H. Sowa, *Quellen zur Transformation der Antiphonen. Tonar- und Rhythmusstudien* (Kassel, 1935), pp. 81–154.

short anonymous treatise beginning 'Grecam litteram ideo moderni maluerunt ponere quam latinam', which is also preserved only in Leipzig, Cod. 1492.[225] This treatise was used by the author of the lengthy *Commentarius anonymus in Micrologum Guidonis Aretini* – a south-German commentary on Guido's *Micrologus* dating from the third quarter of the eleventh century.[226] Aribo in turn quoted from the anonymous commentary in his treatise and teaching *sententiae*.[227]

The south-German theorists, whether well-known figures or anonymous, were connected by their shared perception of music theory as the science of singing. Their emphasis on the practicality of musical studies grew out of the central role played by music in monastic life and was consolidated by movements such as the Gorze reform, which stressed the importance of the *vita communis*. From Reichenau the teaching of Bern and Herman was disseminated through centres such as St Emmeram in Regensburg, influencing a new generation of theorists. Many of these theorists were united by their reform sympathies, an attribute reflected by the growing contribution of the Hirsau movement to the dissemination of music theory manuscripts. It was ultimately the institutional and friendship networks that existed in eleventh- and twelfth-century Germany that made possible the work of the south-German circle of music theorists.

---

[225] *Grecam litteram ideo moderni maluerunt ponere quam latinam*, ed. H. Sowa, *Quellen zur Transformation der Antiphonen*, pp. 154–60.

[226] T. J. H. McCarthy, 'The origins of *Commentarius anonymus in Micrologum Guidonis Aretini* in the medieval glossing tradition', *Revue d'Histoire des Textes* n.s. 3 (2008), 219–22.

[227] T. J. H. McCarthy, 'Aribo's *De musica*, *Commentarius anonymus in Micrologum Guidonis Aretini* and Guido of Arezzo: textual correspondence and scholastic method', *Mediaevistik. Internationale für interdiszplinäre Mittelalterforschung* 20 (2007), 154.

2

Ancient doctors and modern masters: the south-German circle at work

Classical sources for music theory

The influence of antiquity upon the thought of the Middle Ages is well known to historians. The very place of music in the curriculum of the seven liberal arts was itself a legacy of late-Classical thought. The range of Classical sources on music was diverse. Encyclopaedists such as Cassiodorus (*c*. 487–*c*. 580) and Isidore of Seville (*c*. 560–636) transmitted much information – and speculation – on ancient music and its rudiments.[1] St Augustine (354–430), whose pervasive influence touched most aspects of medieval thought, wrote on music, though the six books of his *De musica* were concerned solely with rhythm and metrics.[2] The treatises of the south-German circle, however, show relatively little dependence on these authorities. A solitary echo of St Augustine occurs when Aribo compares the forms

---

[1] On Cassiodorus see L. W. Jones, 'The influence of Cassiodorus on mediaeval culture', *Speculum* 20 (1945), 433–42; 'Further notes concerning Cassiodorus' influence on mediaeval culture', *Speculum* 22 (1947), 254–6; H. J. Abert, *Die Musikanschauung des Mittelalters und ihre Grundlagen* (Halle, 1905; repr. Tutzing, 1964); J. J. O'Donnell, *Cassiodorus* (Berkeley, 1979); W. Bürgsens (trans), *Institutiones divinarum et saecularium litterarum. Einführung in die geistlichen und weltlichen Wissenschaften* (Freiburg, 2003). On Isidore see B. Bischoff, 'Die europäische Verbreitung der Werke Isidors von Sevilla', in B. Bischoff, *Mittelalterliche Studien. Ausgewählte Aufsätze zur Schriftkunde und Literaturgeschichte* 1 (Stuttgart, 1966), pp. 171–94. S. A. Barney, W. J. Lewis, J. A. Beach and O. Berghof (trans.), *The Etymologies of Isidore of Seville* (Cambridge, 2006).

[2] Augustine, *De musica* (*PL* 32.1081–1194); also M. Jacobsson (ed.), *Aurelius Augustinus De musica liber VI: a critical edition with a translation and an introduction* (Stockholm, 2002). See also W. Bowen, 'St Augustine in medieval and renaissance musical science', in R. R. la Croix (ed.), *Augustine on music: an interdisciplinary collection of essays* (Lewiston and Queenstown, 1988), pp. 29–52; M. Huglo and N. Phillips, 'Le *De musica* de saint Augustin et l' organisation de la durée musicale du IXe au XIIe siecles', *Revue des études*

of the different species of *diatessaron* to the metrical feet.³ It is also Aribo's treatise that contains some of the few references to the encyclopaedists. Aribo, who had read widely and delighted in quoting ancient literature, could find occasion to display this learning only in those sections of *De musica* that explored the lore of music. Hence, in his chapter 'Concerning the moral art of music', he had the opportunity to relate the myth of Orpheus placating Pluto with his lyre, for which he probably drew on Cassiodorus' *Institutiones*.⁴ A similar tale – that of the physician Asclepiades – is found in John's *De musica*.⁵ The source for Aribo's description of the sirens was Isidore's *Etymologies*,⁶ but his additional comment that 'the pleasant and flattering sirens of this world would similarly draw our souls into the most dangerous shipwreck', is also found several times in the letters of Peter Damian, which were widely circulated and imitated in Germany.⁷ These Classical authorities remained peripheral on account of their limited relevance to the issues considered important by the south-German theorists. (The important influence of Platonism, which was transmitted by Calcidius, Martianus Capella and Macrobius, will be discussed in Chapter 4.) A significant but complicated exception to this is Boethius.

Boethius

Boethius (*c.* 480–*c.* 525) was one of the most influential of the Classical authors. His influence on music theory resided in his treatises *De institutione arithmetica* and *De institutione musica*. These works, which

---

Footnote 2 (*cont.*)

    augustiniennes 20 (1985), 117–31; P. le Boeuf, 'La tradition manuscrite du "De musica" de saint Augustin et son influence sur la pensée et l'esthétique médiévales' (Doctoral Dissertation, École Nationale de Chartres, Paris, 1986), pp. 107–15; 'Un commentaire d'inspiration érigénienne du "De musica" de saint Augustin', *Recherches Augustiniennes* 22 (1987), 243–316; N. Phillips, 'Classical and late Latin sources for ninth-century treatises on music', in A. Barbera (ed.), *Music theory and its sources: antiquity and the Middle Ages* (Notre Dame, Ind., 1990), pp. 120–6; A. Keller, *Aurelius Augustinus und die Musik. Untersuchungen zu 'De musica' im Kontext seines Schrifttums* (Würzburg, 1993).

³ Aribo, *De musica*, ed. J. Smits van Waesberghe, *Aribonis De musica* (Rome, 1951), p. 25.4; cf. Augustine, *De musica* 2.8, *PL* 32.1108–1109.

⁴ Aribo, *De musica*, p. 47.14; cf. Cassiodorus, *Institutiones* 2.5.9, ed. R. A. B. Mynors, *Cassiodori senatoris institutiones* (Oxford, 1937), p. 148.20.

⁵ John, *De musica* 17, ed. J. Smits van Waesberghe, *Johannes Affligemensis De musica cum tonario* (Rome, 1950), p. 114; cf. Isidore of Seville, *Etymologiae* 4.13.3, ed. W. M. Lindsay, *Isidori Hispalensis episcopi Etymologiarum sive originum libri XX* (Oxford, 1911); Cassiodorus, *Institutiones* 2.5.9, pp. 148–9.

⁶ Aribo, *De musica*, p. 37.7; cf. Isidore, *Etymologiae* 11.3.

⁷ Peter Damian, *Letters* 31, 66, 112, ed. K. Reindel, *MGH Briefe. Die Briefe des Petrus Damiani* 1, pp. 303.21–304.2; 2, p. 266.20–2; 3, pp. 278.18–279.1.

Boethius intended as an attempt to translate Greek thought into Latin, offered to medieval theorists the most significant and detailed account of ancient thought on the closely related disciplines of arithmetic and music. *De arithmetica* and *De musica* were widely disseminated in Germany. The manuscript tradition of *De musica* shows that it was copied in centres such as Freising, Tegernsee, St Emmeram and Bamberg from the ninth to the twelfth centuries.[8] Similarly, copies of *De arithmetica* were becoming more easily available in this period, originating in Lotharingian centres such as Echternach and Toul, as well as Freising and Tegernsee in Bavaria.[9] The appearance of *De arithmetica* in an abbreviated version points to the popularity of this work, while the evidence of numerous gloss collections shows that ninth- and tenth-century clerks were engaging with Boethius at first hand.[10] One twelfth-century manuscript – now Oxford, Trinity College, D. 47 – which contains both *De arithmetica* and *De musica*, has glosses giving the opinions of a certain 'Manegaldus', among others. This is surely the Gregorian polemicist and scholar Manegold of Lautenbach, teacher of Theoger of Metz and author of a number of commentaries on the Classical school texts.

Nevertheless, the widespread availability of and interest in Boethius during the eleventh century is not matched by a comparable prominence in the treatises of the south-German circle. According to Guido of Arezzo, Boethius was useful only to philosophers and not to singers.[11] Though none of the German theorists voiced such an opinion, Guido's comment seems aptly to sum up their attitude to Boethius too, for he does not play a

---

[8] See M. Masi, 'Manuscripts containing the *De musica* of Boethius', *Manuscripta* 15 (1971), 89–95; C. M. Bower, 'Boethius' *De institutione musica*: a handlist of manuscripts', *Scriptorium* 42 (1988), 205–51.

[9] J. Schroeder, *Bibliothek und Schule der Abtei Echternach um die Jahrtausendwende* (Luxemburg, 1977), pp. 69–88; R. Kottje, 'Klosterbibliotheken und monastiche Kultur in der zweiten Hälfe des 11. Jahrhunderts', *Zeitschrift für Kirchengeschichte* 80 (1969), 145–62; C. Eder, 'Die Schule des Klosters Tegernsee im frühen Mittelalter im Spiegel der Tegernseer Handschriften', *SMGBZ* 83 (1972), 24–6.

[10] A. White, 'Boethius in the medieval quadrivium', in M. Gibson (ed.), *Boethius: his life, thought and influence* (Oxford, 1981), pp. 168–9, 176–7; M. Teeuwen, *Harmony and the music of the spheres: the ars musica in ninth-century commentaries on Martianus Capella* (Leiden, 2002), pp. 156–83. See also M. Bernhard and C. M. Bower (eds), *Glossa maior in institutionem musicam Boethii*, 3 vols (Munich, 1993, 1994, 1996). For a twelfth-century commentary see A. Rausch, 'Der Boethius-Kommentar in der Handschrift St. Florian XI 282', *Studien zur Musikwissenschaft* 49 (2002), 7–83.

[11] Guido of Arezzo, *Epistola ad Michahelem*, ed. and trans. D. Pesce, *Guido d'Arezzo's Regule rithmice, Prologus in antiphonarium and Epistola ad Michahelem: a critical text and translation* (Ottawa, 1999), p. 530.

central role in their treatises. It is as if they do not know what to make of him. William of Hirsau, for example, can find occasion to mention him only in criticism when advocating the double function of the pitches D and d.[12] Herman of Reichenau has obviously derived his information about Ptolemy and the mode beginning on the note a from *De institutione musica*,[13] but elsewhere makes only occasional references to Boethius, one of which involves pulling him up because of 'a certain inconsistency in defining the species of *diapente*'.[14] The first chapter of Frutolf's *Breviarium de musica* – 'Concerning the invention and order of the notes' – is an elaborate patchwork of Classical allusion and quotation from *De institutione musica*.[15] Elsewhere, Frutolf adduces the authority of Boethius in his monochord measurements.[16] Yet all of this remains tangential to the main interest of Frutolf's *Breviarium*, for its subject matter is preoccupied with non-Boethian concerns: the theory of singing correctly. Aribo mentions Boethius only when naming the tetrachords, and this is probably so that the reader will understand the ancient note names should he come across them.[17] This pattern is also followed by Theoger of Metz and John.

This state of affairs is explained by the nature of Boethius' treatises. For Boethius arithmetic was the science of number, not of calculation; music was that of harmonic theory, that is, the science of number applied to sound. Consequently, it was as an authority on intervals and consonances

[12] William of Hirsau, *Musica* 16, ed. D. Harbinson, *Willehelmi Hirsaugensis Musica* (Rome, 1975), pp. 42–4.
[13] Herman of Reichenau, *Musica* 9, ed. and trans. L. Ellinwood, *Musica Hermanni Contracti* (Rochester, NY, 1936), pp. 35–6.
[14] Ibid. 16, p. 51: Videtur autem Boethius quadam in definiendis diapente speciebus labi inconstantia.
[15] Frutolf of Michelsberg, *Breviarium de musica* 12, ed. C. Vivell, 'Frutolfi *Breviarium de musica et Tonarius*', Akademie der Wissenschaften in Wien. Philosophische historische Klasse, Sitzungsberichte 188/2 (1919), 27–32.
[16] Ibid., 93–7. Chapter 17 of Vivell's edition, entitled 'De proportionibus semitonii speculatio subtilior' (109–12), is not present in the earliest recension of *Breviarium de musica* (Munich, Bayerische Staatsbibliothek, Clm 14965b), but in the fourteenth-century manuscript Brussels, Bibliothèque Royale, 5266, where it is headed 'Amico suo T. V. haec operari interius, quod habitus profitetur exterius'. It is likely that this superscription refers to Frutolf's friend and collaborator, Thiemo of Michelsberg, who added the text as a gloss or commentary to Frutolf's original in an earlier manuscript. The subject matter of this addition is clearly based upon Boethius, *De institutione musica* 2.27, 3.11, ed. G. Friedlein, *Anicii Manlii Torquati Severini Boetii De institutione arithmetica libri duo, De institutione musica libri quinque. Accedit geometria quae fertur Boetii* (Leipzig, 1867; repr. Frankfurt am Main, 1966), pp. 259–60, 285–6.
[17] Aribo, *De musica*, p. 11.

that he was most consistently invoked. A pertinent example of this is the third chapter of Bern's *Prologus in tonarium*. *Prologus* 3 is concerned with the musical consonances – specifically the *diatessaron*, *diapente* and *diapason* – and their mathematical proportions. Bern's equation of the *diatessaron* and *diapente* with the sesquitertiary and sesquialter closely follows *De institutione musica* 1.7 and 2.25.[18] Similarly, his discussion of the ratio generated from the *diatessaron*-plus-*diapason* (8:3) – with the added comment that the Pythagoreans deny it to be a consonance – is obviously rooted in *De institutione musica* 2.27.[19] When explaining this proportion in more detail, Bern took his example of 8:3 as a double-superbipartient from *De institutione musica* 1.4, while his explanation of the property of the *diapason* as a consonance quotes from *De institutione musica* 5.10.[20]

Abbot Bern's *Prologus in tonarium* offers a number of examples of Boethius' direct influence upon an eleventh-century theorist. It would, however, be misleading to assess Boethius' impact solely on such examples, for he also exerted considerable indirect influence on the eleventh century. He did this through the medium of the Carolingian treatises, which represented the first step towards the systematization of medieval music theory. These treatises used Boethian terminology to describe a very different type of music, that is, western European ecclesiastical chant. Perhaps the earliest example is *Musica disciplina* by Aurelian of Réôme (*fl.* 840–50), the first section of which is a compilation of quotations from Boethius, Cassiodorus and Isidore. Aurelian assumed that Boethius was relevant to plainchant and in the second chapter of his treatise applied Boethian mathematical proportions to the intervals, demonstrating each by citing examples from the chant repertory.[21] In the second half of *Musica disciplina* he adopted the names of the Greek *tonoi* for the eight medieval modes. Aurelian's example was followed in other treatises, among them the anonymous tenth-century *Alia musica*, which appropriated Boethius' table of octave-species for each *tonos* to furnish names for the modal octaves, in the process inverting Boethius' layout.[22] So too theorists like Hucbald of St Amand (*c.* 850–930)

---

[18] Bern of Reichenau, *Prologus in tonarium* 3, ed. A. Rausch, *Die Musiktraktate des Abtes Bern von Reichenau. Edition und Interpretation* (Tutzing, 1999), pp. 36–7; cf. Boethius, *De institutione musica* 1.7, p. 194; 2.25, p. 258.
[19] Bern, *Prologus* 3, p. 37; cf. Boethius, *De institutione musica* 2.27, p. 259.
[20] Bern, *Prologus* 3, p. 37; cf. Boethius, *De institutione musica* 1.4, 5.10, pp. 192, 360.
[21] Aurelian of Réôme, *Musica disciplina* 2, ed. L. Gushee, *Aureliani Reomensis Musica disciplina* (Rome, 1975), pp. 62–4.
[22] Anon., *Alia musica* 15–20, ed. J. Chailley, *Alia musica (Traité de musique du IXe siècle). Edition critique commentée avec une introduction sur l'origine de la nomenclature modale pseudo-grecque au Moyen-Age* (Paris, 1965), pp. 107–11; E. B. Heard, '"Alia musica": a

appropriated the note-names, tetrachords and species from Boethius.[23] The usefulness of the species of *diatessaron* and *diapente* in analysing the modes was first appreciated by the Carolingian theorists, who thus provided a basis for the south-German approach to music theory.

The influence of the Carolingian theorists

The influence of Boethius in our period is intertwined with that of his Carolingian interpreters. He provided the vocabulary for music theory, while they provided the model for its use. This is clearly demonstrated in the case of Bern of Reichenau, who developed his theory from the Carolingians. The treatise and tonary by Regino of Prüm (*c.* 842–915) – which Bern must have studied while a monk of Prüm – provided an obvious model for Bern's own works. Also discernible is the influence of Hucbald of St Amand, from whom Bern derived his teaching on the modes and *toni medii*.[24] The influence of the Carolingian theorists frequently manifests itself in close textual parallels. In *Prologus* 1, for example, Bern states that the concept of conjunction is what is meant by the Greek word *synemmenon*. The *synemmenon* tetrachord (a ♭ c d) had its origins in the ancient Lesser Perfect System, but was constantly called upon to provide pitches needed in many of the melodies that Bern encountered: his articulation of this device was drawn primarily from Hucbald's treatise.[25] Elsewhere, Bern's reliance on Hucbald is even more obvious. His explanation of the different intervals found in chant (*Prologus* 2) parallels that of Hucbald closely, even extending to the identical citation and analysis of the chant *Missus est Gabriel*.[26]

Footnote 22 (*cont.*)
   chapter in the history of medieval music theory' (Ph.D. Dissertation, University of Wisconsin, 1966), p. 179.

[23] See Hucbald of St Amand, *Musica* 29–30, 49–51, ed. Y. Chartier, *L'Œuvre musicale d'Hucbald de Saint-Amand. Les compositions et le traité de musique* (Montreal, 1995), pp. 168, 200–2 for example.

[24] H. Oesch, *Berno und Hermann von Reichenau als Musiktheoretiker. Mit einem Überblick über ihr Leben und die handschriftliche Überlieferung ihrer Werke* (Bern, 1961), pp. 106–14.

[25] Bern, *Prologus* 1, p. 33: In medio horum solet interseri V^{tum} tetrachordum, quod dicitur synemenon, id est coniunctum. Cf. Hucbald, *Musica* 39, p. 186: . . . necesse est, ut suo nomine tetrachordo nuncupato dicatur decurrere, quod uocatur synemenon, id est coniunctum.

[26] Bern, *Prologus* 2, p. 34: Primus modus est in brevissimo duarum vocum spacio, et fit in semitonio, ut hoc liquet exemplo in gravitate et acumine in illa antiphona: A. *Missus est Gabrihel*, ad id loci *Mariam*, item *virginem*. Secundus iam perceptibilioris est intervalli,

Hucbald's treatise, however, was not the only source consulted by Bern. In addition to the anonymous *Alia musica* and pseudo-Bernelinus' *Cita et vera divisio monochordi*, Bern was also influenced by aspects of the anonymous treatises *Musica enchiriadis* and *Scolia enchiriadis*: the description of the upper extent of the authentic modes in *Prologus* 7 echoes the pattern outlined by *Scolia enchiriadis*, and close parallels are also to be observed on the subject of transposing melodies by a fourth.[27]

Nevertheless, direct Carolingian influence is not very apparent among Bern's eleventh-century successors, for there are very few references to the Carolingian theorists in their treatises. Herman mentions *Musica enchiriadis* by name, but only to criticize its tetrachordal arrangement for confounding the authority of nature.[28] Elsewhere, music theorists who referred to *Enchiriadis* or *Enchiriadon* frequently meant *Dialogus de musica*, which was generally misattributed to Abbot Odo of Cluny. (It has been shown by Michel Huglo that it was written in Lombardy, probably in the late tenth century.[29]) Pseudo-Odo – or *Musica Ottonis* as it was more generally known in Germany – circulated fairly widely in German manuscripts and was the most frequently cited pre-eleventh-century text.[30] There were exceptions, of course, such as the author of *Quaestiones in musica*, who copied extensively from *Scolica enchiriadis* in the second part of his treatise.[31] For the most part, though, resonances of the Carolingian

> et fit in tono, ut in hoc: A. *Missus est*. Tertius adhuc parvo diductior, hoc est in tono et semitonio, ut in hoc: A. *Missus est. ad Mariam virginem*. Quartus hoc quoque protensior, qui fit in duobus tonis. . . Cf. Hucbald, *Musica* 7, p. 142: Primus modus est, cum sibi duae uoces breuissimi spatii diuisione cohaerent, adeo ut uix discrimen inter eas sentiatur, ut inest in antiphona *Missus est Gabriel ‹angelus›* ad id loci 'Mariam'. Item 'uirginem'. Secundus iam perceptibilioris est interualli. Vt in hoc *Missus ‹est›*. Item *Angelus*. Tertius adhuc paruo diductior. Vt in hoc *Missus est ‹Gabriel› ad Mu-*. Item *riam virginem*. Quartus hoc quoque protensior.

[27] Bern, *Prologus* 7 and 9, pp. 48–53, 55; cf. *Scolica enchiriadis*, ed. H. Schmid, *Musica et scolica enchiriadis, una cum aliquibus tractatulis adiunctis* (Munich, 1981), pp. 82.319–23, 85.365–71; also R. Erickson (trans.), *Musica enchiriadis and Scolica enchiriadis* (New Haven and London, 1995), pp. li–lii.

[28] Herman, *Musica* 3, pp. 23–4.

[29] M. Huglo, 'L'Auteur du Dialogue sur la Musique attribuée à Odon', *Revue de musicologie* 55 (1969), 119–71; *Les Tonaires. Inventaire, analyse, comparaison* (Paris, 1971), pp. 183–224; 'Der Prolog des Odo zugeschriebenen "Dialogus de Musica"', *Archiv für Musikwissenschaft* 28 (1971), 134–46; K.-W. Gümpel, 'Pseudo-Odo', *MGG. Personenteil* 13 (2005), cols 1012–15.

[30] See Chapter 5, p. 203.

[31] *Quaestiones in musica*, ed. R. Steglich, *Die Quaestiones in Musica. Ein Choraltraktat des zentralen Mittelalters und ihr mutmaßlicher Verfasser Rudolf von St. Trond (1070–1138)* (Leipzig, 1911; repr. 1971), pp. 74–84.

theorists owe much to Bern of Reichenau, the primary source for earlier theory: the *accessus* that was *Prologus* obviated the need for the south-German circle to address the Carolingian theorists independently.

The influence of Bern of Reichenau upon the south-German circle

Prologus in tonarium, the longer of Bern's two treatises, exerted a considerable influence on subsequent generations of German music theorists. It was the most frequently copied German treatise of the eleventh and twelfth centuries.[32] The provenances and origins of these eleventh- and twelfth-century manuscripts show it to have been widely disseminated in southern Germany. *Prologus in tonarium* was, therefore, the single most important German music treatise of the period. Nevertheless, the history of its reception is not straightforward because its teaching, while providing the model for subsequent theorists, was at the same time modified extensively by them. This process was started by Bern's pupil Herman of Reichenau. Herman's amendments – outlined in his treatise *Musica* – were a decisive influence upon the development of German music theory in the eleventh century. The points raised by Herman also influenced the production of parts of an interpolated version of Bern's *Prologus*, which survives in a number of recensions. The study of Bern's influence is, therefore, the study of the different layers of eleventh-century interpretations of his theory. The fact that numerous monks and clerks devoted time to developing their understanding of the teaching set out in *Prologus* is a hint of the high regard in which its author was held.

The impact of Herman of Reichenau upon the reception of Prologus in tonarium

Prologus in tonarium comprises twelve chapters prefaced by a letter of dedication to Archbishop Pilgrim of Cologne. Bern started *Prologus* by describing the monochord. (This instrument, which showed the division of the gamut, was central to medieval pedagogy.) According to the instruction of that 'most insightful and excellent person Boethius', it encompasses fifteen notes from which all 'harmony' occurs.[33] The monochord – or we might call it the gamut, for this is what it represents – is divided into the

---

[32] Rausch (ed.), *Die Musiktraktate des Abtes Bern*, pp. 17–24, 71; Oesch, *Berno und Hermann*, pp. 43–5. See also Chapter 1, pp. 21–2.

[33] Bern, *Prologus* 1, p. 32: Omnis igitur regularis monochordi constitutio secundum preclaram disertissimi viri Boetii instructionem in XV chordis consistit, per quas totius armoniae vis rata connexione decurrit, si tamen synemenon non desit.

tetrachords of the *graves, finales, superiores* and *excellentes* (with the addition of the conjunct *synemmenon* tetrachord supplying the pitch b-flat when necessary).[34] This opening, with its emphasis on the monochord and tetrachords, would influence the south-German theorists greatly. Bern's lead was followed by Herman of Reichenau, whose first two chapters describe the monochord in much greater detail.[35] Like Bern, Herman states that the monochord encompasses fifteen notes, though he makes an important terminological connexion with the art of arithmetic by calling this a *quadruplum* (the quadruple proportion produces the double-octave).[36] The implications of this elaboration are explicit in William of Hirsau's *Musica*, which also began by discussing the monochord: 'The whole regular structure of the monochord consists of fifteen notes in two distinct octaves'.[37] This sentence synthesizes Bern's fifteen notes and Herman's two octaves. William then followed Bern by dividing the monochord into tetrachords.[38] Theoger of Metz, too, started – after a very short introduction – with the monochord. He says that in ancient times the monochord consisted only of eight notes and that the fifteen-note monochord is a more recent modification, which he explains as a true and natural reflexion of the difference between the vocal ranges of men and boys.[39] After describing how the monochord is to be measured – and digressing on the ratios arising from this division – he confirms Bern's division of it into tetrachords.[40] The importance of the monochord is readily apparent from the beginning of Aribo's *De musica*, though his treatment is largely concerned with the faults of a visual representation of it called *quadripartita figura modernorum*. Nevertheless, the substance of his

---

[34] Ibid., p. 33: Quae in quatuor dividuntur tetrachorda, his nominibus discreta: Tetracordum gravium, tetracordum finalium, tetracordum superiorum, tetracordum excellentium. . .In medio horum solet interseri V^{tum} tetrachordum, quod dicitur synemenon, id est coniunctum.

[35] Herman, *Musica* 1–2, pp. 18–21.

[36] Ibid. 1, p. 18: . . .quod omnis eius integritas quadruplo, id est bis diapason comprehenditur.

[37] William, *Musica* 2, p. 14: Tota regularis monochordi structura constat quindecim chordis in duo diapason distinctis.

[38] Ibid., pp. 15–16.

[39] Theoger of Metz, *Musica* 2, ed. and trans. F. C. Lochner, 'Dietger (Theogerus) of Metz and his "Musica"' (Ph.D. Dissertation, University of Notre Dame, 1995), p. 10: Procedente autem tempore, musice artis scientia proficiente, intellegentes eius gnari ad eiusdem artis experientiam prodesse multum, si augeretur numerus chordarum, octo addiderunt, non alias (quod natura prohibebat) ponentes, sed easdem repetentes, grauitate et acumine (sicut se habet uirilis uox ad puerilem) tantum differentes.

[40] Ibid. 9, p. 19.

criticisms of this figure (and advocacy of his own alternative called *caprea*) owes much to the exemplars of Bern and Herman: Aribo criticizes the apparent disjunction and misplacement of tetrachords in the *quadripartita figura* and extols their proper and natural constitution in his *caprea*.[41] Aribo follows this excursus by emphasizing the teaching of Bern: the monochord consists, not of one or three octaves, but of two, and is divided in tetrachords.[42] Even though the character of Aribo's elaborate arguments differs from that of Bern's simple opening chapter, the principles he uses have their origin in *Prologus* 1.

'Species theory' – a distinctive feature of German theory – was an area where Herman made substantial and influential amendments to Bern's teaching. Bern developed his species theory from the Carolingian theorists: his description of the species in *Prologus* 5, for example, was prefigured by the anonymous *Alia musica* and Pseudo-Bernelinus' *Cita et vera divisio monochordi*, which he followed closely.[43] The prominent position that Bern gave to the species derived from his development of another theme present in the Carolingian treatises: that of the connexion between the species and the modes, which he emphasized at the beginning of *Prologus* 5.[44] Bern described the species in the following manner:

Bern, *Prologus* 5
Therefore the first species of *diatessaron* is constituted from tone, semitone and tone, beginning at *lichanos meson* [G] and finishing at *lichanos hypaton* [D]; which if there were added a tone above, you would have the first species of *diapente*. The second species is constituted from two tones and a semitone, starting at *mese* [a] and finishing at *hypate meson* [E]; which if there were added a tone above, there would be the second species of *diapente*. The third is constituted from a semitone and two tones, starting at *trite diezeugmenon* [c] and finishing at *lichanos meson* [G]; to which to the tone below is appended, that there might be made the third species of *diapente*. The fourth species of *diapente* is constituted from the first species of *diatessaron*, with the tone below having been added; not however, beginning from the same note, but from another, that is, *paranete diezeugmenon* [d]; so if it descends by tone, semitone and tone to *meson* [a], the ascent from the tone below will reveal four species of *diapente*. The species of *diapason* are easy to

[41] Aribo, *De musica*, pp. 1–6; see Chapter 4, pp. 162–8.
[42] Aribo, *De musica*, pp. 7–8.
[43] *Alia musica* 17–19, pp. 108–10; Pseudo-Bernelinus, *Cita et vera divisio monochordi*, GS 1, p. 313.
[44] Bern, *Prologus* 5, p. 41.

perceive: if one begins at *proslambanomenos* [A] and proceeds until *mese* [a], there is the first species; thus repeating by going always a semitone or a tone higher, there are seven species finishing at *paranete hyperbolaeon* [g]. If, however, the beginning is made from *hypate hypaton* [B], the end will be at *paramese* [b].[45]

In this passage, as in all of his music-theory writings, Bern used the Greek note names instead of the more modern letter notation. The species system that results from this description is as follows:

Figure 2.1: The species according to Bern of Reichenau

	Species of diatessaron	Species of diapente	Species of diapason
first	D E F G	D E F G A	A B C D E F G a
second	E F G a	E F G a b	B C D E F G a b
third	G a b c	F G a b c	C D E F G a b c
fourth		G A b c d	D E F G a b c d
fifth			E F G a b c d e
sixth			F G a b c d e f
seventh			G a b c d e f g

This system was modified significantly by Herman of Reichenau. Like Bern, he valued species theory for its potential to act as a means of understanding the modes. Herman would have read in *Prologus* 6 (and in Bern's *Tonarius*) that the modes were made up from combinations of the species of *diatessaron* and *diapente*: authentic *protus*, for example, 'from the first species of *diapente* and from the first species of *diatessaron* above';[46] plagal

[45] Ibid., pp. 41–2: Ergo prima species dyatesseron constat ex tono, semitonio et tono, exordium sumens a lichanos meson et finiens in lichanos ypaton; cui si adieceris tonum superius, oritur tibi prima species dyapente. Secunda species ex duobus tonis et semitonio, incipiens a mese et finiens in ypate meson; cui si adieceris tonum superius, erit secunda species dyapente. Tertia ex semitonio et duobus tonis, incipiens a trite dyezeugmenon et finiens in lychanos meson; cui adhibendus est tonus inferius, ut fiat tertia specie dyapente. Quarta species dyapente constat ex prima specie dyatesseron, adiecto tono inferius, non quidem per eiusdem nominis cordam, sed altius idest a paranate dyezeugmenon incipiens, ac sic per tonum, semitonium et tonum in meson descendit, assumptoque inferius tono, quartam speciem dyapente perficit. Dyapason vero species facile est pervidere. Si enim a proslambanomenos incoeperis, usque in mese prima species erit, sicque semper semitonio vel tono altius per ordinem repetendo, septimae speciei finis in paranete yperboleon erit. Sin autem exordium sumis ab ypate ypaton, erit finis in paramese.

[46] Ibid. 6, p. 44: Protus constat ex prima specie dyapente et ex prima specie dyatessaron superius.

protus 'from the same species of *diapente* and from the same species of *diatessaron* below'.[47] The problem with this pattern was its inconsistency with the description of the species that Bern had given in *Prologus* 5. It is readily apparent from Figure 2.1 that the species of *diatessaron* and *diapente*, when combined as they are, do not form the species of *diapason*. Bern's system required, therefore, a certain amount of transposition of the species of *diatessaron* to make it work. This is exactly what Herman did out of a desire to harmonize the inconsistencies apparent between *Prologus* 5 and 6.

Herman's answer was the simultaneous relocation of the three species of *diatessaron* to a lower position in the gamut and the introduction of a fourth species of *diatessaron*. In *Musica* 5 he wrote that the first species of *diatessaron* is A–D, consisting of tone, semitone and tone.[48] The second and third are B–E and C–F respectively. Then he introduced the new fourth species of *diatessaron*: the tone, semitone and tone from D to G, identical to the first in its arrangement (tone-semitone-tone), but 'fourth in its constitution and power'.[49] Herman then spelled out the reason for having it: it 'duly concludes by the proper letters the seven distinct pitches [the octave]'.[50] Now the species of *diatessaron* and *diapente*, when combined, would correspond with the species of *diapason*.[51]

This adaptation of Bern's species theory influenced all subsequent members of the south-German circle. It is to be seen behind the delineation

Figure 2.2: The species according to Herman of Reichenau

	Species of *diatessaron*				Species of *diapente*					Species of *diapason*							
first	A	B	C	D	D	E	F	G	a	A	B	C	D	F	F	G	a
second	B	C	D	E	E	F	G	a	b	B	C	D	E	F	G	a	b
third	C	D	E	F	F	G	a	b	c	C	D	E	F	G	a	b	c
fourth	D	E	F	G	G	A	b	c	d	D	E	F	G	a	b	c	d
fifth										D	E	F	G	a	b	c	d
sixth										E	F	G	a	b	c	d	e
seventh										F	G	a	b	c	d	e	f
eighth										G	a	b	c	d	e	f	g

[47] Ibid.: Subiugalis eius ex eadem specie dyapente et ex eadem specie dyatessaron inferius.
[48] Herman, *Musica* 5, p. 27.
[49] Ibid.: Quarta .D.G. in positione prima, in constitutione et potestate quarta.
[50] Ibid.: . . . regulariter propriis literis septena vocum discrimina determinat hoc modo.
[51] See Chapter 3, pp. 126–30.

of the species by William of Hirsau and by his pupil Theoger of Metz, who for good measure added a description of the identical arrangement at the higher octave.[52] It is discernible too in Aribo's *De musica*: the following textual comparison shows how his arrangement is closely based upon that given by Herman.

Example 2.1: The derivation of Aribo's species theory from Herman of Reichenau

Herman, *Musica* 5   Aribo, *De musica* [51]: Quod oppositio quoque sit in specibus diatessaron et diapente.

Sunt igitur hae graves sive principales .A.B.C.D.; finales hae .D.E.F.G. Est igitur necessario prima species diatesseron .A.D. constans tono, semitonio, tono; propriis comprehensa literis. Secunda .B.E. constans semitonio, tono, tono, propriis hinc inde conclusa literis. Tercia .C.F. constans tono, tono, semitonio, suis utrimque munita literis. Quarta .D.G. in positione prima, in constitutione et potestate quarta . . .

. . . Prima species diatessaron tono, semitonio, tono intenditur ab .A. in .D. Quarta eodem modo remittitur a .G. in .D. Secunda intenditur a .B. in .E. semitonio, ditono. Tercia remittitur ab .F. in .C. semitonio, ditono.[54]

De musica [56]: De quatuor speciebus diatessaron.

. . . Prima diatesseron species constat ex prima gravi et ex prima finali .A.D.; secunda ex secunda gravi et ex secunda finali .B.E.; tercia ex tercia gravi et ex tercia finali .C.F.; quarta ex quarta gravi et ex quarta finali .D.G.[53]

Diatessaron species prima incipit a prima gravium .A., desinit in primam finalium .D. Secunda species diatessaron incipit a secunda gravium .B., desinit in secunda finalium .E. Tercia species diatessaron incipit a tercia gravium .C., desinit in terciam finalem .F. Quarta species diatessaron incipit et

---

[52] William, *Musica* 7, p. 22; Theoger, *Musica* 15, p. 23.
[53] Herman, *Musica* 5, p. 27.
[54] Aribo, *De musica*, p. 25.99.

(These, therefore, are the *graves* or principal [notes]: A B C D; these the *finales*: D E F G. Therefore, the first species of *diatessaron* is, of necessity, A to D, comprising tone, semitone, tone and indicated by the appropriate letters. The second, B to E, comprises semitone, tone, tone and is indicated by its appropriate letters. The third, C to F, comprises tone, tone, semitone, again marked by its letters. The fourth, D to G, is first in its position but fourth in its contitution and power . . .

The first species of *diatessaron* consists of the first of the *graves* and the first of the *finales*, A and D; the second from the second of the *graves* and the second of the *finales*, B and E; the third from the third of the *graves* and the third of the *finales*, C and F; the fourth from the fourth of the *graves* and the fourth of the *finales*, D and G.)

desinit a quarta et in quartam .D.G.[55]

(That opposition also exists among the species of *diatessaron* and *diapente*.
. . . The first species of *diatessaron* is extended from A to D by tone, semitone and tone. The fourth in the same way is remitted from G to D. The second is extended from B to E by semitone and two tones. The third is remitted from F to C by semitone and two tones.

Concerning the four species of *diatessaron*.
The first species of *diatessaron* starts at the first of the *graves*, A, and ends at the first of the *finales*, D. The second species of *diatessaron* starts at the second of the *graves*, B, and ends at the second of the *finales*, E. The third species of *diatessaron* starts at the third of the *graves*, C, and ends at the third of the *finales*, F. The fourth species of *diatesaron* starts and ends at the fourth and fourth [of the *graves* and *finales*], D and G.)

The chief benefit of Herman's amendment was that the species of *diatessaron*, *diapente* and *diapason* now reflected exactly the operation of the modes. So, for example, the authentic version of the *deuterus* mode

[55] Ibid., p. 26.16.

(E–e) – which is equivalent to the fifth species of *diapason* – comprises 'the second species of *diapente* [E–b] and the second species of *diatessaron* above [b–e]'; the plagal version of *deuterus* (B–b) – or the second species of *diapason* – is constituted from 'the same species of *diapente* [E–b] and from the same species of *diatessaron* below [B–E]'.[56] Thus the thrust of *Prologus in tonarium*, that the species provide a codified and logical method for recognizing the modes, had been realized by Herman. This now enabled Herman to set out in an orderly and detailed fashion the relationship between the species and the modes. If we compare Herman's description of *protus* with Bern's, the extent of Herman's codification becomes clear:

Example 2.2: Herman of Reichenau's codification of Abbot Bern's modal theory

Bern, *Prologus* 6	Herman, *Musica* 8
Protus constat ex prima specie dyapente et ex prima specie dyatessaron superius. Subiugalis eius ex eadem specie dyapente et ex eadem specie dyatessaron inferius. Quod autem dico, tale est: Primus tonus a suo finali idest lichanos ypaton habet licentiam ascendendi in dyapente hoc est in mese, a mese in paranete dyezeugmenon, quod est prima species dyatessaron, constans ex tono, semitonio et tono. Secundus vero tonus, qui dicitur eius subiugalis, in eandem dyapente ascendit, sed descendit per eandem speciem dyatessaron inferius per tonum, semitonium ac tonum, a lichanos ypaton in proslambanomenos . . .[57]	Protus cum suo subiugali, quia primi sunt, necessario omnia quae prima sunt requirunt, primas videlicet in omnibus quadrichordis literas, quae sunt .A.D.a.d., primas species diapason quae sunt .A.a. et .D.d., primam speciem diapente quae est .D.a. primam speciem diatesseron quae est .A.D. Quae generalis institutio utrique nunc secundum suam proprietatem specialiter subdividatur. Ex quatuor praedictis literis autenticus tres sibi vendicat, id est .D.a.d., et est diapason .D.d. in quarum una altissime quantum ad legem ascendit, in altera finit, in .a. media saeculorum amen canit. Habet diapente .D.a., diatesseron .a.d. in superioribus. Quomodo hae constant species superius petendum est. Subiugalis similiter

---

[56] Bern, *Prologus* 6, p. 45: Deuterus constat ex secunda specie dyapente et secunda specie dyatessaron superius. Subiugalis eius ex eadem specie dyapente et eadem specie dyatessaron inferius.

[57] Ibid., pp. 44–5.

tribus formatur literis .A.D.a., et est diapason .A.a., id est eius acutissimum et gravissimum; .D. vero media finit eum cum magistro, cum quo etiam idem diapente communitur diatesseron vero id ipsum quod magister accipit in gravibus. Quo modo ergo protus cum suis tantum modo principalibus informatus est literis; sic et caeteri omnes secundum suum ordinem.[58]

(*Protus* consists of the first species of *diapente* and of the first species of *diatessaron* above; its plagal of the same species of *diapente* and of the same species of *diatessaron* below. Which is to say: the first tone from its final, that is *lichanos hypaton* [D], has licence to ascend a fifth, that is to *mese* [a]; and from *mese* [a] to *paranete diezeugmenon* [d], which is the first species of *diatessaron*, comprising a tone, semitone and tone. The second tone, which is called its plagal, ascends through the same *diapente*, but descends by tone, semitone and tone through the same species of fourth below from *lichanos hypaton* [D] to *proslambanomenos* [A] . . .)

(*Protus* and its plagal, since they are first, necessarily require all that is first: namely the first letters in all the tetrachords, which are A D a d; the first species of *diapason*, which are A–a and D–d; the first species of *diapente*, which is D–a; and the first species of *diatessaron*, which is A–D. This general arrangement is now to be subdivided according to the special property of each. From the four above-mentioned letters the authentic appropriates three for itself, that is, D a d, and the *diapason* is D–d; on one of these [letters] it ascends to its highest legitimate point, on another it ends and on the middle a it sings the *saeculorum amen*. It has the *diapente* D–a and, in the *superiores*, the *diatessaron* a–d. The manner in which these species are formed is to be sought above. Similarly, the plagal is formed from the three letters A D a, and the *diapason* is A–a, that is, its highest and lowest points. D in the middle, however, finishes with its master [authentic form], with which

---

[58] Herman, *Musica* 8, pp. 32–3.

it even shares the same *diapente* and accepts the same *diatessaron* as its master, but in the *graves*. In the manner in which *protus* is formed, in so far as the principal letters are concerned, so also are all the others formed according to their own order.)

Herman's development of Bern's model is to be seen behind the description of the modes in Chapters 12 and 13 of William of Hirsau's *Musica*. In *Musica* 12 William states that 'authentic *protus*, which ranges from D to d, has a middle distinction at a'.[59] This is a clear echo of Herman's comment that 'from the above-mentioned letters the authentic form appropriates three for itself, that is, D–a–d; and the octave is D, d'.[60] Similarly William's statement that plagal *protus* occupies the range A–D–a mirrors Herman's, and like Herman he emphasizes that that *protus* occupies the first letters in the tetrachords.[61] William's more detailed description of the role played by the species in the formation of the modes (*Musica* 13) is also closely based upon Herman.[62] The same arrangement is outlined by Theoger, though he omits the extensive explanations of Herman and William.[63] The influence of Bern as filtered through Herman and William is also to be seen in Aribo's discussion of this point. He repeats the stress

[59] William, *Musica* 12, p. 33: Autenticus protus qui est a .D. in .d. mediam distinctionem habet in .a.
[60] Herman, *Musica* 8, p. 32.
[61] William, *Musica* 12, p. 33: Subiugalis eius qui est ab .A. in .a. mediam distinctionem ponit in .D. Qui si iungantur, ut indifferenter sit protus, ascendit ab .A. in .d. duas continens distinctiones medias, id est .D. et .a. Quae quatuor litterae sive chordae singulorum tetrachordorum sunt primae.
[62] Ibid. 13, p. 36: In ultimo enim tramite, qui proto praetitulatur, primis omnibus collectis, et ab invicem ita ut in monochordo proportionaliter seiunctis, liquido inspicitur us .A. et .D. sicut in constitutione specierum dictum est, primam speciem diatessaron, .D. et .a. primam speciem diapente, .a. et .d. iterum primam speciem diatessaron, et rursum .A. et .a. primam speciem diapason. Itemque .D. et .d. primam speciem diapason concludant, et ut autenticus protus ex ipsa prima specie diapason, quae est a .D. in .d. constet, mediam distinctionem faciens in .a. et ab eadem .a. diatessaron superius, diapente autem habens inferius; et quomodo subiugalis eius ex illa prima specie diapason, quae est ab .A. in .a. subsistat, mediam distinctionem statuens in .D. et supra eamdem .D. diapente, infra vero diatessaron assumens; et quemadmodum hae duae species diapason protum indifferenter conficiant duabus mediis distinctionibus dilatatum, et quam omnino mirando moderamine naturae omnis primarum chordarum operatio solum protum construat.
[63] Theoger, *Musica* 20–7, pp. 26–8.

on the functions of the first notes of the tetrachords in *protus* (and similarly the respective cardinals in the other modes),[64] but also emphasizes the mediating function of the *finales* in the plagal ranges (which run from the *graves* to the *superiores*) and of the *superiores* in the authentic ranges (which run from the *finales* to the *excellentes*).[65]

Herman of Reichenau, therefore, was central to the reception of Bern by the south-German circle. His modifications to Bern's species theory, which tied it even more closely to the modes, definitively established the centrality of the species for German theorists from the second half of the eleventh century. Even those theorists who copied extensively from Bern – the Wolf Anonymous and the author of *Quaestiones in musica* – relied on Herman for species theory. As Bern was the filter through which much of the Carolingian theory reached the south-German circle, so Herman was the lens through which they viewed much of the teaching set out in Bern's *Prologus*. Herman's important contributions also seem to have influenced the compilers of the interpolated version of *Prologus in tonarium*.

The interpolated version of Prologus in tonarium

The interpolated recension of Bern's *Prologus* is transmitted in six manuscripts: Karlsruhe, Badische Landesbibliothek, 504; Munich, Bayerische Staatsbibliothek, Clm 14663; Melk, Stiftsbibliothek, 950; Rochester, NY, Eastman School of Music, ML 92/1100; Trier, Stadtbibliothek, 1897/18; Vienna, Österreichische Nationalbibliothek, Cod. 2502.[66] The Karlsruhe recension, copied by Frutolf of Michelsberg and dating from the second half of the eleventh century, is the earliest and probably served as the archetype for the others.[67] The Rochester and Trier codices (both from the eleventh century) are the closest to Karlsruhe. The Munich manuscript belonged to St Emmeram in Regensburg and, like the Vienna manuscript, was copied during the twelfth century.[68] The Melk codex is a late witness and has been dated to 1462.[69]

---

[64] Aribo, *De musica*, p. 15.46: Prima finalium, prima superiorum, prima excellentium principales sunt in prima specie autenticorum cantuum, id est in primo tono, quem principaliter constituunt.

[65] Ibid., p. 27.24: Sicut istae quatuor species diapason, id est quatuor plagarum constant gravibus et superioribus, dimidiantur autem finalibus, prima primis, secunda secundis, tercia terciis, quarta quartis: sic quatuor sequentes ad autenticos pertinentes claudentur finalibus et excellentibus, dimidiantur autem vel vinculantur superioribus . . .

[66] Rausch (ed.), *Die Musiktraktate des Abtes Bern*, p. 24.

[67] Ibid., p. 124.

[68] *RISM B* 3/3, pp. 118–19; *RISM B* 3/1, pp. 42–3.

[69] Huglo, *Les Tonaires*, p. 267.

The interpolations are extensive: in Gerbert's edition – where they are printed as part of the text – they add three chapters to the twelve properly contained in *Prologus*. They do not, however, consist solely of extra chapters: many take the form of short clauses added for the purpose of explanation. These interpolations function like the short glosses to medieval texts that help the reader's understanding by offering qualification and methodological analysis. By the same token, the longer interpolations resemble the extended glosses frequently appended at the beginnings or ends of sections in a text, which orientate the reader by explaining the nature of the new material or by providing exegesis of what has just been read.

The characteristics of the interpolations suggest that they may well have started out as glosses on the basic text of *Prologus*, and the wider researches of textual historians show that this is not an unsuitable interpretation. Beryl Smalley, in the context of medieval biblical studies, pointed out that exegesis could be undertaken through marginal and interlinear glossing as well as through independent commentaries, and that the distinction between the two often became blurred.[70] The scholar Robert of Tombelaine (who died about 1090) sent an autograph of his commentary on the *Song of Songs* to a friend with the request that it be copied 'not just in the margins, as it is here, but continuously in pages, as other expositions are usually written'.[71] Smalley (and later Margaret Gibson) also pointed to the appearance of the same work as a continuous commentary in one manuscript, and as a marginal and interlinear gloss in another: Lanfranc of Bec on St Paul, for example.[72] As with these examples, so too with the *Prologus* interpolations. If we assume that Karlsruhe, 504 represents the stage at which glosses on Bern's text were copied 'not just in the margins . . . but continuously in pages, as other expositions are written' we shall see one aspect of scholarly practice described by Robert of Tombelaine in the study of the *sacra pagina* occurring also in the study of music.

The character of the interpolations reveals much about attitudes to Bern's teaching. The first four chapters of *Prologus in tonarium* – where

---

[70] B. Smalley, *The study of the Bible in the Middle Ages*, 2nd edn (Oxford, 1952), p. 66.
[71] Ibid., pp. 66–7; Robert of Tombelaine, *Prologus in Cantica Canticorum*, ed. J. Mabillon, *Vetera analecta, sive collectio veterum aliquot operum & opusculorum omnis generis, carminum, epistolarum, diplomatum, epitaphiorum, &c* (Paris, 1723; repr. Farnborough, 1967), p. 128: Quod si librum istum tibi scribere libuerit, non ita in marginibus, sicut hic habetur scribas: sed continuum in paginis, sicut aliae expositiones scribi solent.
[72] Smalley, *The study of the Bible*, p. 67; M. Gibson, 'Lanfranc's commentary on the Pauline epistles', *Journal of Theological Studies n. s.* 22 (1971), 86–95.

Bern described the monochord, the consonances and the significance of number and proportion – seem to have satisfied scribes as they stood, for they elicited very few comments. By far the greatest proportion of scribal commentary is centred on Bern's species and modal theory (*Prologus* 5 and 6), the same topics that were extensively amended by Herman of Reichenau. The simplest interpolations are merely line-of-thought pointers, designed to clarify the text. Such an example occurs in *Prologus* 6, where Bern's explanation that authentic *tetrardus* mode (G–g) 'consists of the fourth species of *diapente* and the fourth species of *diatessaron* above' is glossed with the comment 'which is the seventh mode' (indicated here by italics):

> Example 2.3: Simple explanatory gloss (interpolation) to *Prologus* 6, Karlsruhe, Badische Landesbibliothek, 504, fol. 7r
> Tetrardus autentus *qui est tonus septimus* constat ex | quarta specie diapente et †ex† prima specie dia|tessaron superius . . .[73]

The description of the fourth species of *diapente* in *Prologus* 5 prompted a similar explanatory comment. According to Bern the fourth species of *diapente* consists of the 'first species of *diatessaron*, with the tone below having been added' (that is C–G); it does not, however, begin at the same note, but 'at another, that is *paranete diezeugmenon* [d]'.[74] The resulting *diapente* (G–d) has exactly the same form as the one from C to G: tone-tone-semitone-tone, working from the bottom to the top. (Bern, following Boethius, described the species from top to bottom.) In Karlsruhe, 504 this is the subject of a clarification: very much in the style of a gloss it draws attention to the identical form, the part of Bern's description most likely to cause confusion (the interpolation is again indicated here by italics):

> Example 2.4: Explanatory gloss (interpolation) to *Prologus* 5, Karlsruhe, Badische Landesbibliothek, 504, fol. 4v.
> Quarta species diapente constat ex prima specie diatessaron, | adiecto inferius tono, non quidem per eorundem nominum chordis, | *sed per eiusdem speciei formam,* altius *scilicet,* id est a paranete | diezeugmenon incipiens . . .[75]

The scribe's comment emphasizes that though the notes change, the form of tones and semitones remains unchanged, albeit transposed higher in the gamut.

---

[73] Cf. Rausch (ed.), *Die Musiktraktate des Abtes Bern*, p. 46.
[74] Ibid., p. 42.
[75] Cf. ibid.

Much longer comments were required to sort out the confusion caused by the divergence between the operation of the species as described by Bern and the modes. These lengthy interpolations, such as this example from *Prologus* 5, probably began as extended glosses to Bern's text.

Example 2.5: 'Extended gloss' (interpolation) on *Prologus* 5, Karlsruhe, Badische Landesbibliothek, 504, fols 4v–5v

Et hęc quidem dispositio specierum in consonantiis secundum uete|res quosdam, sed moderni diligentiores in omnibus in dia|pente et diapason eis aliquatenus consentiunt, diatessaron | uero speciebus et aliud exordium et alium ordinem tribuunt. | Quia enim diapason ex diapente et diatessaron consistit, pri|maque species diapason ab .A. ad .a., id est a proslambano| menos ad mese pertingit, cum prima diapente species a mese | incipiens in lychanos ypaton finiatur, incongruum eis || uisum est ut tetrachordum grauium quod est ab eadem lycha|nos ypaton usque ad proslambanomenos, in quo diatessaron | continetur, uelut otiosum et inutile ab his speciebus exclu|datur, hacque de causa statuerunt, ut prima diatessaron speci|es ab .A. usque .D. protendatur, et ex eadem .D. prima diapente | species in acutam .a. producatur, sicque prima diapason species | in his duabus speciebus ab .A. in .a. contineatur. | Est igitur prima species diatessaron .A.B.C.D. a proslam| banomenos uidelicet ad lychanos ypaton, constans ex | tono, semitonio et tono; secunda species .B.C.D.E. quę | est semitonium et ditonus; tercia .C.D.E.F., ditonus | scilicet et semitonium; et sic per omnem seriem chordarum | computando per quaternas, has alternatim tres species inuenies, ex|ceptis duobus locis, scilicet inter parypate meson et para|mese, et inter trite synemenon et nete diezeugmenon. |

Diapente uero species prima sicut et supra dictum est continetur | .D.E.F.G.a., tono, semitonio, ditono; secunda .E.F.G.a.b., | semitonio et tribus tonis, ab ypate meson scilicet ad paramese; | tercia .F.G.a.b.c., tribus tonis et semitonio, a parypa|te meson ad trite diezeugmenon; quarta .G.a.b.c.d., | ditono, semitonio et tono, a lychanos meson ad para|nete diezeugmenon. Has si diligenter inspicias, tonorum | et ‹s›emitoniorum positione inuenies diuersas, et per seriem | uocum in totius monochordi constructione alternatim | dispositas, exceptis tribus locis, uidelicet inter ypate ypa|ton et parypate meson, et inter ypate meson et trite | synemenon, et inter parameson et trite yperboleon. || Diapason autem quoniam his duabus consonantiis completur, tot | habet formas quot sub his continentur. Septem igitur continet | species, per diapente quatuor, per diatessaron tres. Quarum | prima inter .A. et .a. id est proslambanomenos et mese continetur; | secunda ab ypate ypaton ad paramese porrigitur; tercia par|ypate ypaton et trite

75

diezeugmenon terminatur; quarta | a lychanos ypaton ad paranete diezeugmenon protenditur; | quinta ypate meson et nete diezeugmenon limitatur; | sexta a parypate meson ad trite yperboleon intenditur; | septima a paranete yperboleon ad lychanos meson remit|titur. Quas omnes si tonorum et semitoniorum situm inspexeris, | a se inuicem distantes uidebis. Quod si octauam a mese per pa|ramese et trite diezeugmenon intendendo ad nete yperbo|leon adieceris, a prima non dissentire uidebis. Si uero ab | eadem mese per trite synemenon et paranete synemenon ascende|ris, eandem quintę notabis. Sic igitur diapason septem habet | species, unam minus quam uoces, in quibus octo modorum diuer|sa fit positio, quod sequens expediet oratio. Septem uero tan|tum modos secundum diapason species primum fuisse, sed Pto|lomeum octauum superaddidisse Boetium in musica scimus | tradidisse. Quorum nomina diuersitatemque, quoniam breuitati | studemus, secundum ęcclesiasticum usum expediamus.[76]

In Example 2.5 the glossator begins by describing Bern's explanation as a 'disposition of the species according to others of old' ('secundum ueteres'). This he contrasts with the moderns, who understand the *diatessaron* and *diapente* as constituents of the *diapason* ('sed moderni . . . alium ordinem tribuunt'), an opinion that clearly derives from Herman of Reichenau. In Bern's system, where the species of *diatessaron* were in different places, it was impossible for them and the species of *diapente* to form the species of *diapason*, and consequently the modes. It is with this inconsistency that the scribe finds greatest difficulty. He points out that since the first species of *diapason* is A–a and since – by Bern's reasoning – it contains the first species of *diapente* (D–a), the incongruity of Bern's description is to be seen in the fact that the tetrachord of the *graves* (A–D), which contains a *diatessaron*, has been ignored ('incongruum eis uisum est . . . ab his speciebus excludatur'). The scribe knows that the first species of *diatessaron* is A–D and that the first species of *diapente* is produced 'from the same D to the higher a', which – when combined with the *diatessaron* – produces the first species of *diapason* ('hacque de causa statuerunt, ut prima diatessaron species . . . ab .A. in .a. contineatur'). The only possible outcome was that Bern's scheme should be rejected. Indeed, this happens in the very next sentence when the scribe emphatically lists the species of *diatessaron* according to the pattern with which he was familiar. These species can occur in all places 'except two, namely between *parhypate meson* (F) and *paramese* (b), and between *trite synemmenon* (♭) and *nete diezeugmenon* (e)': either would, of course, result in a tritone ('et sic per

---

[76] Ibid., pp. 43–4.

omnem seriem . . . nete diezeugmenon'). The species of *diapente* present fewer problems for the scribe, and all that needs to be done is to reverse Bern's order, so that each is named from the bottom up ('Diapente uero species . . . ad paranete diezeugmenon'). Again, the places where a tritone would result are clearly marked as prohibited ('exceptis tribus locis . . . et trite yperboleon'). For these extended comments the scribe relied on the roughly contemporary treatise Anonymous I, which he copied as commentary to Bern's text. Unlike Bern, who spelled out only the first species of *diapason* explicitly, the scribe took care to delineate all seven meticulously with the added comment that if one were to extend an octave from a (*mese*) to ^a_a (*nete hyperboleon*), the arrangement would be the same as the first species ('Quod si octauam a mese . . . a prima non dissentire uidebis').

In *Prologus* 6 Bern discussed the connexion between the species and the modes. The scribe anticipated this when leaving his discussion of the species of *diapason*, where he took the opportunity to introduce the modes in brief, again using Anonymous I (Example 2.5). He comments that there are seven modes (one for each of the species of *diapason*), but that Ptolemy has added another, giving eight in total ('Septem uero tantum modos . . . sed Ptolomeum octauum superaddidisse'). He tells the reader that there are competing systems of nomenclature for the modes but, excusing himself with the rhetorical device of *epistolaris brevitas*, states that he will speak of them 'according to ecclesiastical use' ('Quorum nomina diuersitatemque, quoniam breuitati | studemus, secundum ęcclesiasticum usum expediamus'). Before *Prologus* 6, however, there is another section in Karlsruhe, 504, which seems like an extended gloss designed as a preparation for what is to come.

Example 2.6: 'Extended gloss' (interpolation) before *Prologus* 6, Karlsruhe, Badische Landesbibliothek, 504, fols 5v–6r

Octo itaque cantionum modis, quos abusiue tonos uocamus | ordo ęcclesiasticus utitur, quorum quatuor excelsiores mo|nochordi uoces sortiti sic uocantur: autentus protus | id est primus magister, autentus deuterus id est secundus magister, | autentus tritus id est tercius magister, autentus tetrardus || id est quartus magister. Authentos enim greci magistros | dicunt, quasi auctoratos, id est auctoritate preditos, | quorum uidelicet precellit auctoritas. Vnde a comparatio|ne altioris gradus, hos modos ita uocari obtinuit usus. | Alii uero quatuor inferiora loca possidentes sic uocantur. | Plagis proti, id est lateralis primi subauditur autenti, quasi | sub latere eius contineatur et inferior sit. Simili ratione | plagis deuteri, plagis triti, plagis tetrardi. Sed nos eorum regulas dantes, | latinis utamur nominibus, et excelsiores magistros, inferiores uero discipulos nominemus. | Sed antequam eorum intensiones uel remissiones incipiamus, | finales omnium neruos ostendamus. Quatuor sunt uoces | quę uocantur finales, eo quod in una qualibet harum | regulares finiantur cantiones, uidelicet .D.E.F.G., | quę sunt lychanos ypaton, ypate meson, parypate | meson, lychanos meson. Quę idcirco ex omnibus electę | sunt finales, quod inter septem uocum discrimina inueni|antur sonoriores. Extra quas si uel uetus uel noua cantio | finiatur, irregularis et non legitimus sine dubio iudicatur. | Cantus igitur magistri eiusque discipuli id est primi et secundi modi | .D. finitur; secundi magistri eiusque discipuli id est tercii | et quarti modi in .E.; tercii magistri eiusque subiecti id est | quinti et sexti modi in .F.; quarti magistri eiusque disci|puli id est septimi et octaui modi in .G. Sed quia nomi|na et finales eorum diximus, intensionis et remissionis limi|tes aperiamus.[77]

This gloss (Example 2.6) starts by explaining that there are eight modes 'which we improperly call tones' – repeating a dictum common among contemporary scholars ('Octo itaque cantionum modis, quos abusiue tonos uocamus').[78] The scribe then lists them, first the authentic forms of *protus*, *deuterus*, *tritus* and *tetrardus* 'which the Greeks call magisterial, as if authoritative'; then the plagal versions 'occupying the lower positions' ('Authentos enim greci . . . inferiora loca possidentes sic uocantur'). But the scribe prefers the comparison of 'master' and 'pupil' to describe the hierarchy and relationship of the authentic and plagals, an analogy that would not have been lost among his contemporaries ('Sed nos eorum regulas dantes, latinis utamur nominibus, et excelsiores magistros, inferiores uero discipulos nominemus').[79] One thing remains to be explained 'before we start on their *intensio* and *remissio*': the importance of the tetrachord of the *finales* ('Sed antequam eorum intensiones uel remissiones incipiamus, finales omnium neruos ostendamus'). This is important because all the modes – whether plagal or authentic – have as their final a note from this tetrachord, which he then explains for each of the modes.

---

[77] Ibid., p. 44.
[78] See C. Atkinson, ' "Harmonia" and the "Modi, quos abusive tonos dicimus" ', in A. Pompilio (ed.), *Atti del XIV congresso della Società internazionale di musicologia. Trasmissione e recezione delle forme di cultura musicale* (Turin, 1990), pp. 485–500.
[79] This analogy is also found in the second of the two short treatises attached to the ninth-century 'Metz tonary' in Metz, Bibliothèque municipale, Cod. 351. See W. Lipphardt, 'Der Karolingische Tonar von Metz', *Liturgiewissenschaftliche Quellen und Forschungen* 43 (1965), 62.

When we come to *Prologus* 6 itself, we again find that the scribe has been busy annotating Bern's text (see Example 2.7 below). 'Protus constat ex prima specie diapente' becomes 'Protus *itaque autentus id est primus magister* constat ex prima specie diapente', in a reference to the extended gloss that preceded the chapter. The subsequent clause – 'et ex prima specie diatessaron superius' – which refers to Bern's description of the species of *diatessaron* – required a reference back to the gloss on this point in *Prologus* 5, for we have seen the differences between Bern's system and that familiar to the scribe.[80] The scribe commented here 'not that the first species of it begins here, but that it has the form and similitude of this first species, which is below it'. He was pointing out, therefore, that though Bern's *diatessaron* bore the same form of tone-semitone-tone, it was not the same as the generally accepted *diatessaron*. The chapter continues with similar additions, offered by way of clarification and explanation (these scribal interpolations in Bern's text indicated by italics):

Example 2.7: Scribal interpolations in *Prologus* 6, Karlsruhe, Badische Landesbibliothek, 504, fols 6r–7r.

Protus *itaque autentus id est primus* | *magister* constat ex prima specie diapente et ex || prima specie diatessaron superius, *non quod ibi prima eius spe|cies exordiatur, sed quod forma et similitudo primę illius | speciei, quę inferius est hic sub eadem chordarum dispositio|ne contineatur, tono scilicet et semitonio et tono.* Subiu|galis uero eius constat ex eadem specie diapente et ex eadem | specie diatessaron inferius. Quod autem dico, tale est. | Primus tonus a suo finali id est a lychanos ypaton habet | licentiam ascendendi in diapente hoc est in mese, et a mese | in paranete diezeugmenon, quod est prima species dyatessaron | *eo modo quo predictum est* . . . itemque protus infra finalem suum descendit | in sonum sibi uicinum, aliquando in tercium, numquam uero *in* | *legitimis cantibus* in quartum. Similiter et alii tres auten|tici iuxta ordinem finalium suorum. Deuterus constat ex | secunda specie diapente et secunda specie diatessaron superius, | *illo scilicet modo quo supra taxatum est*; subiugalis eius ex ea|dem specie diapente et ex eadem specie diatessaron | inferius. Ex superiore autem sermone potes et istud | comprehendere. Tritus *autentus qui est tonus quintus* | constat ex tercia specie diapente et tercię speciei | diatesseron forma superius, subiugalis eius ex | eadem specie diapente et ex eadem specie diatessaron || inferius. Tetrardus *autentus qui est tonus septimus* constat ex | quarta specie diapente, et †ex† prima specie dia|tessaron superius † †; subiugalis eius ex ea|dem specie diapente et ex prima specie diatessaron infe|rius. |[81]

---

[80] See above pp. 76–7.
[81] See Rausch (ed.), *Die Musiktraktate des Abtes Bern*, pp. 45–6.

The subject matter of the glosses on Bern's text centres on the species and modes. The scribe(s) responsible for annotating *Prologus in tonarium* were clearly familiar with the advances made by Herman of Reichenau, who reconciled the operation of the species and modes. They annotated Bern's text where necessary and supplemented it with large portions of Anonymous I when longer commentary was required.

In this reconstruction, I have assumed the existence of a glossed manuscript that was the direct ancestor of Karlsruhe, 504, fols 1–14. Alexander Rausch has argued that the *Prologus* interpolations originated with Frutolf of Michelsberg, owing to the fact that Frutolf copied Karlsruhe, 504, fols 1–14 and incorporated parts of the interpolations into his own *Breviarium de musica*.[82] Rausch's important suggestion, however, overlooks that fact that there are textual differences between the 'original' *Prologus* interpolations and their reappearance in Frutolf's *Breviarium de musica*. Furthermore, these differences are similar in character to the textual differences that exist between Frutolf's copying of other authors and their original texts.[83] Had Frutolf been the author of the interpolations, he would probably have copied them unaltered. Although he may not be the author of the interpolations, it is more than possible that he was responsible for copying a glossed *Prologus* as continuous text. The intermediate sources do not survive, but the conjecture presents an interesting perspective on the contemporary transmission of texts and on the importance of *Prologus in tonarium* for eleventh-century scholars.

The influence of Guido of Arezzo

It would be difficult to underestimate the influence exerted by Guido of Arezzo upon eleventh- and twelfth-century music theory. The great number of surviving manuscripts containing copies of his treatises points to the importance of his reputation and teaching for later generations. Some 118 manuscript copies of *Micrologus* survive while Guido's other treatises – *Regule rithmice*, *Prologus in antiphonarium* and *Epistola ad Michahelem* – are transmitted in seventy manuscripts. Nevertheless, despite the abundance of source material, relatively little work has been done on the influence of Guido in the eleventh and twelfth centuries. Joseph Smits van Waesberghe's 1955 edition of *Micrologus* is in many respects dated, while the same author's *De musico-paedagogico et theoretico Guidone Aretino* and

[82] Ibid., p. 124.
[83] See below, pp. 97–106.

Hans Oesch's *Guido von Arezzo* remain the only full-length studies of this important author.[84] These monographs have been supplemented by a number of specialized studies.[85] Recent research by Delores Pesce provides valuable information about the manuscript tradition of Guido's *Regule rithmice*, *Prologus in antiphonarium* and *Epistola ad Michahelem*, but the scope of her edition precluded an analysis of his influence and reception.[86] The only other recent set of studies is that edited by Rusconi.[87] A detailed study of Guido's influence cannot be attempted here. Nevertheless, it is both necessary and useful to analyse his impact upon the south-German circle of music theorists. This will make it possible to understand more about the extent and nature of their response to his music theory.

Knowledge of Guido's teaching was certainly widespread in eleventh-century Germany. The early twelfth-century historiographers provide useful snapshots of his influence. In the encyclopaedic *Liber de illustribus viris*, Sigebert of Gembloux spoke of Guido as being pre-eminent among musicians and remarked how 'even young boys and girls could more easily learn an unknown chant by his rules than from the voice of a master or from the use of any other instrument'.[88] This is a reference to the notation and

[84] Guido of Arezzo, *Micrologus*, ed. J. Smits van Waesberghe, *Micrologus Guidonis Aretini* (Rome, 1955); J. Smits van Waesberghe, *De musico-paedagogico et theoretico Guidone Aretino eiusque vita et moribus* (Florence, 1953); H. Oesch, *Guido von Arezzo. Biographisches und Theoretisches unter besonderer Berücksichtigung der sogenannten odonischen Traktate* (Bern, 1954).
[85] See for example D. Pesce, *The affinities and medieval transposition* (Bloomington, Ind., 1987), pp. 18–26 and K.-J. Sachs, 'Tradition und Innovation bei Guido von Arezzo', in W. Erzgräber (ed.), *Kontinuität und Transformation der Antike im Mittelalter. Veröffentlichung der Kongressakten zum Freiburger Symposion des Mediävistenverbandes* (Sigmaringen, 1989), pp. 233–44; C. Meyer, 'La tradition du "Micrologus" de Guy d'Arezzo. Une contribution à l'histoire de la réception du texte', *Revue de musicologie* 83 (1997), 5–31.
[86] Guido, *Epistola ad Michahelem*, ed. Pesce.
[87] A. Rusconi (ed.), *Guido d'Arezzo, monaco pomposiano. Atti dei Convegni di studio, Codigoro (Ferrara), Abbazia di Pomposa, 3 ottobre 1997, Arezzo, Biblioteca Città di Arezzo, 29–30 maggio 1998, a cura di Angelo Rusconi* (Florence, 2000).
[88] Sigebert of Gembloux, *Liber de illustribus viris* 145, ed. R. Witte, *Catalogus Sigeberti Gemblacensis monachi de viris illustribus. Kritische Ausgabe* (Bern and Frankfurt am Main, 1974), pp. 92–3: Guido Aretinus monachus post omne pene musicos in ecclesia claruit, in hoc prioribus perferendus, quod ignotos cantus etiam pueri et puelle facilius discunt [vel docent] per eius regulam quam per vocem magistri aut per usum alicuius instrumenti, dummodo sex litteris vel sillabis modulatim appositis ad sex voces, quas solas musica recipit, hisque vocibus per flexuras digitorum leve manus distinctis per integrum dyapason se oculis et auribus ingerunt intente et remisse elevationes vel depositiones earundem vocum.

solmization system that Guido developed in *Prologus in antiphonarium* and *Epistola ad Michahelem* (also known as *Epistola de ignoto cantu directa*), and which was received enthusiastically across Europe. Sigebert mentions two other Guidonian innovations: 'the six letters or syllables apposite to the six notes' (that is, the hexachord worked out by Guido) and the 'Guidonian hand' – a pedagogic device which, though not actually devised by Guido, was universally associated with him. It seems clear from the technical detail in Sigebert's description that he had read Guido. Sigebert recycled much of this passage for his *Chronicon* (written between 1105 and 1110), where he devoted the entire entry for the year 1028 to Guido, further attesting his fame.[89] Another twelfth-century historian, the anonymous author of the continuation to Rudolf of St Trond's *Deeds of the abbots of St Trond* recorded that Rudolf, when master of the school, taught the boys 'not only *dictamen* and metrics . . . but music following the principles laid down by Guido of Arezzo'.[90]

Guido and Herman of Reichenau

Engagement with Guido's teaching occurs on different levels in the south-German treatises. Although Sigebert of Gembloux hinted that Abbot Bern of Reichenau may have been acquainted with Guido's works, it is unlikely that this was so, for there are no such indications in either of Bern's two treatises (*Epistola de tonis* and *Prologus in tonarium*).[91] Scholars have remained divided on whether or not Bern's pupil Herman of Reichenau knew Guido's works. Hans Oesch found no incontrovertible evidence to support this and so concluded that he did not.[92] This conclusion, however, fails to explain adequately the references that Herman makes to ideas that are explicitly Guidonian in origin.

A recurring theme of Herman's *Musica* is its author's desire to formulate a system that aids the recognition of the modes, in pursuit of which he went far beyond the precedent established by his teacher Bern. This led Herman to tackle the issue of hexachords, or as Richard Crocker aptly termed it, his 'major sixth'.[93] Guido had suggested a very similar arrangement in his *Epistola ad Michahelem* of c. 1032.[94] In *Musica* 19 Herman introduces 'one

---

[89] Sigebert of Gembloux, *Chronicon* 1028, *MGH SS* 6, p. 356.
[90] *Gesta abbatis Trudonensis* 8 (*Continuatio* 1), *MGH SS* 10, p. 273.
[91] Sigebert of Gembloux, *Liber de illustribus viris* 157, p. 98.
[92] Oesch, *Berno und Hermann*, pp. 212, 215–16, 229, 234–48.
[93] R. L. Crocker, 'Hermann's major sixth', *Journal of the American Musicological Society* 25 (1972), 19–37.
[94] Guido, *Epistola ad Michahelem*, pp. 438–531. On its dating see pp. 1–3.

rule for recognizing the modes which has hitherto been dug out as a rough mass . . . by previous writers'.[95] (The only person to whom 'previous writers' could refer in this context is Guido of Arezzo.) Herman proceeds from what he has already established in outlining this new concept, writing that if one take a tetrachord (he chooses that of the *graves* – A B C D) and add a tone at both ends, one then has 'the limits of the modes, which form the seats of the tropes'.[96] He continues 'there are four tropes and as many modal voices', which clearly echoes Guido's earlier *Micrologus* (written between 1026 and 1032).[97] The major sixth that results from this description (Γ A B C D E) is essentially the same as that described in Guido's *Epistola ad Michahelem*. Although it is impossible to be certain that Herman is pointing to Guido in these references (since he does not quote him as he does the Carolingian treatise *Musica enchiriadis* elsewhere in his treatise), it is highly probable that this is an echo of Guido's work. It would not be stylistically incongruous for Herman to refer to Guido without quoting him explicitly: Herman's *Chronicon* shows that where he relied on the chronicle of Regino of Prüm, he displayed a marked habit of paraphrasing rather than quoting his source.[98] The fact remains that Herman's knowledge of Guidonian hexachordal theory is so detailed that it can be explained adequately only by the conclusion that Herman knew it at first hand.

Herman, in subsequent passages, can be seen to criticize Guido's reasoning overtly by accusing 'previous writers' of lack of clarity. Guido has erred because he has 'failed to notice the oft-mentioned double aspect of D'.[99] He commits what is for Herman a cardinal error by not observing 'how the modes are interconnected'.[100] Herman further complains that by 'regularly laying out the three modes on A, B and C, but denying the existence of the fourth mode; and seeking again a sequence of the abovementioned modes by similar rule on D, E and F, they fixed the fourth mode

[95] Herman, *Musica* 19, p. 57.
[96] Ibid.: Accipe tetrachordum quodcumque volueris, verbi gratia gravium, addito utrinque tono, habes terminos modorum qui fiunt sedes troporum.
[97] Ibid.: Sunt autem quatuor tropi, et totidem vocum modi; cf. Guido, *Micrologus* 7, pp. 117–18: Cum autem septem sint voces, quia aliae ut diximus, sunt, eaedem, septenas sufficit explicare, quae diversorum modorum et diversarum sunt qualitatum. Primus modus vocum est, cum vox tono deponitur et tono et semitonio duobusque tonis intenditur, ut .A. et .D. Secundus modus est, cum vox duobus tonis remissa, semitonio et duobus tonis intenditur, ut .B. et .E. Tertius est qui semitonio et duobus tonis descendit, duobus vero tonis ascendit, ut .C. et .F. Quartus vero deponitur tono, surgit autem per duos tonos et semitonium, ut .G.
[98] I owe this reference to Professor I. S. Robinson.
[99] Herman, *Musica* 19, p. 59.
[100] Ibid.

finally on G alone, making it fall a tone and rise two tones and a semitone'.[101] This error, he protests, 'is threefold . . . because they did not set this same mode off against its opposite, that is, *protus*, in the way we have described; secondly, they extended it beyond the pattern and exceeded the legitimate limit beyond the six pitches, which begins on C and stretches to a; and finally they make this extension with no established species'.[102] This criticism can be identified as another reference to *Micrologus* 7.[103] Richard Crocker has interpreted this and Herman's other criticisms of Guido's work as pointing to a common concern 'to express the interval set within which the ascents and descents around the finals are identical in their several locations'.[104] He has suggested that Guido argued that three finals are all there really are. This helps to explain Herman's particular anxiety about Guido's arrangement: he would rather emphasize four finals within the major sixth (A B C D).[105]

The essential difference is that Herman's approach is inductive, Guido's deductive; they approach the issue from opposite standpoints. The importance that Guido accorded the octave allowed him to adumbrate the hexachord: he deduced it from his *scala*, or 'ladder of notes'. (Indeed in the later Middle Ages, when the concept of the hexachord had been formalized, the positions of the soft, natural and hard hexachords were called the deductions or *deductiones*.)[106] Herman, in contrast, proceeded from the bottom up, from the tetrachordal theory that was so central to his reasoning. 'Take any tetrachord you wish': he induced the idea of the hexachord from this starting-point. Hence, though he was aware of Guido's idea, the genesis of his own was very different. Critical of what he saw as the weaknesses of Guido's system, Herman's own work on 'modal voices' is in many ways the culmination of *Musica*. Herman was probably the first south-German theorist to consider Guido's teaching. Already apparent is disagreement rooted in different methodologies: the Guidonian, which sought modal expressions of the gamut in hexachords; and the German,

---

[101] Ibid., p. 60.
[102] Ibid.
[103] Guido, *Micrologus* 7, pp. 118–19: Et nota quod se per ordinem sequuntur, ut primus in .A., secundus in .B., tertius in .C. Itemque primus in .D., secundus in .E., tertius in .F., quartus in .G. Itemque nota has vocum affinitates per diatessaron et diapente constructas: .A. enim ad .D. et .B. ad .E. et .C. ad .F. a gravibus diatessaron, ad acutis vero diapente coniungitur hoc modo.
[104] Crocker, 'Hermann's major sixth', 24.
[105] Ibid., 25.
[106] See K. Berger, *Musica ficta: theories of accidental inflections in vocal polyphony from Marchetto da Padova to Gioseffo Zarlino* (Cambridge, 1987), pp. 2–10.

which proceeded from the building blocks of tetrachords. This disagreement would recur in later German music treatises.

Guido and the wider south-German circle

Differing attitudes towards Guido are apparent among later members of the south-German circle. An analysis of their music treatises reveals that the teachings criticized by Herman continued to meet with disapproval. Nowhere is this more apparent than in William of Hirsau's *Musica*. William followed Herman's teaching in emphasizing the conjunction of the tetrachords around D and d. *Musica* 15 – 'How D and d are double-formed and double-functioned' – is devoted to this point. Here Guido is mentioned in the same breath as pseudo-Odo of Cluny and Boethius as one who does not subscribe to this position.[107] William must also have had Guido in mind with the title of the next chapter: 'How Boethius and other musicians have erred over D and d, and that double aa is assumed to be necessary'.[108] These criticisms of Guido, which are carried through the subsequent chapter,[109] are made explicit in the title of *Musica* 18: 'That lord Guido, while knowing the errors of the ancients, did not correct them'.[110] William states Guido's position as outlined in *Micrologus* 12: 'He [Guido] asserts also in his music treatise that the eight modes in nature are more truly four, and that in each of these four two are contained, that is from *protus* the first and second, from *deuterus* the third and fourth, from *tritus* the fifth and sixth, from *tetrardus* the seventh and eighth'.[111] William then gives a diagram of this arrangement, which is taken from Guido's *Regule rithmice*.[112]

As the diagram shows, Guido only allows D and d one function: they are always *protus* (either authentic or plagal) and never *tetrardus*. William notes this with disapproval, saying that '[Guido] did not understand the double function of D and d. If he had understood this, as well as the first and seventh [functions], the second and eighth would have been noted down in this manner':[113]

[107] William, *Musica* 15, p. 41.
[108] Ibid. 16, p. 42.
[109] Ibid. 17, p. 47.
[110] Ibid. 18, p. 48.
[111] Ibid.: Asserens enim in musica sua quod octo modi verius in natura sint quatuor, et quod ab unoquoque ipsorum quatuor duo contineantur, id est a proto primus et secundus, a deutero tertius et quartus, a trito quintus et sextus, a tetardo septimus et octavus.
[112] Guido took the diagram from pseudo-Odo's *Dialogus de musica*. An abbridged version, for the notes A–c, appears in *Micrologus* 7.
[113] William, *Musica* 18, pp. 48–9: In hac igitur descriptione quantum ad id quod tetrachordis Gravium et Superiorum quartam suam ademit, et quod duplicitatem .D. et .d.

Figure 2.3: Diagram from Guido's *Regule rithmice* quoted by William of Hirsau

I	III	V	I	III	V	VII	I	III	V	I	III	V	VII	I
A	B	C	D	E	F	G	a	b	c	d	e	f	g	aa
II	IIII	VI	II	IIII	VI	VIII	II	IIII	VI	II	IIII	VI	VIII	II

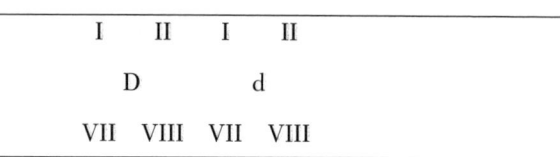

Key: I   authentic protus   V   authentic tritus
      II   plagal protus   VI   plagal tritus
      III authentic deuterus   VII   authentic tetrardus
      IIII plagal deuterus   VIII plagal tetrardus

Figure 2.4: William of Hirsau's correction of Guido's error

I	II	I	II
D		d	
VII	VIII	VII	VIII

By William's arrangement D and d have both a *protus* and *tetrardus* function, since he considered them both the final note of the *graves* (A B C D) and *superiores* (a b c d), as well as the beginning note of the *finales* (D E F G) and *excellentes* (d e f g) respectively.

William's pupil Theoger of Metz provides another example of the matters in which the German theorists were most likely to disagree with Guido. Chapter 12 of Theoger's *Musica*, which is concerned with the *synemmenon* tetrachord, makes what can be identified as a critical reference to Guido, though without mentioning him explicitly.[114] This may be because of the high esteem in which he was held by Theoger, who placed him in the company of Pythagoras and Boethius and described him as 'a most diligent investigator of the notes [of music] and a most reliable commentator and teacher'.[115] Guido had allowed the use of 'soft-b' (b-flat) as well as 'hard-b' (b-natural) in certain circumstances, especially in chants where the pitches F or f recurred frequently.[116] For Theoger, however, the

---

Footnote 113 (*cont.*)
    non intellexit. Si enim intellexisset, utrimque primum cum secundo, et septimum cum octavo partier annotasset hoc modo.

[114] The *synemmenon* tetrachord (a ♭ c d) was used by German theorists to account for the note b-flat, which occurred in certain chants.

[115] Theoger, *Musica* 1, p. 9: Gwido uero monachus extitit uocum indagator diligentissimus et commendator traditorque certissimus.

[116] Guido, *Micrologus* 8, pp. 124–5.

use of soft-b necessitated the introduction of the *synemmenon* tetrachord. The point is plainly made in *Musica* 12: 'Certain musicians do not establish the *synemmenon* tetrachord, but only one note instead, and they call it soft; but rarely are the voices changed in one note without affecting the whole tetrachord, or even more.[117] By insisting on the use of the whole *synemmenon* tetrachord, Theoger was adhering to the practice set out by Bern of Reichenau and followed by German theorists.

Except for these specific criticisms, most of the other references in the south-German treatises evince a positive attitude towards Guido. In Chapter 20 of his treatise, William of Hirsau quotes at length from *Micrologus* 7, which introduces the concept of 'modus vocum', that is, patterns for each mode.[118] The change in William's attitude is reflected not only by the inclusion of a long quotation from *Micrologus*, but in the manner in which Guido is addressed: he is now styled 'venerabilis Guido', 'venerandus Guido' and 'domnus Guido'.[119] Theoger of Metz, too, responded enthusiastically to Guido's 'modus vocum'. The influence of *Micrologus* 7 can likewise be seen behind the heading 'De quatuor modis vocum' that occurs in Chapter 10 of the lengthy treatise *Breviarium de musica* by Frutolf of Michelsberg.[120] When Theoger treats of the four modes he, like William, praises Guido who 'calls them [the tropes] "modes", and establishes four of them for the same purpose for which we have established the species; and through these "modes" he gives form to the four tropes, namely *protus*, *deuterus*, *tritus* and *tetrardus*, just as we did by means of the species'.[121] This statement also contains a hint that Theoger's reception of Guido was not entirely uninfluenced by other sources, for his comment about the species seems to recall the language of Herman's *Musica*.[122]

A different type of reliance on Guido is apparent in Aribo's *De musica*. While *De musica* contains sporadic allusions to Guidonian ideas – for example the statement that songs in which F and f are prominent require *synemmenon* in order to avoid a tritone,[123] and that 'soft- and square-b

---

[117] Theoger, *Musica* 12, p. 20: Quidam musici non ponunt tetrachordum synemni, sed tantum unam chordam, et uocant eam mollem; sed raro mutantur uoces in una chorda, quin potius permeant totum tetrachordum, uel eo amplius.
[118] Ibid. 20, p. 52; cf. Guido, *Micrologus* 7, pp. 117–19.
[119] William, *Musica* 20, pp. 51–2.
[120] Frutolf, *Breviarium* 10, p. 72.
[121] Theoger, *Musica* 19, p. 25; cf. Guido, *Micrologus* 7, pp. 117–19.
[122] See above p. 84 n. 102.
[123] Aribo, *De musica*, p. 10.91: Quapropter .F. et .f. admodum indigent synemmenon, ut gravis supra quartam, acuta habeat quintam ad se resultantem per diapente; cf. Guido, *Micrologus* 8, pp. 124–5.

never meet in a single neume' – it is Aribo's long commentary on aspects of Guido's melodic theory that sets him apart from William, Theoger and Frutolf.[124] *Micrologus* 15 is concerned with the composition of adroit melodies. Guido advocates that the composer think of his melodies as lines of verse: just as syllables, letters, parts, feet and lines are its members, so too melodies have their own analogous members. He says that two or three sounds taken together make a 'syllable'; one or two of these a 'neume', which constitutes a 'part of a melody'; and one or more of these a 'distinction, that is a suitable place to take a breath'.[125] Aribo takes up this idea enthusiastically in *De musica*: 'The sweetness of rejoicing is two-fold, if in this wise the neumes and distinctions be brought together proportionally, just as the notes of the monochord are disposed in the same way, as lord Guido teaches, who is indeed the most modern musician of the time, foremost in usefulness, with whose merit we compare other teachers of the same art, as we do the dumb to the speaking'.[126] He then cites a long passage of *Micrologus* 15 and explains that his purpose is only to 'explain these things for the very simple', as Guido 'has left these directions of his without examples'.[127] He stresses Guido's teaching that the neumes must always correspond to each other either in the number of notes or in the ratio of their durations.[128] Guido's definition of *tenor* is then echoed: it is properly the holding of a voice or *mora vocis*.[129] Aribo links this proportionality to the practice of appending letters such as c*[eleritas]*, t*[arditas]* and m*[ediocritas]* to neumes, though he admits that this procedure is

---

[124] Aribo, *De musica*, p. 28.27: . . . quia nunquam .b. molle atque quadratum in unam convenient neumam; cf. Guido, *Micrologus* 8, pp. 124-5: utramque autem .b. in eadem neuma non iungas.

[125] Guido, *Micrologus* 15, pp. 162-3: Igitur quemadmodum in metris sunt litterae et syllabae, partes et pedes ac versus, ita in harmonia sunt phtongi, id est soni, quorum unus, duo vel tres aptantur in syllabas; ipsaeque solae vel duplicatae neumam, id est partem constituunt cantilenae; et pars una vel plures distinctionem faciunt, id est congruum respirationis locum.

[126] Aribo, *De musica*, p. 48.22: Duplex est iubilandi dulcedo, si ita proportionaliter conferantur neumae distinctionesque, sicut ipsae monochordi voces dispositae, sicut domnus Guido docet, musicus quidem tempore novissimus, utilitate primus, cuius merito alios eiusdem artis praeceptores ita comparamus, ut mutas vocalibus.

[127] Ibid., p. 49.25: Quoniam quidem domnus Guido has praeceptiones suas sine exemplis reliquit, quia eas, ut sunt, satis manifestas credidit, nos eas valde simplicibus pro nostro captu exponemus. See Guido, *Micrologus* 15, pp. 164-9.

[128] Guido, *Micrologus* 15, p. 165: . . . ut cum neumae tum eiusdem soni repercussione, tum duorum aut plurium connexione fiant, semper tamen aut in numero vocum aut in ratione tenorum neumae alterutrum conferantur.

[129] Ibid., p. 163: Tenor vero, id est mora ultima vocis, qui in syllaba quantuluscumque est, amplior in parte, diutissimus vero in distinctione, signum in his divisionis existit.

obsolete.¹³⁰ Examples of chants are then provided to apply his interpretation of Guido and the support of *Rhetorica ad Herennium* is adduced as the proportional interpretation of the neumes is likened to the *colores rhetorici*.¹³¹ Aribo ends his discussion by including a further quotation, this time from *Micrologus* 16, in support of his interpretation.¹³² Aribo's aim in expounding these short portions of *Micrologus*, therefore, is to demonstrate that the neumes should be considered with the proper arithmetical proportion in mind. This proportion is analogous to the feet of prose or verse and the astute musician uses them as the orator or letter writer would the *colores rhetorici*; an equal number of notes finds close analogy in the eleventh-century art of letter writing, where the *color* that used approximately equal numbers of syllables to balance clauses was an especially frequent occurrence.¹³³ Just as any oration is built from the combination of its topics and figures, so too a piece of music is built from its own analogous devices.

These references to Guido suggest that Aribo saw himself as an expositor of Guidonian metrical theory. Other references, however, hint that Aribo considered himself an improver in certain respects. Later in *De musica* he qualifies Guido's statement that almost all of the distinctions should proceed to the principal or final note, because this is 'more rarely than frequently found to be the case',¹³⁴ while in the following chapter we are afforded a valuable glimpse of Aribo's motivation: 'Having set forth the useful ideas relating to melody that we share with lord Guido, not only have we expounded his own words, but also proposed more convenient types of melody about which he has kept thoroughly quiet'.¹³⁵

De musica does not present Aribo's only response to Guido's melodic theory, for this is also the subject of two *sententiae* that he appended to his

---

¹³⁰ Aribo, *De musica*, p. 49.28: Unde in antiquioribus antiphonariis utrisque c. t. m. reperimus persaepe, quae celeritatem, tarditatem, mediocritatem innuunt. Antiquitus fuit magna circumspectio non solum cantus inventoribus, sed etiam ipsis cantoribus, ut quilibet proportionaliter et invenirent et canerent. Quae consideratio iam dudum obiit, immo sepulta est.

¹³¹ Ibid., p. 50.31: Talis consideratio similis est rethorico colori, qui compar dicitur, qui constat fere ex pari numero syllabarum.

¹³² Guido, *Micrologus* 16, p. 181.

¹³³ T. J. H. McCarthy, 'Literary practice in eleventh-century music theory: the *colores rhetorici* and Aribo's *De musica*', *Medium aevum* 71 (2002), 200.

¹³⁴ Aribo, *De musica*, p. 54.66: Hoc tamen rarius invenitur, quam crebrius; cf. Guido, *Micrologus* 15, p. 170.

¹³⁵ Aribo, *De musica*, p. 54.71: Praemissis modulationis utilitatibus cum domno Guidone nobis communibus, quia sua non solum verba exposuimus, sed etiam commodiores motuum species, quas ipse penitus reticuit, proposuimus.

treatise shortly after it was written, perhaps in answer to the questions of a pupil or colleague.[136] The first is entitled 'A useful exposition of some obscure sentences in Guido'. For the first part of the *sententia* Aribo relied upon a source that he had previously used in *De musica*: the contemporary south-German *Commentarius anonymus in Micrologum Guidonis Aretini*.[137] The portion cited in the *sententia* comments upon *Micrologus* 15. Aribo's emphasis, however, is different from his previous discussion of Guido in *De musica*, as the quoted text from the anonymous commentary is concerned with the relationship of what Guido calls the 'brief delays between notes' and proportionality in chant. When Aribo resumes his own commentary, he quotes parts of *Micrologus* 15 not found in his earlier discussion, in addition to expounding *Micrologus* 17.[138] The second of Aribo's *sententiae* takes its subject text from Guido's *Prologus in antiphonarium* and is concerned with the formulas of the modes.[139]

Whereas the treatises of William, Theoger and Frutolf appraise selective aspects of Guido, and whereas that of Aribo is dominated by his concern with Guido's melodic theory, it is John's *De musica*, written sometime in the early twelfth century, that shows its author to be the most consistently enthusiastic proponent of Guido among the south-German circle. In the dedicatory letter that precedes *De musica*, John records the encouragement of his patron and dedicatee, designed to overcome the author's characteristically humble expressions of unworthiness: 'Have I not learned . . . that you have read the music treatises of Boethius and Guido and also of Bern?'[140] This rhetorical question is similar in character to the statement at the beginning of Theoger's *Musica*: by casting Guido as an authority it adds prestige to his teaching. John cites Guido on numerous occasions, frequently picking out the subjects beloved of the German theorists: the numeration of six consonances,[141] or Guido's criticism of calling the modes 'tones'.[142] Like them he too modifies Guido where necessary, an example being in Chapter 11, where he discusses the 'tenors of the modes'.

---

[136] T. J. H. McCarthy, 'Aribo's *De musica*, *Commentarius anonymus in Micrologum Guidonis Aretini* and Guido of Arezzo: textual correspondence and scholastic method', *Mediaevistik. Internationale Zeitschrift für Interdisziplinäre Mittelalterforschung* 20 (2007), 159–61.

[137] *Commentarius anonymus in Micrologum Guidonis Aretini*, ed. J. Smits van Waesberghe, *Expositiones in Micrologum Guidonis Aretini* (Amsterdam, 1957), pp. 99–172.

[138] Aribo, *De musica*, pp. 65–71; cf. Guido, *Micrologus* 15, 17, pp. 164–93.

[139] Aribo, *De musica*, p. 71; cf. Guido, *Prologus in antiphonarium*, pp. 432–3.

[140] John, *De musica*, pp. 44–5.

[141] Ibid. 8, p. 67; cf. Guido, *Micrologus* 4, p. 105.

[142] John, *De musica* 11, p. 76; cf. Guido, *Micrologus* 10, pp. 133–8.

For John a 'tenor' is what Aribo calls a 'principal note': it is 'the place where the first syllable of the *saeculorum amen* of any mode begins'. He observes, however, that Guido uses 'tenor' to describe the delay on a final note, a reference to *Micrologus* 15. John, therefore, uses 'tenor' as a term of modal theory while being aware that Guido had used it with a different meaning for melodic theory.[143]

Guido's exalted status is reflected in the frequency of his appearance, which is apparent from the very beginning of John's treatise. Chapter 1 introduces one of the most enduring of Guidonian legacies: solmization. Here, John writes that six syllables are used in music, which, however, differ among different peoples: the English, French and Germans use ut, re, mi, fa, sol, la; 'the Italians have others, and those who wish to learn them may arrange to do so with these people'.[144] This statement is probably connected to the fact that the five oldest manuscripts of Guido's *Epistola ad Michahelem* gave the syllable set 'Tri-Pro-De-Nos-Te-Ad' as an alternative solmization system, a tradition to which John seems to have had access.[145] John then quotes Guido's mnemonic hymn *Ut queant laxis* in order to explain the solmization syllables.[146]

Chapter 5 affords another glimpse of John's enthusiasm for Guido. He describes the letters of the gamut, discussing the invention and use of Γ by the moderns. This results in the normal gamut of seventeen notes, though Guido 'whom we consider the greatest in our field since Boethius, set up twenty-one notes in his musical system, so that no deficiency might ever find its way into plainchant'.[147] John makes no effort to distinguish between the merits of either system but in his subsequent discussion uses Guido's gamut instead of that common in southern Germany, a clear indication of his attitude. Guido's pedagogic reputation is also evident in Chapter 14, where he is adduced as an authority in criticism of the use of *synemmenon* in the *protus* chant *Gaudendum est nobis*: 'Guido, who was concerned precisely that no notes should be wanting on the monochord, would undoubtedly have intercalated this one had it seemed necessary to him'.[148]

John is the only member of the south-German circle to discuss organum, which he does so briefly in Chapter 23. Here the influence of

---

[143] John, *De musica* 11, p. 82; cf. Guido, *Micrologus* 15, p. 163.
[144] John, *De musica* 1, p. 49.
[145] Smits van Waesberghe, *De musico-paedagogico et theoretico Guidone Aretino*, pp. 101–02; C. V. Palisca (ed.) in W. Babb (trans.), *Hucbald, Guido and John on music: three medieval treatises* (New Haven and London, 1978), pp. 99–100, 104 n. 1.
[146] John, *De musica* 1, pp. 49–50.
[147] Ibid. 5, p. 60.
[148] Ibid. 14, p. 103.

Guido is readily apparent, since his explanation of melodic motion paraphrases *Micrologus* 16, while the overall inspiration can be seen to rest in *Micrologus* 18.[149] These citations and allusions to Guido are but examples from the many contained in John's treatise. The impression gained is of one who has studied Guido's treatises extensively, to the extent that Guidonian references permeate his text. John may, in this respect, be contrasted with a late representative of the south-German circle, the anonymous author of *Quaestiones in musica*. This theorist had certainly read *Micrologus*, as his references contain expressions and terms from it not found in other south-German treatises.[150] *Quaestiones in musica* contains a number of other Guidonian borrowings and allusions.[151] Some, however, seem to have come not directly from *Micrologus*, but through intermediate sources such as Aribo, who is quoted extensively. The title of *Quaestio* 6 ('How the tetrachords of Guido correlate with the tetrachords of Boethius'), for example, suggests that the substance of the answer has been taken at first hand from Guido.[152] But the ensuing text originates with Aribo, who in *De musica* 26 laid out Boethius' and Guido's arrangement of the tetrachords.[153] It is the heading that has been added by the author of *Quaestiones in musica*. A similar explanation of the comments on metrical proportion in singing is possible: on this occasion, Aribo's first *sententia* (and possibly *De musica* 89) seems to have been the source of the Guidonian echoes.[154]

The evidence of the music treatises provides a valuable opportunity to assess the attitude of the German theorists to Guido. It is possible to conclude that knowledge of his writings was widespread in Germany. In this respect, Master Henry of Augsburg (d. 1083) and the Wolf Anonymous (c. 1060) – whose treatises do not contain any real evidence of Guido's influence – must be seen as exceptions. Guido was considered useful, not in his entirety, but in specific matters. John's *De musica*, written sometime in the early twelfth century, is the most thoroughly pro-Guidonian of the treatises. The relative lateness of its composition may have had a bearing on John's attitude, for by the early twelfth century the teaching of Guido

---

[149] Ibid. 16, pp. 157–8; Babb (trans.), *Hucbald, Guido and John*, p. 159.
[150] *Quaestiones in musica* 1, p. 12: Proinde facultas humanae vocis limitem non valet excedere septimi discriminis, quia octavae cordae adiectio primae prorsus est renovatio et repeticio; cf. Guido, *Micrologus* 5, p. 112: Unde verissime poeta dixit: septem discrimina vocum, quia etsi plures sint vel fiant, non est aliarum adiectio, sed earundem renovatio et repetitio.
[151] *Quaestiones in musica* 1.10, 1.20, 2.24, pp. 20, 50–1, 54, 90–2.
[152] Ibid. 1.6, pp.15–16: Quomodo conveniant tetrachorda Guidonis cum tetrachordis Boetii.
[153] Aribo, *De musica*, p. 11.2.
[154] *Quaestiones in musica* 1.22, p. 62.

had become more firmly established than it had been in the mid-eleventh. The gradual encroachment of Guidonian theory among German scholars with the passage of time is a process that can be observed in broad outline through these treatises. Aribo's use of Guido is strikingly individual on account of his preoccupation with melodic theory. But in his application of Guido – which is heavily influenced by the contemporary *Commentarius anonymus in Micrologum Guidonis Aretini* – there lies another important point. As we have already seen in the cases of Theoger of Metz and *Quaestiones in musica*, his use of Guido seems coloured by German sources and ideas. We might say that this 'Germanic' response to Guidonian theory is a shared feature of the south-German treatises.

The transmission of ideas within the south-German circle

The reliance of the south-German theorists upon Bern has already been illustrated, and with it, their reliance upon Herman. The many parallels that exist in the treatises show how the theorists also relied upon each other. Aribo – in addition to being familiar with Herman's *Musica* – was well acquainted with William of Hirsau's work and drew upon the contemporary *Commentarius anonymus in Micrologum Guidonis Aretini* at a number of points in his treatise. John relied similarly upon his predecessors.[155] To this may be added the examples of the treatises that are the Wolf Anonymous and *Quaestiones in musica*, which are obviously dependent on their south-German predecessors. The texts copied by the Wolf Anonymous are a good indication of its relatively early date (*c.* 1060): Anonymous I, Bern and Herman of Reichenau. Additionally, its quotation of a letter attributed to Notker Balbulus (840–912) – knowledge of which was confined to the St Gallen area – places its author firmly within the south-German milieu.[156] By contrast *Quaestiones in musica*, written in the early twelfth century, relies on a wider variety of south-German texts: Anonymous I, Bern and Herman, the Wolf Anonymous and Aribo, though absence of William, Theoger and Frutolf suggests that its author may have been somewhat isolated from the circle in which these theorists circulated freely. This was not so with Frutolf of Michelsberg who, based in Bamberg, offers perhaps the best illustration of the circulation of texts and ideas within the south-German circle.

---

[155] John, *De musica* 12, p. 93; Aribo, *De musica*, pp. 18–20.
[156] Babb (trans.), *Hucbald, Guido and John*, pp. 93–4.

Frutolf of Michelsberg

It is not known precisely when Frutolf wrote his *Breviarium de musica*. A *terminus post quem* in the 1070s can be established on account of his reliance upon William of Hirsau's *Musica* and probable knowledge of Aribo's treatise (see pp. 103-6). The earliest, and only complete, recension of Frutolf's treatise and its accompanying tonary is a manuscript dating from the late eleventh- or early-twelfth century that may have been copied in Bamberg (now Munich, Bayerische Staatsbibliothek, Clm 14965b).[157]

Breviarium de musica begins with a short introduction in which Frutolf announces his aim to make a summary of music that will act as an introduction to the question of 'what we say music is'.[158] Frutolf's answer to this question is firmly within the tradition of his south-German colleagues: 'Music is the science of singing well through long reflexion and constant practice', the science of commanding correctly and according to reason all the elements affecting chant.[159] These elements are the gamut (including the intervals and consonances), the monochord, the tetrachords, and the species of *diatessaron, diapente* and *diapason*, all of which culminate in the theory of the modes. Following in the footsteps of Bern, Herman, William, Aribo and Theoger, Frutolf discusses the significance of the monochord early in *Breviarium*. The second chapter, entitled 'De speculatione monochordi', is largely based upon the description given by Herman of Reichenau, although Frutolf has added some comments and a diagram illustrating the proportions that constitute the double octave span of the monochord.[160] His discussion of proportions is carried on into the third chapter ('De proportionibus'). At this point Frutolf turns to the musical consonances. He describes the origins of the consonances in ancient times, before explaining which intervals qualify as consonances and offering arithmetical reasons for this. In the following chapter ('De speciebus consonantiarum') the species of *diatessaron, diapente* and *diapason*, so

---

[157] E. Klemm, *Die romanischen Handschriften der Bayerische Staatsbibliothek* 1. (Wiesbaden, 1980), p. 22; K. Dengler-Schreiber, *Scriptorium und Bibliothek des Klosters Michelsberg in Bamberg* (Graz, 1979), p. 212.

[158] Frutolf, *Breviarium* 1, ed. Vivell, 26: Compendiosum de musica breviarium collecturi et quasi quamdam introductionem facturi, primum quid sit musica dicamus, ut per ejus definitionem promptiorem ad eam adducamus auditorem.

[159] Ibid.: Musica est bene modulandi scientia per diutinam meditationem frequenti percepta experientia. Bene autem modulari est rata tonorum et intervallorum dispositione per legitimos excursus apta modulatione suaves cantus formare eosque post debitos ascensus et descensus congruo et legitimo fini aptare.

[160] Frutolf, *Breviarium* 2, ed. Vivell, 32-5; cf. Herman, *Musica* 1, 2, pp. 18-21.

important to the study of music for contemporary German theorists, are discussed. Another quintessentially German method of analysing the gamut was that of the tetrachords, which forms the subject-matter of Chapter 5 ('De tetrachordis'). All of the points discussed thus far culminate in two chapters devoted to the modes. The first of these ('De modis vel tropis sive tonis') explains how the modes are formed from the species and tetrachords, while the second ('Quid moderni sentiant de ascensu troporum') discusses what modern theorists think regarding the ranges of the modes. Thus from a beginning largely based on Boethius' description of the intervals of antiquity, *Breviarium de musica* has become steadily more practical in orientation. Frutolf consolidates the practical nature of his treatise in the two following chapters ('De vocibus musicis' and 'De intervallis'). He begins 'De intervallis' by describing the intervals that the singer will encounter and then provides a number of notated mnemonic verses to illustrate the operation of these. They are supplemented by directions for the measurement of the monochord, organ pipes and bells, after which Frutolf compiled a lengthy and detailed tonary. The tonary represented the interface between the theory of melody and its practical application, for after studying the rudiments of chant the student would fully understand the tonary, which classified chants according to their mode. This natural progression is reflected in the structure of Frutolf's work.[161]

Frutolf looked in the first place to Bern of Reichenau when writing *Breviarium de musica*. Like Abbot Bern, Frutolf chose to cast his work in the form of a treatise and tonary. Yet although Frutolf's subject-matter parallels that of Bern in many respects, there is little direct textual dependence upon Bern in *Breviarium de musica*. Frutolf – though indebted to Bern's model in terms of conception and archetype – based the substance of his theory on intermediate authors. The only explicit reference to *Prologus in tonarium* shows Frutolf correcting Bern with theory from Herman of Reichenau. In *Breviarium* 10, Bern is mentioned along with Hucbald as having taught that there were nine intervals: semitone, tone, semiditone, tritone, ditone, *diatessaron, diapente, diapente*-plus-semitone and *diapente*-plus-tone.[162] This is a reference to *Prologus*

---

[161] Vivell's edition of *Breviarium de musica* differs in many respects from the earliest surviving recension. His printing of Thiemo's excursus on the semitone as if it were part of the original text has been mentioned above (p. 58 n. 16). Also of importance is his omission of organ pipe measurements by William of Hirsau (see below, pp. 105–6). In some of the following discussion, the readings of Munich, Bayerishe Staatsbibliothek, Clm 14965b are give in preference to those of Vivell's edition.

[162] Frutolf, *Breviarium* 10, ed. Vivell, 65: Domnus vero Bern abbas Augiensis novem intervalla scripsit, sed Hucbaldum musicum secutus et ipse quidem unisonantiam abscidit, sed

2.¹⁶³ The problem with Bern's list, however, is that the fourth interval is a tritone. Frutolf knew from his study of Herman's *Musica* that the tritone had been dismissed there for 'confounding all harmonic speculation'. He countered Bern's description in the first place with short quotations from Guido of Arezzo's *Regule rithmice* and *Epistola ad Michahelem*.¹⁶⁴ Frutolf continued by stating that 'many authorities' similarly deny the validity of the tritone and offered twelve chant examples in support of this.¹⁶⁵ There was, however, one extant problem for Frutolf: he could not use Guido as an effective rebuttal against Bern, for though Guido rejected the tritone, he taught that there were only six intervals.¹⁶⁶ Here Frutolf was encountering an obstacle that the south-German theorists frequently encountered with Guido: a conceptual difference that often made it difficult to apply Guido to German problems. The resolution to Frutolf's *sic et non* was Herman of Reichenau. Like Bern, Herman held that there were nine intervals, but like Guido, denied the tritone to be among them. Frutolf introduced him as the 'illustrious man lord Herman, in whose writings, through his sharp intelligence, a great spirit of modernity breathes' and praised him for taking the middle way in this dispute, thus bringing consent from dissent.¹⁶⁷ Herman described the nine intervals 'in the verses that he has composed', including the unison in the first place but excluding the tritone. These sets of mnemonic verses circulated widely in contemporary manuscripts and were included in full by Frutolf.¹⁶⁸ Herman was thus used by Frutolf to balance the competing teachings of Bern and Guido.

Footnote 162 (*cont.*)
    tritonum in sexto intervallorum loco posuit, sicque novem intervalla, id est semitonium, tonum, semiditonum, ditonum, tritonum, diatessaron, diapente, diapente cum semitonio, diapente cum tono eisdem fere exemplis, quibus et ille quem secutus est, elucidavit.

¹⁶³ Bern, *Prologus* 2, pp. 34–6.
¹⁶⁴ Frutolf, *Breviarium* 10, ed. Vivell, 65: Sed domnus Guido negat, tritonum in intervallis fieri, cum dicit, quartas voces sibi non nisi per diatessaron jungi, ait enim sic: 'Omnis vox secunda sibi jungitur et tertiae; quartae vero et quintae non jungitur aliter, nisi diatessaron ibi sit vel diapente'. Item: 'Cum vox aliqua movetur ad secundam, aut fit tono aut semitonio; cum vero ad tertiam, semiditono fit aut ditono; ad quartam et quintam non fit nisi per diatessaron aut diapente'. Cf. Guido, *Regule rithmice* lines 107–109, pp. 350–2; *Epistola ad Michahelem* lines 359–63, p. 524.
¹⁶⁵ Frutolf, *Breviarium* 10, ed. Vivell, 65–6.
¹⁶⁶ Guido, *Regule rithmice* lines 110–14, p. 352; *Micrologus* 16, p. 179.
¹⁶⁷ Frutolf, *Breviarium* 10, ed. Vivell, 68: Illustris autem vir domnus Herimannus cuius acuminato ingenio multum in tabulis aspirat favor modernus, quasi medius inter hos regiam viam cedens et neutris ex parte consentiens, neutrisque omnino dissentiens et ipse quidem novem intervalla describit in versibus quos de his composuit.
¹⁶⁸ See M. Bernhard, 'Zur Rezeption der musiktheoretischen Werke des Hermannus Contractus', in Pass and Rausch (eds), *Beiträge zur Musik, Musiktheorie und Liturgie der Abtei Reichenau*, pp. 99–126.

Frutolf's tonary, however, is closely modelled on Bern's *Tonarius*. The following example, which compares extracts from the beginning of each tonary, shows the extent to which Frutolf copied and augmented Bern's exemplar.

Example 2.8: Textual comparison of the tonaries by Bern of Reichenau and Frutolf of Michelsberg

Bern, *Tonarius*	Frutolf, *Tonarius* (Munich, Bayerische Staatsbibliothek, Clm 14965b, fol. 34ra)
Autenticus protus constat ex prima specie diapente et ex prima specie diatessaron superius.[169]	Autentus protus qui et do|rius constat ex prima specie diates|saron superius quę est ab .a. ad .d., id est a mese | ad paraneten diezeugmenon, et ex pri|ma specie diapente inferius, quę est ab | eadem .a., id est a mese, ad .D. quę est lychanos ypa|ton, possidens quartam uel potius quantum ad | modos primam speciem diapason inter .D. | et .d., sed interdum superius et inferius tonum as|sumit, raro autem utrimque semidito|num admittit; hoc est legitime ad | .d. interdum autem ad .e. rarissime uero | ad .f., quę est trite hyperboleon, ascendit | ad .D. autem legitime, ad .C. sepe, | ad .B. quę est hypate hypaton inter|dum descendit. Huius cantus incipitur | sex neruis: .C.D.E.F.G.|.a., in quibus etiam cola et commata, | id est membra et incisiones quas distinc|tiones cantus appellamus tenentur. |
Interpolation in *Prologus in tonarium* (Karlsruhe, Badische Landesbibliothek, 504, fol. 7r)	
Magistri autem id est | primi toni cantus incipitur sex neruis, scilicet .C.D.E.|.F.G.a. habens cola et commata id est me‹m›bra et incisi|ones quas distinctiones cantus appellamus, in eisdem. |	Principales autem eius antiphone ab | ipsa finali chorda sua scilicet .D. | ordiuntur; ultima uero seculorum amen | syllaba per
Bern, *Tonarius* Huius ultima sillaba in *Seculorum amen*	

[169] Bern, *Tonarius*, p. 75.

altius distat a finali diatessaron intervallo.	gutturalem ‹s›emiuocalem | ad parhypaten meson quę est .F. | reclinatur, ut quasi ipsarum | antiphonarum inicio occur|rere uideatur. Distat autem altius | a finali semiditono, ut sequen|ti liquebit exemplo. | [*fol. 34rb*]

NOANNOEANE
Primum querite regnum Dei.
...
Differentia prima, quae a finali quidem incipit, sed mox in quintum sonum ascendit, ut sicut antiphona ab ultima *Seculorum amen* sillaba in gravitate, ita secunda neuma distat diapente a prima in acumine.

SECULORUM AMEN

Lichanos ypaton.

A. Domine Dominus noster quam.
A. Fontes et omnia.
...
Hae antiphonae tono inferius cum subsequenti differentia, quae taliter vadit: *amen*, incipiunt, sed cum superiori post contiguum tonum statim in diapente consurgunt; ideoque in medio ambarum hic eas locavimus, ut cuilibet earum illas attribuas, non delinquas.[170]

NONAN NOEANE |
Primum querite regnum | dei. |
... [*fol. 36ra*]
Differentia prima ab ipsa quidem | finali incipit, sed mox in diapen|te id est ad .a. sicut et ultima saeculorum | amen syllaba consurgit. |

Lichanos hypaton. .D.a.b. |

Seculorum amen. |
Afra priscam raab hierichontem. |
Domine dominus noster. |
Ecce ueniet Deus et homo. |
... [*fol. 36rb*]
Hę uero antiphonę quę se|cuntur cum similibus sibi eiusdem | differentię sunt, sed tono in|ferius, qui secundę differentię lo|cus est incipiunt, mox uero | cum superioribus post contiguum | tonum in diapente, ideoque | quasi medię sunt ambarum dif| ferentiarum, ut cuilibet | eas tribuas non delinquas. | Proprię tamen sunt primę differen|tię. Distant autem ab ul|timo seculorum amen diapente | et tono.[171]

---

[170] Ibid., pp. 75–8.
[171] Cf. Vivell (ed.), 'Frutolfi *Breviarium*', 113–18.

In the above example, Frutolf began by changing the order of Bern's statement that 'authentic *protus* consists of the first species of *diapente* and the first species of *diatessaron* above' ('Autenticus protus constat . . . diatessaron superius') to the following:

> Authentic *protus*, or dorian, consists of the first species of *diatessaron* above, which is from a to d, that is from *mese* to *paranete diezeugmenon*, and from the first species of *diapente* below, which is from the same a, that is *mese*, to D, which is *lychanos hypaton*.

He did this to bring the description into line with the *status quo* arising out of Herman's modifications to Bern's teaching. He also added the alternative name 'dorian' for authentic *protus* and the letter names for the notes, which Bern had never used. He then added further material on the range of authentic *protus*, commenting that melodies in that mode have a legitimate range up to the note d or, perhaps, to e and only 'very rarely' to the note f. This comment was not the invention of Frutolf, but reflects standard thinking at the time; Frutolf, however, chose to add it for the sake of thoroughness. Another source that Frutolf drew upon in this passage was the treatise known today as Anonymous I, which was probably written shortly after Bern's treatise.[172] Anonymous I was a source for the interpolated version of *Prologus in tonarium*, and the passage quoted by Frutolf here ('cantus incipitur sex neruis . . . cantus appellamus') occurs also in the interpolations.[173] It is unclear, therefore, whether Frutolf took this short passage directly from Anonymous I or from his interpolated copy of Bern's *Prologus in tonarium*; parhaps the latter of these two possibilities, since he was working from Bern at this point. Whatever its exact origin, Frutolf modified its beginning and end to suit his purposes before returning to Bern's *Tonarius* for more material.

The difficulty in distinguishing Frutolf's direct or indirect use of material that can ultimately be traced to Anonymous I is a recurring problem in *Breviarium de musica*. Frutolf's discussion of the species in *Breviarium* 5, for example, could have been taken from the *Prologus* interpolations or directly from Anonymous I. Other passages in *Breviarium de musica*, however, are more straightforward, and show that Frutolf had access to an original copy of Anonymous I in addition to the parts of it that circulated in the *Prologus* interpolations (consequently, he must have been well aware

---

[172] T. J. H. McCarthy, 'Anonymous I and *Prologus in tonarium*: changing interpretations of music theory in eleventh-century Germany', *Journal of the Society for Musicology in Ireland* 1 (2005), 26–8.

[173] See above, pp. 76–7.

of the connexion between these sources). In *Breviarium* 4, Frutolf discusses the consonances at some length, relying primarily upon Anonymous I. This example shows Frutolf's willingness to rearrange his sources as he deemed necessary: passages of his own are interspersed with the quotations from Anonymous I. Where portions of Anonymous I are copied, they are frequently augmented or rephrased with qualifications and line-of-thought pointers. This embellished form of copying, which is also evident in the passages of the tonary based upon Bern of Reichenau, can be identified as a distinguishing stylistic trait of Frutolf's work methodology.

Example 2.9: Frutolf's reliance upon and reworking of passages from Anonymous I

Anonymous I, § 6	Frutolf, *Breviarium* 4 (Munich, Bayerische Staatsbibliothek, Clm 14965b, fol. 11r)
Nemo autem existimet, idem esse diatessaron, quod sesquitertium, diapente quod sesquialterum, diapason quod duplum. Nam quod arithmetici sesquitertium dicunt, Musici diatessaron, quod sonat de quatuor: quod sub quaternis voculis talis proportio contineatur.	Nemo autem existimet idem esse diatessaron quod sesquitercium, uel diapente quod sesqualterum | siue diapason quod duplum, sed quod arithmetici sesquitercium dicunt, musici diates|saron uocant, quod sonat de quatuor, quia sub quaternis uoculis talis proportio | continetur, et quod illi dicunt sesqualterum,
Diapente de quinque, quod sub totidem contineatur.	isti diapente quod sonat de quinque, | quia sub totidem chordis constituitur; quod uero illi duplum,
Diapason de omnibus; vel quod harum duarum	isti uocant dia|pason, quod dicitur de omnibus, siue quod harum duarum consonantiarum id est |
omnes voces contineat, vel quod melius puto, omnium vocum discrimina in se concludat. Nam septem dumtaxat sunt vocum distantiae, videlicet	diatessaron et diapente uoces omnes contineat, siue, quod melius puto | omnium uocum discrimina in se concludat. Nam septem dumtaxat sunt uocum | distantię, uidelicet proslambanomenos, hypate hypaton, parhypa|te hypaton, lychanos hypaton, hypate meson, parhypate me|son, lichanos meson, quę notantur litteris his:
.A.B.C.D.E.F.G.	.A.B.C.D.E.|.F.G. uel secundum

quodsi octavam, quae est .H. tetigeris, eandem invenies primae. Unde nullius scientiae ignarus inquit Virgilius: Obloquitur numeris septem discrimina vocum. Aliarum autem nomina haec scienti sunt manifesta.[174]	quorumdam annotationem .F.G.A.B.C.D.E. | Quod si octauam tetigeris quę est mese et a quibusdam notatur .a. ab | aliis autem .f. eandem inuenies quę est et prima. Vnde nullius scientię | ignarus ait uirgilius: Obloquitur numeris septem discrimina uocum. | Aliarum autem nomina hęc scienti poterunt esse manifesta.[175]

Frutolf, like other members of the south-German circle, considered the monochord a pedagogic device of considerable importance. He had pointed to its significance already in his introduction, saying that the monochord was 'very necessary' for understanding the art of music.[176] When it came to providing his own description of the monochord and its proportions, Frutolf could have based himself upon a number of *auctores*: Bern, Herman and William had all begun their treatises by describing the monochord. He did not bother with Bern or William, however, but chose instead the most detailed account of the monochord available: the first two chapters of Herman's *Musica*.[177] Unlike in the previous examples, Frutolf made very few changes to Herman's text: in addition to adding an opening sentence and some closing material, his only other contribution was to add a diagram illustrating the double octave span of the monochord.[178] It is hard to resist speculating that Frutolf saw little need to add to Herman's masterful account.

Frutolf also possessed a copy of William of Hirsau's *Musica*, and made good use of it in *Breviarium de musica*.[179] William first appears in *Breviarium* 6 - 'De tetrachordis' - where Frutolf explains the differences between the two sets of tetrachords (that is between the tetrachords *hyperbolaeon*, *diezeugmenon*, *meson* and *hypaton*, characterized by the interval form semitone-tone-tone, and the modern tetrachords of the *graves*, *finales*, *superiores* and *excellentes* that were used in

[174] Anonymous I, § 6, *GS* 1, p. 335.
[175] Cf. Vivell (ed.), 'Frutolfi *Breviarium*', 43.
[176] Frutolf, *Breviarium*, ed. Vivell, 27: In hujusmodi vero artis disciplina monochordi notitia est valde necessaria, in cujus frequenti exercitio consonantiarum et modorum ceterorumque ad hanc artem pertinentium plene percipi potest cognitio.
[177] Herman, *Musica* 1, 2, pp. 18-21.
[178] See Vivell (ed.), 'Frutolfi *Breviarium*', 34.
[179] Ruf (ed.), *MBDS* 3/3, p. 360.

south-German music theory).[180] William, following Herman of Reichenau, had already explained this in *Musica* 2 and it was this explanation that Frutolf used. As with his use of Bern in his tonary and Anonymous I in *Breviarium* 4, Frutolf augmented and abridged the source text to suit his purpose.

Example 2.10: Frutolf's reliance upon William of Hirsau's *Musica*

William, *Musica* 2	Frutolf, *Breviarium* 6 (Munich, Bayerische Staatsbibliothek, Clm 14965b, fol. 14r)
Specie quoque discrepant, quoniam illa semitonium habent in ultimo, ista in medio. Illa bina et bina in utroque diapason coniuncta, quia Guidonem in litterarum positione sequimur, .e. et .E. synaphen, tonum vero supra mese proximum diezeuxin habebunt. Ista simili modo si copulentur, .D. et .d. synaphen, tonum autem infra mese proximum diezeuxin designabunt. In illorum enim duali coniunctione, sive singulari dispositione de utroque diapason tonus remanet, in illorum inferius, in istorum superius. Ex illis enim primum descendit ab .aa. in .e. secundum ab .e. in .b. et ibi remanente seu disiungente tono, tertium demittitur ab .a. in .E. quartum ab .E. in .B. itemque tonus supererit. Econtra ex istis primum ascendit ab .A. in .D. secundum a .D. in .G. ubi tono restante	. . . ista uero secundum constructionem troporum | a grauibus progredientia semitonium habent in medio, illa | bina et bina in utroque diapason coniuncta .e. et .E. id est neten | diezeugmenon et hypaten meson, synaphen, tonum uero supra mesen | proximum diezeuxin habent et supra proslambanomenon, ista simili | modo si copulentur .D. et .d. id est lychanos hypaton et paranete | diezeugmenon, synaphen, et tonum infra mesen et infra ne|ten hyperboleon proximum diezeuxin designant. In illorum duali || coniunctione de utroque diapason tonus remanet inferius, in istorum | superius, quiaprimum ex illis descendit ab .aa. in .e. secundum ab .e. in .b. et ibi | remanente seu disiungente tono III^{um} demittitur ad .a. in .E. quar|tum ab.E. in .B. itemque tonus supererit; econtra uero primum ex istis ascendit ab .A. | in .D. secundum a .D. in .G. ubi tono restante seu

---

[180] See Chapter 3, pp. 122–4.

tertium scandit ab .a. in .d. quartum a .d. in .g. tono item superfluo. Illa sunt notabilia. Ista nomino sicut et sunt principalia. Hae sunt specificae tetrachordorum differentiae. Musica enim species est quaedam habitudo diversae positionis tonorum et semitoniorum.[181]	disiungente III^(um) scan|dit ab .a. in .d., quartum a .d. in .g. tono iterum remanente. He sunt speci|ficę tetrachordorum differentię. Musica enim species est habitudo | quędam diuersę positionis tonorum et semitoniorum.[182]

This pattern is also repeated in *Breviarium* 10 – 'De musicis intervallis' – where Frutolf relies closely on passages of *Musica* 21.[183]

To Bern, Herman, Anonymous I and William, who are the main sources for *Breviarium de musica*, others may be added. There are good reasons for believing that Frutolf knew Aribo's *De musica*. His description of the joining of the tetrachords of the *superiores* and *excellentes* at the note d as 'medietatis uinculo' quotes Aribo's exact turn of phrase.[184] In addition, one of the diagrams that appears in *Breviarium* 4 closely resembles a diagram from the latter part of Aribo's treatise. As with many medieval authors, Frutolf used diagrams to summarize and illustrate his teaching. Many of these were reworked from the Boethian diagram tradition, such as the one shown in Plate 1, which consists of a number of interlocking circles that illustrate how the consonances of the *diatessaron*, *diapente* and *diapason* are proportionally related to each other.[185]

Aribo's diagram (Plate 2) shows the same relationship of the *diatessaron*, *diapente* and *diapason*, with the difference that instead of one outer circle there are two. A comparison of the diagrams reveals that the Frutolf's version is in effect a distillation of Aribo's original.[186]

But perhaps the most significant pieces of evidence connecting Frutolf and Aribo is found in the section of *Breviarium de musica* containing

---

[181] William, *Musica* 2, p. 15.
[182] Cf. Vivell (ed.), 'Frutolfi *Breviarium*', 50–1.
[183] Frutolf, *Breviarium* 10, ed. Vivell, 64–5; cf. William, *Musica* 21, pp. 54–5.
[184] Frutolf, *Breviarium* 7, ed. Vivell, 53; cf. Aribo, *De musica*, p. 14.
[185] Frutolf, *Breviarium* 4, ed. Vivell, 40. The reproduction of the diagram in Vivell's edition is incorrect, as it misrepresents the original by implying that sesquialter proportion is equal to twice the sesquiterciary proportion.
[186] This diagram is not printed in Smits van Waesberghe's edition of Aribo's *De musica*, but is only given – along with a number of other important omitted diagrams – in an unclear manuscript plate. The diagram occurs in both full recensions of Aribo's treatise: Rochester, Eastman School of Music, ML 92/1200, fol. 28r and Salzburg, Stiftsbibliothek St. Peter, a. V. 2, fol. 141r.

Plate 1 The proportions of the gamut. Diagram from Frutolf of Michelsberg's *Breviarium de musica*. Munich, Bayerische Staatsbibliothek, Clm 14965b, fol.9v

various sets of directions for the measurement of organ pipes. The south-German treatises, as well as the music theory manuscripts they circulated in, frequently contain directions for the measurement of the monochord, organ pipes and bells. These texts demonstrate the application of harmonics, and whether they deal with the monochord, organ pipes or bells, their essential aim is to show the appropriate ratios of string length, of pipe length and diameter, or of bell size and diameter to produce the notes of the gamut. Many different sets of directions circulated: some were attributed – with varying degrees of accuracy – to well-known theorists; most were anonymous. Frutolf included two sets of organ pipe measurements and one set of bell measurements in *Breviarium de musica*. The second set of organ pipe measurements, which is not printed in Vivell's edition, is attributed by Frutolf to William of Hirsau with the heading 'Alia regula domni Willihelmi de fistulis'.[187] This set of measurements circulated in a number of manuscripts during the eleventh and twelfth centuries, but only some attribute it to William of Hirsau: those transmitting it as part of Aribo's *De musica*.

[187] Munich, Bayerische Staatsbibliothek, Clm 14965b, fol. 31v. Vivell did not publish these measurements on the grounds that they had already been published by Martin Gerbert in *GS* 2, p. 280 (where they are attributed to Eberhard of Freising): Vivell, (ed.), 'Frutolfi *Breviarium*', 107 n. 4.

ANCIENT DOCTORS AND MODERN MASTERS

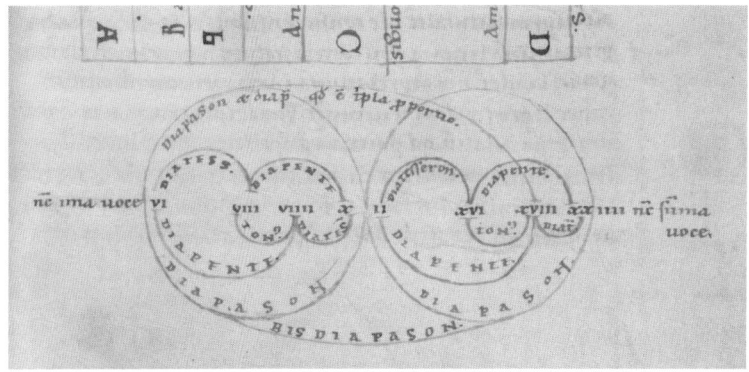

Plate 2   The proportions of the gamut. Diagram from Aribo's *De musica*. Rochester, Eastman School of Music, Sibley Music Library, ML 92/1200, fol. 28r

Aribo clearly identifies William as the author with the announcement that 'lord William, formerly a monk of St Emmeram in Regensburg but now venerable abbot elsewhere, has discovered a new measurement of pipes . . . which he has communicated to me'.[188] Aribo, as he mentions in *De musica*, was on friendly terms with William: their closeness verifies that these measurements can be assigned to William of Hirsau with confidence. Frutolf, therefore, must have got these measurements from Aribo's treatise, since it is the only source identifying William as their author. A comparison of the measurements in both sources shows that Frutolf continued his distinctive habit of augmenting and inserting line-of-thought pointers as he copied into his own work. Even the first line of this example contains an interjection that is immediately identifiable as Frutolf's own: 'Therefore, the size of the first pipe, *that is its length*, is to be divided in eight'.[189] This comment is stylistically consistent with countless other examples from *Breviarium de musica*.

Example 2.11: Frutolf's organ pipe measurements, derived from those of Aribo

| Aribo, *De musica* | Frutolf, *Breviarium* 16 (Munich Bayerische Staatsbibliothek, Clm 14965b, fol. 31v) |

---

[188] Aribo, *De musica*, p. 42.
[189] See K.-J Sachs (ed.), *Mensura fistularum. Die Mensurierung der Orgelpfeifen im Mittelalter* 1 (Stuttgart, 1970), pp. 84–9 for an edition of these measurements giving all the variant manuscript readings. Noteworthy is the consistent individuality of Frutolf's version compared to the others.

Primae igitur fistulae quantitatis
in octo dividatur, eique
octava pars cum octava
diametri apponatur, et erit secunda.
  Secundae item longitudo
in octo partiatur, additaque
octava cum diametri octava,
erit tercia.
  Prima autem in tres
dividatur, additaque tercia cum
tercia diametri,
habebis diatesseron
in ipsa quarta peractum. In hac
ipsa incipit integer minor ordo
priorque. Tercia item fistula in octo
dividatur, additaque octava
cum octava diametri, synemmenon
reperitur. Item prima in duo
dividatur, additaque medietate
diametri, quinta
perficitur. Secundae item longitudo
in duo partiatur, additaque
medietate cum medietate diametri,
sexta peragitur. Tercia
similiter in geminas partes dividatur,
appositaque altera cum altera
diametri parte, septima producitur.
Octava a prima sic
inveniatur. Prima duplicetur, insuper
integrum diametrum apponatur,
et octavareperitur. Et sicut per
primam inventa est octava, eodem
modo omnes subsequentes
facillime reperire poteris,

tantum si singulis integrum
diametrum apposueris.[190]

Primę ergo fistulę quantitas id est
longi||tudo eius in octo diuidatur,
eique octaua pars cum octaua
parte | diametri apponatur, et
erit secundam eritque inter has
tonus. | Secundę autem longitudo
item in octo diuidatur, additaque
octaua | cum octaua diametri, erit
tercia et est item tonus. |
Prima item in tres partes
diuidatur, additaque tercia cum
tercia | diametri, erit quarta,
et habebis diatesseron integram, |
in ipsa peractam. In hac
ipsa etiam incipit integer ordo minor
et | prior. Tercia item fistula in octo
diuidatur, additaque octaua |
cum octaua diametri, synemenon
inuenitur. Item prima in duo
diuidatur, | additaque medietate
eius cum medietate diametri, quinta
perficitur. | Secundę item longitudo
in duo partiatur, additaque
medietate cum me|dietate diametri,
sexta formatur. Tercia item in
geminas par|tes diuidatur,
appositaque altera cum altera
parte diametri, | septima producitur.
Octaua autem per primam sic
inueniatur. | Prima duplicetur insuper
diametrum eius integrum ei apponatur
et | octaua reperit. Sicut autem per
primam inuenta est octaua, eodem
modo | omnes subsequentes
facillime poteris reperire,
scilicet max|imo spacio,
minimaque numeri quantitate
tantum si singulis | fistulis
diametrum integrum apposueris.

---

[190] Aribo, *De musica*, p. 43.

Like the eleventh- and twelfth-century compilers of music theory textbooks, Frutolf attached great value to mnemonic verses as a means of pedagogy.[191] Having begun the chapter entitled 'De interuallis' by describing the intervals that the singer will encounter, he provided a number of notated didactic verses to illustrate their operation. The first of these begins 'Ut cantor iunctis deriues singula punctis' and may well have been composed by Frutolf himself. It is accompanied by letter notation and neumes above the words. The next two sets of verses are by Herman of Reichenau: 'Ter tria iunctorum' teaches recognition of the different intervals and 'Ter terni sunt modi' concerns the modes. Both are accompanied by neumes and Herman's didactic notation. The fourth verse, which is preceded by the heading 'De quatuor modis uocum', summarizes Herman's teaching about *modi vocum*.[192] Although its author is unknown, it also has been supplied with Herman's notation. It is tempting to suggest that Frutolf himself was responsible for this. A third verse by Herman of Reichenau – the key to his notational system – follows before an elaborate set of mnemonics composed by Frutolf himself. Frutolf designed these verses to complement the others, a point underlined by the self-deprecating rhyming couplet with which he prefaced them:

> Frutolf the dullard had played with these dirges,
> Yet adding many suitable things to the eight modes.[193]

Frutolf's verses, which are notated with letters and neumes, proceed in order through the eight modes listing their *differentiae* and citing chant examples for each.[194] They have frequently and incorrectly been described by modern scholars as Frutolf's 'first' or 'versified tonary', supposedly in contrast to the 'proper' tonary that follows *Breviarium de musica*.[195] Although a superficial glance may suggest parallels with a tonary, their

---

[191] See Chapter 5, p. 211.
[192] Frutolf, *Breviarium* 10, ed. Vivell, 72–3; cf. Herman, *Musica* 19, p. 57; Guido, *Micrologus* 7, pp. 117–8. Although Herman's articulation of this concept was based upon Guido of Arezzo's, Frutolf's terminology indicates that Herman was the direct influence here.
[193] Munich, Bayerische Staatsbibliothek, Clm 14965b, fol. 22v: Frutolfus neniis ceu stultus luserat istis | Dans tamen octonis congrua multa modis; cf. Vivell (ed.), 'Frutolfi *Breviarium*', 75.
[194] The *differentiae* are the different cadences available for each of the psalm tones, used to enable a smooth transition between the end of the psalm and the repetition of its attendant antiphon. See D. Hiley, *Western plainchant: a handbook* (Oxford, 1993), pp. 58–61.
[195] M. Huglo, 'Frutolfus of Michelsberg', *NG* 9, p. 302; A. Rausch, 'Frutolf von Michelsberg', *MGG. Personenteil* 7, col. 211; A. M. Busse-Berger, *Medieval music and the art of memory* (Berkeley, 2005), p. 65.

content reveals that they were designed to augment the verses that preceded them in this section of *Breviarium de musica*. Judging from Frutolf's self-effacing remarks – an expression of *humilitas* common in the monastic context – his didactic verses may well have been inspired by Herman of Reichenau's example.

Frutolf's *Breviarium de musica* is a treatise that could not have been written without access to a variety of eleventh-century sources. It is not, however, the mere compilation that is suggested in some of the general modern accounts, but a skilful and thorough guide to the science of singing correctly. Its overall plan and subject matter was inspired by Bern's *Prologus in tonarium* and *Tonarius*, but the substance of much of its theory came from Herman of Reichenau, Anonymous I, Aribo and William of Hirsau. Frutolf's debt to Herman of Reichenau and William of Hirsau – great men of his time in the world of music theory – can be compared to the reliance of polemicists such as Manegold of Lautenbach upon Bernold of Constance and the canonical researches of his circle,[196] or to the use of Anonymous I, Bern, Herman, the Wolf Anonymous and Aribo by the author of *Quaestiones in musica*. This affinity of purpose, shared use of sources and textual interdependence is a salient feature of the south-German circle of music theorists as a whole.

---

[196] See I. S. Robinson, 'The friendship circle of Bernold of Constance and the dissemination of Gregorian ideas in late eleventh-century Germany', in J. Haseldine (ed.), *Friendship in medieval Europe* (Stroud, 1999), pp. 190–4.

3

Dialectic and the theory of music

The study of dialectic in the late eleventh and early twelfth centuries, which was seen by contemporary thinkers as a species of logic, was largely dependent on Classical texts.[1] The Aristotelian logical works known in this period were *Categories*, *De interpretatione* and *Isagoge*. *Categories* was sometimes called *Liber predicamentorum*, and in the eleventh century was usually studied in a composite version derived from Boethius' final translation of it and from another translation which may have been an earlier draft also by Boethius.[2] *De interpretatione* generally went by the contemporary title *Perihermenias*. *Isagoge* is not actually by Aristotle, but an introduction to his *Categories* by the third-century Neoplatonist Porphyry. It was widely available in the translation by Boethius and was extremely popular. According to Peter Abelard's *Dialectica*, written between 1114 and 1120, these works were augmented by Boethius' *On division*, *On topical differentiae*, *Categorical syllogisms* and *Hypothetical syllogisms*.[3]

---

[1] A number of contemporary manuscripts show similar divisions: see Munich, Bayerische Staatsbibliothek, Clm 9921, fol. 13v and Leipzig, Universitätsbibliothek, Cod. 1493, fol. 90r for example.

[2] J. Marenbon, 'Medieval Latin commentaries and glosses on Aristotelian logical texts before *c.* 1150 AD', in C. Burnett (ed.), *Glosses and commentaries on Aristotelian logical texts* (London, 1993), p. 78 n. 5.

[3] Peter Abelard, *Dialectica*, ed. L. M. de Rijk, *Dialectica. Petrus Abaelardus*, 2nd edn (Assen, 1970), p. 146.10–17: Sunt autem tres quorum septem codicibus omnis in hac arte eloquentia latina armatur. Aristotilis enim duos tantum, *Predicamentorum* scilicet et *Periermenias* libro‹s›, usus adhuc Latinorum cognovit; Porphirii vero unum, qui videlicet *De quinque vocibus* conscriptus . . . introductionem ad ipsa preparat *Predicamenta*; Boetii autem quatuor in consuetudinem duximus, *Librum* videlicet *Divisionum* et *Topicorum* cum *Sillogismis* tam *Cathegoricis* quam *Ypoteticis*.

Dialectical texts in German libraries

A survey of German library catalogues from the eleventh and twelfth centuries provides a useful context for Abelard's testimony. These catalogues show that the texts considered necessary by Abelard for the study of dialectic were also available in German libraries. They suggest that the curriculum of logical studies in the Empire broadly corresponded with that in northern France, the area that would come to lead western Europe in dialectical studies as the twelfth century progressed.

Several library catalogues from the middle of the twelfth century indicate the types of works commonly found in German centres. The catalogue of books compiled at the abbey of St Martin at Muri (founded in 1027) shows that a good selection of Classical authors was held in the library in addition to many glossed texts. We find works by Sedulius, Arator, Cato, Prudentius, Martianus Capella, Ovid, Sallust, Statius, Donatus and Priscian, as well as a gloss on Priscian and glosses on many books of the Bible. There is also a book on dialectic, a 'Liber divisionum' (by which Boethius' *De divisione* is probably intended), and a 'Glose de decem predicamentis' (which may well have been a gloss on *Categoriae decem*, a paraphrase of *Categories* wrongly attributed to St Augustine that had been especially popular in the ninth and tenth centuries).[4] The catalogue continues with the music treatises of Hucbald of St Amand, William of Hirsau and Bern of Reichenau, as well as 'Musica Ottonis', which probably means *Dialogus de musica* by pseudo-Odo of Cluny.[5] The catalogue of the monastic library at nearby Pfäfers, compiled in 1155, shows that similar resources were available there. Its holdings in Classical literature are comparable to Muri, while in the domain of dialectic there was a copy of Cicero's *Topics*, 'the *Predicamenta* and *Perihermenias* of Aristotle in one volume' and 'the two books of Porphyry

---

[4] L. Minio-Paluello (ed.), *Categoriae vel predicamenta* (Aristoteles Latinus 1/1–5; Leiden, 1961), pp. xii–xxii; 'Note sull' Aristotele latino medievale: XV. Dalle *Categoriae decem* pseudo-agostiniane (temistiane) al testo vulgato aristotelico boeziano', *Revista di filosofia neoscolastico* 54 (1962), 137–47.

[5] P. Lehmann (ed.), *MBDS* 1, p. 212: Liber Job cum glosis. Glosa super epistolas Pauli. Gdbose super apocalipsim et cantica cantorum. Glose super Matheum. Glose super Priscianum. Priscianus. Duo libri Prudencii et in uno ex his psichomachia. Sedulius in uno volumine. Tres libri Aratoris, Prosper, constructiones Prisciani. Higinus, Cato et Avianus in uno libello. Esopus. Duo libri de Walthario. Duo libri Homeri. Maximianus. Conputus Helpricus. Donatus. Marcianus. Ovidus epistolarum. Salustius. Stacius Achilleòs. Dyalecotia. Liber divisionum. Liber questionum. Glose de decem predicamentis. Musica Hupaldi et geometria. Musica Wilhelmi. Musica Bern. Musica Ottonis.

with the commentaries of Boethius' (that is, the two books of the *Isagoge*).[6] The library of St Mary's Abbey at Engelberg (founded in 1120) seems to have been stocked along these lines from the outset, giving an indication of those dialectical volumes considered most necessary in a monastic library at this time. A catalogue of Engelberg's books survives from the time of Abbot Frowin, 1142-78. It shows that the library contained many glosses on the Classical works in addition to Priscian, Porphyry, *Categories*, *De interpretatione*, Cicero's *Topics*, Boethius' *Topics*, an introduction to dialectic, a gloss on Porphyry, *Categories, Analytics* and a book on syllogisms.[7] Another catalogue from the middle of the twelfth century is that of the abbey of St George at Prüfening, which was founded in 1109. Its holdings on logic included a book on dialectic, Boethius' *Topics*, Porphyry's *Isagoge* and Cicero's *Topics*.[8]

These examples of the frequent and widespread dissemination of logical textbooks in south-German libraries illustrate the continuation of a tradition that can be traced back at least to the early eleventh century. The monastery of St Emmeram in Regensburg was founded in 739 and by the end of the tenth century boasted a fine library. The inventory taken under Abbot Ramwold in 993 shows the extent of its holdings in the Classics. It lists the commentary by Remigius of Auxerre on Martianus Capella, as well as Sedulius, Prudentius, Donatus and the music treatises of Augustine and Boethius.[9] There follows a very extensive collection of logical works: a commentary on *Isagoge*, Cicero's *Topics*, Aristotle's *De interpretatione* and *Categories*, a commentary on Cicero's *Topics*, commentaries on *De interpretatione* and *Categories*, two commentaries by Boethius on *Isagoge*, Book 4 of Martianus Capella's *De nuptiis Philologiae et Mercurii* (on dialectic), as well as Porphyry in the collection of a monk named Walter.[10] The

---

[6] Ibid., p. 486: Beda de metrica arte. Item liber de metrica ratione. Topica Tullii. Predicamenta Aristotilis et peri erminias in uno volumine. Duo libri Porphirii cum commentis Boecii. Liber geometriae.

[7] Ibid., p. 33: Liber Tullii de rhetorica . . . Prudentius psichomachie . . . Priscianum constructionum . . . Porfirius predicamenta, periermenie, topica Tullii, topica Boetii sub uno volumine. Introductiones dialectie. Glosse super retoricam Tullii. Regule de retorica. Expositio Timei. Regula de grammatical . . . Dialectice derivationes. Glosse super Porfirium et predicamenta . . . Retorica Tulli ad Erennium . . . Porfirius: predicamenta, periermenie, analitica. Liber silogismorum.

[8] C. E. Ineichen-Eder (ed.), *MBDS* 4/1, p. 420: Priscianus maior. Boethius. Glosę Prosperi, Prudentii . . . Dialectica. Topica Boetii. Ysagogę Porfirii . . . Topica Tullii.

[9] Ibid., pp. 145-6.

[10] Ibid., pp. 148-9: Commentum super ysagogas . . . Topica Ciceronis. Periermenias Aristotelis. Cathegorię Aristotelis. Commentum super topica Ciceronis. Commentum super periermenias Aristotelis. Commentum super cathegorias Aristoteils. Commenta

eleventh-century catalogue from the monastery of Sts Stephen and Michael at Weihenstephan near Freising shows that Aristotle's 'Dialectica' (perhaps meaning his *Categories*) with a commentary was to be found in its library,[11] while a list compiled in the second half of the eleventh century at the important south-German monastery of Tegernsee mentions a 'commentary on *Perihermenias*...Tully's [Cicero's] *Topics* with the commentary of Boethius and a book on differences and on division and much concerning rhetoric and syllogisms in one volume'.[12] The records of other German libraries show them to have been similarly constituted. The catalogue of the monastery of Sts Peter and Paul at Oberaltaich made at the beginning of the twelfth century records the presence of two anonymous books of excerpts on dialectic, Porphyry with a commentary, a 'Dialectica' by Boethius and Porphyry's *Isagoge*.[13] As early as 1000 the cathedral library at Bamberg possessed a copy of *Isagoge* with Boethius' commentary,[14] and the neighbouring monastery at Michelsberg (founded in 1015) had a very extensive collection by the early twelfth century. The following extract from the Michelsberg catalogue shows the library to have been strong in works of dialectic:

> A gloss on Porphyry, *Categories*, *Periermenias*, *Topics* and *De divisione* in one volume. Another gloss on Porphyry, *Categories* and *Periermenias* in one volume. Another gloss on Porphyry. Porphyry with the *Categories* in one volume . . . Boethius' *Musica*. His *Arithmetica* in two volumes. Boethius' commentary on Porphyry's *Isagoge* and Porphyry in one volume. Also another commentary on Porphyry. Tully's [Cicero's] *Rhetoric*. His *Topics* as well . . . Remigius on Donatus . . . Arguments on Donatus and Porphyry. *Categories*, *Periermenias* and *Topics* with Porphyry in one volume. The book of Aristotle on the *Ten Categories*.[15]

Footnote 10 (*cont.*)
    duo super ysagogas Boetii. Arithmetica Boetii . . . Marcianus de nuptiis Philologiae. Dialectica eius . . . Commentum super retoricam Ciceronis . . . Isti sunt libri Vualtherii monachi . . . Decem eglogas. Georicon. Boecius I . . . Particulum Porfirii I. Priscianus minor I.
[11] B. Bischoff, W. Stoll (eds), *MBDS* 4/2, p. 650: De VIII partibus orationis. Dialectica. Aristotelis cum commento . . . Musice due enchiriadis.
[12] Ibid., pp. 750–1: Commentum in perhiermenias . . . Topica Tullii cum commentis Boetii et librum differentiarum et divisionum et multa de rethorica et de sillogismis in uno corpore.
[13] C. E. Ineichen-Eder (ed.), *MBDS* 4/1, p. 84: Liber Virgilii. Excerpto in dialecticam . . . II Porfirii cum commento . . . Dialectica Boetii. Liber ysagogarum Porfirii.
[14] P. Ruf (ed.), *MBDS* 3/3, p. 340.
[15] Ibid., p. 358: Glose super Porphirium, cathegorias, periermenias, topica et divisiones in uno voluminare. Item glose super Porphirium, cathegorias et periermenias in uno volu-

In addition to Michelsberg, the monasteries of Gorze and Toul show extensive holdings of dialectical works,[16] while the cathedral library at Cologne also contained a selection of these works during the eleventh century.[17] From the evidence of library catalogues it is possible to conclude that the texts of the *ars logica* were widely disseminated in German centres from the second half of the tenth century. This fact suggests that dialectical texts were considered a necessary part of the educational curriculum both by monks and by secular clerks.

Attitudes to dialectic in the eleventh century

A survey of eleventh-century intellectual history indicates that the availability of these dialectical sources was matched by their use. The place of dialectic in the intellectual life of the eleventh-century Empire has been much debated by historians. The older literature emphasizes the resistance of reformers to the encroaching hegemony of dialectic. J. A. Endres, for example, identified pro- and anti-dialectic groups of contemporary thinkers: Anselm of Besate and Berengar of Tours among the former; Manegold of Lautenbach, Peter Damian, Otloh of St Emmeram and

mine. Item glose super Porphirium. Porphirius cum cathegoriis in uno volumine; p. 359: Musica Boecii. Arithmetica in duobus voluminibus. Commentum Boecii in ysagogas Porphirii et Porphirius in uno volumine. Item aliud commentum super Porphirium. Item pars commenti super Porphirium. Rethorica Tullii. Topica eiusdem . . . Remigius super Donatum . . . Argumentum super Donatum et super Porphirium. Cathegorias, periermenias et topica cum Porphirio in uno volumine. Liber Aristotilis de decem predicamentis.

[16] M. Manitius, *Handschriften antiker Autoren in mittelalterlichen Bibliothekskatalogen*, ed. K. Manitius (Leipzig, 1935), p. 277. Gorze: Commentum Boecii super Isagogas Porphirii . . . Cathegoriae Aristotelis et commentum Boetii in uno codice. Commentum eiusdem de topicis differentiis. Ysagogae Porphirii . . . commentum eius super Ysagogas Kategorias et Periermenias in uno vol. Commentum ipsius super Ysagogas Porphirii ceptum. Commentum ipsius in topica Ciceronis. See also G. Morin, 'Le catalogue des manuscrits de l'Abbaye de Gorze au XIe siècle', *Revue Bénédictine* 22 (1905), 9–11. Toul: Ysagoge categoriae perymenie topica Ciceronis et topica differentiae vol. I. ysagoge Porphirii. Boethius super ysagogas et categorias vol. I. item Boetius super topica Ciceronis cum libris de divisione et diffinitione et de topicis differentiis et de categoricis et ypoteticis syllogismis. primum commentum Boetii super pery ermenias. item commentum Boetii super peryermenias. See also G. H. Becker, *Catalogi bibliothecarum antiqui* (Bonn, 1885), pp. 153–4.

[17] M. Manitius, *Handschriften antiker Autoren*, p. 277; see also E. Dümmler, 'Cölner Bücherkatalog', *Zeitschrift für deutsches Altertum und deutsche Literatur* 19 (1876), 467: Isagogas . . . Commentum minus isagogarum, maius etiam in easdem in duobus voluminibus. Minus commentum Boetii in librum periiermenias Aristotelis et partem commenti eiusdem in Kategorias.

Lanfranc of Bec among the latter.[18] More recent studies, however, have qualified this crude distinction. While Endres identified the influence of Peter Damian behind the rejection of dialectic by German clerks, F. Dressler – like M. Grabmann before him – has emphasized that Peter Damian did not eschew dialectic in principle: rather, was he careful to subordinate its meaning in relation to theology when questions of the faith were being treated.[19] A more recent study of Peter Damian's treatise *De divina omnipotentia* has shown that Damian was concerned with the right relationship between Christian wisdom and pagan learning: on the basis of his own dialectical approach to questions of divine power, it is unfair to characterize him as an anti-dialectician for whom all pagan learning was superfluous.[20]

Peter Damian's influence was considerable in eleventh-century Germany, where his works were widely copied and admired. In Endres' classic interpretation this influence perpetuated hostility towards dialectic and pagan literature. The important papal polemicist Manegold of Lautenbach, who was well acquainted with Peter Damian's works, has also been portrayed as an enemy of dialectic and pagan literature. His *Liber contra Wolfelmum* – written in 1085 at the height of the Investiture Contest in condemnation of a *libellus* by Wenrich, *scholasticus* of Trier – denounces pagan philosophy, especially certain Platonic and Macrobian beliefs. The reason for Manegold's vehemence was his staunch Gregorianism and the danger he perceived in the use of pagan learning to undermine the Gregorian position. As with many contemporary polemicists, Manegold delivered his opprobrium in exaggerated terms, using the rhetorical devices of hyperbole and *vituperatio*. Like Peter Damian before him, however, his attack was not upon dialectic *per se*, but upon those who used sophistry to undermine the faithful. He could thus reconcile the charge that Master Wenrich wrote 'in the manner of the rhetoricians of the schools', with the resonances of dialectic that occur in his own *Liber contra Wolfelmum*.[21] Manegold continued his attack on Wenrich in *Liber ad*

---

[18] J. A. Endres, 'Die Dialektiker und ihre Gegner im 11. Jahrhundert', *Philosophisches Jahrbuch* 19 (1906), 20–33; 'Studien zur Geschichte der Frühscholastik', *Philosophisches Jahrbuch* 26 (1913), 164–9; *Forschungen zur Geschichte der frühmittelalterlichen Philosophie* (Münster, 1915), pp. 42–9.

[19] F. Dressler, *Petrus Damiani. Leben und Werk* (Rome, 1954), pp. 175–6; M. Grabmann, *Die Geschichte der scholastischen Methode* 1 (Freiburg, 1909; repr. Darmstadt, 1956), pp. 232–3.

[20] I. M. Resnick, *Divine power and possibility in St Peter Damian's De divina omnipotentia* (Leiden, 1992), pp. 113–14.

[21] Manegold of Lautenbach, *Liber contra Wolfelmum* 14, 22, 24, ed. W. Hartmann, *MGH Quellen* 8, pp. 76, 96–7, 107; cf. Boethius, *De differentiis topicis* 3 (*PL* 64.1198D); *In*

Gebehardum, which he wrote shortly afterwards. Here, as Wilfried Hartmann has noted, not only did Manegold use aspects of dialectic to confute Wenrich, but he applied the rules of right reason in order to elucidate the predicates of the tradition that he was defending.[22] His defence, like that of Lanfranc against Berengar, entailed exploiting the tecnhiques he deplored in the works of others.

Neither is blind hostility to dialectic discernible among Manegold's contemporaries. The leading Gregorian William of Hirsau, renowned as one of the foremost scholars of his generation, believed that without the dialectical exposition of Scripture, neither the Bible nor the Fathers could be understood fully.[23] (In this respect his view concurs with that of Lanfranc of Bec, who exploited dialectic in his exposition of the Pauline epistles.[24]) William's friend and colleague Otloh of St Emmeram – while frequently dismissive of liberal studies – had himself used dialectic where he thought it appropriate.[25] Abbot Siegfried of Tegernsee, another leading Gregorian, similarly advocated the suitability of such inquiry when rightly used.[26] The *Vita* of Bishop Meinwerk of Paderborn (d. 1036) provides a useful, if highly stylized picture of the ideal patron of learning. Its author recounts in verse that scholarship flourished in Meinwerk's entourage, and is especially careful to mention the arts both of the trivium and of the quadrivium.[27] Though the picture is an idealized one, there is no hint of hostility to dialectic in the account. As the intellectual turmoils of the Investiture Contest spurred Manegold into action, so the eucharistic controversy generated by Berengar of Tours prompted responses that

Isagogen Porphyrii commenta 1.25, 2.7, ed. S. Brandt and G. Schepss, *Corpus scriptorum ecclesiasticorum latinorum* 48 (Vienna and Leipzig, 1906), pp. 76, 97.

[22] W. Hartmann, 'Manegold von Lautenbach und die Anfänge der Frühscholastik', *DA* 26 (1970), 123–9.

[23] B. Pez (ed.), *Thesaurus anecdotorum novissimus, seu veterum monumentorum praecipue ecclesiasticorum, ex Germanicis potissimum bibliothecis adornata collectio recentissima. Omnia cum praefationibus, observationibus [&c] publici juris facta, a B. Pezio* 6 (Augsburg, 1729), p. 260.

[24] T. J. Holopainen, *Dialectic and theology in the eleventh century* (Leiden, 1996), pp. 157-8; M. Gibson, 'Lanfranc's "Commentary on the Pauline Epistles"', *Journal of Theological Studies* n.s. 22 (1971), 102–12.

[25] H. Schauwecker, *Otloh von St. Emmeram. Ein Beitrag zur Bildungs- und Frömmigkeitsgeschichte des 11. Jahrhunderts* (Munich, 1964), pp. 224–32.

[26] Pez, *Thesaurus anecdotorum novissimus* 6, p. 85.

[27] *Vita Meinwerci episcopi Patherbrunnensis, MGH SS* 11, p. 140.24–30: Studiorum multiplicia sub eo floruerunt exercitia . . . quando ibi musici fuerunt et dialectici, enituerunt rhetorici clarique grammatici; quando magistri artium exercebant trivium, quibus omne studium erat circa quadruvium; ubi mathematici claruerunt et astronomici; habebantur phisici atque geometrici.

exploited the *ars logica*, not only from Lanfranc of Bec, but also from German scholars: *De veritate corporis et sanguinis Domini* by the Gregorian apologist Bernold of St Blasien and *De corpore et sanguine Domini* by Haimo, prior of Hirsau, are two such examples.[28] The use of dialectic is also apparent in the roughly contemporaneous *De misericordia et iustitia* by Alger of Liège.[29]

A state of affairs very different from that described by Endres is apparent from the evidence. He polarized the role of reason and authority in the eleventh century, turning each into something it was not. By casting 'dialecticians' as thorough-going rationalists who rejected revelation as a source of knowledge it was easy to portray Peter Damian, Manegold of Lautenbach – and by extension those who supported reform in the eleventh century – as 'anti-intellectual'.[30] This flawed outlook, which has characterized much historical writing on the period, has been justly dismissed as 'utterly misleading'.[31] In the light of codicological evidence it becomes even more so.

The ars logica *in eleventh-century literature*

John Marenbon has interpreted the existence of numerous glosses and commentaries on Aristotle and Boethius as further evidence for the pervasive influence that dialectic exerted upon the intellectual life of the eleventh and early twelfth centuries.[32] Works such as the anonymous *Excerpta Categoriarum et Isagogarum* contained in the manuscript Rome, Biblioteca Apostolica Vaticana, Reg. lat. 1281, fols 9v–18v and *Glossae super Porphyrium a magistro W. collectae*, which is to be found in the manuscript Erfurt, Wissenschaftliche Allgemeinbibliothek, Ampl. Oct. 5, fols 1r–18v and 16r–36v, are examples of contemporary responses to the Classical texts.[33]

---

[28] Bernold of St Blasien, *De veritate corporis et sanguine Domini*, ed. H. Weisweiler, 'Die vollständige Kampfschrift Bernolds von St. Blasien gegen Berengar', *Scholastik* 12 (1937), 58–93; Haimo of Hirsau, *De corpore et sanguine Domine* (*PL* 118.0815–18).

[29] Alger of Liège, *De misericordia et iustitia*, ed. R. Kretzschmar, *Alger von Lüttichs Traktat De misericordia et iustitia. Ein kanonistischer Konkordanzversuch aus der Zeit des Investiturstreits. Untersuchungen und Edition* (Sigmaringen, 1985), pp. 58–9, 61.

[30] Holopainen, *Dialectic and theology in the eleventh century*, p. 156.

[31] Ibid., see pp. 1–5 for a lucid introduction to the historiography. The influence of the older historiography is still apparent in the account given by F. C. Lochner in Theoger of Metz, *Musica*, ed. and trans. F. C. Lochner, 'Dietger (Theogerus) of Metz and his "Musica"' (Ph.D. dissertation, University of Notre Dame, 1995), pp. 215–42, esp. pp. 236–42.

[32] Marenbon, 'Medieval Latin commentaries', p. 77; 'Supplement to the working catalogue', in J. Marenbon, *Aristotelian logic, Platonism and the context of early medieval philosophy in the West* (Aldershot, 2000), pp. 128–40.

[33] Y. Iwakuma, ' "Vocales", or early nominalists', *Traditio* 47 (1992), 42.

Other works of this type are the pseudo-Raban commentary (found in its oldest version in the manuscript Oxford, Bodleian Library, Laud Lat. 67, fols 9v–14v and dated to the 1060s or 1070s) and the eleventh-century commentary on Porphyry found in Munich, Bayerische Staatsbibliothek, Clm 14458, fols 83r–93r (a manuscript that belonged to the monastery of St Emmeram in Regensburg).[34] Though these commentaries contain some original material, the ideas expressed in them are closely based upon their Boethian exemplars.[35] Nevertheless, they demonstrate clearly the direct engagement of contemporary scholars with dialectic.

In addition to the practice of glossing and commenting upon the Classical texts, a small number of new treatises on logic were written in the central Middle Ages. Like the glosses and commentaries, they also seem to have been based closely upon Boethius. The treatise named *Dialectica*, written by the Burgundian clerk Garland of Besançon *c*. 1100, is good indicator of the type of logical thought current in the late eleventh and early twelfth centuries: much of it is based closely upon Porphyry and Boethius, though its discussion of *in voce* exegesis makes for an important original contribution.[36] Master Alberic of Monte Cassino, a 'most eloquent and erudite man', is another example of one engaged in the study of the *artes*.[37] Alberic's pupil, Peter the Deacon, testifies in the *Chronicle* of Monte Cassino to his master's authorship of a dialogue on music, a book on the arts of letter writing and salutation – undoubtedly his widely studied *Flores rhetorici* – and a book on dialectic (which he links with Alberic's presence in Rome between November 1078 and February 1079 at the synod that condemned the eucharistic doctrine of Berengar of Tours).[38]

---

[34] Marenbon, 'Medieval Latin commentaries', p. 106.

[35] Iwakuma, ' "Vocales" , or early nominalists', 42.

[36] Garland [of Besançon], *Dialectica*, ed. L. M. de Rijk, *Garlandus Compotista Dialectica* (Assen, 1959). De Rijk's identification of the author with Garland the Computist (pp. i–xxii, xxxii, xlii, xlix) is no longer accepted: see B. de Vergille, *Dictionnaire d'histoire et de géographie ecclésiastique* 20 (Paris, 1984), pp. 883–7 and Iwakuma, ' "Vocales" , or early nominalists', 47–54.

[37] U. Chevalier, *Répertoire des Sources Historiques du Moyen Age. Bio-Bibliographie* 1 (Paris, 1905), p. 98; M. Manitius, *Geschichte der lateinischen Literatur des Mittelalters* 3 (Munich, 1939), pp. 300–5.

[38] *Chronica Monasterii Casinensis*, MGH SS 34, pp. 410.30–411.07: Per idem tempus Albericus diaconus vir disertissimus ac eruditissimus ad hunc locum habitaturus advenit. Hic in hoc monasterio positus composuit librum de virginitate sancte Marie. Librum dictaminum et salutationum. In musica dialogum . . . Librum de dialetica. Temporibus vero eius facta est sinodus in urbe Roma adversus Berengarium diaconem ecclesie Andecavensis, qui inter multa, que astruere nitebatur, dicebat sacrificium corporis et sanguinis Domini figuram esse.

Finally, it is possible to see the influence of dialectic in contemporary letter collections. Examples from two eleventh-century letter collections – those from Regensburg and Worms – display quite specific and deliberate applications of the *ars logica* outside the genre of dialectical writings. Eleven letters from the Regensburg collection often incorporate dialectical material in their text. They show knowledge on the part of their authors of Boethius' *De differentiis topicis*,[39] *Commentarius in topica Ciceronis*,[40] *Perihermenias*,[41] *Introduction to categorical syllogisms*,[42] *Categorical syllogisms*,[43] and *Hypothetical syllogisms*.[44] Sometimes this knowledge is in the form of a simple quotation or allusion, as in the case of the maximal proposition 'contraries are suited to contraries' taken from *De differentiis topicis* and quoted in letter 1,[45] or a quotation from *Perihermenias* in letter 20 on whether words are to be considered products of the trachea or as the conjunction of syllables.[46] Letter 6 from the Regensburg collection is long and intellectually sophisticated, incorporating extensive quotation from both pagan and Christian authors. One paragraph clearly alludes to *De differentiis topicis* in the context of an argument for the inerrancy of the Church. Here, however, the Boethian statement that it is not possible to have an effect without a cause is closely intertwined with the pseudo-Isidorian canonical sentence that introduces the topic of the paragraph.[47]

---

[39] *Regensburg letter collection* 1, ed. N. Fickermann, *Briefsammlungen der Zeit Heinrichs IV. Die Regensburger rhetorischen Briefe*, MGH Briefe 5, p. 274; 5, p. 284; 6, pp. 288, 293; 10, pp. 323, 325; 22, p. 349; 34, p. 365.

[40] Ibid. 5, pp. 282, 284; 23, p. 352; 28, pp. 358–9.

[41] Ibid. 8, p. 307; 20, p. 344.

[42] Ibid. 18, p. 338.

[43] Ibid. 31, p. 365.

[44] Ibid.

[45] Ibid. 1, p. 274: . . . quisquis torpori et inertię se tradit, minus studiosum esse recte vivendi. Contraria namque contrariis conveniunt. Parum fuit, quod olim studio florente percepi. See Boethius, *De differentiis topicis* 2 (*PL* 64.1191C).

[46] *Regensburg letter collection* 20, p. 344: . . . non ut vox eius per quasdam gutturis partes, quę arterię vocantur, audiatur aut per syllabarum coniunctionem? See Boethius, *Commentariorum in librum Aristotelis περὶ ἑρμνείας secundae editionis*, ed. K. Meiser, *Commentarii in librum Aristotelis περὶ ἑρμνείας* 2 (Leipzig, 1880).

[47] *Regensburg letter collection* 6, p. 288: Nullum reprehensibile sancta ęcclesia admittit. Se enim admiteret, sine macula et ruga non esset. Omne autem vitium reprehensibile est. Quod enim ex omni parte inhonestum est, cum effectus sine causa esse non possit, consequentia declarat, quod antecedens non contradicat. Liquet igitur, quia nullum vitium sancta ęcclesia admittit. Quod autem sancta ęcclesia non admittit, extra ęcclesiam est. Quod est extra ęcclesiam, est extra communionem. Nullum delatorem ęcclesia ammittit. Ergo extra ęcclesiam est. Igitur extra communionem. Cui enim secundum apostolum ave non est dicendum, ne sit infra regnum communionis, excludutur. See Boethius, *De differentiis topicis* 3 (*PL* 64.1199B).

Letter 10, on the subject of the corrupting influence of friendship with laymen and the authority of the ecclesiastical over the secular, also cleverly interlaces its dialectical references with a mass of Patristic and biblical allusion.[48] The only surviving fragment of letter 28 is a detailed discussion on incompatible propositions based closely on *Commentarius in topica Ciceronis*,[49] while letter 31 includes a substantial discussion on dialectic that is heavily dependent on Boethius' *Hypothetical syllogisms, Categorical syllogisms* and *De differentiis topicis*.[50]

The smaller Worms collection also evinces knowledge of dialectical texts on the part of its authors. Letter 32 – from 'G.' to 'E.', master of the cathedral school at Worms, thanking him for a copy of Victorius' *Calculus* – includes a comment by the sender on Boethius' *In categorias Aristotelis*, with which he was experiencing some difficulty.[51] A quotation from *Commentarius in topica Ciceronis* is to be found in letter 60, addressed to Master Wolzo of Worms.[52] Letter 52 from the collection is a long and erudite example written by a clerk of Worms to Bishop Azecho, 1025-44.[53] The central concern of the letter is the proper natural order of the world and the Church. This is expressed in Platonic terms, with particular reference to the theory of harmony and proportion outlined in Boethius' *De institutione arithmetica* and *De institutione musica*, both of which were obviously well known to the writer. He devotes considerable space to detailed explanation of the musical proportions and of the symphonies, declaring that the *diapason, diatessaron* and *diapente* mirror the numerical proportions of the binary, sesquitertia and sesquialter.[54] This statement

---

[48] *Regensburg letter collection* 10, pp. 323-5. See Boethius, *De differentiis topicis* 2 (*PL* 64.1191), 3 (*PL* 64.1199). See I. S. Robinson, 'The "Colores rhetorici" in the Investiture Contest', *Traditio* 32 (1976), 209-38 for a discussion of the purpose of letter 10.

[49] *Regensburg letter collection* 28, pp. 358-9. See Boethius, *Commentarius in topica Ciceronis* 5 (*PL* 64.1134C).

[50] *Regensburg letter collection* 31, p. 365. See Boethius, *De differentiis topicis* 3 (*PL* 64.1197), 4 (*PL* 64.1210); *De syllogismo hypothetico* 1 (*PL* 64.0844), 2 (*PL* 64.0876C); *De syllogismo categorico* 2 (*PL* 64.0821).

[51] *Worms letter collection* 32, ed. W. Bulst, *Die ältere Wormser Briefsammlung, MGH Briefe* 3, pp. 58-9. See Boethius, *In categorias Aristotelis* 4 (*PL* 64.0294B).

[52] *Worms letter collection* 60, p. 102. See Boethius, *Commentarius in topica Ciceronis* 1 (*PL* 64.1041A).

[53] *Worms letter collection* 52, pp. 89-93.

[54] Ibid., pp. 90-1: Eandem autem proportionum habitudinem et in symphoniis spectare licet. Nam quod in numeris proportio duplaris efficit, hoc idem in consonantiis diapason reddit. Quod vero sesqualtera et sesquitertia pensant in numeris, hoc idem diapente et diatessaron resonant in melicis. Has ipsas consonantias in supradictis numerorum summulis reperire valemus. Binarius etenim ad i diapason, iii diapente ad ii, iiii vero diatessaron ad iii resonabunt. Hac itaque proportionum habitudine et maiores fungi numeros

contains an implicit message: the musical proportions are a natural manifestation of divine ordinance; this proper reflexion can, and should, be manifest in other areas of human life. In other words, the musical proportions are derived from the numerical ones, and this derivation happens accidentally. This 'accidental' derivation, however, proceeds according to the rules of reason for, in the clerk's words, 'whatsoever is predicated in the second place is not done so *per se*, but accidentally'.[55] He gives the example of animal: what exists *per se* is the 'animate substance'; the genus, which comes in the second place, is accidental. This example is taken from Boethius' commentary on Porphyry's *Isagoge*.[56] The author's second exploitation of dialectic comes after a passage enthusiastically furnished with allusions to the ancient poets. The subject here is universal propositions and *differentiae*, and again the author quotes Boethius' commentary on *Isagoge*.[57]

The examples from the Regensburg and Worms letter collections illustrate the extent to which knowledge of those dialectical texts available in the libraries of southern Germany was utilized by clerks writing in a non-dialectical genre. They provide what is perhaps the most pertinent evidence of the influence exercised by dialectic upon the intellectual life of the eleventh century, and a valuable context for the discussion of its exploitation in the music treatises of the south-German circle. We thus possess a considerable amount of evidence for the active study and use of dialectic in the German schools in the generations preceding the rise of the subsequently more famous schools of northern France.

Dialectic in the south-German music treatises

As with these authors, so too with the music theorists from the south-German circle: their treatises show obvious signs of having been influenced

Footnote 54 (*cont.*)
   non negamus, sed prenominatis principaliter ascribimus, illis vero, maioribus videlicet, quorum esse ab istis derivatur, proportionaliter in invicem comparari secundo loco et per hoc accidentaliter contingere astruimus.
[55] Ibid. p. 91: Illud namque exigit ratio, ut quęcumque secundo loco predicantur, non per se sed accidentaliter dicantur, velut animal, cum sit per se substantia animata sensibilis, secundo loco vero genus et ideo accidenter nomen generis possidet, quoniam de pluribus specie differentibus in eo quod quid sit predicatur.
[56] Boethius, *In Isagogen Porphyrii commenta* 2.4, pp. 179–80.
[57] *Worms letter collection* 52, p. 92: . . . quoniam ad maiorem partem respexi, non ignoret, qua responsione dialectici sepenumero sophisticas argumentorum importunitates effugere solent. Cum enim universaliter proponatur: differentia est, quę de pluribus specie differentibus in eo quod quale sit in substantia predicatur, hęc propositio,

by studies in the *ars logica*. This influence is manifested in the first place in the language used by the theorists. Terminology that also possessed a dialectical meaning had been used in music treatises from the Carolingian period: the species of *diatessaron*, *diapente* and *diapason* are found in the tenth-century *Alia musica* and, in a more developed form, in pseudo-Bernelinus' *Cita et vera divisio monochordi*.[58] These terms occur too in Bern of Reichenau's *Prologus in tonarium*,[59] but their specifically dialectical implication seems to have been more fully realized by Bern's pupil Herman. A study of Herman's *Musica* suggests that his use of dialectical terminology – while partly inherited – was significant in itself, for he exploited dialectic as a tool in his division of the gamut.[60] His lead was followed by others from the south-German circle. William of Hirsau, writing before 1069, used the vocabulary of dialectic extensively in his treatise, speaking of the *differentiae* of genera and the properties of species.[61] Aribo's *De musica* – written sometime between 1070 and 1078 – abounds with dialectical terms, and in places this aspect is emphasized by conscious allusion to the textbooks of the *ars logica* in a manner comparable with that of the examples from the Regensburg and Worms letter collections discussed above. References to dialectic are also apparent in Frutolf of Michelsberg's *Breviarium de musica*.[62] The appearance of dialectical terminology so widely in these music treatises suggests that it held some significance for theorists, and was not merely the affected usage of sophisticated language.

It is possible to distinguish two categories of dialectical usage in the music treatises: the implicit and the explicit. Implicit usage refers to ideas that are expressed with reference to dialectic or that take the form of their

quoniam gravitas de sola terra, levitas de solo igne et cetera plura non nisi de uno solo predicantur, a limine veritatis velut falsa excluderetur, nisi respectus ad maiorem partem a falsitate illam separaret. See Boethius, *In Isagogen Porphyrii commenta* 4.10, pp. 266–7.

[58] *Alia musica* 17–19, ed. J. Chailley, *Alia musica (Traité de musique du IXe siècle). Edition critique commentée avec une introduction sur l'origine de la nomenclature modale pseudo-grecque au Moyen-Age* (Paris, 1965), pp. 108–10; Pseudo-Bernelinus, *Cita et vera divisio monochordi*, *GS* 1, p. 313.

[59] Bern of Reichenau, *Prologus in tonarium*, ed. A. Rausch, *Die Musiktraktate des Abtes Bern von Reichenau. Edition und Interpretation* (Tutzing, 1999), pp. 35, 39, 40, 44, 46, 62, 66.

[60] See Chapter 2, pp. 62–72.

[61] William of Hirsau, *Musica*, ed. D. Harbinson, *Wilhelmi Hirsaugiensis Musica* (Rome, 1975), pp. 15, 23, 26, 30, 53, 58, 65, 67.

[62] Frutolf of Michelsberg, *Breviarium de musica*, ed. C. Vivell, 'Frutolfi Breviarium de musica et Tonarius', *Akademie der Wissenschaften in Wien. Philosophische historische Klasse, Sitzungsberichte* 188/2 (1919), 33, 36, 37, 42, 47, 51–7, 86.

methodology from dialectic, but which do not quote the source texts. The explicit usage of dialectic occurs occasionally in the treatises, usually to prove specific points. As in the examples from the letter collections, the music theorists will often quote a passage from one of the standard texts of the *ars logica* that supports the point being made. Instances of this strengthen the case for believing an implicit understanding of the correlation between dialectic and music theory to have been widespread among south-German theorists. This case has already been made in a study of the influence exerted upon music theorists by Boethius' influential treatise *De divisione*.[63] But the evidence concerning the state of dialectic in eleventh-century Germany that has been set out above implies a broader context than the narrow interpretation offered by that study. It is thus possible to detect the resonance of a number of dialectical works in the music treatises from the south-German circle.

The two sets of tetrachords

The south-German treatises show that tetrachords were the basis for dividing the gamut of the monochord. Herman of Reichenau explained the reason for this: the gamut encompasses the *quadruplum* of two octaves (fifteen notes), which in turn embraces twice seven pitches.[64] This division is further divided into groups of four notes that are called the tetrachords of the *graves, finales, superiores* and *excellentes*.

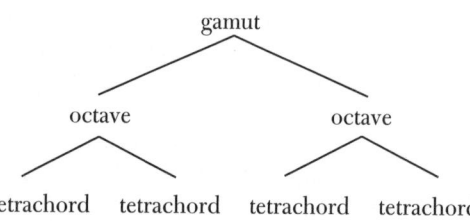

Figure 3.1: The hierarchical division of the gamut

The tetrachord of the *graves* comprises the tone, semitone and tone from A to D and that of the *finales* the tone, semitone and tone from D to G. This arrangement is repeated identically an octave higher by the *superiores* (a to d) and the *excellentes* (d to g).

---

[63] W. D. Deason, 'A taxonomic paradigm from Boethius' *De divisione* applied to the eight modes of music' (Ph.D. dissertation, Ohio State University, 1992).

[64] Herman of Reichenau, *Musica* 3, ed. and trans. L. Ellinwood, *Musica Hermanni Contracti* (Rochester, NY, 1936), p. 22.

Figure 3.2: The tetrachords of the *graves*, *finales*, *superiores* and *excellentes*

Thus did Herman name the tetrachords and add that 'these names indicate their particular genealogy, like children born in their parent's likeness'.[65] In making this comment, Herman was echoing the second definition of genus in Porphyry's *Isagoge*. Porphyry defined genus in three ways: a collection of things related to one another because each is related to some one thing in a particular way; the source of each man's birth, whether from his father or from the place of birth; that to which the species is subordinate, that is, the genus is a source of the species.[66]

There were, however, two different sets of tetrachords. A little further on in his *Musica*, Herman writes of tetrachords being formed in two ways, with one set being marked off on the right-hand side of the monochord and the other on the left-hand side.[67] The first set – with Latin names – comprises the tetrachords of the *graves*, *finales*, *superiores* and *excellentes* that have just been mentioned; these tetrachords have the interval-form tone, semitone, tone. The second set – with Greek names – consists of *hyperbolaeon*, *diezeugmenon*, *meson* and *hypaton*; these tetrachords are characterized by the interval-form semitone, tone, tone. (This second set of tetrachords was an historical hangover from ancient Greek music theory.)

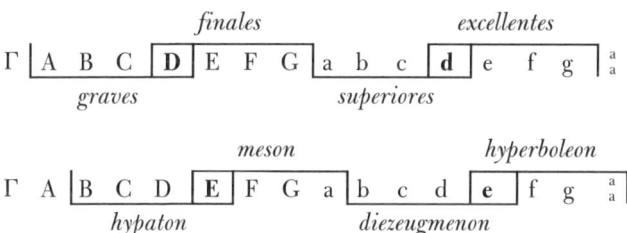

Figure 3.3: The two sets of tetrachords

---

[65] Herman, *Musica* 3, p. 22: . . . propriam velut filii ad parentum vultus nati generositatem demonstrant.

[66] Porphyry, *Isagoge* 1.20–2.11, ed. L. Minio-Paluello, *Isagoge. Translatio Boethii* (Leiden, 1966), p. 6; trans. E. W. Warren, *Porphyry the Phoenician: Isagoge* (Toronto, 1975), pp. 28–9.

[67] Herman, *Musica* 4, p. 26.

Herman was not alone in distinguishing two such sets: he was followed in this by William of Hirsau later in the eleventh century. William expressed his description of this point in terms of the *ars logica*. He began his treatise by stating that the 'regular structure of the whole monochord consists of fifteen notes in two distinct octaves', and added that in these two octaves the tetrachords may be found, which 'in their names, genera and species are truly diverse'.[68] He explains that the species of tetrachord differ because some have a semitone at the extremity, others in the middle. Having elaborated on this point, he states in conclusion that various forms of tones and semitones are the specific logical *differentiae* of the two sets of tetrachords.[69] William's choice of language here is avowedly dialectical. In other words, genus is predicated of 'tetrachord', which differs in its species: those of the form tone, semitone, tone; and those of the form semitone, tone, tone; namely the first and second group of tetrachords. Porphyry's *Isagoge* defined species in three ways. First: species designates the shapeliness of an individual. Secondly: species is that under the defined genus. Thirdly: species is what is ordered under the genus and what the genus is predicated of essentially; or, species is that predicated essentially of many things that differ in number.[70] The point being made by William here is that the two sets of tetrachords form species ordered under the genus. A *differentia* is an attribute that distinguishes a given species from other species belonging to the same genus. Hence, the two sets are distinguished from each other by the *differentia* of the order of tones and semitones.[71] This point was repeated by Aribo, for whom the two sets of tetrachords differed in name, quality and species.[72] Frutolf of Michelsberg also divided the two sets according to their *differentiae*.[73] A division according to logic, therefore, provided the means to explain and distinguish these two sets of tetrachords.

[68] William, *Musica* 2, p. 14: Tota regularis monochordi structura constat quindecim chordis in duo diapason distinctis . . . In ipsis quindecim chordis inveniuntur tetrachorda nominibus, genere, specie valde diversa, id est, tetrachordum Hypaton, Meson, Diezeugmenon, Hyperboleon. Item tetrachordum Gravium, Finalium, Superiorum, Excellentium.
[69] Ibid. p. 15: Hae sunt specificae tetrachordorum differentiae.
[70] Porphyry, *Isagoge* 4.1–10, pp. 8–9; trans. Warren, pp. 34–5.
[71] See Boethius, *De divisione*, ed. J. Magee, *Anicii Manlii Severini Boetii De divisione liber: critical edition, translation, prolegomena and commentary* (Leiden, 1998), p. 16 (*PL* 64.0880).
[72] Aribo, *De musica*, ed. J. Smits van Waesberghe, *Aribonis De musica* (Rome, 1951), p. 10.99.
[73] Frutolf, *Breviarium* 6, p. 51: Hae sunt specificae tetrachordorum differentiae. Musica enim species est habitudo quaedam diversa positionis tonorum et semitoniorum. Cf. William, *Musica* 2, p. 15.

Tetrachords and the 'seats of the modes'

Of these two sets of tetrachords, only the first set, with its symmetrical form of tone, semitone and tone, was of practical use to the south-German theorists. Each note of these tetrachords also corresponds to a Greek ordinal indicating a mode. Hence, in the tetrachord of the *graves* A is called *protus*, B *deuterus*, C *tritus* and D *tetrardus*. These positions are the same for the tetrachords of the *finales*, *superiores* and *excellentes*.

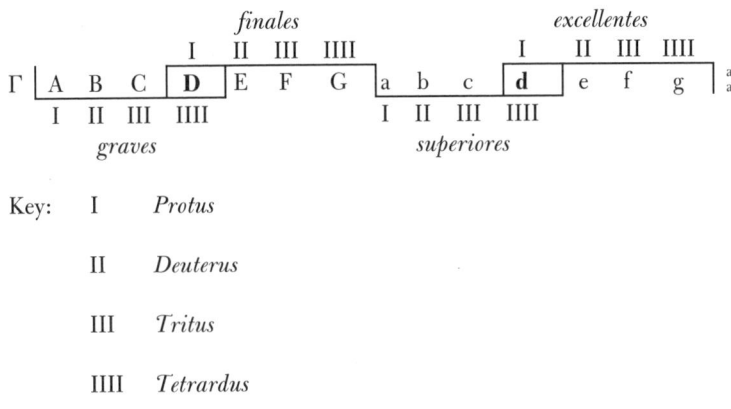

Key: I   Protus

II   Deuterus

III Tritus

IIII Tetrardus

Figure 3.4: The modal properties of the tetrachords

A mode was defined by Herman of Reichenau as a modulation of many notes within any one octave, as determined by fixed intervals and fitted into one whole.[74] He followed this by stating that there are four modes which are further subdivided with reference to low and high ranges or ambit.[75] Those with a high ambit were called 'authentic' by the theorists and those with a low ambit 'plagal'. Hence, the *protus*, *deuterus*, *tritus* and *tetrardus* note of each tetrachord formed a fulcrum for the authentic or plagal form of each mode. Herman of Reichenau coined the phrase *sedes troporum* – 'seats of the modes' – to describe this and was followed in turn by others from the south-German circle.[76] Modes were regarded by the theorists, therefore, as species of octaves (*diapason*). From this it was apparent that different patterns of tones and semitones surrounding the modal seat could be identified within an interval of a fourth or a fifth,

---

[74] Herman, *Musica* 8, p. 31: Tropus est inter unumquoque diapason multarum vocum ratis effecta intervallis apta in unum corpus modulatio.
[75] Ibid.
[76] Ibid., p. 57; William, *Musica* 28, 35, pp. 59, 60, 65; Aribo, *De musica*, p. 13.18.

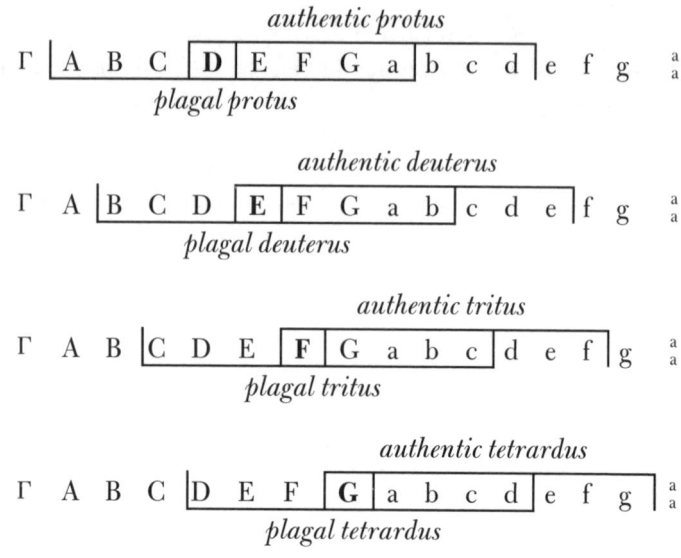

Figure 3.5: The seats of the modes

which became a boundary interval. The differing patterns within the boundary interval – which can also be seen as logical *differentiae* – gave rise to several varieties of fourth and fifth.[77] These varieties of fourth, fifth and octave were called 'species' by the theorists.[78]

'Species' theory

The use of the word 'species' is significant, as it has a logical meaning.[79] Although it was used in Carolingian music treatises, the dialectical implications of its meaning seem to have been exploited in particular during the eleventh century. In the system worked out by Herman of Reichenau and adopted by subsequent theorists there are four species of *diatessaron* (species of fourth).[80] Aribo's *De musica* describes the first species as beginning on the first of the *graves* and ending on the first of the *finales*, that is A and D. The second species of *diatessaron* begins on the second note of the *graves* (B) and ends on the second note of the *finales* (E), while the third and fourth species of *diatessaron* begin and end on the

---

[77] Deason, 'A taxonomic paradigm', pp. 53–4.
[78] See Chapter 2, pp. 64–7.
[79] See below, pp. 128–30.
[80] See Chapter 2, pp. 65–7.

DIALECTIC AND THE THEORY OF MUSIC

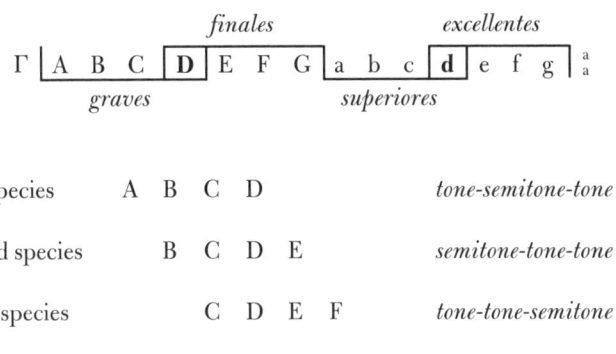

Figure 3.6: The species of *diatessaron*

third and fourth notes of the *graves* and *finales* respectively (C and F, D and G).[81]

There are also four species of *diapente* (species of fifth). These are made by combining each note of the tetrachord of the *finales* with its corresponding note from the tetrachord of the *superiores*. Hence the first species of *diapente* is from D to a and the second from E to b, while the third and fourth species of *diapente* extend from F to c and G to d. Aribo explains both this fact and the species' form of tones and semitones at once, by taking us through the tone, semitone and two tones encountered as the first species ascends (D to a) and then through the tone, semitone and two tones as the fourth species descends (d to G), before treating the second and third species in a like manner.[82]

Finally, there are the species of *diapason* (species of octave). The generally accepted theory from the period was that the species of *diapason* were formed by marrying the first, second, third and fourth species of *diatessaron* to the corresponding species of *diapente*.[83]

---

[81] Aribo, *De musica*, p. 26.15: Diatessaron species prima incipit a prima gravium .A., desinit in primam finalium .D. Secunda species diatessaron incipit a secunda gravium .B., desinit in secunda finalium .E. Tercia species diatessaron incipit a tercia gravium .C., desinit in terciam finalem .F. Quarta species diatessaron incipit et desinit a quarta et in quartam .D.G.

[82] Aribo, *De musica*, p. 25.2: Prima species diapente ascendit tono, semitonio, ditono a .D. finali in .a. superius. Quarta descendit tono, semitonio, ditono a .d. superiori in .G. finalem. Secunda suspenditur ab .E. finali in .b. superius, semitonio, tritono. Tercia deponitur semitonio, tritono a .c. superiori in .F. finalem.

[83] Aribo, *De musica*, p. 26.12. See also Herman, *Musica* 7, pp. 30–1; William, *Musica* 9, pp. 25–30; Theoger, *Musica* 17, p. 24: Nam prima species dyapason constat ex prima specie dyatessaron, et ex prima specie diapente, et fit ab .A. graui usque in .a. acutum, et

MUSIC, SCHOLASTICISM AND REFORM

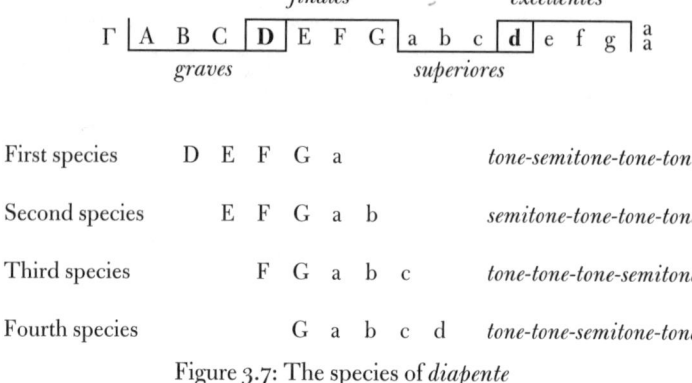

Figure 3.7: The species of *diapente*

Porphyry says that philosophers explain genus as that predicated essentially of many things which differ in species.[84] Hence, the genus 'animal' differs in a variety of species such as 'horse', 'cat' and 'dog'.[85] In the theory of the gamut, if the *diatessaron* is considered a genus, then it differs in its species, namely first, second, third and fourth; that is, the quality of being *diatessaron* is predicated of the first, second, third and fourth species of *diatessaron*. As in the case of the two sets of tetrachords, the species of *diatessaron* are divided by a *differentia*. The *differentia* in this case is also the order of tones and semitones. The first species (A to D) has the form tone-semitone-tone; the second (B to E) semitone-tone-tone; the third (C to F) tone-tone-semitone. The fourth species of *diatessaron* has a form identical to the first, so at this point the process of division seems to break down: the *differentia* of form does not adequately distinguish the first and fourth species. Such a problem had, however, been discussed by Boethius in *De divisione*. In this treatise he had pointed to the necessity for levels of *differentiae* in order that objects might be defined adequately. He took 'name' as an example and in his first division came up with 'significative

---

Footnote 83 *(cont.)*
habet medium terminum .D., quod etiam finale est proti. Secunda species dyapason constat ex duabus secundis speciebus, id est ex secunda specie dyatessaron et ex secunda specie dyapente, et fit a .B. graui usque in .b. acutum, et habet medium terminum .E. graue, quod etiam finale est deutri. Tertia species dyapason constat ex duabus tertiis speciebus, id est ex tertia specie dyatessaron et ex tertia specie dyapente, et fit a .C. graui usque in .c. acutum, et habet medium terminum .F., quod etiam finale est triti. Quarta species dyapason constat ex duabus quartis speciebus, id est ex quarta specie dyatessaron et ex quarta specie dyapente, et fit a .D. graui usque in .d. acutum, et habet medium terminum .G., quod etiam finale est tetrardi.

[84] Porphyry, *Isagoge* 2.15, pp. 6–7; trans. Warren, pp. 29–30.
[85] Ibid.

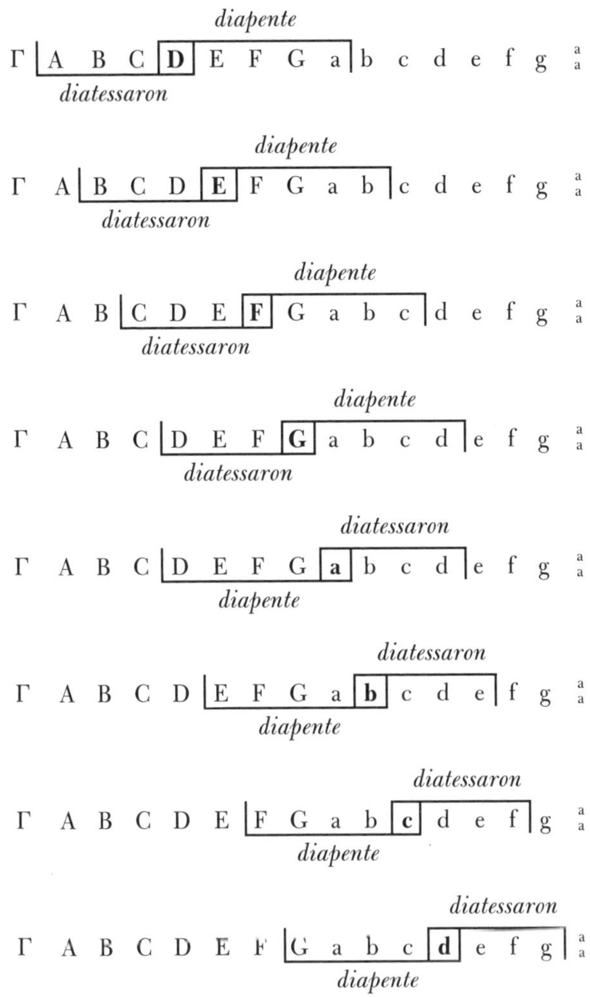

DIALECTIC AND THE THEORY OF MUSIC

```
                 diapente
Γ  A   B   C  D  E   F   G   a   b   c   d   e   f   g   aa
   diatessaron

                    diapente
Γ  A   B   C   D  E   F   G   a   b   c   d   e   f   g   aa
       diatessaron

                       diapente
Γ  A   B   C   D   E  F   G   a   b   c   d   e   f   g   aa
           diatessaron

                          diapente
Γ  A   B   C   D   E   F  G   a   b   c   d   e   f   g   aa
               diatessaron

                             diatessaron
Γ  A   B   C   D   E   F   G  a   b   c   d   e   f   g   aa
                   diapente

                                diatessaron
Γ  A   B   C   D   E   F   G   a  b   c   d   e   f   g   aa
                       diapente

                                   diatessaron
Γ  A   B   C   D   E   F   G   a   b  c   d   e   f   g   aa
                           diapente

                                      diatessaron
Γ  A   B   C   D   E   F   G   a   b   c  d   e   f   g   aa
                               diapente
```

Figure 3.8: The species of *diapason*

spoken sound'.[86] This, however, was inadequate as the genus 'spoken sound' and the *differentia* 'significative', when added together, did not produce only 'name'; Boethius pointed out that the result could justly include certain spoken sounds that designate states of mind or grief, but which were not names.[87] Thus, more division was needed to arrive at a

---

[86] Boethius, *De divisione*, p. 34 (*PL* 64.0886C).
[87] Ibid.

129

correct definition. If we return to the *diatessaron* and apply the principles outlined by Boethius, it is also possible to reach a definition that adequately explains the different species. The species of *diatessaron*, therefore, require two *differentiae*: the form of the intervals and the position in the gamut. Only with both is it possible to have four species of *diatessaron*. Using the same approach, so too the *diapente* and *diapason* differ in their species.

Taxonomy of modes

The relationship between the authentic and plagal modes was often expressed with reference to dialectic. The south-German theorists divided *protus*, *deuterus*, *tritus* and *tetrardus* according to quality into authentic and plagal versions. They explained the relationship between authentic and plagal versions by using metaphors like father and son, master and slave, or authority and subjugation. If *protus*, *deuterus*, *tritus* and *tetrardus* are considered genera, then their authentic and plagal versions can be seen as species. In authentic *protus*, the *diapente* (D E F G a) comes first, followed by the *diatessaron* (a b c d); in plagal *protus*, however, the *diatessaron* (A B C D) is followed by the *diapente* (D E F G a). The *differentia* that divides authentic *protus* and plagal *protus*, therefore, is the order of the species of *diatessaron* and *diapente*. This is an example of what Boethius, in *De divisione*, termed division through the opposition of contraries.

Boethius identified four oppositions and deemed it necessary to know by which particular opposition a genus was divided: contraries, possession and privation, affirmation and negation, relation.[88] The fourth opposition – relation – occurs between 'father and son, master and slave, double and half, sensible and sense', to use Boethius' example.[89] This fourth opposition is echoed by the south-German theorists' conception of the relationship of the authentic and plagal modes. Nevertheless, Boethius stated that when dividing, the opposition of relation was always to be rejected in favour of divisions from possession and privation or from contraries.[90]

So we return to the authentic and plagal modes which, while possessing the opposition of relation, may be divided more correctly by the opposition of contraries: the order of the *diatessaron* and the *diapente* is inverted. Boethius' teaching on oppositions influenced Aribo, for there are numerous references to it in *De musica*. One chapter – entitled 'The opposition

---

[88] Ibid., p. 20 (*PL* 64.0882A).
[89] Ibid., p. 28.9: Quartam uero oppositionem diximus quae est secundum ad aliquid, ut pater filius, dominus seruus, duplex medium, sensibile sensus (*PL* 64.0884B).
[90] Ibid. This point is neglected in Deason, 'A taxonomic paradigm', pp. 32–4 and in the author's subsequent discussions, pp. 63, 76–7.

of tetrachords' – uses this concept to show how the tetrachords of the *finales* and *excellentes* oppose the *graves* and *superiores*.[91] They are opposite, argues Aribo, because the species of *diatessaron* and *diapente* begin in some and end in others; thus the opposition of contraries may be used to divide the tetrachords. In subsequent chapters Aribo extends this concept to the species of *diatessaron* and *diapente*, eventually likening the opposition of the species to the opposition of types of metrical feet.[92]

But taxonomies can be disrupted by what is known as an 'accident'. Aristotle, Porphyry and Boethius agree on the definition of an accident as a difference that can be separated from the subject without changing the nature of the subject. This point has relevance in the theory of the gamut when applied to the *synemmenon* tetrachord. Use of the *synemmenon* tetrachord was advocated by Bern of Reichenau in his *Prologus in tonarium*. The *synemmenon* tetrachord (a ♭ c d) was the tetrachord from the ancient Greek Lesser Perfect System that was frequently used to provide the pitch b-flat in many of the melodies that Bern encountered.[93] Bern was not the first to see the advantage of such a tetrachord: the idea was taken directly and without theoretical elaboration from Hucbald of St Amand, writing most likely in the 890s.[94] Following Bern, other south-German theorists also discussed this tetrachord, which was to all intents and purposes a *deus-ex-machina*-type appendage to the gamut. In authentic *protus*, authentic *tritus* and plagal *tritus*, the use of 'round' b in place of 'square' b can be termed an accident; in any other of the modes it is a *differentia* because, as Guido of Arezzo had taught, its use changed the nature of the mode.[95] If 'round b' were used in plagal *protus*, for example, the form of the tones and semitones at the beginning would change from tone-semitone-tone to semitone-tone-tone, which would then be the same as authentic *deuterus*: hence the mode would have undergone a *transformatio*.[96] In authentic *protus*, however, 'round b' is an accident, because whichever b should occur, it

[91] Aribo, *De musica*, p. 24.90.
[92] Ibid., p. 25.96.
[93] Bern, *Prologus* 1, p. 33: In medio horum solet interseri V^{tum} tetrachordum, quod dicitur synemenon, id est coniunctum. See also R. L. Crocker, 'Hermann's major sixth', *Journal of the American Musicological Society* 25 (1972), 26.
[94] Hucbald of St Amand, *Musica*, ed. Y. Chartier, *L'Œuvre musicale d'Hucbald de Saint-Amand. Les compositions et le traité de musique* (Montreal, 1995), p. 186: necesse est ut suo nomine tetrachordo nuncupato dicatur decurrere, quod uocatur synemenon, id est coniunctum.
[95] Guido of Arezzo, *Regule rithmice, Epistola ad Michahelem*, ed. and trans. D. Pesce, *Guido d'Arezzo's Regule rithmice, Prologus in antiphonarium and Epistola ad Michahelem: a critical text and translation* (Ottawa, 1999), pp. 348, 510.
[96] Deason, 'A taxonomic paradigm', pp. 64, 71–2.

remains authentic *protus*. Thus, as Boethius had written, the division of men by different colours – black, white and intermediate colour – involved a division *secundum accidens*, for 'these are accidents for men, not species of men, and Man is their subject, not their genus'.[97] In other words, the essence of the subject remains intact.

This analysis of the gamut has involved, for the most part, a reconstruction of a thought process influenced by dialectic. The question remains whether such a reconstruction is anachronistic when applied to eleventh-century music theory. We have seen echoes of dialectical thought in the music treatises of the south-German circle. These echoes, which include the use of dialectical terminology and sporadic references to dialectical texts, suggest that the *ars logica* informed the work of the south-German circle. Three case studies, focusing on the explicit application of dialectic in the treatises by Master Henry of Augsburg, the Wolf Anonymous and Aribo, will show that the south-German theorists were indeed thinking in such terms.

The division of music according to Henry of Augsburg

A conscious application of dialectic to the understanding of music occurs in the treatise *Musica* written by Henry, who was master of the cathedral school at Augsburg until 1077. The treatise, written as a dialogue between master and pupil, shows that he viewed music in terms of a hierarchy of genera and species. The most obvious inspiration for this approach lies in the teaching of *Isagoge*, where Porphyry states that in moving through the levels in between the highest and the lowest classes of species and genera, the intermediate classes will be species of the anterior classes, but genera of the posterior classes.[98]

The pupil begins by asking whether music is a genus or a species, to which the master replies 'it is a species, and a subaltern genus'.[99] When asked to explain, the master then responds that, as with many sciences, music is also to be divided according to logic. In fact, it is a subaltern genus divided into three species: earthly, human and artificial.[100] This

---

[97] Boethius, *De divisione*, p. 10.3: . . . haec enim accidenta sunt hominibus, non hominum species, et homo his subiectum, non horum genus est (*PL* 64.0878B).
[98] Porphyry, *Isagoge* 4.15, p. 9; 5.7, p. 16; trans. Warren, pp. 35, 36.
[99] Henry of Augsburg, *Musica*, ed. J. Smits van Waesberghe, *Musica domni Heinrici Augustensis magistri* (Buren, 1977), p. 35: D[iscipulus]. Estne musica genus an species? M[agister]. Species est et subalternum genus.
[100] Ibid.: Scientia artificialis, cum in multa, etiam in musicam [speciem] dividitur. Est autem subalternum genus, quia in tres species subdividitur, quarum prima est mundana, secunda humana, tertia artificiosa.

classification was certainly not novel, as it was no doubt inspired by the famous passage from the beginning of Boethius' *De institutione musica*.[101] Nevertheless, Master Henry's decision to cast it in specifically dialectical terms is significant in itself. Turning to the next level below, 'earthly, human and artificial' music now become genera.

So Master Henry continues his exposition starting from the highest level. Having divided the genus 'music' into three species, each of these species now becomes a genus that in turn may be further subdivided. Thus, according to Master Henry, if one take artificial music as the genus, its species are those things fashioned by the handiwork of men: the species of music by touch, as in strings; the species of music by blowing, as in organs; the species of music by percussion, as in bells and tibia.[102] If one take the genus of human music to the level below – that is, music produced by singing – then the three species themselves become genera, giving diatonic, chromatic and enharmonic. This point was also expressed in another south-German treatise written a few years later: *De musica* by the otherwise unknown John.[103] Henry, like his contemporaries, traces his division through diatonic music. He cites the authority of Macrobius to dismiss the chromatic genus as too soft and the enharmonic genus as being too difficult to be useful.[104]

The dialogue proceeds in this manner, with the pupil asking questions that take Henry in a progressive descent through the classes. The pupil asks whether or not music exists in reference to itself (*per se*), or exists in reference to something else (*ad aliquid*): the master answers 'to something else'. When the pupil asks for a reason, Master Henry responds that the first begetting of music (by which he means human music) consists in the

---

[101] Boethius, *De institutione musica* 1.2, ed. G. Friedlein, *Anicii Manlii Torquati Severini Boetii. De institutione arithmetica libri duo, De institutione musica libri quinque. Accedit geometria quae fertur Boetii* (Leipzig, 1867; repr. Frankfurt am Main, 1966), pp. 187–9.

[102] Henry of Augsburg, *Musica*, p. 35: D. Quae est artificiosa? M. Quae arte hominum composita, aut tactu, ut in fidibus, aut flatu, ut in organis, aut percussione, ut in cymbalis et tibiis perficitur.

[103] John, *De musica*, ed. J. Smits van Waesberghe, *Johannis Afflighemensis De musica cum tonario* (Rome, 1950), p. 58: . . . tria sint musicae melodiae genera, enharmonicum, diatonicum, chromaticum.

[104] Henry of Augsburg, *Musica*, p. 36: D. Sive quis voce, sive artificiis musicam exerceat: quot cantilenae generibus uti poterit? M. Uno tantum. D. Quo? M. Diatonico. Nam teste Macrobio chromaticum genus propter infamem mollitiem, enharmonicum vero propter nimiam sui difficultatem ab usu recessit. See Macrobius, *Commentarius in Somnium Scipionis* 2.4.13, ed. J. Willis, *Ambrosii Theodosii Macrobii Commentarii in Somnium Scipionis* (Leipzig, 1963), p. 109.

reason of numbers and proportions, which are represented by the intervals.[105] Hence, like Herman of Reichenau, Master Henry too echoes Porphyry's second definition of genus; which is why, when asked at the beginning, he classified music as a species and a subaltern genus.[106] Henry of Augsburg, therefore, explains music in a manner that is centred upon a dialectical understanding of the hierarchy of its elements: music is seen as a spectrum of subaltern genera and species.

It is not surprising that Henry, as a *scholasticus*, should have favoured such a discussion of music, for his teaching in the cathedral school at Augsburg must have heightened his awareness of the close connexions between the arts of the trivium and quadrivium. The content of one contemporary manuscript – now Leipzig, Universitätsbibliothek, Cod. 1493 – reveals a similar preoccupation on the part of one of the clerks responsible for its production. This codex of ninety folios is written in two very similar eleventh-century minuscules. The similarity of the two hands, as well as the presence of distinctive decorated capitals in orange throughout the codex, suggests that it was the work of one scriptorium. The first scribe copied Boethius' *De institutione musica* on fols 1r–46r (Book 1 begins mid-sentence, which implies that there were originally more folios before the present beginning). A second scribe copied the remainder of the codex: Bern of Reichenau's *Prologus in tonarium* and *Tonarius* (fols 47r–60r), Notker of St Gallen's monochord and organ pipe measurements in Old High German (fols 60r–61v),[107] Alcuin's *Dialogus de rhetorica et virtutibus* (fols 62v–74v) and *De dialectica* (fols 80r–89v), as well as a number of annotated diagrams showing the division of the subjects of the curriculum into their parts (fols 75r–80r). Like Master Henry, this scribe was interested not only in music and logic, but in the division of disciplines into their species. His interest was probably kindled by Alcuin's *De dialectica*. This treatise – cast as a pious and learned dialogue between Charlemagne and Alcuin – begins with Charlemagne asking into how many species 'physics' and 'logic' are divided. Alcuin responds that 'physics' is divided into four (arithmetic, geometry, music and astronomy) and 'logic' into two (dialectic and rhetoric).[108]

[105] Henry of Augsburg, *Musica*, p. 37: D. Utrum est musica per se, an ad aliquid? M. Ad aliquid. D. Quare? M. Quia prima eius genitura in ratione numerorum et proportionum consistit.
[106] See above p. 132 n. 99.
[107] See F.-J. Pensel and I. Stahl, *Verzeichnis der deutschen mittelalterlichen Handschriften in der Universitätsbibliothek Leipzig* (Berlin, 1998), p. 191.
[108] Leipzig, Universitätsbibliothek, Cod. 1493, fol. 80v: K. In quot species phisica diuiditur? A. In quatuor: arithmeticam, geometricam, musicam, astronomiam. K. Logica in quot

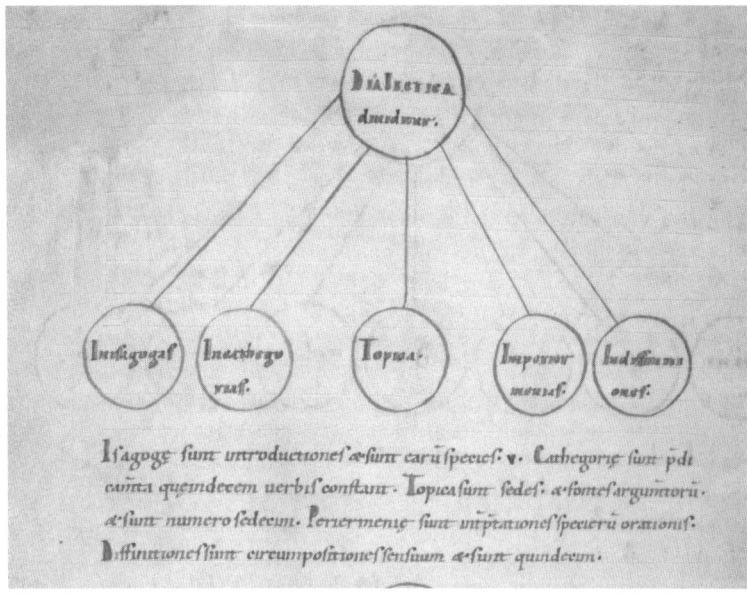

Plate 3 The division of dialectic into its species. Leipzig, Universitätsbibliothek, Cod. 1493, fol 78v

These comments are glossed by the scribe in the margin with the pointers *Species phisicę* and *Species logicę* respectively. In an annotated diagram on fol. 78v (Plate 3), the scribe shows how dialectic can be divided into five species, each of which can be further subdivided in turn.

The questions asked by Charlemagne in *De dialectica* are reminiscent of those asked by the pupil in Master Henry's *Musica*. The interests and comments of the scribe responsible for that part of the Leipzig codex provide a useful parallel for understanding Master Henry's dialectical approach to music.

Anonymous I and the Wolf Anonymous on the species of consonance
The use of dialectic is apparent in a passage discussing the species of consonance, which appears in two of the south-German treatises: Anonymous I and the Wolf Anonymous. Anonymous I, writing sometime after Bern of Reichenau, appears to have been the source of this passage for the Wolf

species diuiditur? A. In duas: in dialecticam et rethoricam. In his quippe generibus tribus: philosophię et iam eloquia diuina consistunt (*PL* 101.0949).

Anonymous.[109] In the sixth section of Anonymous I, the author considers what constitutes a species of consonance.[110] His definition of consonance is taken from Boethius: consonance is a mixture of diverse sounds falling sweetly and uniformly upon the ears.[111] He then proceeds to list the species of consonances: *diatessaron, diapente, diapason, diapason*-plus-*diapente* and double-*diapason*. He mentions that if, according to the teaching of Ptolemy, one were to include the *diapason*-plus-*diatessaron* in this list, there would be six species of consonance.[112] The text of the Wolf Anonymous, as the following textual comparison shows, is clearly based on that of Anonymous I.

Anonymous I, § 6
Consonantia est diversarum vocum concentus suaviter et uniformiter accidens auribus, ut si in lira vel alio aliquo musico instrumento diligenter tensis et remissis nervis, primam et quartam, seu primam et quintam, vel primam et octavam simul ferias vocem: quarum prima, quae et minima, diatessaron dicitur; secunda diapente, tono maior; tertia ex his duabus compacta diapason; quarta diapason et diapente; quinta bis diapason, vel disdiapason.

Quibus si secundum Ptolomaei rationabile iudicium diapason et diatessaron adiicias; sex habebis consonantias. Sed cum haec et nomen et diffinitionem sui generis recipiat, cur excludatur, ratio nonapportat.

Wolf Anonymous, *Musica*
Consonantia est diversarum vocum concentus suaviter et uniformiter accidens auribus; veluti si in aliquo musico instrumento, diligenter intensis nervis, primam et quartam, primam et quintam, primam et octavam simul tetigeris chordam. Inter species igitur consonantiarum diatessaron ponitur prima, quae habetur et minima, diapente secunda diatessaron una superans chorda, quae tonus exstat proportione sesquioctava; ex his duabus composita diapason constituitur tertia, diapason et diapente quarta, bis diapason ponitur quinta. His quinque speciebus, si diapason et diatessaron adicias, sex habebis consonantias. Quam Pythagoras quidem praetermisit, sed Ptolemaeus rationabili iudicio apposuit.

---

[109] T. J. H. McCarthy, 'Anonymous I and *Prologus in tonarium*: changing interpretations of music theory in eleventh-century Germany', *Journal of the Society for Musicology in Ireland* 1 (2005), 29–31.

[110] Anonymous I, § 6, *Musica*, *GS* 1, p. 333b.

[111] Boethius, *De institutione musica* 1.8, p. 195.

[112] Anonymous I, § 6, *Musica*, *GS* 1, p. 333b.

Nam si equus est substantia animata sensibilis, pro certo speciebus intererit animalis: quod si diapason et diatessaron est diversarum vocum concentus suaviter et uniformiter accidens auribus, iure interponetur consonantiae speciebus; sed eam hoc esse nemo negare poterit; igitur consonantiis intererit.[113]	Quod si quis hanc neget esse speciem, cum generis sui subiaceat diffinitioni, facillime convinci poterit ratione. Si enim homo est substantia animata, rationabilis, sensibilis, procul dubio speciebus intererit animalis. Si autem diapason et diatessaron est diversarum vocum concentus suaviter et uniformiter accidens auribus, iure interponetur consonantiae speciebus. Sed hoc eam esse nemo est, qui possit inficere, si rei veritatem studeat perpendere.[114]

Although both texts are very similar, the Wolf Anonymous has expanded Anonymous I in parts: he adds that the Pythagoreans oppose the inclusion of the *diapason*-plus-*diatessaron*, a fact not mentioned by Anonymous I. This piece of information he found in *De institutione musica* 5, where Boethius recorded Ptolemy's demonstration that the *diapason*-plus-*diatessaron* was a consonance.[115] Immediately after this comment comes a passage in both sources that consciously uses dialectic to refute the Pythagoreans: the version of the Wolf Anonymous, which uses 'man' rather than 'horse' as the example of an animate substance, is given in translation here ('Si enim homo. . . .. interponetur consonantiae speciebus').

Which, if a person deny this [the *diapason*-plus *diatessaron*] to be a species, since it lies below the definition of its genus, he can very easily be refuted by reason. For if man is an animate substance, rational and sentient, he will differ from the species [called] animal. If, however, the *diapason* and the *diatessaron* are a concord of diverse voices falling sweetly and uniformly upon the ears, then they [the *diapason* and *diatessaron*] are justly placed among the species of consonance.[116]

---

[113] Anonymous I, § 6, *GS* 1, pp. 333-4.
[114] Wolf Anonymous, *Musica*, pp. 212-13.
[115] Boethius, *De institutione musica* 5.9, pp. 358-60.
[116] Cf. Porphyry, *Isagoge* 11.1, p. 17.17: . . . homo enim ab animali plus habet rationale et mortale. Animal enim neque ipsum nihil horum est (nam unde habebunt species differentias?); trans. Warren, p. 46.

The terminology for this passage was undoubtedly taken from one of the dialectical works of Boethius: the terms used (whether horse or man) occur in Boethius' commentary on Aristotle's *Categories* and in Porphyry's *Isagoge* (which, of course, was available in the translation of Boethius). In addition to echoing *Isagoge* 11.1, this example also recalls an earlier passage of that work. In *Isagoge* 2.15 Porphyry gave as an example of genus 'animal', of species 'man' and of the *differentia* 'rational'.[117] Since rationality is the *differentia* that distinguishes man from the other species of animal, then it must be present in man. Consequently, the Wolf Anonymous argues that since the *diatessaron* and *diapason* are species of consonance, when added together their product will retain this characteristic and so be a species of consonance. The application of a dialectical 'proof' to this question seemed appropriate to Anonymous I and the Wolf Anonymous because of their firm conviction that music ought to obey the rules of right reason and reflect the natural order that governed it: the original author of the passage stressed that those who denied the proposition should be refuted by 'reason'. As in other disciplines, dialectic provided a means to analyse the order of music.

Dialectic in Aribo's De musica

An intriguing example of the application of the *ars logica* in a music treatise is provided by Aribo's *De musica*. Aribo, a clerk of Freising who may subsequently have been a monk of Hirsau, displays a wide variety of learning in his treatise. It comes as no surprise, therefore, that he should be especially enthusiastic about dialectic. The use of dialectic is particularly apparent in those parts of *De musica* where Aribo deals with conjunct and disjunct tetrachords. The music theorists from the south-German circle repeatedly emphasized the necessity for the conjunction of the tetrachord of the *graves* with the tetrachord of the *finales* (at the pitch D), and a repetition of this between the tetrachords of the *superiores* and the *excellentes* at the higher octave.[118] By this the theorists reconciled the division of the gamut into tetrachords with the self-evident principle of octave replication.

The necessity for the tetrachords to be conjunct in this manner was first recognized by Herman of Reichenau. Like Aribo later in the century, he was deeply influenced by the belief that reason and perception were concordant, a Platonic theme stressed repeatedly in Boethius' *De institutione musica*. Herman's dismissal of disjunct tetrachords, particularly those of

---

[117] Porphyry, *Isagoge* 2.15, p. 31.
[118] See Chapter 2, pp. 83–6.

the Carolingian treatise *Musica enchiriadis*, is most revealing in this respect. He condemned disjunct tetrachords because they destroyed 'the structure of the whole monochord by upsetting its regular order' and were not capable of the octave replication, which was 'endorsed both by the united opinion of all and by the insurmountable law of nature'.[119] Consequently, Herman took the tetrachords of the *graves, finales, superiores* and *excellentes*, and fitted them into the double octave (*quadrupulum*). This, of necessity, involved the use of conjunct tetrachords. As there are seven distinct pitches in the octave, to fit two tetrachords into this space it is necessary for them to have a pitch that 'is both the highest note of the first tetrachord and the lowest of the second'.[120] Herman's conclusion was that 'this function of mediation must relate to D alone' since it is around this pitch that the form of the tetrachords with regard to tones and semitones is symmetrical.

Herman's emphasis was repeated by William of Hirsau. William's interlocutor, Otloh of St Emmeram, raised the question of the double aspect of the pitch D by observing that whereas G can be assigned only to the fourth place of a tetrachord (*tetrardus*), D could potentially belong to the first or fourth place (*protus* or *tetrardus*).[121] When William treats of this issue, he mentions that D and d have two functions: they operate in both tetrachords.[122] He cautions that many authors, both ancient and modern (even Guido of Arezzo and pseudo-Odo of Cluny), have erred in this matter since they have ignored this double function.[123] Not only is this state of affairs confusing, but it is not supported by the layout of the monochord.[124] The

[119] Herman, *Musica* 3, p. 24: . . . ipsius medietatis troporum quod impossibile est duplicavit, et ita produorum naturali positione tonorum continuum tritonum incurrit, sicque totius monochordi structuram regulari eius ordine disturbato destruxit . . . quippe ubi nulla eiusdem dispositionis chorda in octava eadem esse reperitur; quod tamen quia oporteat et unanimi omnium assertione, et insuperabili naturae veritate comprobatur.

[120] Ibid., p. 23: . . . nos coniunctionem possumus dicere, ut videlicet superioris sit quarta vel auctissima posterioris vero prima vel gravissima.

[121] William, *Musica* 7, p. 24: Sed .D. quia ut iam dixi biformis est, tam inter primas quam inter quartas numeratur; .G. vero simpliciter quartis ascribitur.

[122] Ibid. 14, p. 40.

[123] Ibid. 15, p. 41: Interius igitur mirabilem ipsarum .D. et .d. naturam speculantes, secundum id quod in quolibet biformitatis et duplicitatis suae modo faciunt utraque unum, non inconvenienter eas lapides angulares dicimus, secundum id vero quod omnes musici graviter in eis offenderunt, non immerito lapides offensionis, et scandali petras nominamus. Quod ut indubitanter probemus, quam fortiter in his maximus antiquorum Boetius, ac modernorum potissimi Otto et Guido offenderint, in memoriam reducamus.

[124] Ibid. 17, pp. 46–7: . . . et hac intentione naturalem coadunationem coniunctionemque primae ac quartae in .D. et .d. non satis cauta nec bene provisa interpositione toni disiecit, sicque totius monochordi structuram regulari eius ordine disturbato destruxit;

most objectionable feature of these theorists, however, is that their denial of the double function of D and d confounds all harmonic speculation and is contrary to natural order, separating and dividing what is naturally together. Drawing on the teaching of Herman, William too notes the seven distinct pitches in the octave; D must be concurrently the fourth and first note of a tetrachord, as must d an octave above it.[125] A little later, William points to the fact that his description of the seven distinct notes is capable of octave replication.[126]

These arguments in favour of regarding the pitches D and d as double-functioned are, for the most part, grounded in observation, and use the layout of the monochord as their primary point of reference. Aribo, however, felt the need to add to these already powerful arguments in a manner similar to the example of Anonymous I and the Wolf Anonymous above. Chapters 64–71 of *De musica* show – through their repeated use of dialectical terminology – that he chose to use the self-sufficiency of dialectic to bolster the established theory. He acknowledged the implications of his choice by saying 'nevertheless, we wish to bring to bear upon them the force of sufficiency, even though not furnishing an abundance of necessary arguments'.[127] This 'abundance of necessary arguments' had already been furnished by Herman and William: the powerful weapon of dialectic would additionally compel the understanding.

Aribo, therefore, was faced with the task of proving that the notes D and d are simultaneously the final notes of the tetrachords of the *graves* and *superiores* and the beginning notes of the tetrachords of the *finales* and *excellentes*; in other words, that they are both *protus* and *tetrardus* at the same time. (A consequence of this is that the octave from D to d can form either an authentic or a plagal mode.) Aribo starts by mentioning that 'our ancestors, considering carefully that any of the tropes, hitherto indivisible, consisted of the four principal notes. . .divided them into authentics and plagals, calling the authentics authoritative and more dignified, but the

---

Footnote 124 (*cont.*)
et tam eam quae est secundum antiquos atque modernos, quam eam quae est secundum ipsius naturae auctoritatem, harmoniae speculationem omnem confu[n]dit.

[125] Ibid., p. 46: et cum tetrachorda Gravium et Finalium in .D. concurrant, ita ut eadem et quarta sit Gravium et prima Finalium, eodemque modo tetrachorda Superiorum et Excellentium in .d. conterminent, ita ut eadem et quarta sit Superiorum et prima Excellentium.

[126] Ibid. 18, p. 49: Quantum ad id vero quod in eadem descriptione septem vocum discrimina secundum antiquissimos adeo non intendit, quin octavum modum recipiat.

[127] Aribo, *De musica*, p. 33.68: tamen adhuc ipsi sufficientiae violentiam volumus inferre, etiam non necessariorum copiam ministrantes argumentorum.

plagals lateral and subordinate'.[128] Like Herman and William before him, he notes that they did not foresee that 'the double-formed D and d are powerful letters naturally creating either an authentic or plagal species'.[129] This he contrasts with the 'perceptive moderns', who 'investigating more carefully the nature and efficacy of the aforementioned mode, have attributed to it plagal formula or *differentiae*'.[130] Here the word 'difference' is used in its dialectical sense, as William had used it to distinguish the two groups of tetrachords. Aribo sees the problem, therefore, as denial by the ancient theorists of the plagal possibilities of D and d. After two very brief chapters, he begins to show (*De musica* 67) how the mode beginning on D may have a plagal form in addition to an authentic one.

Aribo, *De musica* [67]: That the same mode may have the material of a plagal.

Since the same mode may have the material of a plagal, we may compose the plagal form from this, or if we can, we might naturally deny D to be the fourth of the *graves* and d to be the fourth of the *superiores*, or else we may grant this to be so. If we deny it, we will be constrained by an opponent using the following argument: every note that is a *synemmesis*, that is a conjunction of two tetrachords, is the end of one and the beginning of yet another. But D is the *synemmesis* of the tetrachords of the *graves* and of the *finales*. If it is the end of the tetrachord, it is the fourth note. But it is the end, therefore the fourth, since every final of a tetrachord is fourth. The maximal proposition is the argument from genus: what holds in all holds also in one. From the preceding argument we can gather that if in a tetrachord the final is the fourth note, the beginning of it is the first note. But this is the case. Therefore D, according to this reasoning, is both the fourth of the *graves* and the first of the *finales*. From this argument itself it may be gathered that d is the fourth of the *superiores* and the first of the *excellentes*.[131]

---

[128] Ibid., p. 29.39: Maiores nostri perpendentes quemlibet tropum adhuc indivisum quatuor principalibus ita chordis consistere, ut altrinsecus collectae duas diapason species possent conficere, diviserunt eos in autentos et plagas, autentos vocantes auctorales et digniores, plagas autem laterales et subiectos.

[129] Ibid., p. 30.45: Sed quia eundum modum prius in proto autenticam speciem diapason, id est, tonum primum facerunt, recusaverunt illum in tetrardo vel habere vel appellare plagalem, non providentes, quod .D.d. biformes sint litterae potentes naturaliter tam plagalem quam autenticam constituere speciem.

[130] Ibid., p. 31.48: Sollertius autem praelibati modi naturam et efficatiam iuniores intuentes plagales sibi formulas vel differentias attribuerunt.

[131] Ibid., pp. 31.53–32.58: Cum idem modus habeat plagalis materiam, plagalem ex hac componamus formam, aut si possimus, naturaliter negemus, .D. non esse quartam

The style of this passage betrays the influence of the *ars logica*. Aribo speaks in terms of 'arguments' and 'reasoning', while his reference to being 'constrained by an opponent' gives the passage the flavour of a scholastic disputation. The dialectical approach was the basis of the discipline of disputation that developed in the schools involving the division and distinction of individual issues and their consideration from different points of view.[132] It is made explicit by Aribo's use of a maximal proposition: what holds for all holds also for one. The inspiration for this reference was undoubtedly Boethius' commentary on Cicero's *Topics*.[133] Since every final note of a tetrachord is fourth, D, being a final note, is fourth and consequently must behave like a fourth note.

Aribo then goes on to introduce a dialectical term that he had discussed earlier in *De musica*: property. Porphyry defined property in four ways. First, property is what occurs in one species only, although not in every member of the species, as healing and measuring occur in man. Secondly, property is what occurs in the entire species and not in it only, as being two-footed occurs in man. Thirdly, property is what occurs in the entire species, in it only and at some time, as becoming grey in old age occurs in every man. Fourthly, property is what occurs in the entire species, in it only and always, as the capacity to laugh occurs in man.[134] An example from an earlier part of *De musica* shows the importance Aribo accorded to property in the question 'What is the property of being *diatessaron*?'.

Aribo, *De musica* [35]: That the beginning of the similarity lies in these things.

If anyone should ask me what is a *diatessaron* or a *diapente*, and I should respond 'four notes' or 'five notes', I should not be speaking cautiously with the four notes being a♭ b c and nevertheless including a semiditone;

Footnote 131 (*cont.*)
> gravium, .d. non esse quartam superiorum, aut esse concedamus. Si negabimus, ab adversario subsequente constringemur argumentatione: Omnis chorda, quae duorum synemmesis, id est coniunctio, est tetrachordorum, alterius est finis, alteriusque est principium. Sed .D. synemmesis est tetrachordi gravium et finalium. Si finis est tetrachordi, quarta est chorda. Sed finis est, ergo quarta, quia omnis tetrachordi finalis quarta est. Argumentum a genere maxima propositio: Quod in omnibus valet, valet et in uno. Ab argumento praecedenti possumus colligere, quia si in tetrachordo finis est quarta chorda, principium est in eo prima chorda. Sed hoc est. Ergo .D. secundum hanc rationem et quarta est gravium et prima finalium. Hac ipsa argumentatione sit probatum, quod .d. sit quarta superiorum, prima excellentium.

[132] G. Constable, *The reformation of the twelfth century* (Cambridge, 1996), pp. 130–1.
[133] Boethius, *Commentarius in topica Ciceronis* 2 (*PL* 64.1069).
[134] Porphyry, *Isagoge* 12.15; trans. Warren, p. 48.

DIALECTIC AND THE THEORY OF MUSIC

or with the five notes being B C D E F and they containing a *diatessaron* and a semitone. On that account we say: a *diatessaron* is a semitone with two tones in it that are separate and a *diapente* is a semitone with three tones in it that are separate. I say this, moreover, that the tone which is from a to b with that tone which is from ♭ to c partakes of the same space of that from ♭ to b, which is the greater part of a tone and is called *apotome* since otherwise it could be proved that a semitone is a *diatessaron* and a *diatessaron* is a *diapente*.[135]

Hence the property of being *diatessaron* is not four notes but a semitone and two separate tones. In this case, 'four notes' is what *Isagoge* would have termed an accident, that is, what can belong or not belong to the same thing, or what is neither a genus, nor a difference, nor a species, nor a property, but which always exists in a substratum.[136] In *De musica* 69, however, the reference to 'property' is made explicit by the title: 'Concerning the property of *protus*, *deuterus*, *tritus* and *tetrardus*'. The four short verses of this chapter designate the property of each as the form of ascent (*intensio*) and descent (*remissio*).

Aribo, *De musica* [69]: Concerning the property of *protus*, *deuterus*, *tritus* and *tetrardus*.

The property of *protus* is to concord in elevation by a fifth, in deposition by a tone. The property of *deuterus* is in making whole a *diatessaron* by *intensio*, a ditone by *remissio*. The property *tritus* is to concord in *intensio* by a ditone, in *remissio* by a *diatessaron*. The property of *tetrardus* is to oppose *protus*, whose elevation may be its remission.[137]

---

[135] Aribo, *De musica*, pp. 16.53-17.55: Si aliquo me interrogante, quid est diatessaron vel diapente, respondebo, quatuor chordae, quinque chordae, non caute dixero, cum quatuor sint chordae .a.♭.b.c. et tamen non contineant nisi semiditonum; cum quinque chordae sint, .B.C.D.E.F. et non cohibeant nisi diatessaron et semitonium. Idcirco dicamus: diatessaron est semitonium cum duobus tonis in nullo participantibus; diapente est semitonium cum tribus tonis in nullo participantibus. Hoc dico propterea, quia tonus, qui est ab .a. in .b. cum illo tono qui est a ♭. in .c. participat spacium, quod est a ♭. in .b., quod est maius toni spacium, quod apotome dicitur, quia aliter poterit probari et semitonium esse diatessaron, et diatessaron esse diapente.
[136] Porphyry, *Isagoge* 13.1; trans. E. W. Warren, p. 49.
[137] Aribo, *De musica*, p. 32.62-66: *De proprietate protorum, deuterorum, tritorum, tetrardorum*. Proprietas est protorum, ut concordent in elevatione per diapente, in depositione per tonum. Proprietas est deuterorum cum integra diatessaron per intensionem, ditono per remissionem. Proprietas est tritorum, ut concordent intensione ditono, diatessaron remissione. Proprietas est tetrardorum, ut protis opponantur, quatenus horum elevatio istorum sit remissio.

De musica 70 fleshes out the argument in prose. Aribo acknowledges that although it may have been satisfactorily proved that D and d can have a plagal mode, he wishes to bring upon those who doubt the 'force of sufficiency, even though not furnishing an abundance of necessary arguments'.[138] He begins by admitting that it is not possible to 'invent powerful arguments about their property' and by stating that 'neither have we thought rationally of overlooking the property of the tropes'.[139] Aribo is, therefore, thinking very much in dialectical terms. He continues by asking whether D and d can have both the 'property' of *protus* and of *tetrardus*: 'the property of *tetrardus* is that the *intensio* of *protus* may be its *remissio*'. He follows this by stating that 'D is so remitted by tone, semitone and tone in the same way as A of *protus* is extended by tone, semitone and tone'. Hence, if because of *intensio* A is *protus*, and if the *remissio* of D have the same form, then D must be *tetrardus*, because Aribo has already stated that 'the property of *tetrardus* is that the *intensio* of *protus* may be its *remissio*'.

But this reasoning is of limited use to Aribo, who wants to prove that D has the property both of *protus* and *tetrardus*. In the next chapter – aptly entitled 'That the species and properties predicate equally of themselves' – he begins with a quotation from Boethius' *De differentiis topicis*.[140]

> Aribo, *De musica* [70]: That the species and properties predicate equally of themselves.
>
> Every man is capable of laughter and everything capable of laughter is a man. Every *tetrardus* is remissible by tone, semitone and tone, and everything remissible by tone, semitone and tone is *tetrardus*. But D and d are remitted through tone, semitone and tone. Therefore, they are *tetrardus*. If *tetrardus*, then they are either authentic or plagal. But it is necessary that they be plagal, since no authentic consits of *graves* and *superiores*. These irrefutable arguments having been transacted, and the lengthy scrutiny of their nature having been finished, we may baptize this same mode in the name of hypomixolidian, so that it is doubly-named, as he of the two forms with whom we have become acquainted.[141]

---

[138] Ibid., p. 33.68.
[139] Ibid., p. 33.69.
[140] Boethius, *De differentiis topicis* (*PL* 64.1175C); trans. E. Stump, *Boethius's De topicis differentiis* (Ithaca and London, 1978), p. 32.
[141] Aribo, *De musica*, p. 33.71: *Quod aequaliter de se praedicentur species et propria.* Omnis homo risibilis est, et omne risibile homo est. Omnis tetrardus per tonum, semitonium, tonum remissibilis est, et omnis remissio toni, semitonii, toni tetrardus est. Sed .D.d. remittitur tono, semitonio, tono. Ergo tetrardus est. Si tetrardus est, aut autentus aut pla-

DIALECTIC AND THE THEORY OF MUSIC

Boethius, however, had relied closely on a corresponding passage in *Isagoge*. Following Porphyry's example, Aribo argues that the characteristics of *tetrardus* – being remissible by tone, semitone and tone – are properties in the strict sense, because they are convertible. Porphyry had said that if there is a horse there is the capacity to neigh, and conversely, if there is the capacity to neigh there is a horse.[142] In this situation, if there is remissibility by tone, semitone and tone, then there is *tetrardus*. D and d are therefore *tetrardus*, as they display the property of remission through tone, semitone and tone. Aribo next points out, however, that if D and d are *tetrardus*, then they must be either authentic or plagal, since each note of the tetrachord of the *finales* (*protus*, *deuterus*, *tritus* and *tetrardus*) has an authentic and plagal version. Consequently, Aribo states that in this case the authentic version cannot consist of the *graves* and the *superiores*, but must – by implication – consist of the *finales* and the *excellentes*. Since D and d can only function within the *finales* and the *excellentes* as *protus*, then returning to the 'convertibility' of which Porphyry speaks, if there is the capacity to be of the *graves* and *superiores*, then there is *tetrardus*. Aribo's approach was obviously appreciated by the early twelfth-century author of *Quaestiones in musica*, for he incorporated these chapters in abridged form into his treatise, taking particular care to retain in his abridgement the references to Boethius' *In topica Ciceronis* and *De differentiis topicis*.[143]

Conclusion

A reliance on dialectic, therefore, is apparent in these examples from the the south-German circle. They show the theorists to have been aware of the possibilities for applying the methods of the *ars logica* to the *ars musica*. This use of dialectic is a valuable indication of the learning that influenced the theorists. The explicit quotations and allusions to the textbooks of dialectic, obvious in the case studies above, provide the strongest evidence for believing dialectically-based thinking to have been widely applied to the theory and division of the gamut. In light of the evidence that points to the wide dissemination of logical texts in Germany at this time, it is not

galis. Sed necesse est, ut sit plagalis, quia nullus autentus gravibus et superioribus constat. Irrefragabilibus transactis argumentationibus, et prolixo naturae suae finito scrutinio, baptizemus eundem modum, nominantes eum yppomixolidium, ut sic sit binomius, sicut eum biformem novimus.

[142] Porphyry, *Isagoge* 12.20; trans Warren, p. 48.
[143] *Quaestiones in musica*, ed. R. Steglich, *Die Quaestiones in Musica. Ein Choraltraktat des zentralen Mittelalters und ihr mutmaßlicher Verfasser Rudolf von St. Trond (1070–1138)* (Leipzig, 1911; repr. 1971), p. 26.

surprising that the *ars logica* should have influenced the *ars musica*: contemporary intellectuals were imbued with a love of definition, division and distinction. This realization has implications not only for our understanding of music theory, but for our appreciation of its intellectual context: it again shows music to have been an intellectual discipline deeply influenced by studies in the other *artes*. As we have seen, the treatise entitled *De animae exsilio et patria* by Honorius Augustodunensis portrays the student of the arts as a symbolic traveller journeying through numerous cities. The third of these cities is dialectic. The picture of dialectical studies sketched by Honorius concurs in large measure with the evidence regarding the availability of logical texts in Germany during the eleventh century. He further mentions that the city of dialectic has five gates: genus, species, *differentia*, property and accidents.[144] The content of the music treatises from the south-German circle indicates how easily these theorists would have recognized all five.

---

[144] Honorius Augustodunensis, *De animae exsilio et patria* 4: Tertia civitas est dialectica, multis quaestionum propugnaculis munita, per quam iter est ad patriae atria. Haec per quinque portas adventantes recipit, scilicet per genus, per species, per differens, per proprium, per accidens; unde et isagogae introductiones dicuntur, quia per has repatriantes introducuntur. Arx hujus urbis est substantia; turres circumstantes novem sunt accidentia. In hac duo pugiles sunt et litigantes certa ratione dirimunt: cathegorico et hypothetico syllogismo quasi praeclaris armis viantes muniunt. Quos Aristoteles in topica recipit, argumentis instruit, in perihermeniis ad latum campum syllogismorum educit. In hac urbe docentur itinerantes haereticis, et aliis hostibus armis rationis resistere, qui eis, ut olim Amalec populo Dei, in hac via moliuntur obsistere (*PL* 172.1244AB).

4

Plato, his interpreters and the south-German circle

The extent of Plato's influence on the thinking of the central Middle Ages has been the subject of much distinguished scholarship. We have today a subtle and nuanced understanding of many of the different strands of Platonic thought current at this time, as well as of their respective origins.[1] Historians are also beginning to distinguish different types of engagement with Plato: recent research cautions that documentary references to Plato in this period need not imply substantive engagement with him or his ideas.[2] Plato's name was frequently used in the 'accommodative' sense, much as Otloh of St Emmeram used biblical citation to add lustre and gravity to his prose. Although references to Plato by name are rare in the south-German treatises – Aribo mentions him three times and John once – he nevertheless was an important influence on the south-German circle. This influence, which goes far beyond accommodative use, is manifested in the recurrence of Platonic metaphor and vocabulary in the treatises. It was made possible both by the availability of Plato and his interpreters in libraries, and by a glossing and commentary tradition that sought to apply them to music theory.[3]

---

[1] See B. W. Switalsky, *Des Chalcidius Kommentar zu Platos Timaeus* (Münster, 1902); R. Klibansky, *The continuity of the Platonic tradition during the Middle Ages* (London, 1939); T. Gregory, 'Note e testi per la storia del platonismo medioevale', *Giornale critico della filosofia italiana* 34 (1955), 346–84; 'The Platonic inheritance', in P. Dronke (ed.), *A history of twelfth-century western philosophy* (Cambridge, 1988), pp. 54–80.

[2] J. Marenbon, 'Platonism – a doxographic approach: the early Middle Ages', in S. Gersh and M. J. F. M. Hoenen (eds), *The Platonic tradition in the Middle Ages: a doxographic approach* (Berlin and New York, 2002), pp. 67–89.

[3] See M. Teeuwen, *Harmony and the music of the spheres: the ars musica in ninth-century commentaries on Martianus Capella* (Leiden, 2002), pp. 152–3, 161–83, 344.

Of Plato's works only part of *Timaeus* (17a–53b) was known directly in the eleventh century. This portion was available in the translation by Calcidius (*c.* 256–*c.* 357), whose accompanying commentary incorporated various middle- and Neoplatonic influences from the earlier commentaries of Iamblichus and Porphyry. It was extremely popular in the Middle Ages, but since Calcidius had omitted those sections dealing with man, it was received primarily as a cosmological exposition of the origins and order of the universe.[4] (The translation by Cicero, upon which St Augustine relied, was not widely circulated in the eleventh century.[5]) This was not, however, the only route by which Platonic thought reached the Middle Ages. Boethius had sought to harmonize the philosophy of Plato and Aristotle, and while he was practically the sole means of transmission for most of Aristotle's works until the late twelfth century, he simultaneously perpetuated much of Plato's teaching. In contradistinction to Calcidius, he was a follower of Proclus and thus introduced another shade of Neoplatonism to the Middle Ages.[6] The influence of Plato is to be seen most vividly in Boethius' *Consolation of Philosophy*, which became one of the most enduringly popular works of literature during the Middle Ages: the ninth *metrum* of Book 3 was valued as a summary in twenty-eight verses of Plato's entire cosmology.[7] Plato was also behind much of Boethius' *De institutione arithmetica* and *De institutione musica*. To Calcidius and Boethius should be added Macrobius and Martianus Capella, who also contributed much to the medieval reception of Plato. Our attempt to assess the impact of Platonic thought on the music treatises of the south-German circle begins by tracing the manuscripts of Plato and his interpreters available to the theorists.

Manuscript sources for Platonic texts in eleventh-century Germany

Timaeus *in Calcidius' translation and commentary*

It is plausible to assume a wide familiarity in our period with Calcidius' translation of and commentary on *Timaeus*. Calcidius was available at Reichenau by the second half of the ninth century, and by the twelfth

---

[4] M. D. Chenu, 'The Platonisms of the twelfth century', in M. D. Chenu, *Nature, man and society in the twelfth century: essays on new theological perspectives in the Latin west*, 2nd edn, ed. and trans. J. Taylor and L. K. Little (Toronto, 1997), pp. 65–6.

[5] Ibid., p. 65 n. 29.

[6] Ibid., p. 73; P. Courcelle, *Les lettres grecques en occident de Macrobe à Cassiodore* (Paris, 1948), pp. 257–312.

[7] Chenu, 'The Platonisms of the twelfth century', pp. 64–5.

century appears in the libraries of Engelberg, Michelsberg and St Peter in Salzburg.[8] But as is so often the case, the library catalogues paint only an imperfect picture that must be supplemented by manuscript evidence.[9] Among the Latin manuscripts of *Timaeus* are a considerable number of German origin: a tenth-century manuscript from Tegernsee formerly in the collection of Sir Thomas Phillipps (now Austin, Tx., Harry Ransom Humanities Research Center, MS 29) contains *Timaeus* on fols 12v–24r,[10] while three eleventh-century sources now in the British Library are also of German origin.[11] To these should be added four eleventh-century codices now in Bamberg, Cologne, Munich and Vienna,[12] as well as numerous twelfth-century copies.[13] One of these manuscripts – Munich, Bayerische Staatsbibliothek, Clm 14663 – is of particular interest for the study of Platonism in the context of music theory. This manuscript of fifty-one folios, which was copied during the second half of the twelfth century, belonged to the great monastery of St Emmeram in Regensburg. It is an example of a music theory 'textbook codex'; among its contents are Guido's works, pseudo-Odo, the anonymous commentary on *Micrologus*, excerpts from Aribo's *De musica*, a partial copy of Bern's *Prologus in tonarium* and – on fols 34r–51v – Calcidius' translation of and commentary on *Timaeus*.[14] The inclusion of Plato here is suggestive of his perceived relevance to music theory in the twelfth century; it might also sum up the attitudes of the eleventh. Another St Emmeram manuscript – Munich, Bayerische Staatsbibliothek, Clm 14689 – bears witness to both interest in

[8] P. Lehmann (ed.), *MBDS* 1/1, pp. 32, 266; P. Ruf (ed.), *MBDS* 3/3, p. 362; G. Möser-Mersky and M. Mihaliuk (eds), *MBÖ* 4, p. 72.

[9] See especially Plato, *Timaeus*, ed. J. H. Waszink, *Timaeus a Calcidio translatus commentarioque instructus*, 2nd edn (London, 1975), pp. cvi–clxvii.

[10] Ibid., p. cxii. See also H. Schenkl, 'Bibliotheca patrum latinorum Britannica 4', *Sitzungsberichte der kais. Akademie der Wissenschaft. Philosophisch-historische Klasse* 126/4 (Vienna, 1892), pp. 26–7.

[11] London, British Library, Harl. 2610, Harl. 2652, Add. 19968. Waszink (ed.) in Plato *Timaeus*, pp. cvii, cxv.

[12] Bamberg, Staatsbibliothek, Msc. Class. 18; Cologne, Dombibliothek, 192; Munich, Bayerische Staatsbibliothek, Clm 6365; Vienna, Österreichische Nationalbibliothek, Cod. 443. On the Bamberg manuscript see F. Leitschuh and H. Fischer, *Katalog der Handschriften der königlichen Bibliothek zu Bamberg* 1/2 (Bamberg, 1895; repr. Wiesbaden, 1966), pp. 18–19. On the Cologne manuscript see P. Jaffé and G. Wattenbach, *Ecclesiae metropolitanae Coloniensis codices manuscripti* (Berlin, 1874), pp. 80–1.

[13] Berlin, Staatsbibliothek zu Berlin, Preußischer Kulturbesitz, Lat. qu. 202 (copied at the monastery of Sts Ulrich and Afra in Augsburg); Lat. oct. 8 (provenance to Worms); Bern, Universitätsbibliothek, 681; Munich, Bayerische Staatsbibliothek, Clm 514, Clm 14663; Vienna, Österreichische Nationalbibliothek, Cods 176, 278, 2376.

[14] *RISM B* 3/3, pp. 118–19.

Timaeus and its relevance to the quadrivium. This codex of 127 folios is written in numerous early twelfth-century hands and contains works on arithmetic and music by Gerbert of Aurillac, Heriger of Laubach, Herman of Reichenau and William of Hirsau among others.[15] Fols 88r–96r contain a commentary on musical aspects of the world's order based upon *Timaeus*.

Macrobius' Commentarius in Somnium Scipionis

Two versions of Macrobius were current in eleventh-century Germany: a full recension and an abbreviated form that contained only the central cosmological section. It has been suggested that this second version originated at Auxerre in 809.[16] It was very popular in Germany, appearing in Freising during the tenth century.[17] This version contained the sections on astronomy, music, geography, the zodiac and the passage on the gate of dreams. It was also this version that elicited an extensive apparatus of glosses. Here it is possible to discover something of the interests and propensities of different readers. Macrobius' discussion of the significance of the numbers four and seven in the elements and lunar phenomena generated considerable interest, as did his doctrine on the musical harmonies in the world soul, which was used hand in hand with Calcidius.[18] The glosses show that the Neoplatonic approach of *Commentarius in Somnium Scipionis* aroused little hostility. Rather, clerks seem to have felt comfortable enough with Macrobius to make critical contributions in the form of comments and diagrams.[19]

The special relevance of *Commentarius in Somnium Scipionis* to music theory is attested by its appearance in a number of music textbook codices. One such is an early twelfth-century example possibly from Bamberg: Munich, Bayerische Staatsbibliothek, Clm 14965a. Its thirty-nine folios contain treatises by pseudo-Odo, Guido of Arezzo and Bern of Reichenau, in addition to portions of Aribo's *De musica* and the types of miscellaneous texts that usually occur in such textbooks.[20] A short

---

[15] Ibid., pp. 119-20.
[16] A. White, 'Glosses composed before the twelfth century in manuscripts of Macrobius' *Commentary* on Cicero's *Somnium Scipionis*' (D.Phil. thesis, University of Oxford, 1981), p. 4.
[17] N. Daniel, *Handschriften des zehnten Jahrhunderts aus der Freisinger Dombibliothek. Studien über Schriftcharakter und Herkunft der nachkarolingischen und ottonischen Handschriften einer bayerischen Bibliothek* (Munich, 1973), pp. 86-7, 140, 152-3.
[18] White, 'Glosses composed before the twelfth century', pp. vii, viii.
[19] Ibid. See also A. Hüttig, *Macrobius im Mittelalter. Ein Beitrag zur Rezeptionsgeschichte der Commentarii in Somnium Scipionis*, pp. 63-8 for more generalized remarks.
[20] See Chapter 5, pp. 200, 203-14.

extract from Macrobius is copied on fols 29v–30r, immediately after a treatise on the measurement of organ pipes. This extract, taken from the beginning of *Commentarius in Somnium Scipionis* 2, lists the six ratios (the sesquitertia, sesquialtera, double, triple, quadruple and super-octave [9:8]) and then explains the arithmetical derivation of intervals that 'unite to produce music out of the innumerable variety of numerical combinations'.[21] Whereas the preceding organ-pipe measurements describe the theory for making pipes to sound the intervals, this portion of Macrobius seems to have been chosen by the scribe because it offered a complementary explanation of the intervals' generation. A similar example occurs in a contemporary manuscript that is mainly devoted to Frutolf of Michelsberg's *Breviarium de musica*: Munich, Bayerische Staatsbibliothek, Clm 14965b. After a diagram showing the *ars rhetorica*, the manuscript begins with a short treatise entitled 'De numeris musicis et de consonantiis'. The first part of this treatise is virtually identical to the extract from Macrobius copied in the previous manuscript.[22] It fulfils the 'de numeris musicis' requirement of the title, after which the author moves on to describing the constitution of the intervals. This particular section of *Commentarius in Somnium Scipionis* also appears in the twelfth-century textbook Kassel, Landesbibliothek, 4° Mss Math. 1, fols 22v–23r.[23] The occurrences of Macrobius in these textbook codices show the limited extent to which he could be applied directly to the nuts-and-bolts of music theory. His main use, as we shall see later, was as a channel for Platonic thought. In this guise the fantastic style of his commentary had a considerable influence upon the members of the south-German circle.

Martianus Capella's De nuptiis Philologiae et Mercurii

Historians have noted with some surprise that *De nuptiis Philologiae et Mercurii* was absent from European libraries until the ninth century, when it appears to have been introduced at centres such as Laon and Auxerre by

---

[21] Macrobius, *Commentarius in Somnium Scipionis* 2.1.14–20, ed. J. Willis, *Ambrosii Theodosii Macrobii Commentarii in Somnium Scipionis* (Leipzig, 1963), pp. 97–8.

[22] Ibid., 2.1.14–21, pp. 97–8.

[23] The Kassel manuscript has the same heading as the short treatise in Munich, Bayerische Staatsbibliothek, Clm 14965b, indicating a probable connexion between the two manuscripts. See Chapter 5, p. 210; C. Meyer, 'Aus der Werkstat des Kompilators. Bermerkungen über zwei musiktheoretische Schriften des 11. Jahrhunderts', in M. Bernhard (ed.), *Quellen und Studien zur Musiktheorie des Mittelalters* 2 (Munich, 1997), pp. 1–12.

John Scottus Eriugena and other Irish scholars.[24] Its subsequent popularity is perhaps explained by viewing it as one of the 'four master-books that could transmit directly to the Latin Middle Ages the teachings scholars needed to know, whether they were admirers or opponents of ancient philosophy'.[25] Of *De nuptiis*, Books 7 and 9 – devoted to arithmetic and to the technical content of music respectively – were most relevant for the study of music theory, along with the narrative of the first two books where the numerical ratios of creation resound in the music of the sacred Appollonian grove and of the heavenly spheres.[26] *De nuptiis* is contained in two tenth-century manuscripts that were probably copied in a Lotharingian scriptorium and subsequently entered the cathedral library at Bamberg: Bamberg, Staatsbibliothek, Msc. Class. 7, where it accompanies Boethius' *De institutione arithmetica*, and Msc. Class. 9, where it accompanies Hucbald and Boethius on music.[27] It appears throughout southern Germany, with known copies at Einsiedeln, Benediktbeuren, St Emmeram, Tegernsee and St Gallen during the eleventh century, and at Admont and Prüfening in the twelfth.[28]

Platonic influence in the south-German music treatises

The significance of number

The earliest responses to Platonic thought from the south-German circle are to be found in Bern of Reichenau's *Prologus in tonarium*. Already in the dedicatory letter to Archbishop Pilgrim of Cologne it is possible to detect the influence of Plato filtered through Boethius' *De institutione musica*. Following Boethius, Bern extols the importance of the 'four mathematical disciplines' and repeats the Platonic dictum that 'the whole structure of our soul and body had been joined by means of musical

---

[24] J. Préaux, 'Les manuscrits principaux du *De nuptiis Philologiae et Mercurii* de Martianus Capella', in G. Cambier, C. DeRoux and J. Préaux (eds), *Lettres latines du moyen âge et de la Renaissance* (Brussels, 1978), pp. 85–90.

[25] E. Jeauneau, 'L'héritage de la philosophie antique durant le haut moyen âge', in *Settimane di studio del Centro italiano di studi sull'alto medievo, XXII, 1974* (Spoleto, 1975), pp. 17–56.

[26] Teeuwen, *Harmony and the music of the spheres*, p. 154.

[27] C. Leonardi, 'I codici di Marziano Capella', *Aevum* 34 (1960), 5–6. H. Hoffmann, *Bamberger Handschriften des 10. und des 11. Jahrhunderts* (Hanover, 1995), pp. 126–7.

[28] Admont, Stiftsbibliothek, Cod. 390; Einsiedeln, Stiftsbibliothek, Cod. 266; Munich, Bayerische Staatsbibliothek, Clm 4559 (Benediktbeuren); Clm 14271, Clm 14401 (St Emmeram); Clm 19413 (Tegernsee); St Gallen, Stiftsbibliothek, Cods 381, 872; Vienna, Österreichische Nationalbibliothek, Cod. 12600 (Prüfening). See Leonardi, 'I codici di Marziano Capella', 1, 31–2, 90–1, 94–5, 97–8, 452–3, 461–2, 490.

coalescence'.²⁹ The distinguished teacher Hugh of St Victor would echo this sentiment in the early twelfth century.³⁰

In *Prologus* 4, Platonic number theory informs Bern's handling of the modes. *Timaeus* stressed the importance of numbers in the constitution of the universe, among which the quaternary was accorded pre-eminent significance. It was from the elements 'which are four in number' that the body of the world was made and harmonized by proportion.³¹ The significance of the quaternary lay not only in four elements, but also the motion of the cosmos, which was dependent on two sets of four numbers (the first – 1, 2, 4, 8 – producing double intervals and the second – 1, 3, 9, 27 – triple intervals).³² The creator of the world had also ordained four genera of beings: the heavenly beings, the birds of the air, the fish of the sea and the creatures of the land.³³ Bern would have found Plato's emphasis on the quaternary accentuated further in Calcidius' commentary, which was available to him at Reichenau, and which stressed in particular the mathematical and geometrical design behind the universe.³⁴ This was of considerable importance because Bern held that there were four modes, each divided into plagal and authentic, and having their finals (D, E, F, G) in the tetrachord of the *finales*. He considered this tetrachord to possess a natural virtue because 'from its four notes, the origin of all the modes or tones can

---

²⁹ Bern of Reichenau, *Prologus in tonarium*, ed. A. Rausch, *Die Musiktraktate des Abtes Bern von Reichenau. Edition und Interpretation* (Tutzing, 1999), pp. 31–2: Quod ego perpendens haut facile indagare valeo, quid causae extiterit, quod tu quem non solum quatuor metheseos disciplinarum speculatio quadratum . . . quoniam tota nostrae animae corporisque compago musica coaptatione coniungitur, animus quoque tuus sonora artis huius dulcedine suauius delectetur. Cf. Boethius, *De institutione musica* 1.1, ed. G. Friedlein, *Anicii Manlii Torquati Severini Boetii. De institutione arithmetica libri duo, De institutione musica libri quinque. Accedit geometria quae fertur Boetii* (Leipzig, 1867; repr. Frankfurt am Main, 1966), p. 179: Unde fit ut, cum sint quattuor matheseos disciplinae, ceterae quidem in investigatione veritatis laborent, musica vero non modo speculationi verum etiam moralitati coniuncta sit; p. 186: . . . id nimirum scientes quod tota nostrae animae corporisque compago musica coaptatione coniuncta sit.

³⁰ Hugh of St Victor, *Didascalicon* 2.13: Musica inter corpus et animam: est illa naturalis amicitia qua anima corpori non corporeis vinculis, sed affectibus quibusdam colligitur ad movendum et sensificandum ipsum corpus (*PL* 176.0756D).

³¹ Plato, *Timaeus* 32c, p. 25.6: Atque ita ex quattuor supra dictis materiis praeclaram istam machinam uisibilem contiguamque fabricatus est amica partium aequilibritatis ratione sociatam.

³² Ibid. 35bc, 43d, pp. 27, 39.

³³ Ibid. 40a, pp. 32.20–33.3: . . . sic deus in hoc opere suo sensili diuersa animalium genera statuit esse debere constituitque quattuor, primum caeleste plenum diuinitatis, aliud deinde praepes aeriuagum, tertium aquae liquoribus accommodatum, quartum quod terrena soliditas sustineret.

³⁴ Calcidius, *Commentarius* 1.14, 1.32, in Plato, *Timaeus*, pp. 66, 82.

be seen to proceed', just as from the four elements the fabric of the Platonic universe proceeds. For this reason the tetrachord of the *finales* was to be 'considered carefully' before all others.[35]

The quaternary, however, was not the only number of importance to Bern, for his statement also hints at the Platonic concept of unity. In *Timaeus*, unity, or the number one, was special. The world that Plato sought to expound was 'solitary, like a perfect animal'; it was the work of a single creator who made 'not two worlds or an innumerable number of them . . . but a single [world].[36] In *Commentarius in Somnium Scipionis* Macrobius interpreted this more explicitly. He called one the monad (μονάς), 'that is unity . . . itself not a number, but the fount and origin of numbers'.[37] Being perfect – 'the beginning and ending of all things' – unity referred ultimately to the creator. Macrobius' commentary, which is quoted and paraphrased in the subsequent lines of *Prologus in tonarium*, is clearly the main source for Bern's number theory at this point.[38] He writes that 'one, therefore, not a number but the beginning, is the fount and origin of all numbers'.[39] Bern may well have popularized this use of the phrase 'fount and origin' for it reappears, often devoid of the technical sense it has in Macrobius, in the later writings of the south-German circle.[40] In contrast to Abbot Bern, William of Hirsau stressed the importance of the tetrachord of the *graves* over that of the *finales*, by describing it as the 'fount and origin' of the other tetrachords.[41] In

---

[35] Bern, *Prologus* 4, p. 38: Inprimis tetracordum finalium diligentius est intuendum, cui tanta quaedam naturalis sonorum inest virtus, ut ex IIII cordarum eius origine omnis modorum seu tonorum potestas videatur procedere.

[36] Plato, *Timaeus* 31b, p. 24.2: Ut igitur exemplari, cuius aemulationem mutuabatur, etiam in numero similis esset, idcirco neque duo nec innumerabiles mundi sed unicus a deo factus est.

[37] Macrobius, *Commentarius in Somnium Scipionis* 1.6.7, p. 19: Unum autem quod μονάς id est unitas dicitur et mas idem et femina est, par idem atque impar, ipse non numerus sed fons et origo numerorum.

[38] F. C. Lochner in Theoger of Metz, *Musica*, ed. And trans. F. C. Lochner, 'Dietger (Theogerus) of Metz and his "Musica"' (Ph.D. dissertation, University of Notre Dame, 1995), p. 219 n. 491 ascribes Bern's use of 'fons et origo' to the *Geometria* sometimes attributed to Boethius. This is unlikely, as it was much simpler for Bern to have taken the term from Macrobius, to whom he was referring at this point.

[39] Bern, *Prologus* 4, p. 38: Unum ergo, non tam numerus quam principium, fons et origo est omnium numerorum, quod medio et fine caret, nisi forte pro sui perfectione sicut principium, ita et finis dicatur.

[40] The term 'fons et origo' occurs widely in Patristic sources and is used many times in the Middle Ages. Its use in this context, however, is unique to Macrobius, and is not reflected in any of its other appearances.

[41] William of Hirsau, *Musica*, ed. D. Harbinson, *Willehelmi Hirsaugensis Musica* (Rome, 1975), p. 20.

a further extension of the metaphor he interpreted the return of the species to their own tetrachord as being a return 'to the fount of their origin'.[42] William's pupil, Theoger of Metz, followed his teacher by attributing importance to the tetrachord of the *graves*; he considered it first because 'it is indeed the beginning, fount and origin of the other three [tetrachords]'.[43]

Bern's statement that the tetrachord of the *finales* is the 'origin of all the modes' carries with it a double implication. It implies an emphasis on the power of both unity and quaternary. The tetrachord of the *finales* functions as a quaternary by virtue of its four notes; it functions as a unity by virtue of the modes that originate from it. This reasoning presupposes that there is some intimate relationship between the numbers one and four that would enable such a state of affairs. Abbot Bern again looked to Macrobius' exposition of Plato to find this. It would have been apparent to him that four – the first square – was the third number of the series outlined in *Timaeus* 35bc, and he may have derived inspiration from two separate passages of Macrobius when he wrote 'one and one make two with the same added, that is two and two, makes four' by way of explanation.[44] In the end, however, he repeats the metaphysical explanation of the sacred Pythagorean tetrad offered by Macrobius in *Commentarius in Somnium Scipionis* 1.6.41.[45]

The concern to link unity and quaternary is also apparent in Herman's *Musica*, which similarly explains the quaternary's relevance to the gamut. Following Boethius and Macrobius, Herman used the term *quadruplum* (the ratio 4:1) to describe the two octaves of the gamut.[46] He believed this proportion 'more suitable than any other for the whole system of music'.[47] Herman did not quote Macrobius as his teacher had done, though the influence of *Commentarius in Somnium Scipionis* is clearly discernible in his treatise. 'The generation of the quadruplum stands among the first roots from which all numbers emerge, that is, one and two. For the ratio of one to two furnishes the duplum or octave.'[48] He continues that 'two

[42] Ibid. 8, p. 25.
[43] Theoger of Metz, *Musica* 14, p. 22. See also pp. 219–20 for the editor's commentary.
[44] Bern, *Prologus* 4, pp. 38–9: Unum et unum faciunt duo; quod si dixeris bis unum, creantur similiter duo, quae simul iuncta, idest duo et duo, faciunt IIII. Cf. Macrobius, *Commentarius in Somnium Scipionis* 1.6.23, 2.2.9, pp. 22, 100.
[45] Bern, *Prologus* 4, p. 39; cf. Macrobius, *Commentarius in Somnium Scipionis* 1.6.41, p. 25.
[46] Herman of Reichenau, *Musica*, ed. and trans. L. Ellinwood, *Musica Hermanni Contracti* (Rochester, NY, 1936), p. 18.
[47] Ibid. 2, p. 19: . . . quare musicae integritati quadrupla magis quam alia conveniat proportio.
[48] Ibid.: . . . quod ipsius quadrupli genitura statim inter primas omnium numerorum radices id est I et II mirabiliter emergit. Unum enim ad II comparatum duplum atque ideo diapason reddit.

multiplied by itself gives four, which, collated with one produces the quadruplum, that is, the double octave'.[49] It is possible that *Commentarius in Somnium Scipionis* 2.2.18 was the inspiration for this passage.[50] A little later Herman states his case in more explicitly Platonic terms: music lays claim 'to what the primordial nature of numbers created in the finest proportion'.[51] Herman's phrase 'primordial nature' alludes to the perfect pattern that the creator had in mind before he made the world.[52] The following sentence, which sums up Herman's position, is replete with Platonic significance:

> This, I declare, is that which, beginning from a position of unity, ended in squaring off the number four so that it cannot move; which, being the first of all [numbers] to rest on two mediants, unites the contention of the elements and tempers the diversity of the times, since it is most necessary in music, insofar as it [music] cannot in any respect be contrary or inconsonant with man, who exists by it, just as he does by the four elements.[53]

Herman stresses the path from one to four, just as his teacher Bern had done in *Prologus* 4. Four is created from a position of unity and is the first number to have two means. The authority for this statement is *Commentarius in Somnium Scipionis* 1.6.23. According to Macrobius a mean binds the extremities of a number together (as in the case of three, the first number to possess a mean); how much stronger, therefore, is the number four, which has two means.[54] Macrobius continues by explaining that the creator used the means to bind the elements together 'with an

---

[49] Ibid.: Binarius vero per se multiplicatus generat IV; cui unum collatum restituit quadruplum, quod est bis diapason.

[50] Macrobius, *Commentarius in Somnium Scipionis* 2.2.18, p. 102: Nam duo ad unum dupla sunt, de duplo autem διὰ πασῶν symphoniam nasci iam diximus, tria vero ad duo hemiolium numerum faciunt, hinc oritur διὰ πεντε, quattuor ad tria epitritus numerus est, ex hoc conponitur διὰ τεσσαρων; item quattuor ad unum in quadrupli ratione censentur, ex quo symphonia δις διὰ πασῶν nascitur.

[51] Herman, *Musica* 2, p. 20: Igitur breviter ac manifeste patet, quod id sibi merito musica dignitas vendicavit, quod primordialis numerorum natura excellentissimis proportionibus creavit.

[52] Plato, *Timaeus* 28a–29b, pp. 20–2.

[53] Herman, *Musica* 2, p. 20: Id inquam illud est, quod a principali unitatis incipiens positura, ne vacillare possit in quaternarii finivit quadratura; qui primus omnium duabus nitens medietatibus, elementorum foederat conpugnantiam, temporumque contemperat diversitatem, qui etiam musicae necessarius est quam maxime, quatenus homini ex ea sicut ex IV elementis existenti, in nullo contraria vel inconsonans possit haberi.

[54] Macrobius, *Commentarius in Somnium Scipionis* 1.6.23, p. 22.

unbreakable chain, as was affirmed in Plato's *Timaeus*'.[55] It is just possible to imagine Herman's excitement as he absorbed these texts through meticulous study; the result is the fusion of these influences in parts of his *Musica*.

One matter concerning the modes remained: the four modes could be divided into plagal and authentic varieties, giving eight tones. Bern again explains this in Platonic language. Eight is the first cube,[56] made from a 'doubling of that number that is begotten and begets, namely four'.[57] Elsewhere Macrobius referred to eight as 'a solid body' and Bern probably had these words in mind when he wrote that 'twice two twice is a solid body, which is eight'.[58] He could now state confidently the final part of his argument, which had connected unity, quaternary and octonary.

Therefore, it is very clear that the power of the fourfold number is so immense – albeit not without the help of the divine gift – that the harmony of all music arises from it and returns to it as if to the origin of its beginning; therefore, compelled by justice, the eight tones always return two by two to one of the four final notes as if returning to their parent.[59]

The significance of the quaternary is a recurrent theme of eleventh-century music theory. Herman's response has been noted, but the quaternary looms large in William of Hirsau, Aribo and Theoger of Metz. Its continuing importance as a subject in music theory is to be seen in *quaestio* 14 of the anonymous *Quaestiones in musica*. The text of the response, like much of *Quaestiones in musica*, is an amalgamation of sources, but the first section is copied closely from *Prologus* 4, omitting only one sentence.[60] The lengthy question title is, however, the author's own invention.

[55] Ibid. 1.6.24, p. 22: Quas ab hoc numero deus mundanae molis artifex conditorque mutatus, insolubili inter se vinculo elementa devinxit, sicut in Timaeo Platonis adscrtum est. Cf. Plato, *Timaeus* 32, pp. 24–5.
[56] Martianus Capella, *De nuptiis Philologiae et Mercurii*, ed. J. Willis, *Martianus Capella opera* (Leipzig, 1983), p. 268.
[57] Macrobius, *Commentarius in Somnium Scipionis* 1.5.15, p. 17.
[58] Bern, *Prologus* 4, p. 39: . . . bis II bis solidum corpus, quod est VIII; cf. Macrobius, *Commentarius in Somnium Scipionis* 1.5.11, p. 16: Ex his apparet octonarium numerum solidum corpus et esse et haberi. Si quidem unum apud geometras puncti locum obtinet . . .
[59] Bern, *Prologus* 4, p. 40: Ergo . . . satis claret non sine magno divini muneris nutu hanc vim quaternario esse ingenitam, ut totius armoniae concentus ab eo oriatur, et in eundem velut ad principii sui originem revertatur, quemadmodum illi VIII toni semper bini et bini ad unam ex IIII finalium cordis quadam dictante iustitia velut ad parentem redeunt. Cf. Plato, *Timaeus* 32c, p. 25.6: Atque ita ex quattuor supra dictis materiis praeclaram istam machinam uisibilem contiguamque fabricatus est.
[60] Ibid., pp. 27–9.

What may be the virtue and what the perfection of the quaternary number, that its disposition may be seen to constitute all harmony, since there are principally only four tetrachords, four species of *diatessaron*, four of *diapente*, four of *diapason* and ultimately there are only four modes according to nature and to the constitution of the ancients?[61]

The number theory of *Timaeus*, and especially the exegesis of Macrobius, furnished Bern of Reichenau with an explanation for the validity of the modal system he sought to describe. In this system the eight tones reverted to four modes, which in turn reverted to the unity of the tetrachord of the *finales*. It was for Bern a mirror of the cosmological and metaphysical order described in *Timaeus*. It would be incorrect to believe that a love of ancient philosophy in general was the driving force behind Bern's rationalization of the modes. Rather, was it Platonism – filtered through Macrobius in this instance – that offered him the opportunity to locate the modal system within the patterns of the natural world. For Bern, as for the eleventh-century clerk of Worms who compared the propriety of the musical proportions to the proper order of sacred and secular power in the world, music was a manifestation of natural order.[62]

Platonic metaphor and vocabulary

Eleventh-century responses to the Platonic inheritance involved not only number theory but also a distinct type of metaphor. Bern's use of the expression 'fount and origin' to describe the number one – taken directly from Macrobius – has already been mentioned, as has its subsequent modification by William of Hirsau. William uses the word 'fount' seven times in his treatise, sometimes separate from 'origin', which accompanies it in Macrobius' original version. It is always used to express the notion of natural propagation and progression. It is one example of the metaphor of generation that punctuates the writings of the south-German circle and frequently complements Platonic number theory.

Of the many ideas latent in *Timaeus*, that of generation held a particular attraction in the Middle Ages. Plato emphasized in his cosmological

---

[61] *Quaestiones in musica*, ed. R. Steglich, *Die Quaestiones in Musica. Ein Choraltraktat des zentralen Mittelalters und ihr mutmaßlicher Verfasser Rudolf von St. Trond (1070–1138)* (Leipzig, 1911; repr. 1971), p. 27: Quae virtus quaeve perfectio quaternarii sit numeri, ut eius dispositione tota fere armonia videatur constituti, cum et principaliter quatuor tantum sint tetracorda, quatuor species diatessaron, quatuor diapente, quatuor diapason et ad summam quatuor tantum sint modi secundum naturam et constitutionem antiquorum.
[62] *Worms Letter Collection* 52, ed. W. Bulst, *Die ältere Wormser Briefsammlung, MGH Briefe* 3, pp. 89–93. See above Chapter 3, pp. 119–20.

outline the importance of 'birth' for the universe: it is described as a 'world of generation' made by the creator.[63] Elsewhere it is said to have three natures: that which is generated; that in which the generation takes place; that from which similarity draws and borrows what is generated.[64] Towards the end of the portion of *Timaeus* known in the eleventh century, the main protagonist announces that 'being, space and generation . . . existed in their three ways before the heaven' and that 'the nurse of generation' was responsible for the combination of the elements.[65] The metaphor of generation is a recurrent one in the central Middle Ages. (Giles Constable has observed how the writers of saints' *Vitae* constantly used metaphors of generation, growth and a rich vocabulary of *topoi* from Antiquity in their works.[66]) It was used extensively by the south-German theorists. As with so much of the Platonic influence, they would have found the orientation of *Timaeus* strengthened in other sources, such as Boethius who, in the second book of *De institutione arithmetica*, introduced the procession of numeric series as 'a profound and admirable speculation, relevant both to Plato's generation of the soul in *Timaeus* and to the intervals of the discipline of harmony'.[67] Theorists such as Bern of Reichenau would have found the Platonic metaphors of generation emphasized in his reading of Macrobius, who used them quite extensively. In *Prologus* 4, as we have seen, Bern speaks of the modes 'proceeding' from four notes,[68] uses the verbs *generare* and *procreare* to describe how the number eight – the first cube – derives from the binary,[69] and emphasizes the generative power of the quaternary with the metaphor of the eight modes returning to the four

[63] Plato, *Timaeus* 29e, p. 22.17: Dicendum igitur, cur rerum conditor fabricatorque geniturae omne hoc instituendum putauerit.

[64] Ibid. 50d, p. 48.12: At uero nunc trinum genus animo sumendum est: quod gignitur, item aliud in quo gignitur, praeterea tertium ex quo similitudinem trahit mutuaturque quod gignitur.

[65] Ibid. 52d, p. 51.6: Haec est meae quidem sententiae mens esse et ante mundi quoque sensilis exornationem fuisse tria haec: existens locum generationem. Igitur generationis nutriculam humectatam modo, modo ignitam, terraeque item et aeris formas suscipientem ceterasque pedissequas passiones perpetientem omniformem uisu uideri.

[66] G. Constable, *The reformation of the twelfth century* (Cambridge, 1996), p. 125.

[67] Ibid., p. 219. Boethius, *De institutione arithmetica*, 2.2, ed. Friedlein, p. 80.5: Est autem quaedam in hac re profunda et miranda speculatio et ut ait Nicomachus enmusotaton theorema proficiens et ad Platonicam in Timaeo animae generationem et ad intervalla armonicae disciplinae.

[68] Bern, *Prologus* 4, p. 38: . . . ut ex IIII cordarum eius origine omnis modorum seu tonorum potestas videatur procedere.

[69] Ibid., p. 39: Adde etiam quod idem quaternarius a binario, quem supra diximus principium esse, generatur, a quo et octonarius, qui est primus cubus, procreatur.

finals 'as if returning to their parent'.[70] It recalls Macrobius who spoke of four as a number that 'is both begotten and begets'[71] and of arithmeticians honouring 'odd numbers with the name "father" and even ones with the name "mother"'.[72]

Bern's pupil Herman of Reichenau develops this imagery, probably owing to the influence both of his teacher and of his studies in Platonic literature. He applies the metaphor of generation to the gamut, declaring that the two octaves of the monochord are said not 'to be born twice, but that those already born, in the manner of the seven days of the week, are repeated or renewed'.[73] Of particular interest is his use of the verb *nasci* (to be born). The four tetrachords are explained by Herman in a similar manner: 'these names [*graves, finales, superiores* and *excellentes*] indicate their particular genealogy, like children born in their parent's likeness'.[74] In later passages of his treatise Herman again exploits the metaphor of generation: 'the generation of the principal tetrachord begets all the species of *diatessaron*';[75] when the species of *diatessaron* are reproduced in the higher octave the resulting species is 'not born from another generation' but is a mere repetition.[76] The same preoccupation with birth and origin is continued in William's *Musica*, which contains numerous examples of the generation metaphor – employed through such verbs as *nasci* and *generare*.[77] It is also apparent in the treatise of his pupil Theoger of Metz.

[70] Ibid., p. 40 (see p. 157 n. 59 for text); cf. Plato, *Timaeus* 32c, p. 25.6: Atque ita ex quattuor supra dictis materiis praeclaram istam machinam uisibilem contiguamque fabricatus est.

[71] Macrobius, *Commentarius in Somnium Scipionis* 1.5.16, p. 18: . . . aut de duplicato eo qui et generatur et generat id est quattuor – nam hic numerus quattuor et nascitur de duobus et octo generat.

[72] Ibid. 1.6.1, p. 18: Nam impar numerus mas et par femina vocatur, item arithmetici imparem patris et parem matris appellatione venerantur.

[73] Herman, *Musica* 1, pp. 18–19: Ubi intuendum non alias atque alias denuo nasci; sed semel natas more VII septimanae dierum iterum repeti sive innovari.

[74] Ibid. 2, p. 22: Quae quia tam chordarum numero quam continua successione nec non etiam tropica institutione solum quaternarium repraesentant; propriam velut filii ad parentum vultus nati generositatem demonstrant.

[75] Ibid. 5, p. 27: Videsne quaeso ut principalis quadrichordi genitura omnes diatessaron species propriis comprehensas literis procreet.

[76] Ibid., p. 29: . . . sciendum est quod si quis ea quae dicta sunt in secundo diapason facere tentaverit, non aliam genituram diatessaron nasci, sed eam quae iam dicta est repeti . . .

[77] William, *Musica* 5, p. 19: Hoc siquidem in inferiori diapason duplicatum generat ex se tetrachordum Finalium; 7, p. 22: Media item tetrachorda Finalium dico et Superiorum, si conferantur, omnes diapente species eodem naturae et ordinis decore nascuntur; p. 23: Vel quid ipsarum consummatio, nisi tetrachordi Finalis ex principali genitura quaedam productio?

Theoger who, before embracing the monastic life, had studied in the secular schools with the distinguished master Manegold of Lautenbach, probably devoted much energy to reading Plato, Martianus Capella and Macrobius.[78] He speaks of the structure of the tetrachords being 'brought forth through arithmetical generation'.[79] Worthy of note is his use of the verb *gignere*, patterned after Calcidius' translation of the three natures of creation in *Timaeus* 50d.[80]

The metaphors of generation that are repeatedly used by the south-German circle possess a teleological implication. They suggest the existence of a world that is the outcome of generation, a world that is governed by numerical ratios and an organic order. One distinguished scholar has recognized at this time a growing perception of the world as an entity.[81] He has identified the spread of the word *universitas* to designate the world in descriptions and treatises, especially in those of twelfth-century authors such as Honorius Augustodunensis (*c.* 1080-*c.* 1140), Gerhoh of Reichersberg (1093-1169) or Hugh of St Victor (*c.* 1096-1141).[82] But in truth the beginnings of this trend occur in the eleventh century. It is in William of Hirsau's *Musica* that *universitas* is first found. In Chapter 5 William speaks of the 'natural universe'[83] and when he begins Chapter 14 by stating 'it is to be understood as universal that all authentic [modes], beginning at the *finales*, ascend to the *excellentes* and finish in the *superiores*',[84] he is emphasizing the universality of the dogma, not of its understanding. It is universal because it describes the universal or 'natural' and correct order to which music is subject. The natural universe, in so far as it pertained to music, was most frequently represented by the monochord. The connexion is made explicit by William in two passages where he refers

[78] Lochner in Theoger of Metz *Musica*, pp. 236-42.
[79] Ibid., pp. 225-6.
[80] Theoger, *Musica* 14.2, p. 22: Nam gignit tetrachordum finalium dimensionis proportione sesquitertia, tetrachordum uero superiorum dupla; see also ibid. p. 217. Compare Plato, *Timaeus* 50d, p. 48.12: At uero nunc trinum genus animo sumendum est: quod gignitur, item aliud in quo gignitur, praeterea tertium ex quo similitudinem trahit mutuaturque quod gignitur.
[81] M. D. Chenu, 'Nature and man: the renaissance of the twelfth century', in Chenu, *Nature, man and society in the twelfth century*, p. 5.
[82] Ibid., pp. 5-7. See Honorius Augustodunensis, *Liber XII quaestionibus* 2, 4, 12 (*PL* 172.1179, 1180, 1184-5); Gerhoh of Reichersberg, *De aedificio Dei* 1 (*PL* 194.1193); Hugh of St Victor, *Commentaria in Hierarchiam coelestem S. Dionysii Areopagitae* 3 (*PL* 175.0980).
[83] William, *Musica* 5, p. 19.
[84] Ibid. 14, pp. 37-9: Universaliter autem hic notandum est, quod omnes autentici a Finalibus incipientes ad Excellentes ascendunt, et in Superioribus distinguuntur.

to the universal nature or structure of the monochord,[85] but the idea was widespread among the south-German theorists. The monochord appears in their writings as an instrument that embodies natural order. Music treatises frequently begin with an analysis of the monochord (the treatises by Bern, Herman, William and Theoger, for example) and we will see that texts devoted to its measurement were a staple of music theory 'textbook codices'.[86] The monochord, then, was the embodiment of each and every theoretical system and a paradigm of universal and natural order. Nowhere are the Platonic implications of this more apparent among the treatises of the south-German circle than at the beginning of Aribo's *De musica*.

Aribo and Platonic language

A popular theorem for understanding the division of the monochord underwent a detailed analysis and critique in Aribo's treatise. It was called the *quadripartita figura* and is attributed to a monk of Regensburg called Otker in its only surviving source, a manuscript from the south-German monastery of Benediktbeuren (now Munich, Bayerische Staatsbibliothek, Clm 4622).[87] This manuscript, however, was copied after Aribo wrote *De musica*, for it purports to transmit a set of monochord measurements 'according to Aribo'.[88] A diagrammatic representation of the quadripartite figure occurs, without mention of Otker, in William of Hirsau's *Musica*, which was written in St Emmeram before he became abbot of Hirsau in 1069. This diagram, which at first William calls *figura monochordi*, but later *cribrum monochordi* and *theorema troporum*, is virtually identical to that discussed by Aribo.[89] For these reasons it seems plausible to trace Aribo's knowledge of the diagram to William's *Musica* (see Plates 4 and 5). Aribo called it *quadripartita figura modernorum* ('the quadripartite figure of the

---

[85] Ibid. 5, 19, pp. 19, 50.
[86] See Chapter 5, pp. 211–12.
[87] Munich, Bayerische Staatsbibliothek, Clm 4622, fols 178v–179r; *RISM B* 3/3, p. 91; M. Bernhard (ed.), 'Otkeri Ratisbonensis monachi aetatis incertae mensura quadripartitae figurae', in M. Bernhard, *Clavis Gerberti. Eine Revision von Martin Gerberts Scriptores ecclesiastici de musica sacra potissimum (St. Blasien 1784)* (Munich, 1989), pp. 199–200.
[88] Munich, Bayerische Staatsbibliothek, Clm 4622, fol. 178v: 'Organica dispositio secundum aribonem'. What the scribe attributed to Aribo, however, was in fact copied from a short anonymous treatise on the measurement of the monochord found in two other contemporary sources without attribution to Aribo: the eleventh-century Tegernsee manuscript, Munich, Bayerische Staatsbibliothek, Clm 18914, fol. 41r, and a lost twelfth-century manuscript from St Blasien. The measurements were published by Martin Gerbert, *GS* 1, p. 347a, based upon the St Blasien copy. See T. J. H. McCarthy, 'Aribo's *De musica* and Abbot William of Hirsau', *Revue bénédictine* 116 (2006), 74–5.
[89] William, *Musica* 14, 40, 41, pp. 37–40, 70–5.

Plate 4   *Figura monochordi* from William of Hirsau's *Musica*. Vienna, Österreichische Nationalbibliothek. Cod. 51, fol. 1v

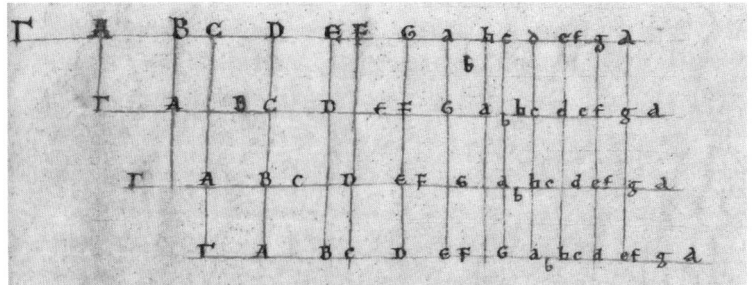

Plate 5   The *Quadripartita figura modernorum* criticized by Aribo. Darmstadt, Universitäts- und Hochschulbibliothek, 1988, fol. 171r

moderns'), perhaps in deference to the learned abbot of Hirsau, whom elsewhere he called 'the greatest among musicians, without doubt the Orpheus and Pythagoras of the moderns', and with whom he was certainly friendly.[90]

Aribo writes that this diagram is constructed so 'that the first series contains the measure of the first and second modes at the same time, the second [series] the third and fourth modes, the third [series] the fifth and sixth modes and the fourth [series] the seventh and eighth modes'.[91] Its purpose, therefore, is to aid the recognition of the modes, which from the time of Herman of Reichenau had been a central concern among German music theorists.[92] Aribo, however, perceived inconsistencies in the diagram. He criticized it on two counts: because of its 'perverse

[90] Aribo, *De musica*, ed. J. Smits van Waesberghe, *Aribonis De musica* (Rome, 1951), p. 42.57: Nam meam dilexit parvitatem ultra parvitatis dignitatem, qui est musicus primus, modernus videlicet Orpheus et Pithagoras.
[91] Ibid., p. 1.8: Quae ita construitur, ut una series primi insimul et secundi toni mensuram contineat, secunda tercii et quarti, tercia quinti et sexti, quarta septimi et octavi.
[92] Herman, *Musica* 19, p. 57.

tetrachordal arrangement' and because of the 'perverse disjunction' that results from this.[93] The figure, therefore, is visually misleading and shows an apparent disjunction between the fourth note of the *graves* and the first note of the *finales*, and again between the fourth note of the *superiores* and the first note of the *excellentes*. According to the natural structure of the monochord, however, these notes should occupy one and the same place or, in other words, be conjunct. William of Hirsau fully endorsed the principle of conjunct tetrachords within the octave as first outlined by Herman of Reichenau, and devoted the four chapters of his *Musica* following the introduction of *cribrum monochordi* to a discussion of the necessity for conjunction around D and d (in the process openly censuring Boethius and Guido of Arezzo for failing to recognize the double function of these pitches).[94] It seems, however, that Aribo was disturbed by the apparent visual distortion in the diagram: a point of pedantry, perhaps, but an ensuing discussion that is rich in Platonic metaphor and vocabulary.

The significance of the Platonic influence in this example lies in the language of Aribo's argument.

> Men are accustomed very much to disapprove whenever they see anyone degenerate from the virtue of his parent. We know indeed that each and every musical figure took the origin of its birth from the primitive disposition of the rule of the monochord. When, however, we see here collected those things which are there dispersed and here dispersed which are there collected, surely this figure degenerates from its parent, namely the measure of the monochord?[95]

The image of a parent recurs throughout *Timaeus*, where it is often used as a personification for the idea of the perfect pattern in reflexion of which the world is formed.[96] We have already seen it used by Bern and Herman

---

[93] Aribo, *De musica*, pp. 3.22: *De perversa tetrachordorum collectione*; 3.26: *De perversa diezeuxi, id est disiunctione*.

[94] William, *Musica* 15-18, pp. 40-9.

[95] Aribo, *De musica*, p. 2.18: Solent homines admodum inprobare, cum vident aliquem de parentum virtute degenerare. Scimus autem et istam et omnem musicam figuram nativitatis suae primordium sumpsisse de primitiva regularis monochordi dispositione. Cum autem hic videamus collecta, quae ibi sunt dispersa, hic dispersa quae ibi sunt collecta, nonne ista degenerat figura a sua genitrice, monochordi videlicet mensura?

[96] Plato, *Timaeus* 28a-29b. Plato considers two alternatives: that the creator fashioned his work after an unchangeable pattern, of necessity fair and perfect; that he looked to a created pattern, neither fair nor perfect. This dichotomy might also be posed by asking – as Plato does – whether the world has a beginning or is always in existence. The Christian is obliged to answer that the world was created, but fortunately Plato though likewise. Hence the creator framed the world in likeness of that which is apprehended by

of Reichenau. From the idea of the perfect and unchangeable pattern comes the requirement that the beginning of everything should be according to nature.[97] In the case at hand we can consider the monochord to be a copy formed in the likeness of the unchangeable pattern. It, being the tangible representation of this pattern, can be personified as the parent of musical figures. This is exactly what Aribo does. The 'quadripartite figure', however, 'degenerates from its parent'. This is because it confuses the order of certain things, which is in direct opposition to the nature of God's world. God, following the perfect pattern, brought order out of disorder.[98]

In the three subsequent chapters Aribo sets out the faults of the quadripartite figure in detail.

Aribo, *De musica* [6]: Concerning the perverse collection of tetrachords.

In this figure all of the *graves* and all of the *finales* are collected in one place. Similarly with all of the *superiores* and even all of the *excellentes*. What the nature of the monochord does not at all yield is to share out different places for each of the four tetrachords.[99]

Aribo, *De musica* [7]: Concerning the perverse *diezeuxis*, that is disjunction.

In this figure the fourth of the *graves* and the first of the *finales*, the fourth of the *superiores* and the first of the *excellentes* are disjunct, though in the natural structure of the monochord they hold one and the same place, as in one and the same letter.[100]

---

reason and mind and is unchangeable. There is still a difference, however, because these attributes are external to the *demiurgos* (literally 'the craftsman'). Boethius, in *metrum* 9 of *De consolatione philosophiae* 3 minimizes this difference, regarding the creator as one who creates out of his own nature.

[97] Plato, *Timaeus*, 29b, pp. 21.24–22.2: Et quoniam rationem originis explicare non est facile factu, distinguendae sunt imaginis exempliqué naturae.

[98] Ibid., 30a, pp. 22.24–23.3: . . . omne uisibile corporeumque motu importuno fluctuans neque umquam quiescens ex inordinata iactatione redegit in ordinem sciens ordinatorum fortunam confusis inordinatisque praestare.

[99] Aribo, *De musica*, p. 3.22: *De peversa tetrachordum collectione*. In ista figura collectae sunt in unum locum omnes graves, in unum locum omnes finales. Similiter in unum omnes superiores, omnes etiam excellentes. Quod penitus non concedit monochordi natura, quae cuilibet tetrachordorum quatuor diversa partitur loca.

[100] Ibid., p. 3.26: *De peversa diezeuxi, id est disiunctione*. In ista figura disiunctae sunt quarta gravium, prima finalium, quarta superiorum, prima excellentium, quae in monochordi naturali structura unum et eundem obtinet locum, ut pote in una et eadem littera.

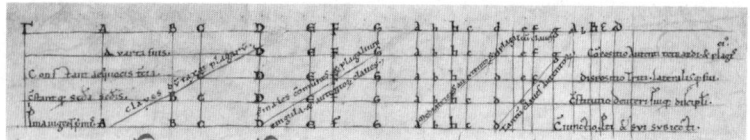

Plate 6   Aribo's *Caprea*. Darmstadt, Universitäts- und Hochschulbibliothek, 1988, fol. 171v

Aribo, *De musica* [8]: Concerning the unnaturally high position of *protus* and the inappropriately low position of *tetrardus*.
In this same quadripartite figure *protus* is in the highest position, *tetrardus* in the lowest; and how contrary it is to the nature of the monochord anyone can very easily contemplate, even if he is only imbued with a mediocre knowledge of these matters.[101]

Beyond the technical matters that Aribo points out, the recurrent theme of his criticism is that the quadripartite figure is wrong because it goes against the nature of the monochord. The monochord, as we have seen, is the manifestation of the universal nature, which in the words of *Timaeus* 'never departs from her own nature'.[102] It contravenes what Aribo would have understood as the third of three natures outlined by Plato.[103] Aribo's point is that the quadripartite figure does not resemble what occurs naturally. His answer to this state of affairs was his own amended version of William's *cribrum monochordi*, proposed out of a desire to reconcile the discordance of the quadripartite figure with the manifestation of *natura* in the monochord (Plate 6).

Aribo chose an allegorical title for this new diagram: *caprea* (a goat or roe). His chapter entitled 'Quare caprea tali nomine censeatur et quid praesuli offeratur' ('Why *caprea* may be called by such kind of name and why it is offered to the bishop') contains two quotations from Genesis 27, which relate the story of the appropriation by Jacob of Esau's birthright.[104] Jacob offered two kids from the herd of goats to Isaac and hence Aribo's *caprea* may be seen not only as a new 'offering', but also as a learned allusion to its

---

[101] Ibid., pp. 3.28: *De acumine non naturali proti, et gravitate tetrardi non competenti*. In hac eadem quadripartita figura, protus est acutissimus, tetrardus gravissimus, quod quam contrarium sit naturae monochordi, potest quivis etiam mediocriter his inbutus facillime contemplari.

[102] Plato, *Timaeus* 50bc, p. 48.6:. . . in quam imprimuntur uaria signacula, moueturque et conformatur omnimode ab introeuntibus, ipsa nec formam nec motum habens ex natura sua.

[103] Ibid., 50d, p. 48.12: At uero nunc trinum genus animo sumendum est: quod gignitur, item aliud in quo gignitur, praeterea tertium ex quo similitudinem trahit mutuaturque quod gignitur.

[104] Aribo, *De musica*, p. 5.46; Gen. 27.20, 27.31.

superseding the older or 'first-born' quadripartite figure. The language he uses to advocate his *caprea* again makes use of the Platonic vocabulary.

When I reflect upon these things in my own mind with constant wonder, and consider what might occur more naturally, I have found *caprea* very like a mother ... She has *protus* in the lowest position and *tetrardus* in the highest, so that they do not lose the nature that they possess in the bosom of the mother in the dwelling place of the daughter.[105]

The inspiration for Aribo's language here is *Timaeus* 50d, where Plato likens the 'receiving principle' to a mother, the source or spring to a father and the intermediate nature to a child.[106] It is easy for a Christian reading Plato to identify the father: he is God. Aribo's use of the feminine – following that of Plato – indicates that *caprea* is the mother. We might also call her a reflexion of *natura*. The nature that the figures of music possess in *caprea* is also that which they possess in reality; their forms 'which enter into and go out of her are the likenesses of truly existing things'.[107] Aribo has drawn very closely on Platonic themes to express his argument. But he has done this in a very Christian context, for nature remains subservient to the will of God. This is made perfectly clear in the following passage.

But thanks and praise be to the Father of lights from whom comes 'every best gift and every perfect gift' [James 1.17] for our diagram, or rather His diagram (that we may say with the psalmist 'not unto us, O Lord, not unto us: but to Thy name give glory' [Ps. 113.9]), which lays down the divisions of the tropes well and proposes clearly according to the monochord their natural difference of low and high position.[108]

---

[105] Ibid., p. 4.31: Haec cum diutina mecum admiratione revolverem et, si quid naturalius occurreret, indagarem, inveni capream matri simillimam. Quae habet in uno loco quartam gravium, primam finalium, quartam superiorum, prima excellentium. Quae habet in quatuor locis diversis, graves, finales, superiores, excellentes. Quae habet protum gravissimum, tetrardum acutissimum, ut naturam, quam in principali genitricis gremio possideant, in filiae mansiunculis non amittant.

[106] Plato, *Timaeus* 50d, p. 48.14: Decet ergo facere comparationem similitudinemque impertiri illi quidem quod suscipit matris, at uero unde obuenit patris, illi autem naturae quae inter haec duo est prolis.

[107] Ibid. 50c, p. 48.8: Quae uero ingrediuntur, formas mutant aliasque alia et diuersa cernuntur, eademque quae introeunt et egrediuntur simulacra sunt uere existentium rerum miro quodam uixque explicabili modo formata ab isdem uere existentibus rebus.

[108] Aribo, *De musica*, p. 5.40: Sed gratia lausque sit patri luminum a quo est omne datum optimum et omne donum perfectum, nostra immo sua ut dicamus cum psalmista: Non nobis domine, non nobis sed nomini tuo da gloriam, et bene divisiones troporum constituit, et naturalem secundum monochordorum gravitatis et acuminis eorum differentiam evidenter proponit.

Caprea is His diagram because it is a reflexion of the perfect order after which God fashioned the world. Thus the content of Plato's *Timaeus* is here cast in a Christian die by Aribo. The dedication of his treatise to Bishop Ellenhard of Freising may well have influenced his approach, for this section seems to be especially addressed to Aribo's patron. The criticism of the quadripartite figure and praise of *caprea* using the Platonic concepts of natural order is an extension of reasoning to be found in the writings of many of his contemporaries, but the extent to which Aribo dwells and delights on this subject may well have been inspired by a desire to indulge in a display of sophisticated erudition for his patron.

God and natura

Two aspects of eleventh-century Platonism that have already been broached remain to be discussed: the expression of Platonic thought in a Christian context and the personification of *natura*. In reality they are closely linked. Theoger of Metz, in one passage of his *Musica* that echoes Calcidius, states that 'We have most rightly called "natural" those pitches and intervals for which the creative nature who formed all things in number, weight and measure provided such underlying exemplars, or impressed such exemplars upon them'.[109] Theoger uses the term *creatrix natura* to refer to the mother of creation who is presented as an important figure from *Timaeus* 50 onwards.[110] This passage also contains an instructive example of how the theorists (and their contemporaries) were seeking to interpret Plato in a Christian context, for in addition to echoing *Timaeus* it quotes Wisdom 11.21: 'But thou hast ordered all things in measure, weight and number'. The importance of measure and number was implied by *Timaeus* and additionally reinforced by Calcidius' commentary, which takes the numerical-philosophical postulations of *Timaeus* and applies them to sensible matter.

The science of music was that of ordering the proportions relating to sound. The importance of Wisdom 11.21 – quoted by Theoger – had not been lost on music theorists. 'Thou', of course, refers to God; but in

---

[109] Theoger, *Musica* 8.13, p. 17: Rectissime igitur diximus uoces uel uocum modos naturales, quibus creatrix natura, quae omnia formauit in numero, pondere et mensura, talia substrauit uel impressit exemplaria; see also p. 228. Cf. Calcidius, *Commentarius* 29, in Plato *Timaeus*, p. 79.

[110] Plato, *Timaeus* 50b, p. 48.4: . . . recepit enim cuncta nec ullam ex isdem formam trahit, et cum uelut intra gremium eius formentur quae recipiuntur; 51a, p. 49.7: Ideoque facit generati uisibilis animalis matrem corporeaeque substantiae receptaculum neque terram neque aquam . . .

Timaeus Plato had spoken of a being very like unto a God: of a creator who 'made this world of generation'.[111] Martianus Capella identified this creator as the monad.[112] Macrobius did not go this far, but spoke more reasonably and repeatedly of a divine creator. Boethius built upon this in the opening chapters of *De institutione arithmetica*: 'All things that are built from the primeval nature of things seem to be shaped according to the law of number. For this was the principal archetype in the mind of the Maker'.[113] Bern of Reichenau described an *artifex natura* as a real creative power under the control of the creator, similar to the Platonic *demiurgos*: 'Upon the creator's command the artificer nature associated itself with the number four for good reason'.[114] It was in four books that the Gospel has 'gone out into all lands and unto the ends of the earth'.[115] Bern further Christianized the Platonic significance of the quaternary by quoting Ps. 46.7, which employs a pertinent quadruple form of the rhetorical color *repetitio*: 'Psallite Deo nostro, psallite; psallite regi nostro, psallite sapienter'. The Christian interpretation of Platonic philosophy is felt strongly in William's *Musica*. At the beginning of the dialogue Otloh asks William to 'reveal the hidden origin and nature of the art of harmony, in as much as the author of nature allows it'.[116] William then reminds his interlocutor that this discussion must take place 'in the name of Jesus' before embarking on the subject-matter of the treatise.[117] He explains the principality of the four tetrachords as being 'what nature, or indeed the author of nature wished to bring forth first through the quaternary'.[118] The tacit implication of God 'the author of nature' underpins William's many references to nature as a force in the

[111] Plato, *Timaeus* 30a.
[112] Martianus Capella, *De nuptiis Philologiae et Mercurii* 7.731; 9.992, pp. 262, 383.
[113] Boethius, *De institutione arithmetica* 1.2, p. 12.14-17.
[114] Bern, *Prologus* 4, p. 39: Quaternarius vero, qui duas medietates obtinuit. Et quia tunc arcius extima vinciuntur, quando medietas geminatur, merito artifex natura iussa creatoris hunc sibi numerum adscivit (this is a difficult sentence, the text of which may well be corrupt). See also Lochner in Theoger, *Musica*, p. 229. Lochner incorrectly states that Herman referred to a 'creative nature' explicitly. Nevertheless, the presence of a creative nature is implicit in Herman's language.
[115] Romans 10.18. Bern, *Prologus* 4, p. 40: Sub huius numeri mysterio consonus evangelistarum sonus in omnem terram exivit, et in fines orbis terrae dulcissima predicationis eorum vox processit.
[116] William, *Musica* 1, p. 13: . . . ipsius etiam harmonicae artis originem et naturam, quantum auctor naturae concesserit, adhuc latentem proferas.
[117] Ibid.: . . . respirationi atque meditationi reliquum diei concedatur spatium, et cras in nomine Iesu congregemur, sicque ipso nos mediante ac ducente propositum iter incipiamus.
[118] Ibid. 3, p. 16: Illud est quod natura, immo naturae auctor primo per quadrupla proferri voluit.

realm of music theory.[119] Like Aribo, he too uses the Biblical phrase 'Father of lights' in referring to God's presence behind and in nature.[120] Both theorists were in fact using a commonplace metaphor associating light with the supreme being (described in *Timaeus* and its commentators) that had been used by Christians from the time of St Augustine.[121]

These attempts to apply the Platonic inheritance in a Christian context resulted in the gradual appearance of a being called *natura*. *Timaeus* 50 hinted at such a construct: 'a universal nature that receives all bodies . . . who never departs from her own nature'.[122] It is also likely that such a figure was made more appealing to the eleventh-century minds by the personification of philosophy as the lady who visited the incarcerated and disconsolate Boethius of the *Consolation of Philosophy*. *Natura*, therefore, became a sort of governess or mistress of music in the south-German treatises: she fulfils the function of the mother figure implied in Aribo's discourse on the quadripartite figure and *caprea*. She is the bequeather of music and consequently it owes her obedience. Only that which conforms to her rules is to be accepted. This view is to be seen in Herman of Reichenau's rejection of a certain notational system for being 'contrary to the laws of nature herself'.[123] It is also apparent in Aribo's rejection of the quadripartite figure for being 'against the nature of the monochord', as well as in the final commendatory words of *De musica* that assert 'by no means does nature speak of one thing and my *caprea* of another'.

The personification of nature is not a phenomenon unique to music theory, but is also to be found in contemporary literature. The prolific and widely-read author Honorius Augustodunensis speaks of a similar artisan who made the universe 'like a great zither upon which he placed strings to yield a variety of sounds'.[124] In a roughly contemporary work by the French

---

[119] Ibid. 4–10, 16, pp. 17–31, 42. In the light of this Lochner's statement (Theoger, *Musica*, p. 230) that William does not consider *natura* a spontaneously active force is in need of modification.

[120] James 1.17. William, *Musica* 9, p. 26: Quod tum in promptu erit, si Patre luminum donante lucidam ut incepi non solum specierum diapason quam postulas, sed et omnium pari modo memorabilium quatuor rerum seriem indissociabiliter sibi coherentem ex tam purissimo quam verissimo fonte naturae produxero.

[121] See Chenu, 'The Platonisms of the twelfth century', pp. 51–2. See also R. Bultmann, 'Zur Geschichte der Lichtsymbolik im Altertum', *Philologus* 97 (1948), 1–36.

[122] Plato, *Timaeus* 50c, p. 48.

[123] Herman, *Musica* 18, p. 56: . . . immo contra ipsius iura naturae eadem signa in nona potius quam in octava regione veniant.

[124] Honorius Augustodunensis, *Liber XII quaestionibus* 2 (*PL* 172.1179B): Summus namque opifex universitatem quasi magnam citharam condidit, in qua veluti varias chordas ad multiplices sonos reddendos posuit. Chenu, 'Nature and man', p. 8.

abbot Arnold of Bonneval, the Platonic concepts of the supreme artisan are firmly linked with God, though the ideas of *Timaeus* remain: 'God distributed the things of nature like the members of a great body, assigning to all their proper places and names, their fitting measures and offices'. Arnold continues that 'nothing is confused to God', for to use the phraseology of *Timaeus*, He followed a perfect pattern in creation; 'the entire fabric of the world . . . solid and concordant, perseveres in its lawful and ordered manner'.[125] In the world of music, this *natura* manifests herself in the monochord, her instrument, and the yardstick by which all arrangements of the gamut are measured.

Contemporary understanding of this is shown to striking effect in a picture contained in a twelfth-century music theory manuscript copied at the monastery of Sts Ulrich and Afra in Augsburg: Wolfenbüttel, Herzog-August Bibliothek, Gud. lat. 334 8°, fol. 2v (Plate 7). The picture, one of a number at the start of the codex (also included are St Gregory the Great and Pythagoras), shows a female figure seated at the monochord that has the notes of the gamut marked on its side. Above her is the name *musica*, perhaps inspired by the goddess described in Book 9 of Martianus Capella's *De nuptiis Philologiae et Mercurii*. She might also be called *natura*.

Conclusion

Early in 1085 the staunch Gregorian polemicist Manegold of Lautenbach published his *Liber contra Wolfelmum* which, among other things, attacked certain Platonic doctrines on the world soul. Macrobius was singled out along with Plato as one who presumed to illuminate the divine obscurities.[126] Though Martianus Capella is not mentioned, it can be assumed that he too was intended in Manegold's attack. The warnings of *Liber contra Wolfelmum* were partially designed to comfort Gregorian partisans by using a frequently exploited theme of reform rhetoric: the snares of pagan literature. This theme had already been elucidated by Peter Damian, whose writings were widely admired and copied in Germany

---

[125] Arnold of Bonneval, *De operibus sex dierum* (*PL* 189.1515A–1516C): Et [Deus] quasi magni corporis membra, rerum naturas, distinguens propria loca, et nomina, congruas mensuras et officia assignavit . . . tota illa mundi fabrica . . . et solida et concors in sua lege perseverat et ordine. Chenu, 'Nature and man', p. 9.

[126] Manegold of Lautenbach, *Liber contra Wolfelmum* 2, ed. W. Hartmannm, *MGH Quellen* 8, p. 48: Si quis vero ea audire desideret ab eodem Platone sive a Macrobio, qui easdem tenebras quodam modo elucidandas suscepit, hec animadvertere poterit; Hüttig, *Macrobius im Mittelalter*, pp. 69–74.

Plate 7   *Musica* personified and seated at the monochord. Wolfenbüttel, Herzog-August Bibliothek, Gud. Lat. 334 8°, fol. 2v

during the eleventh century.[127] Its influence is to be seen in figures such as Otloh of St Emmeram, who lamented the sway that pagan literature had held over him. But such reactions signal the extent to which Plato and his commentators had gripped the imaginations of eleventh-century clerks. Manegold, in his youth, had been an avid student of Plato and other pagan authors, possibly composing a commentary on *Timaeus*.[128] Eleventh-century letter collections like those from Worms, Regensburg, Hanover and Hildesheim contain numerous references to Platonic doctrines of nature and creation.[129] The references to Macrobius by eleventh-century authors such as Thietmar of Merseburg, Manfred of Magdeburg and Adam of Bremen call attention to demand for his works.[130] The monastery of Blaubeuren – a house with close connexions to Hirsau and the reform movement – received its copy of Macrobius in the late eleventh century.[131]

It was not so much pagan literature as its improper use that frightened Manegold. Under no circumstances might it be used to explain creation in a way that would enable it to compete with Christianity. In the hands of the south-German theorists this was not the case. Their reaction to Plato and the other ancient authors shows them to have been acutely aware of the need to harmonize Platonic ideas with Christian dogma. This is apparent in their avoidance of Plato's 'world soul' in favour of identifying the creator with God. They concentrated their efforts on applying a rich variety of Platonic themes to music: unity and quaternary proportions, generation and birth, and natural order as the arbiter of music theory. In this Boethius and Calcidius were important Platonic conduits, but the most influential intermediate author was Macrobius. *Commentarius in Somnium Scipionis* offered far less in the way of technical music theory than did Martianus Capella's *De nuptiis Philologiae et Mercurii*, but far more metaphysical discussion of the role of number and proportion in the creation of the world. For this reason it was of greater use to the eleventh-century theorists who found the ancients valuable primarily for their number theory and not for their theories of melody. This, perhaps, explains why Martianus Capella rarely appears in music theory 'textbook' codices and why his influence is

[127] J. Gonsette, *Pierre Damien et la culture profane* (Louvain, 1956), pp. 5–43.
[128] M. Manitius, *Geschichte der lateinischen Literatur 3* (Munich, 1931), p. 179; M. Gibson, 'The study of the "Timaeus" in the eleventh and twelfth centuries', *Pensamiento* 25 (1969), 184–5.
[129] *MGH Briefe* 3, pp. 31, 90; 5, pp. 118–19, 126, 280–1, 330, 334, 355, 361–4.
[130] White, 'Glosses composed before the twelfth century', p. 12.
[131] P. Lehmann (ed.), *MBDS* 1/1, pp. 19–20.

less palpable than that of Macrobius; more useful theories of melody were available in the synthesis of Carolingian theorists produced by Bern of Reichenau. The only part of Macrobius to appear in the textbook codices was, as we shall see, the discussion of interval proportions at the beginning of *Commentarius in Somnium Scipionis* 2. This shows the limited extent of Macrobius' direct influence upon the theory of melody. But upon the broader understanding of Platonic metaphysics his influence was more dominant. It was in *Timaeus* and its subsequent interpretations that ideas of natural proportion and order so important to music theory had the origin of their birth.

5

'Textbook codices': music theory manuscripts of the eleventh and twelfth centuries

Most of the south-German music treatises owe their survival to the copying activity of scribes in German monasteries and cathedrals during the eleventh and twelfth centuries. Of the six surviving manuscripts that transmit all or part of William of Hirsau's *Musica*, for example, five originated in German centres during this time; the sixth manuscript – Bologna, Civico Museo Bibliografia Musicale A43 – is an eighteenth-century copy of a twelfth-century manuscript that was destroyed in the great fire that engulfed the south-German monastery of St Blasien in 1768.[1] Similarly, the treatise by William's pupil, Theoger of Metz, survives in eight manuscripts, all of eleventh- or twelfth-century German origin.[2] In addition to their common geographical origin, these manuscripts are linked by another feature: many are compilations of treatises and excerpts on music theory by different authors.

The textbook codex tradition

The phenomenon of compilation manuscripts is not restricted to music theory. Rather, its occurrence here reflects widespread practice in the central Middle Ages. During the tenth century it became a popular and convenient way of arranging collections of material in disciplines such as canon law. One manuscript from St Emmeram (now Munich, Bayerische Staatsbibliothek, Clm 14628) contains a collection of conciliar and patristic canons – often in abbreviated form – in addition to extracts from the

---

[1] G. Gaspari, *Catalogo della Biblioteca del Liceo Musicale di Bologna* 1 (Bologna, 1890), pp. 185–268; William of Hirsau, *Musica*, ed. D. Harbinson, *Willehelmi Hirsaugensis Musica* (Rome, 1975), p. 9.

[2] *RISM B* 3/3, pp. 20, 37, 48, 70, 86, 105, 142, 212.

175

Admonitio generalis and Merovingian canons;³ while another, with a provenance to an unidentified German centre (now Wolfenbüttel, Herzog-August Bibliothek, Gud. Lat. 454), is a compilation of extracts from the *False decretals*, Regino of Prüm's *Liber synodalis*, conciliar canons and the acts of the Roman Council of 964.⁴ The processes of compilation evident in these early examples seem to have been precipitated in the eleventh century by the intensification of canonical studies in the Empire, an intensification pioneered by distinguished figures such as Burchard, bishop of Worms, 1000–25 and Wazo, bishop of Liège, 1047–8. Burchard's *Decretum*, in particular, became the standard text for canonists and in consequence was frequently excerpted by German clerks. The anonymous eleventh-century *Summa de iudiciis omnium peccatorum* – which is closely based on Burchard – survives in the compilation codex Munich, Bayerische Staatsbibliothek, Clm 12205 along with canon law texts by other authors,⁵ while the collection known as *Collectio XII partium* – similarly excerpted – survives complete in eleventh-century codices from Salzburg and Tegernsee, as well as in five twelfth-century codices of German origin.⁶

Bernold of St Blasien: a compiler and adapter of texts

Johanne Autenrieth has drawn attention to the importance of the cathedral library at Constance as an intellectual centre during the second half of the eleventh century. Her studies of codices belonging to this library have demonstrated that its biblical, patristic and canon-law manuscripts were intensively researched and glossed during this period.⁷ Among the glossators was Bernold of Constance, later a monk of St Blasien and Schaffhausen respectively. Basing himself upon the glossed passages in the Constance manuscripts, Bernold compiled numerous manuals of canonical and patristic *sententiae*, which served as the basis for his treatises and which would also be used by other Gregorian

---

³ P. Fournier and G. le Bras, *Histoire des collections canoniques en Occident depuis les Fausses décrétals jusqu'au Décret de Gratien* 1 (Paris, 1931), pp. 292–5.
⁴ Ibid., pp. 301–2.
⁵ Ibid., pp. 432–4.
⁶ Ibid., pp. 434–5.
⁷ J. Autenrieth, *Die Domschule von Konstanz zur Zeit des Investiturstreits. Die Wissenschaftliche Arbeitsweise Bernholds von Konstanz und zweier Kleriker dargestellt auf Grund von Handschriftenstudien* (Stuttgart, 1956), pp. 30–115; 'Bernold von Konstanz und der Codex Sangallensis 676', in *Friedrich Baethgen zu seinem 65. Geburtstag* (Munich: MGH Typrscript, 1955), pp. 1–17.

polemicists.[8] One of three surviving codices that can be attributed to him is Stuttgart, Württembergische Landesbibliothek, HB. VI. 107. This codex of 102 folios is actually a binding of two separate manuscripts: one dating from the end of the eleventh century, the other from the end of the eighth.[9] The contents of both manuscripts form a complementary collection of texts that should be seen as a handbook of Gregorian doctrine. The most influential canon-law collections are well represented: the Gregorian *Collection in seventy-four titles* (fols 1v–52r); the *Decretum* of Pope Gelasius I (fols 52r–54v); a compilation in forty-seven rubricated chapters entitled *De ecclesiis* – purporting to be from a *Decretum* of Pope Felix IV, but which is actually based upon the *Decretum* by Burchard of Worms and the collections of Ivo of Chartres and Bishop Anselm II of Lucca – (fols 54v–61r); six chapters from the anonymous tenth-century *Collection in ninety-eight chapters* (fols 82rv and 83rv);[10] and excerpts from Burchard's *Decretum* (fols 164r–173r). In addition, the codex contains excerpts from penitentials by Theodore of Canterbury, an anonymous Roman author and Raban Maur; a set of rules for priests on penance; numerous conciliar canons; a text on the prohibited degrees of consanguinity – *De illicitis coniunctionibus* – based closely on Burchard, Regino of Prüm and Ivo of Chartres; a Roman ordinal, and two letters by Gregory I as well as extracts from Augustine and Gelasius I. Additionally, Bernold copied three of his own works into this codex: a treatise on excommunication (fol. 58v), *De damnatione scismaticorum* (fols 112r–141v) and his *Apologeticus super excommunicacionem Gregorii septimi* (144r–164r).[11]

The contents of this handbook represent the preoccupations of a Gregorian partisan, with the collections of canons having been carefully selected to justify Gregorian ecclesiology. It is significant that the most Gregorian of these – the *Collection in seventy-four titles* – was the only one copied in full. Older collections, such as those by Burchard of Worms or Ivo of Chartres, which emphasized the traditional rights and jurisdictions of individual bishops, were quarried more selectively. To them were added conciliar texts favourable to Gregorian ideals, as well as some of the most up-to-date products of the reform canonists, namely the writings of Anselm

---

[8] I. S. Robinson, 'The Bible in the Investiture Contest: the south-German Gregorian circle', in K. Walsh and D. Wood (eds), *The Bible in the medieval world: essays in memory of Beryl Smalley* (Oxford, 1985), pp. 66–7.
[9] J. Autenrieth, *Die Handschriften der ehemaligen Hofbibliothek Stuttgart. Codices iuridici et politici (HB VI 1–139), Patres (HB VII 1–71)* (Wiesbaden, 1963), pp. 100–5.
[10] See Fournier and le Bras, *Histoire des collections canoniques* 1, pp. 290–2.
[11] *MGH Libelli* 3 pp. 26–58, 58–88, 599–601.

II, bishop of Lucca. In view of Bernold's interest in liturgy, it is not surprising that he should have included a Roman ordinal to go with these 'Roman' texts: here was another area where Gregorian ideas might be asserted. The inclusion of numerous penitentials reflects the attitude of worldly contempt espoused by many reformers.[12] This pessimistic view of the world also explains, perhaps, the inclusion by Bernold of his treatise on the fate of schismatics and texts on excommunication, including his 'apology' for Pope Gregory VII's excommunication of King Henry IV in 1076. (Lay investiture represented for Bernold and his partisans the sullying of the spiritual order by secular worldliness.) The construction of the Stuttgart codex is typical of the handbook format, which brings together in one volume a number of complementary texts and excerpts for a particular purpose: in this case Bernold's purpose was the elucidation of the rights of the Reform Papacy through the compilation of canonical and patristic authority.

Doctrinal handbooks

The struggle between Empire and Papacy evidently stimulated the intellect, not only of Bernold, but of many others in Germany, for the production of theological textbooks became very popular during the last quarter of the eleventh century. Munich, Bayerische Staatsbibliothek, Clm 19126 is a twelfth-century example of a doctrinal handbook from the south-German house of Tegernsee.[13] Its forty-five folios are a compilation of material on theological and ecclesiastical subjects. *Sententiae* by St Augustine against the Manichean and Pelagian heresies are included. So too are tracts on the genealogy of Christ and the heresy of the Jews, an explanation of the name 'Adam' and the names of four stars, *dicta* of St Ambrose and other Fathers, as well as extracts from *De civitate Dei* and further works by St Augustine. The contents of this codex are completed by an exegesis of St Matthew attributed to Pope Gregory I, expositions of the Pauline epistles, the Passion story and various other biblical passages, questions on Genesis and on Augustine, excerpts from conciliar decretals, *dicta* of Gregory VII and other popes, and an account of the eucharistic dispute between Lanfranc and Berengar of Tours, as well as Berengar's *Confessio fidei*. The manuscript was undoubtedly compiled as a handbook of theological and doctrinal material in a milieu sympathetic to reform, judging from the

---

[12] See C. Morris, *The papal monarchy: the Western Church from 1050 to 1250* (Oxford, 1989), pp. 98–101.

[13] C. Halm, F. Keinz, G. Meyer, G. Thomas, *Catalogus codicum latinorum bibliotheca Regiae Monacensis* 2/3 (Munich, 1878), pp. 233-4.

appeal to St Gregory as an authority, the account of the eucharistic controversy of 1070 and the inclusion of *dicta* by Gregory VII. This manuscript is one of a number of similar doctrinal handbooks: further examples are the twelfth-century codices Vienna, Österreichische Nationalbibliothek, Cod. 1050, Bamberg, Staatsbibliothek, Msc. Patr. 30 and Würzburg, Universitätsbibliothek, M. p. th. q. 62.[14]

Hartwic of St Emmeram

Compilation manuscripts were not solely the preserve of canon law and doctrine: they were also produced in the other arts. Early examples are the manuscripts that a monk of St Emmeram named Hartwic copied while studying with the distinguished teacher Fulbert of Chartres in the first third of the eleventh century, and which became part of the monastic library at St Emmeram on his return to Regensburg.[15] Of these six or possibly seven manuscripts, two are of particular interest: Munich, Bayerische Staatsbibliothek, Clm 14436 and Clm 14272. The first is a manuscript of 118 folios that contains a compilation of material on diverse topics.[16] It was partly in existence by the time Hartwic acquired it: fols 34–61 contained fragments and excerpts of works on the linguistic and mathematical arts.[17] Grammar is represented by a fragmentary treatise on division and quantity in metrics entitled *De syllabarum quantitate*; astronomy by part of the second book of Macrobius' *Commentarius in Somnium Scipionis*, excerpts from Pliny's *Natural history* and diagrams of the planetary systems. To this

---

[14] *Tabulae codicum manu scriptorum . . . in bibliotheca palatina Vindobonensi asservatorum* 2 (Vienna, 1868), p. 183; F. Leitschuh and H. Fischer, *Katalog der Handschriften der Königlichen Bibliothek zu Bamberg* 1 (Leipzig, 1887), pp. 385–7; H. Thurn, *Die Handschriften der Universitätsbibliothek Würzburg* 5 (Wiesbaden, 1994), pp. 65 6.

[15] B. Bischoff, 'Literarisches und künstlerisches Leben in St. Emmeram (Regensburg) während des frühen und hohen Mittelalters', in B. Bischoff, *Mittelalterliche Studien. Ausgewählte Aufsätze zur Schriftkunde und Literaturgeschichte* 2 (Stuttgart, 1967), pp. 82–4.

[16] C. Halm, F. Keinz, G. Meyer, G. Thomas, *Catalogus codicum latinorum bibliotheca Regiae Monacensis* 2/2 (Munich, 1876), p. 172; see also Bischoff, 'Literarisches und künstlerisches Leben', pp. 82–4; H. P. Lattin, 'The eleventh-century MS Munich 14436: its contribution to the history of co-ordinates, of logic, of German studies in France', *Isis* 38 (1948), 205–25.

[17] B. C. Barker-Benfield, 'The manuscripts of Macrobius' Commentary on the *Somnium Scipionis*' 2 (D.Phil. thesis, University of Oxford, 1975), pp. 410–11 has identified fols 62–82 (containing Boethius' commentary on Porphyry's *Isagoge*) as an independent eleventh-century manuscript that owes its place in Clm 14436 to the present binding, which dates from *c.* 1500.

manuscript, Hartwic added most of the material on fols 1–33 and 89–118.[18] The contents of the existing portion obviously influenced Hartwic's copying activity, for he continued the emphasis on the linguistic and mathematical arts. He copied the pseudo-Ciceronian *Rhetorica ad Herennium*, a compilation derived from the fourth book of Boethius' *De differentiis topicis* that went by the title *Speculatio de rhetorice cognatione*,[19] Julius Severianus' *Praecepta artis rhetoricae* and some of Julius Victor's *Ars rhetorica*. Turning to the quadrivium, he completed Macrobius, copied two extracts from Bede's *De temporum ratione*, Gerbert of Aurillac's treatise *De numerorum divisione* (as well as a commentary on his *Regulas abaci*) and a fragment from Heriger of Laubach's *Regulae de numerorum abaci rationibus*.[20] Hartwic completed the codex with his *Vita* of St Emmeram on fol. 118.

Hartwic's interests also included music, a fact clearly indicated by the contents of Munich, Bayerische Staatsbibliothek, Clm 14272.[21] Like Clm 14436, this manuscript is devoted to the mathematical and linguistic arts, though here music features prominently. The first sixty-two of its 192 folios are occupied by Boethius' *De institutione musica*, which contains glosses that may have originated in the circle of Fulbert of Chartres.[22] The other music treatises copied by Hartwic are all by anonymous authors: the Carolingian *Musica enchiriadis* and *Scolica enchiriadis*, *Commemoratio brevis de tonis et psalmis modulandis* and a tonary. (The tenth-century treatise *Alia musica*, which is also found in the codex, is in another hand.) Hartwic also copied a text on the measurement of the monochord on fol. 174v.[23] For Hartwic, working in the early eleventh century, these treatises would have represented an up-to-date collection, touching on the most important aspects of music: the authority of Boethius with contemporary interpretation through glosses, the theory of the gamut and the modes, the

---

[18] Ibid.
[19] R. McKeon, 'Rhetoric in the Middle Ages', *Speculum* 17 (1942), 10.
[20] On Hartwic's completion of Macrobius see Barker-Benfield, 'The manuscripts of Macrobius' Commentary on the *Somnium Scipionis*' 2, p. 414; T. J. H. McCarthy, 'Literary practice in eleventh-century music theory: the *colores rhetorici* and Aribo's *De musica*', *Medium Aevum* 71 (2002), 205 n. 19.
[21] See *RISM B* 3/3, pp. 110–12; Bischoff, 'Literarisches und künstlerisches Leben', pp. 80–1. All of this codex has been copied by Hartwic except fols 10v–16v, 29r, 30v, 31r (lines 8–14) and 175r–181v (to line 23).
[22] *RISM B* 3/3, p. 111.
[23] R. Schlecht, '*Musica Enchiriadis* von Hucbald, übersetzt und mit kritischen Anmerkungen begleitet', *Monatshefte für Musikgeschichte* 6 (1874), 167; H. Schmid, *Musica et scolica enchiriadis, una cum aliquibus tractatulis adiunctis* (Munich, 1981), pp. 179–81.

measurement of the monochord and a tonary listing chants according to their mode.

In addition, Hartwic found room for other quadrivial material: he copied Adelbold of Utrecht's letter to Gerbert on the volume of a sphere (fol. 182r),[24] Adalbero of Laon's letter to Fulk, bishop of Amiens (fol. 182v), and an anonymous text on measurement (fols 153r–154v).[25] The linguistic arts are represented by treatises on dialectic by Aristotle, Cicero and Boethius (fols 65r–153r), some notes on grammar and Priscian's *De constructione*, which is the last work in the codex.[26] As in the case of Clm 14436, the works were not copied in any particular order, but presumably they were chosen by Hartwic as examples worthy of study. Though Hartwic's compilations were intended in the first place for personal use, it seems certain that they were also used by later generations of scholars. Numerous marginal diagrams suggest active use of Hartwic's codices after his return to Germany: in the margin of the tonary copied on fols 62v–64v, for instance, a tonary identical to one in the tenth-century manuscript Einsiedeln, Stiftsbibliothek, Cod. 79 has been added by another monk.[27]

Textbooks in the linguistic arts

Hartwic's interest in the trivium was continued by clerks of subsequent generations. The considerable interest among German clerks in the *ars dictandi*, represented by the production of textbooks containing letters that were carefully selected for their stylistic merits, has been highlighted by I. S. Robinson.[28] Munich, Bayerische Staatsbibliothek, Clm 19473 – a twelfth-century Tegernsee codex – is an example of a grammar textbook.[29] It contains Cicero's *De amicitia*, the third book of Donatus' *Barbarismus*,

[24] Gerbert of Aurillac, *Opera*, ed. N. M. Bubnov, *Gerberti postea Silvestri II papae Opera mathematica (972–1003). Accedunt aliorum opera ad Gerberti libellos aestimandos intelligendosque necessaria per septem appendices distributa* (Berlin, 1899; repr. Hildesheim, 1963), pp. 303–09.

[25] Ibid., p. 42.

[26] H. Keil (ed.), *Grammatici latini* 3 (Leipzig, 1880), pp. 107–49.

[27] M. Huglo, *Les tonaires. Inventaire, analyse, comparaison* (Paris, 1971), pp. 59, 62, 68–9, 253; *RISM B* 3/1, pp. 74–5.

[28] I. S. Robinson, 'The "Colores rhetorici" in the Investiture Contest', *Traditio* 32 (1976), 209–38. Didactic rhetorical collections of the eleventh and twelfth centuries include the *Codex Udalrici* (compiled by Udalric of Bamberg, c. 1125), the Regensburg, Hanover and Wolfenbüttel collections. See I. S. Robinson, 'The sources and method of papal and anti-papal polemic: 1073–1112' (D.Phil. thesis, University of Oxford, 1975), p. 40; C. Erdmann, 'Die Bamberger Domschule im Investiturstreit', *Zeitschrift für bayerische Landesgeschichte* 9 (1936), 27–8.

[29] Halm et al., *Catalogus codicum latinorum bibliotheca Regiae Monacensis* 2/3, p. 249.

a collection of rhetorical expositions of the psalms, Alcuin's *Dialogus de philosophia* and a commentary on Ovid's *Metamorphoses* into which Servius' commentary on Virgil has been inserted. The presence of Donatus among these literary works suggests that they were considered as examples of style and as applications of the teaching set out in *Barbarismus*.

Medieval library catalogues frequently allude to the existence of textbooks. Munich, Bayerische Staatsbibliothek, Clm 18541a, fol. 1r contains a booklist from the second half of the eleventh century recording the books that the monk Reginfrid left 'to God and to St Quirinus of Tegernsee'. Among these was 'Tully's [Cicero's] *Topics* with the commentary of Boethius and books on *differentiae* and division and much concerning rhetoric and syllogisms in one volume'.[30] A good example of such a dialectical textbook is the twelfth-century St Emmeram codex Munich, Bayerische Staatsbibliothek, Clm 14516.[31] It contains Porphyry's *Isagoge* with some later workings, Boethius' commentary on *Isagoge* and his first book on Aristotle's *Categories*. Another textbook codex that represents an interesting coalescence of dialectic and rhetoric is Oxford, Bodleian Library, Laud Lat. 49.[32] This codex, possibly from Würzburg, contains 176 fols and dates from the late eleventh century. It is written – three columns to a page – in clear Caroline minuscule and transmits very accurate texts. A number of different though stylistically similar hands recur throughout the codex, suggesting that it was the work of one scriptorium. Its contents include Porphyry's *Isagoge* with Boethius' commentary 'a Mario Victorino translatus'; Boethius' commentaries on Aristotle's *Categories* and *De interpretatione*; Cicero's *Topica* with Boethius' commentary; and *De inventione* with Marius Victorinus' commentary. These works suggest that the codex was put together with an eye to the practice and rhetoric of argument. An extensive corpus of marginal and interlinear glosses in contemporary hands indicates that this textbook was well studied.

Music theory compilations and textbooks

As with the tradition sketched above so too with music theory manuscripts. A survey of German sources from the eleventh century to the twelfth reveals the existence of some sixty manuscripts containing material on music

---

[30] G. Glauche, H. Knaus (eds), *MBDS* 4/2, pp. 750–1.
[31] Halm et al., *Catalogus codicum latinorum bibliotheca Regiae Monacensis* 2/2, p. 186.
[32] H. O. Coxe and R. W. Hunt, *Bodleian Library Quarto Catalogues 2: Laudian manuscripts* (Oxford, 1973), p. xxiii, cols 24–5. See also T. J. H. McCarthy, 'The origins of *Commentarius anonymus in Micrologum Guidonis Aretini* in the medieval glossing tradition', *Revue d'Histoire des Textes* n.s. 3 (2008), 222–6.

theory. From this body of sources it is possible to identify over thirty examples that fit the description of textbooks: codices compiled from selected and related materials for a specific scholarly purpose. Before surveying these codices, however, it will be well to examine one manuscript in detail, for this will enable us to see a twelfth-century scribe at work compiling a textbook for the *ars musica*.

Kassel, Landesbibliothek und Murhardsche Bibliothek der Stadt Kassel, 4° Mss Math. 1

This manuscript of forty-seven folios and of south-German origin contains a broad collection of music theory works, mainly from the eleventh century.[33] Its early protogothic minuscule, which is clearly the work of one very neat and skilful hand, probably dates from the second quarter of the twelfth century.[34] The original ink has faded to dark brown, with headings, initial capitals and rubrication in red. Although the quiring cannot be established – owing to damage in the Second World War and subsequent restoration – there can be no doubt that this manuscript was deliberately planned as a unified entity by its scribe. The way in which it has been compiled suggests that the works included were designed to complement each other in the study of music theory.

The scribe began the manuscript by copying Guido's influential treatise *Micrologus* (fols 1r–9r).[35] He followed this with *Regule rithmice* (fols 9r–12r), *Prologus in antiphonarium* (fols 12r–13v) and *Epistola ad Michahelem* (fols 13v–17v).[36] The inclusion of Guido's œuvre in its entirety at the start of the Kassel manuscript reveals a twelfth-century scholar's attitude to the celebrated Italian theorist. It suggests that Guido's works were highly valued and thought worthy of detailed study. By placing them first, the scribe tacitly acknowledged the status that Guido's teaching had by then attained. For a German clerk, however, Guido's treatises did not constitute a self-sufficient source for the study of music theory. The Kassel scribe would have recognized that the approaches of Guido and the south-German circle were different in their respective emphases: Guido said very little of the

---

[33] *RISM* B 3/3, pp. 67–72; D. Pesce (ed. and trans.), *Guido d'Arezzo's Regule rithmice, Prologus in Antiphonarium and Epistola ad Michahelem: a critical text and translation* (Ottawa, 1999), pp. 100–5.

[34] *RISM* B 3/3, p. 67. C. Meyer, 'Aus der Werkstatt des Kompilators. Bemerkungen über zwei musiktheoretische Schriften des 11. Jahrhunderts', in M. Bernhard (ed.), *Quellen und Studien zur Musiktheorie des Mittelalters* 2 (Munich, 1997), p. 4 dates it to the end of the twelfth century.

[35] Pesce (ed. and trans.), *Guido*, p. 100.

[36] Ibid., p. 101; *RISM* B 3/3, p. 68.

tetrachordal and species theory that was of such importance to the Germans.³⁷ Consequently, texts explaining that theory were indispensable to the pursuit of diligent study in the art of music. It is hardly surprising, therefore, that all of the other texts in this manuscript are of German origin.

Fols 17v–20r contain a number of didactic texts, each complete with a four-line staff and diastemmatic neumes above the words, that can be divided into two groups. The first group of texts (fols 17v–18r) comprises a set of eight mnemonic verses, which are designed to illustrate the melodic characteristics of the eight tones. These examples are followed by a text on the relationship of the intervals of the *diatessaron*, *diapente* and *diapason* to the modes.³⁸ The next text (fol. 18rv) continues the emphasis on the modes and their characteristics. It is concerned with particular interval patterns and provides chant examples to illustrate each case. This is followed by the widely disseminated mnemonic verses of Master Henry of Augsburg, which illustrate the different modes: *Primus ut Exurge . . . Secundus ut Ecce* (fols 18v–19r).³⁹

The second group of texts in this section is made up of Herman of Reichenau's didactic verses, which circulated in a number of south-German manuscripts and which were known to theorists such as Frutolf of Michelsberg.⁴⁰ These mnemonics explain Herman's notational system (which indicated the intervals to be sung from one note to another, rather than the respective pitches of each note), the intervals and the modes. The first verse (*E uoces unisonas*) is preceded by the following heading, presumably the work of the scribe: 'A verse of lord Herman in example of the nine intervals with words and signs that singularly sound the consonances, that is, the unison, semitone, tone, semiditone, ditone, *diatessaron*, *diapente*, semitone-plus-*diapente* and tone-plus-*diapente*.⁴¹ It explains the

---

[37] See Chapter 2, pp. 64–9, 86–7.
[38] Kassel, Landesbibliothek, 4° Mss Math. 1, fol. 18r: Dyapente et Dyatessaron symphonie et intente ac remis|se pariter consonantiam dyapason modulatione consona reddunt | canat cum monochordo incipiens tonum primum currensque ad nouis|simum. Incipiunt toni artis musice auctentus protus id est | auctoritas prima. Pesce (ed. and trans.), *Guido*, p. 101 suggests that there are two separate mnemonics. The manuscript, however, clearly indicates that the scribe conceived the text as one entity.
[39] See Chapter 1, p. 47.
[40] Ibid., p. 33. Frutolf of Michelsberg, *Breviarium de musica*, ed. C. Vivell, 'Frutolfi Breviarium de musica et *Tonarius*', *Akademie der Wissenschaften in Wien, Philosophische historische Klasse, Sitzungsberichte* 188/2 (1919), 69, 72, 82–3; H. Oesch, *Berno und Hermann von Reichenau als Musiktheoretiker. Mit einem Überblick über ihr Leben und die handschriftliche Überlieferung ihrer Werke* (Bern, 1961), p. 136.
[41] Kassel, Landesbibliothek, 4° Mss Math. 1, fol. 19r: Versus domni hermanni ad exempla .viiii. interuallorum c⟨um⟩ uocum | cum notulis quas singule sonant consonancie, id

symbols used in this notational system, which are written above the text. The second verse (*Ter tria iunctorum*) is similar, but is concerned with the different intervals, rather than the notational system. The scribe headed it 'A verse of lord Herman concerning the same thing'.[42] The third verse (*Ter terni sunt modi*), unlike the preceding two, is notated with diastemmatic neumes and not with Herman's system. It is attributed by the scribe to William of Hirsau, with the heading 'Versus Wilhemmi abbatis'.[43] This section of the manuscript ends on fol. 20r with a diagram headed 'Musica est motus uocum'. This diagram properly belongs to *Micrologus* 16, but it is likely that the scribe chose to place it here for a reason.[44] The mnemonic verses that occupy fols 17v–20r have a common purpose: they teach the characteristics of the modes and of the intervals. They are designed to show – as the diagram on fol. 20r underlines – that music is indeed the movement of voices. Thus, it is probable that the scribe decided to place the diagram here because it offered a pertinent encapsulation of their purpose.

Fols 20r–28v contain texts on different matters: measurement and proportion. This part of the manuscript can be divided further into two subsections: the first (fols 20r–22v) is practical in orientation and contains texts on the measurement of organ pipes, bells and geometrical figures; the second (fols 22v–28v) is more theoretical and is concerned with the application of proportions to the theory of intervals.

The scribe began the first subsection by copying a text on the measurement of organ pipes.[45] This text follows the pattern of many similar examples from the sources in giving relative rather than absolute measurements. These directions are designed to produce pipe lengths and diameters that

est, unisonus, semitonium, | tonus, semiditonus, Ditonus, Dyatessaron, Dyapente, Semitonium cum dyapente, | tonus cum dyapente.

[42] Kassel, Landesbibliothek, 4° Mss Math. 1, fol. 19r: Versus domni hermani de eadem Re.
[43] *RISM B 3/3*, p. 68; *GS* 2, p. 152; Oesch, *Berno und Hermann*, p. 138. See Chapter 1, p. 29. This verse is also attributed to William of Hirsau in the fifteenth-century manuscript Berlin, Staatsbibliothek, Preußischer Kulturbesitz, Theol. qu. 74 (Cat. 718), fol. 115v. Huglo, *Les Tonaries*, p. 282 — following doubts expressed by Oesch — believes the attribution to William. H. Möller, *The Zwiefalten Antiphoner: Karlsruhe, Badische Landesbibliothek, Aug. perg. LX. Printouts from an index in machine readable form: a CANTUS index* (Ottawa, 1996), p. xvii believes that William provided the melody to Herman's mnemonic verse 'Ter terni sunt modi'. See M. Bernhard, 'Zur Rezeption der musiktheoretischen Werke des Hermannus Contractus', in W. Pass and A. Rausch (eds), *Beiträge zur Musik, Musiktheorie und Liturgie der Abtei Reichenau. Bericht über die Tagung Heiligenkreuz 6.-8. Dezember 1999* (Tutzing, 2001), pp. 110 n. 22, 115–16.
[44] Pesce (ed. and trans.), *Guido*, p. 102; Guido of Arezzo, *Micrologus*, ed. J. Smits van Waesberghe, *Micrologus Guidonis Aretini* (Rome, 1955), p. 184.
[45] K.-J. Sachs (ed.), *Mensura fistularum. Die Mensurierung der Orgelpfeifen im Mittelalter* 1 (Stuttgart, 1970), pp. 100–12.

will speak in the ratios of the harmonic series, the same ratios upon which the musical intervals are based. The organ-pipe measurements are followed by two sets of bell measurements (fols 20v-21v), one in prose, the other in verse.[46] The scribe probably copied both from Frutolf's *Breviarium de musica*. Instructions for bell making were also frequently copied in contemporary manuscripts, and followed the same mathematical principles as organ-pipe texts. Fols 21v-22v transmit excerpts on geometrical measurements: a text on the measurement of the rotation of a wheel, an astronomical text by Gerbert of Aurillac (later Pope Sylvester II) on the measurement of celestial orbits and a fragment with the title 'Mensura quadre de horis diei' (actually an excerpt from *De utilitatibus astrolabii* 5, possibly also by Gerbert).[47]

The second subsection begins with an extract from Macrobius' *Commentarius in Somnium Scipionis* (fols 22v-23r).[48] This extract, which has been given the title 'De numeris' by the scribe, lists the six ratios (the sesquitertia, sesquialtera, duple, triple, quadruple and super-octave) and then explains the arithmetical derivation of the intervals from these ratios.[49] It is followed by two complementary texts on the theory of intervals: 'De uocibus musicis' and 'Ex quibus proportionum numeris constet symphonia'. Taken together, these three excerpts constitute a unified portion on the musical intervals.[50] They are supplemented with the introduction and first four chapters of Frutolf's *Breviarium*, which the scribe has copied on fols 23v-28v (on the origins and Greek names of the notes, the theory and division of the monochord, arithmetical proportion in music, musical consonances and intervals).[51] This section of the manuscript ends on fol. 28v with an anonymous fragment on the measurement of the *organistrum*.[52]

---

[46] J. Smits van Waesberghe (ed.), *Cymbala: bells in the Middle Ages* (Rome, 1951), pp. 51-2.
[47] Pesce (ed. and trans.), *Guido*, p. 102; *RISM B* 3/3, p. 69; N. M. Bubnov (ed.), *Gerberti postea Silvestri II papae Opera mathematica*, pp. 25-8 (*PL* 139.0155-6); on the authorship of *De utilitatibus astrolabii* see A. van der Vyver, 'Les premières traductions latines (Xe-XIe siècles) de traités arabes sur l'astrolabe', in *Premier Congrès International de Géographie Historique le haut Patronage de S. M. le Roi des Belges* 2 (Brussels, 1931), p. 269 and L. Thorndike, *A history of magic and experimental science* 1 (New York, 1923), pp. 689-91.
[48] Macrobius, *Commentarius in Somnium Scipionis* 2.1.14-2.1.20, ed. J. Willis, *Ambrosii Theodosii Macrobii Commentarii in Somnium Scipionis* (Leipzig, 1963), p. 97.
[49] See Chapter 4, pp. 150-1.
[50] Meyer, 'Aus der Werkstatt des Kompilators', pp. 4-6, 10-12.
[51] Frutolf, *Breviarium* 1-4, pp. 26-45.
[52] *RISM B* 3/3, p. 69; see M. Markovits, *Das Tonsystem der abendländischen Musik im frühen Mittelalter* (Bern, 1977), p. 51.

Having compiled a collection of texts on measurement and proportion, the scribe then appears to have planned a section on the modes. The result of his endeavours is apparent between fols 28v and 39v. The first text, or rather composite text, occupies fols 28v–32v. Its main structure is provided by Chapters 31–45 of *Musica* by Theoger of Metz. To the question 'Why this part of Theoger here?', the answer: 'This part of Theoger's treatise deals exclusively with the modes'. This composite text is itself in two parts, following the division of Theoger's exemplar. Chapters 31–8 of Theoger's *Musica* describe the characteristics of the eight tones, citing example chants in each case. Proceeding according to the rules of logic, Theoger then deduces in Chapters 39–45 general 'rules' for the authentic and plagal chants, as well as for chants that share authentic and plagal characteristics.[53]

Theoger's analysis of the modes individually (*Musica* 31–8) was copied by the Kassel scribe on fols 28v–31v. But the scribe supplemented this part of Theoger's treatise with other material. A study of this supplementary material shows it to have been chosen by the scribe for the specific purpose of adding to Theoger's core text. The composite text begins with a paragraph that, at first glance, appears detached from the overall pattern of this section:

> Kassel, Landesbibliothek, 4° Mss Math. 1, fol. 28v, lines 19–25 Primus tonus intenditur ad acutam .d. raro autem ad .e. | et descendit ad .C. rarissimme uero ad .B. habens inter .D. et .d. quartam | dyapason formam, supra uero et infra chordam ut dictum est rarissime duas | inferius. Penta grece latine dicitur | quinque: inde dyapente dicitur, id est, de quinque sonis. Tessera grece | latine quatuor: inde dyatessaron, id est, ex quatuor sonis. Pan grece latine tonum: inde dyapason dicitur | quasi ex omnibus | uocibus. |

The paragraph is in two parts. The first ('Primus tonus . . . duas inferius') is based upon one of the interpolations in Bern's *Prologus in tonarium*,[54] though it has been abbreviated by the omission of the Greek note names that were in the original interpolation. (The Kassel scribe is presumably responsible for this abbreviation.)[55] The second half of the paragraph sees the Kassel scribe indulge himself as a would-be etymologist: the derivation

---

[53] Theoger, *Musica* 39: Generales regulae autentici cantus; 40: Generalis regulae plagalis cantus; 41: Generalis regula communis cantus, ed. F. C. Lochner, 'Dietger (Theogerus) of Metz and his "Musica"' (Ph.D. dissertation, University of Notre Dame, 1995), pp. 49–51.
[54] A. Rausch (ed.), *Die Musiktraktate des Abtes Bern von Reichenau. Edition und Interpretation* (Tutzing, 1999), p. 46.
[55] This interpolation is itself based upon a passage from § 8 of Anonymous I (*GS* 1, p. 337). The Greek note names were added by the author of the interpolation to explain Bern's

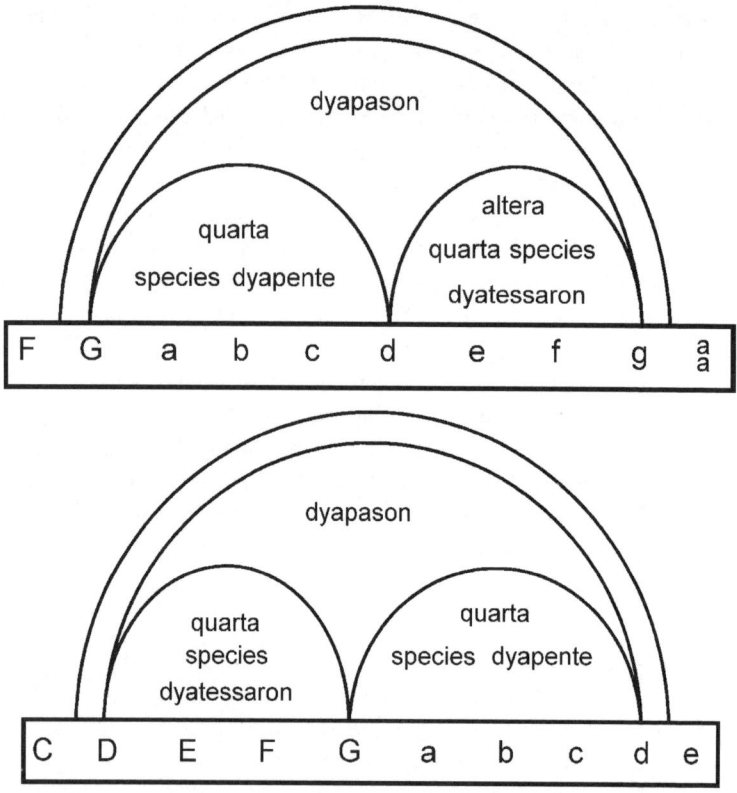

Figure 5.1 Diagram of the seventh and eighth tones from *Musica* by Theoger of Metz

of the *diatessaron*, *diapente* and *diapason*. This paragraph is not, however, detached from the what follows, for it is closely linked with a methodology that is central to the composite text.[56] In his original treatise, Theoger analysed each mode in a particular manner. By means of eight diagrams he split the octave range of each mode into its constituent *diatessaron* and *diapente* (see Figure 5.1).

Footnote 55 (*cont.*)
Prologus, which used these names exclusively. As the passage given by the Kassel scribe no longer fulfilled the function of commentary upon Bern's text, the Greek names were redundant and consequently omitted. The closeness of the Kassel scribe's version to the interpolation indicates that he did not base himself directly upon the passage in Anonymous I.

[56] The description of this part of the Kassel manuscript given by Pesce (ed. and trans.), *Guido*, p. 103 is slightly misleading.

Figure 5.1 gives the diagrams for the seventh and eighth modes, that is, authentic *tetrardus* and plagal *tetrardus*. In the seventh mode (the authentic version), which runs from G to g, the *diapente* (G–d) is followed by the *diatessaron* (d–g). In the eighth mode (the plagal version), which runs from D to d, the *diatessaron* (D–G) is followed by the *diapente* (G–d). (The final for both modes, however, is G.) The opening paragraph is, therefore, an introduction to the whole of the composite text: by introducing the *diatessaron*, *diapente* and *diapason* it prepares the reader for the important role those intervals will play in the subsequent analysis of the modes.

After this introductory paragraph the analysis of the modes begins. In each of the eight sections of the composite text, Theoger's original text and diagram is sandwiched between material that has been added by the Kassel scribe. The first section (on the first mode) is shown in Plate 8.

In Plate 8 the first addition by the scribe has been a group of notated examples beginning 'Primum querite regnum dei'. This is the first of a set of eight mnemonic formulas – one for each of the modes – that was widely circulated in contemporary manuscripts (this set should not be confused with the previous sets of mnemonics quoted by the scribe):

> Primum querite regnum dei.
> Secundus autem simile est huic.
> Tertia dies est quod facta sunt.
> Quarta uigilia ueniat ad eos.
> Quinque prudentes intrauerunt ad nuptias.
> Sexta hora sedit super puteum.
> Septem sunt spiritus ante thronum dei.
> Octo sunt beatitudines.[57]

The scribe used the appropriate line of this octet to begin each section of the composite text. What come immediately after this (and for each of the other modes) are notated chant examples, followed by Theoger's text: in Plate 8 it is the portion appropriate for the first mode (*Musica* 31), beginning 'Primus igitur tonus . . .'. After Theoger's text and diagram the Kassel scribe added more material, possibly from an already circulating tonary to which he had access.[58] He listed the *differentiae* for the first tone, that is,

---

[57] See A. M. Busse-Berger, *Medieval music and the art of memory* (Berkeley, 2005), pp. 69–70.

[58] This text also appears in Darmstadt, Universitäts- und Hochschulbibliothek, 3314/3315, fols 9r–10v, dating from about 1150. See L. Eizenhöfer and H. Knaus (eds), *Die liturgischen Handschriften der Hessischen Landes- und Hochschulbibliothek Darmstadt. Die Handschriften der Hessischen Landes- und Hochschulbibliothek Darmstadt 2* (Wiesbaden, 1968), pp. 162–4.

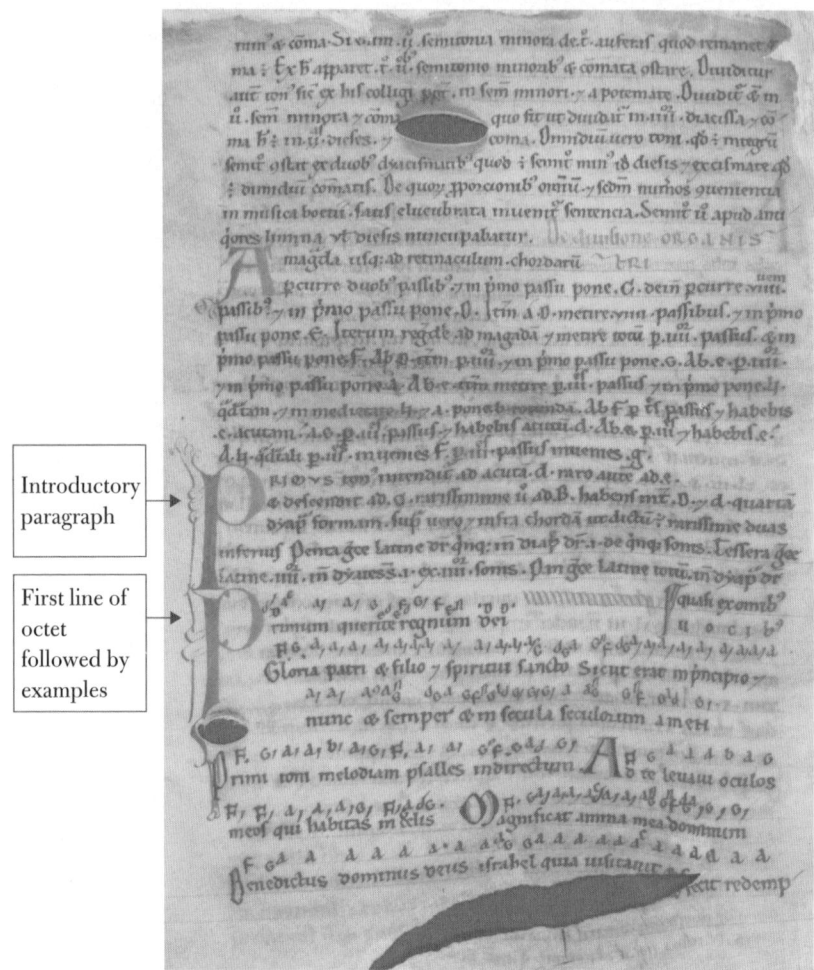

Plate 8   Kassel, Landesbibliothek und Murhardsche Bibliothek der Stadt Kassel, 4° Mss. Math. 1, fols 28v, 29r

the different cadences available for psalmody in that mode. The first psalm tone has six *differentiae*; for the third tone later on the scribe could only find three. The specimen chants provided in each case are accompanied by letter notation in superscript. This pattern is repeated for each of the tones. The scribe then copied Chapters 39–45 of Theoger's *Musica* – without additions – on fols 31v–32v.

Continuing his emphasis on modes, the scribe next copied specific extracts from Aribo's *De musica*. Fols 32v–33r transmit *De musica*

'TEXTBOOK CODICES'

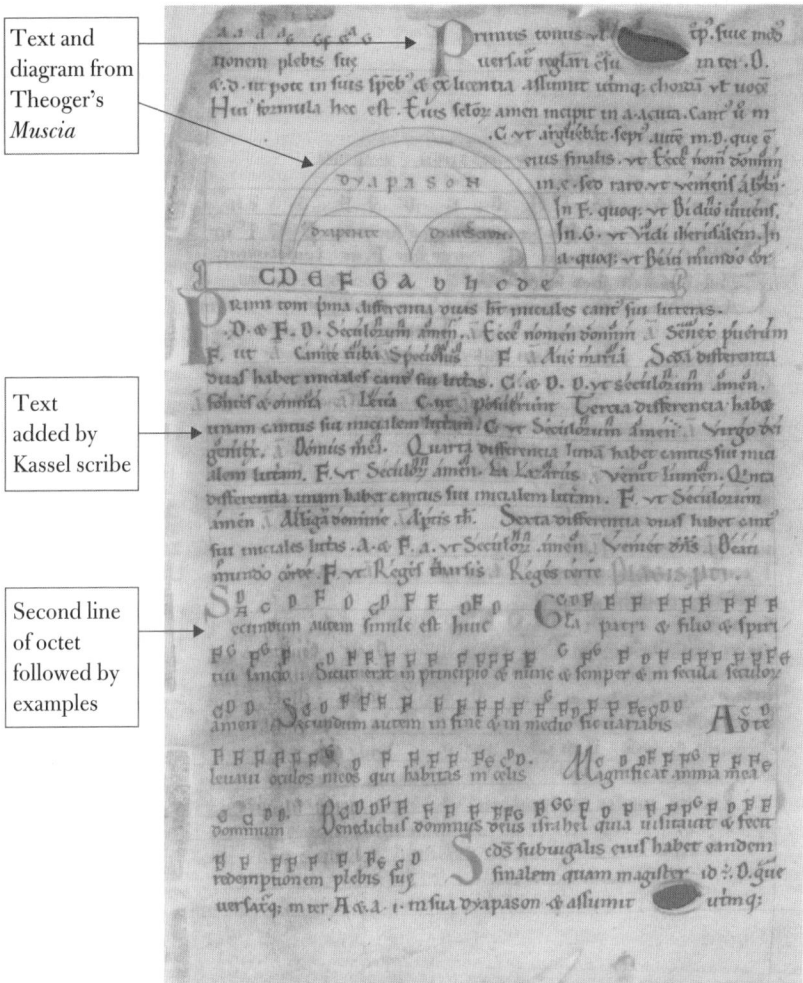

Text and diagram from Theoger's *Muscia*

Text added by Kassel scribe

Second line of octet followed by examples

36–8.[59] In Aribo's original, Chapter 36 is entitled 'De similitudine divitum et pauperum ad tropos utrosque'; in the Kassel manuscript it is given the heading 'De concordia troporum ex similitudine divitum et pauperum'.[60] This short chapter likens the authentic and plagal modes to the rich and the poor: though the rich (the authentics) 'muse in comedy'

---

[59] *RISM B* 3/3, p. 70.
[60] Aribo, *De musica*, ed. J. Smits van Waesberghe, *Aribonis De musica* (Rome, 1951), p. 17; Pesce (ed. and trans.), *Guido*, p. 103.

while the poor (the plagals) 'walk in tragedy', both can expect the same death and end (final note). The title of Chapter 37 – 'De similitudine virilis femineique chori ad authentos et plagas' – is changed by the scribe to 'Item de eadem re'; it also uses allegory by likening the authentic and plagal modes to the 'male and female choral dances'.[61] Chapter 38 – 'De differentia autentorum et plagarum iuxta Horatium Flaccum' – is rendered by the scribe simply as 'Quomodo differunt autenti a plagalibus'.[62] Here, Aribo purports to adduce a quatrain from Horace as he continues to express the relationship between authentic and plagal as one of subservience (only the first couplet is by Horace, however, as the quatrain also contains a quotation from Virgil's *Eclogue* 5.73). It is likely that the scribe chose to change these three chapter headings in order to make them more explicit in the context of his emphasis on modes (these changes provide snapshots of the ways in which subsequent generations understood the south-German theorists). He continued that emphasis by reproducing the four circular diagrams Aribo had used to illustrate the 'male and female choral dances' and their interdependent relationship as an analogy to the authentic and plagal modes (fol. 33rv).[63] Each of the diagrams is accompanied by a brief commentary outlining the species of *diatessaron* and *diapente* that make up each mode. The commentary is taken from various parts of Bern's *Tonarius* and contextualizes Aribo's diagrams (see Plate 9). The combination probably already existed independently: a version of it is also transmitted in Leiden, Bibliotheek der Rijksuniversiteit, BPL 194, fols 39v–41r.

Bern's pupil Herman of Reichenau was also considered useful by the scribe of the Kassel manuscript. Fols 33v–35r transmit an extract from the final section of his *Musica*.[64] It appears to be another highly selective use of a treatise by the scribe, as it has been given the title 'Regula Hermanni Contracti'.[65] The title relates to the sophisticated concept called *modus vocum*: interval patterns around the finals that could be used to aid recognition of the modes.[66] After this extract from Herman, there is a broadening of content in the manuscript. The scribe now returns to Theoger of Metz and, from fols 35r–38r, copies most of the opening two

[61] Aribo, *De musica*, pp. 17–18.
[62] Ibid., p. 21.
[63] Ibid., p. 20.
[64] Herman, *Musica*, pp. 57–66.
[65] *RISM B* 3/3, p. 70.
[66] Herman, *Musica* 19, p. 57; R. L. Crocker, 'Hermann's major sixth', *Journal of the American Musicological Society* 25 (1972), 19–37.

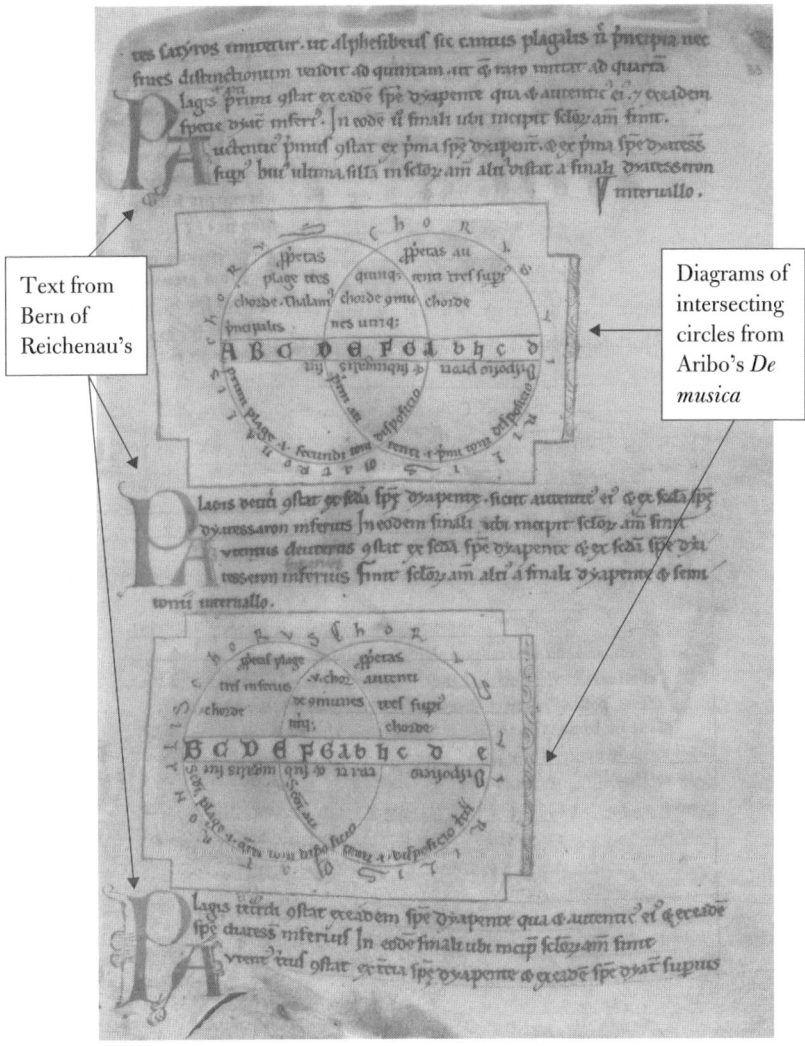

Plate 9 Kassel, Landesbibliothek und Murhardsche Bibliothek der Stadt Kassel, 4° Mss. Math. 1, fol. 33r

thirds of his treatise (*Musica* 6–27). This portion deals with numerical proportion in music (namely the double, *sesquialtera* and *sesquitertia* proportions); the theoretical division of the monochord according to those proportions; the tetrachords; the species of *diatessaron*, *dia-pente* and *diapason*; and the constitution and division of the four modal tetrachords – *protus*, *deuterus*, *tritus* and *tetrardus*.[67] At the end of this second extract the scribe has appended a comment, suggesting why he had included the rest of Theoger at this point: 'But this above-mentioned composition is where to read about the rules for the way and movement of the modes'.[68]

Theoger is followed by an extract from the fourteenth chapter of *Epistola de harmonica institutione* by the Carolingian theorist Regino of Prüm (fol. 38rv).[69] It begins with Regino's explanation of the Greek note names (*proslambanomenos*, *hypate hypaton*, *parhypate hypaton* and so forth), of their position in the medieval gamut and of how the tetrachords are formed from the fifteen notes of the gamut. It continues by showing 'how it is in these fifteen notes that all the consonances are revealed' and demonstrates the way in which they produce the intervals of the *diatessaron*, *diapente*, *diapason* and double-*diapason*, as well as the five tetrachords that in antiquity were called *hypaton*, *meson*, *synemmenon*, *diezeugmenon* and *hyperboleon*.[70] Essentially, this section of Regino's *Epistola* is dedicated to the nomenclature and explanation of the ancient Greek *systema teleion*. The restricted subject matter of this extract again suggests that it represents a selective choice by the compiler of the Kassel manuscript: it was included because he thought it a particularly lucid and accessible account of a potentially confusing aspect of the ancient music theory. (His use of Regino as a 'glossary' is strikingly similar to the use of a short passage from Hucbald of St Amand in the early twelfth-century textbook codex Vienna, Österreichische Nationalbibliothek, Cod. 51, fol. 35r.[71])

Leaving Regino, fols 38v–39r contain two short anonymous fragments on the modes. The first describes the principal (or authentic) versions and the subjugate (or plagal) versions of the modes, while the second attempts to explain the closely related topic of the modal tetrachords (*protus*, *deuterus*, *tritus* and *tetrardus*). This is followed (fol. 39rv) by a fragment on the modality of chants, which uses a notated version of the chant *Petrus autem* as an example, a text headed 'De diuersitate troporum', which discusses in pseudo-Platonic fashion the states of mind associated with partic-

---

[67] Theoger, *Musica* 6–27, pp. 15–31.
[68] Kassel, 4° Mss Math. 1, fol. 38r: Sed hec constitutio supradicta est ubi legitur de regulari cursu et | uersatione troporum.
[69] RISM B 3/3, p. 71; Regino of Prüm, *Epistola de harmonica institutione*, ed. M. Bernhard, *Clavis Gerberti. Eine Revision von Martin Gerberts Scriptores ecclesiastici de musica sacra potissimum* (St. Blasien 1784) (Munich, 1989), pp. 60.5–64.41.
[70] Ibid., p. 63.31: Nunc videamus, qualiter in his quindecim cordis omnes consonantiae reperiantur.
[71] See below, p. 209.

ular modes,[72] and a final passage on the division of the four modes into eight.[73]

Fols 39v–40r contain two texts on the division of the monochord, the instrument of greatest importance to music theorists at this time. The first set of measurements represents received authority, for it is 'according to Boethius' (and is also found in the twelfth-century manuscript Leiden, Bibliotheek der Rijksuniversiteit, BPL 194, fol. 41v).[74] The second set, 'according to the diatonic genus', gives a more modern method.

The texts on the monochord are followed by a lengthy extract from Bern's *Prologus in tonarium*, a treatise with a wide circulation in the eleventh and twelfth centuries (fols 40r–43v).[75] Bern begins his treatise with the monochord, perhaps explaining his inclusion at this point in the Kassel manuscript. The extract includes the greater part of nine of the twelve chapters in *Prologus*. (It breaks off three sentences before the end of *Prologus* 9.) In transmitting the bulk of this treatise, it covers Bern's teaching on the gamut and the monochord, the modes (including references to their ancient meaning and their ecclesiastical use), the intervals, the tetrachords and the species of *diatessaron*, *diapente* and *diapason*.

The final part of the Kassel manuscript (fols 44r–47v) contains a miscellaneous collection of texts and drawings. In it the scribe has copied Frutolf's mnemonic verses on the modes from *Breviarium de musica*,[76] as well as an anonymous tonary containing some examples with neumes.[77] A drawing of the 'Guidonian hand', a diagram that shows the division of the monochord into the chromatic, enharmonic and diatonic genera, and notated examples of the chants *[G]aude visceribus* and *[A]ve speciosissima virgo*, complete the manuscript.[78]

The Kassel manuscript is a compilation of treatises and excerpts on differing but complementary aspects of music theory. Not only does the choice of texts seem to have been highly selective, but the scribe has shown a willingness to adapt excerpts to different contexts. Nowhere is this more apparent than in the section on the modes, where the scribe extracted and matched relevant parts from the treatises of Theoger, Bern, Herman and

---

[72] *RISM B* 3/3, p. 71.
[73] Pesce (ed. and trans.), *Guido*, p. 104 mistakenly categorizes this text as pertaining to the division of the monochord.
[74] *RISM B* 3/1, p. 136.
[75] Bern, *Prologus* 1–9, pp. 32–61. This was copied from an un-interpolated version.
[76] Frutolf, *Breviarium* 10, pp. 75–82; Huglo, *Les tonaires*, p. 286.
[77] *RISM B* 3/3, p. 72; Huglo, *Les tonaires*, pp. 245, 259.
[78] *RISM B* 3/3, p. 72.

Aribo. In doing so he was using the same scholastic techniques as the eleventh-century scribe of a Hirsau codex (now Sélestat, Bibliothèque Municipale, 13) who supplemented one of Bernold of St Blasien's polemical works with two letters by Pope Gregory VII and added generalized rubrics stressing the universal application of papal reforming measures.[79] These characteristics, along with the division of the Kassel manuscript into different thematic elements, suggest that it was compiled with a pedagogic purpose in mind. This manuscript may usefully be seen as one scholar's 'handbook' to music.

Music theory textbooks

Processes and decisions similar to those that influenced the compilation of the Kassel manuscript also shaped the compilation of other music textbooks. From the many surviving German manuscripts of the period, I have chosen a sample of twenty that best reflect the textbook genre. It is a critical choice and cannot provide a definitive representation of contemporary music-theory manuscripts.[80] It excludes, for example, Karlsruhe, Badische Landesbibliothek, 504, a codex of 199 folios that is closely connected with the circle of Frutolf of Michelsberg. This is because Karlsruhe 504 is a binding of numerous individual manuscripts and was not, as it exists today, designed as a textbook. Also excluded are two twelfth-century English textbooks – Cambridge, Trinity College, R. 15.22 (944) and Oxford, Balliol College, 173A – which show obvious signs of having been copied from German exemplars.[81] Other manuscripts might well have been included: the twelfth-century portion (fols 1–75) of Basel, Universitätsbibliothek, F. IX. 36, which appears to have been a rather clumsy attempt to produce a music textbook by a clerk who had access only to a limited number of sources, for example.[82] Some manuscripts have been excluded on account of their date. One of the manuscripts compiled in the early eleventh-

---

[79] Robinson, 'The sources and method of papal and anti-papal polemic', p. 42.
[80] A clearer picture might emerge from a full textual and stemmatic analysis of all relevant manuscripts, an immense project of equivalent stature to that undertaken by Elias von Steinmeyer for Old High German gloss collections: E. Steinmeyer and E. Sievers, *Die althochdeutschen Glossen*, 5 vols (Berlin, 1879–1922).
[81] Pesce (ed. and trans.), *Guido*, pp. 52–5; R. A. B. Mynors, *Catalogue of the manuscripts of Balliol College, Oxford* (Oxford, 1963), pp. 176–8.
[82] RISM B 3/1, p. 69; J. Richter, *Katalog der Musiksammlung auf der Universitätsbibliothek in Basel* (Leipzig, 1892), p. 18. This manuscript is a collection of John's *De musica* (fols 2r–64v), an anonymous treatise and tonary (fols 65r–70r) and a diagram similar to William of Hirsau's *cribrum monochordi* (fol. 27r). The handwriting on fols 76–101 probably dates from the thirteenth century and not the fourteenth, as stated in *RISM B* 3/1, p. 69.

century by Hartwic of St Emmeram (Munich, Bayerische Staatsbibliothek, Clm 14272), while being a classic example of the textbook genre, contains no material by the south-German circle.[83]

Sample of eleventh- and twelfth-century music theory textbooks

B1   Berlin, Staatsbibliothek zu Berlin, Preußischer Kulturbesitz, Lat. qu. 106, fols 157–169
B2   Berlin, Staatsbibliothek zu Berlin, Preußischer Kulturbesitz, Lat. qu. 106, fols 170–185
D1   Darmstadt, Universitäts- und Hochschulbibliothek, 1988, fols 71–146
D2   Darmstadt, Universitäts- und Hochschulbibliothek, 1988, fols 147–189
Ka   Kassel, Landesbibliothek und Murhardsche Bibliothek der Stadt, 4° Mss Math. 1 (47 folios)
L   Leiden, Bibliotheek der Rijksuniversiteit, BPL 194 (46 folios)
Lz   Leipzig, Universitätsbibliothek, Cod. 1493 (90 folios)
M1   Munich, Bayerische Staatsbibliothek, Clm 9921, fols 14–39
M2   Munich, Bayerische Staatsbibliothek, Clm 14523, fols 118–133
M3   Munich, Bayerische Staatsbibliothek, Clm 14663, fols 1–33
M4   Munich, Bayerische Staatsbibliothek, Clm 14965a (39 folios)
M5   Munich, Bayerische Staatsbibliothek, Clm 14965b (73 folios)
M6   Munich, Bayerische Staatsbibliothek, Clm 18914 (43 folios)
M7   Munich, Bayerische Staatsbibliothek, Clm 18937, fols 260–297
M8   Munich, Bayerische Staatsbibliothek, Clm 19421 (58 folios)
R1   Rochester (NY), Eastman School of Music, ML 92/1100 (232 pages)
R2   Rochester (NY), Eastman School of Music, ML 92/1200 (94 folios)
V1   Vienna, Österreichische Nationalbibliothek, Cod. 51 (166 folios)
V2   Vienna, Österreichische Nationalbibliothek, Cod. 2502 (40 folios)
W   Wolfenbüttel, Herzog-August Bibliothek, 334 Gud. Lat. 8° (177 folios)

The codices in this sample range in date from the 1060s (M2) to the last third of the twelfth century (M3). The origins of some are clear: W, for example, was copied at the monastery of Sts Ulrich and Afra in Augsburg.[84] Others, such as V1 and V2, cannot yet be identified with any particular centre, though their contents, handwriting and decoration of initial capitals point unambiguously to southern-Germany.[85] They also vary in size: Lz, R1, R2, V1 and W are the largest of these codices, with

[83] See above, pp. 179–81.
[84] RISM B 3/3, pp. 212–17.
[85] RISM B 3/1, pp. 33–6, 42–4; RISM B 3/6, pp. 61–2, 71–2.

most of the others occupying about forty folios. The large size of some is explained by the presence of long works such as Boethius' *De institutione musica* (**Lz** and **V1**), or by full recensions of a number of treatises: **R2**, an Admont manuscript copied in the first half of the twelfth century, contains full recensions of pseudo-Odo's *Dialogus de musica*, Aribo's *De musica*, Guido of Arezzo's four treatises and Bern's tonary, suggesting a careful plan to bring these treatises together in one volume.[86] **L**, in contrast, is a smaller affair: a neat little book of forty-six folios copied in one tidy hand and dating, most probably, from the late eleventh century. Its provenance is to the monastery of St James in Liège, although we cannot tell whether or not it was copied there. The treatises and excerpts it contains are copied across the quires indicating that it was the deliberate compilation of one clerk, much in the manner of the Kassel manuscript (**Ka**), which may be related to it in part. **R2** and **L**, though differing in length, nonetheless share the characteristic of having been planned textbooks.

Some of the codices are not restricted to works of music theory. **R1** appears to have functioned as a textbook on the quadrivium, for it contains a liturgical calendar, and treatises on the computus, rythmomachia, abacus and astronomy in addition to its musical material.[87] The collection of music treatises in **V1** is accompanied by Cicero's *De inventione*, *Rhetorica ad Herennium*, texts on geometry and Hyginus on astronomy.[88] The whole codex is written in a number of similar and recurring hands, and is additionally unified by its distinctive style of decorative capitals. These characteristics suggest that it was conceived as a textbook on selected *artes*, the deliberately planned work of one scriptorium, with a number of scribes working on its contents simultaneously. A similar conclusion can be drawn about **Lz**, which was produced in an unidentified German scriptorium during the second half of the eleventh century.[89] These codices differ from examples such as **M2**, which was bound together with three independent manuscripts containing other musical and quadrivial material sometime after the end of the thirteenth century.[90]

Other manuscripts, which in their present form are bound together, were originally separate: such are **B1** and **B2**, which belonged to the Lotharingian monastery of Maria Laach. **B1**, containing William of Hirsau's *Musica* (fols

[86] *RISM B* 3/1, pp. 183–6; *RISM B* 3/6, p. 730.
[87] *RISM B* 3/1, pp. 180–3; *RISM B* 3/6, p. 730.
[88] See Chapter 1, p. 46.
[89] See Chapter 3, pp. 134–5; *RISM B* 3/6, pp. 319–21.
[90] *RISM B* 3/3, pp. 113–16; *RISM B* 3/6, pp. 335–6.

157–169) and a diagram of the ancient Greek Greater Perfect System, dates from the last quarter of the eleventh century.[91] **B2**, containing Theoger of Metz's *Musica* and ancillary musical texts, dates from the early twelfth century. The appearance of 'Liber sancte marie lacum' at several places in the codex, suggests that **B1** and **B2** were once in different books and that the present binding is somewhat later. A similar situation obtains with **D1** and **D2**, which belonged to the monastery of St James in Liège, but were bound together by the fifteenth century to form the second and third parts of Darmstadt, Universitäts- und Hochschulbibliothek, 1988.[92]

D2 also illustrates another way in which a textbook might be formed: by the addition of relevant material to an existing manuscript. Most of this manuscript (fols 147–181) is copied in a few closely related hands dating from the early twelfth century. The works contained in this portion of **D2** go across the quires, indicating that the compilation was deliberate and – like **V1** and **Lz** – probably the result of collaboration in a scriptorium. The last quire of four bifolia (fols 182–189) contains a single treatise: the Wolf Anonymous. It is copied in one hand, which is contemporaneous with, but unrelated to the other hands of **D2**. Additionally, it contains red and green rubrication that is absent from the rest of **D2**. At some stage, therefore, this independent quire was added to fols 147–181 of **D2**. It is not anachronistic to suggest that this happened when or shortly after the rest of **D2** was copied. An analogy may be found in the case of Bernold of St Blasien, who added more modern material to the already constituted part of the doctrinal handbook Stuttgart, Württembergische Landesbibliothek, HB. VI. 107.[93] Similarly, the Tegernsee codex **M8** is a binding of three independent manuscripts.[94] The fact that all the material contained in this codex is of the sort found in codices such as **Ka**, **L** or **V1**, warrants the assumption that

---

[91] **B1** contains a quire of two bifolia (fols 157–160) and a quire of four bifolia (fols 161–168). The diagram of the Greater Perfect System (fol. 169) is attached as a fly-leaf fold out.

[92] *RISM B* 3/3, p. 39; G. Ilnitchi, *The play of meanings: Aribo's De musica and the hermeneutics of musical thought* (Lanham, Md., 2005), p. 20.

[93] See above, p. 177.

[94] Various datings have been given for the constituent parts of **M8**. *RISM B* 3/3, p. 143: twelfth century (part 1), end of the eleventh century or beginning of the twelfth century (part 2), end of the eleventh century (part 3); H. Schmid, 'Die musiktheoretischen Handschriften der Benediktiner-Abtei Tegernsee. Ein Beitrag zur Erfassung und Sichtung der musiktheoretischen Hinterlassenschaft des Mittelalters' (Doctoral dissertation, Ludwig-Maximilian University, Munich, 1951), p. 17 dates all parts to the twelfth century; C. E. Eder, 'Die Schule des Klosters Tegernsee im frühen Mittelalter im Spiegel der Tegernseer Handschriften', *SMGBZ* 83 (1972), 107 dates all parts to the third quarter of the eleventh century.

it is another example of a textbook formed through the combination of already existing manuscripts.

M1, which was copied at the monastery of Ottobeuren about the middle of the twelfth century, is remarkable in that its excerpts from the south-German treatises appear as interpolations and marginal glosses.[95] The backbone of its contents is formed by Guido's *Micrologus* and *Regule rithmice*, and the tonary of Udalschalk of Augsburg. To these works, however, has been added an extensive corpus of marginal glosses, mostly comprising extracts from the south-German treatises, measurement texts and didactic verses. As with the scribe of the Kassel manuscript (**Ka**), although in a different form, these additions show a German clerk supplementing and contextualizing Guido with indigenous theory.

Although each of the codices is different, reflecting in a unique way its particular origin and history, the overarching consistency of content and implied didactic purpose across the sample justifies their categorization as textbooks, thereby providing an opportunity to ascertain which authors were considered useful by eleventh- and twelfth-century scribes.

Guido of Arezzo

The scribe of the Kassel (**Ka**) manuscript arranged his material in sections with a clear eye for the content of each. This thematic organization of material can be observed to a greater or lesser extent in the other textbooks. The importance accorded to Guido of Arezzo by the Kassel scribe is mirrored in most of the other codices. Thirteen in total contain some or other part of Guido's works: **D1, Ka, L, M1, M2, M3, M4, M6, M8, R2, V1, V2** and **W**. Seven of these transmit all of Guido's four treatises: **D1, Ka, M3, M4, R2, V1** and **W**.

In all except one of these seven, Guido's treatises have been copied contiguously. In **M3** – a St Emmeram manuscript copied in the last third of the twelfth century – *Micrologus* (fols 1r–11r) is separated from Guido's other treatises, which have been copied together (fols 17r–24v).[96] The interven-

---

[95] *RISM B* 3/1, pp. 103–07; *RISM B* 3/6, pp. 331–2. Pesce (ed. and trans.), *Guido*, pp. 120–5. There has been much confusion over the dating of this manuscript, largely owing to the fact that the codex Clm 9921 is comprised of a number of separate manuscripts of different dates. The handwriting and contents of the part that is **M1** indicate a date around the middle of the twelfth century.

[96] Pesce (ed. and trans.), *Guido*, p. 136; *RISM B* 3/3, pp. 118–19. **M3**, the first constituent manuscript of Munich, Bayerische Staatsbibliothek, Clm 14663, comprises four quires and some singletons: fols 1–8, 9–14, 15, 16, 17–24 and 25–33 (fol. 27 is a singleton). The manuscript was copied by two scribes working in collaboration, except for fols 15 and 16, which were copied in a third but contemporary hand.

ing section of the manuscript (fols 11r–16v) contains three texts: the anonymous treatise *Quomodo de arithmetica procedit musica* on the relationship of arithmetic and music (fols 11r–14v), and two excerpts from *Commentarius anonymus in Micrologum Guidonis Aretini* (fols 15r–16v). The choice of these texts was not an arbitrary one. In the light of Guido's discussion of proportion in *Micrologus*, it is not surprising that the scribe should look for a text that would make explicit the connexion between music and mathematics: *Quomodo de arithmetica procedit musica*, which he copied after *Micrologus*. Folios 15 and 16 are in a different but contemporary hand and were probably inserted between the second and third quires of **M3** because of the complementary material that they contain. The first excerpt from the anonymous commentary deals with arithmetical proportion in music, more specifically that outlined in *Micrologus* 16. Its heading 'Quomodo intelligentur sequentia' emphasizes its didactic purpose at this point. The second excerpt from the commentary continues this theme. These three texts are not designed to split up Guido's treatises. Rather, should they be seen as the efforts of a conscientious and well informed clerk to provide relevant alternative opinions to aspects of Guido's teaching.

A similar pattern is to be observed in **M2**. This mini-textbook is the third of four manuscripts that make up Munich, Bayerische Staatsbibliothek, Clm 14523 and contains works of music theory, mostly by Guido.[97] It was probably in existence by the 1060s and was probably used by William of Hirsau for its Guidonian material: among its different hands is that of Otloh of St Emmeram, the interlocutor of William's music treatise.[98] In **M2** the order of some of the Guidonian material has been changed.

Munich, Bayerische Staatsbibliothek, Clm 14523, fols 118r–133v **(M2)**

fols	118r–125v	*Micrologus*
fols	125v–127r	*Regule rithmice*
fol.	127rv	*Prologus in antiphonarium*, lines 54–126
fol.	127v	*Epistola ad Michahelem*, lines 90–104
fol.	128rv	*Micrologus*
fols	128v–129r	*Prologus in antiphonarium*, lines 1–53

---

[97] Pesce (ed. and trans.), *Guido*, pp. 134–5; *RISM B* 3/3, pp. 113–16. Fols 118–133 comprise one regular quire of four bifolia (fols 118–125) and a mutilated quire (fols 126–131 with fol. 132 and fol. 133 being attached singletons).

[98] Bischoff, 'Literarisches und künstlerisches Leben', p. 94 n. 68.

fol.	129rv	*Epistola ad Michahelem*, lines *1–88*
fol.	129v	Miscellaneous fragment
fols	130r–131v	*Epistola ad Michahelem*, lines *105–388*
fol.	132r	Table of mutations with hexachords on C and G
fols	132r–133v	Didactic verses on the modes ('Regulae tonorum secundum Guidonem')

While *Micrologus* and *Regule rithmice* have been copied integrally, both *Prologus* and *Epistola* have been split. This was probably because it was thought helpful to rearrange the sections of these works along thematic lines. Hence, the excerpts on fol. 127rv are concerned with notation, which explains the matching of lines 54–126 of *Prologus* (where Guido begins to explain his notational system) and lines 90–104 of *Epistola* (the beginning of the section entitled '[Rules] to find an unknown chant'). After having interposed a short extract from *Micrologus*, the scribe paired the opening section of *Prologus* (Guido's admonishment of singers' stupidity) with the similarly disaffected opening of *Epistola* (Guido's complaints about the hardships and jealousy he has endured because of his musical innovations) on fols 128v–129v. He followed this with some comments of his own on fol. 129v, what we might call a gloss of sorts, before copying the remainder of *Epistola* (Guido's demonstration of his notational system to his friend Michael), and providing a table of mutations and hexachords on fol. 132v. This table represents a summary of the teaching just outlined, and provides more evidence of the scribe's engaging with the Guidonian texts. Finally, fols 132v–133v contain didactic verses on the modes with the telling heading 'Regulae tonorum secundum Guidonem'. The conscious rearrangement of authentic Guidonian material and Guidonian-related material across quiring breaks in this manuscript indicates that it was produced with a definite pedagogic purpose in mind.

Only two of the manuscripts that contain Guidonian excerpts do not preserve them as an intact group: the scribes responsible for **M1** and **V2** chose to intersperse other texts among them; nevertheless, in both cases there seems to have been some attempt to keep them together, the interpolated texts generally being brief and relevant to Guido. **L** and **M6** contain parts of *Micrologus* as their only Guidonian material. In **L**, *Micrologus* is interspersed with various commentaries on fols 1v–22v,[99] while the scribe of **M6**, working in the third quarter of the eleventh century at Tegernsee,

---

[99] *RISM B* 3/1, p. 136.

seems only to have been interested in Guido's monochord measurements for he has copied a passage from *Micrologus* 3 on fol. 32r.[100]

Pseudo-Odo of Cluny

Eleventh- and twelfth-century writers believed that the treatise *Dialogus de musica* had been written by Abbot Odo of Cluny.[101] (Michel Huglo has shown that it was written in Lombardy during the late tenth century.[102]) It was fairly popular with German clerks, probably owing to a combination of its supposed author's fame and Guido's admonition at the end of *Epistola ad Michehelem* to 'read the book . . . that the most reverend abbot Odo composed most brilliantly'.[103] *Dialogus de musica* appears complete in six of the sample textbooks: **D1**, fols 101v–110r (where it is attributed to Guido); **L**, fols 22v–39v; **M4**, fols 33r–37v; **M8**, fols 1v–12v; **R2**, fols 1r–11r; **V1**, fols 46r–48v. One further manuscript – **M3** – contains an incomplete recension on fols 21v–24v.

Bern of Reichenau

The important position that Bern of Reichenau held in relation to the south-German circle is mirrored by his relative popularity among the compilers of the music theory textbooks. Bern was the most frequently copied of the German theorists, with twelve of the sample codices containing material by him. (Additionally, the recension of Anonymous I in **V1** is attributed to Bern.) This popularity was based primarily upon his *Prologus in tonarium* and *Tonarius* which, though originally intended as a complementary pair, in practice frequently became separated, perhaps owing to the needs of individual scribes. Three textbooks preserve a full version of Bern's treatise and tonary as one entity: **D2**, fols 147r–167r; **Lz**, fols 47r–60r; **M7**, fols 261r–295r. In **M7**, a Tegernsee codex copied in the second half of the eleventh century, the continuity has been interrupted by the insertion of a table in the same hand showing the Greek Greater Perfect System and a

---

[100] Ibid. 3/3, p. 136. Fol. 41 contains a measurement text from William of Hirsau's *Musica* that carries the marginal heading 'Versus ad mensuram monochordi secundum Guidonem' and an additional fourteenth- or fifteenth-century heading 'Versus Guidonis de mensura monochordi'.

[101] Some eleventh- and twelfth-century authors call pseudo-Odo's treatise *Enchirias de musica*, which can create confusion as to whether they are referring to pseudo-Odo or the Carolingian treatise *Musica enchiriadis*.

[102] M. Huglo, 'L'Auteur du Dialogue sur la Musique attribuée à Odon', *Revue de musicologie* 55 (1969), 119–71; *Les Tonaires*, pp. 183–224; 'Der Prolog des Odo zugeschriebenen "Dialogus de Musica"', *Archiv für Musikwissenschaft* 28 (1971), 134–46.

[103] Pesce (ed. and trans.), *Guido*, p. 530.

short text on the modes (part of which is based upon the anonymous Carolingian treatise *Musica enchiriadis*) on fol. 278rv.[104] These additions, however, should be seen as study aids: the table would have been a helpful concordance to the Greek note names used exclusively by Bern, while the text on the modes recapped important issues before proceeding to the tonary. They were thus designed to link Bern's treatise and tonary, rather than divide them.

The full text of *Prologus* is also transmitted in **V1** (fols 49r–52r), although it is separated from the tonary, of which there are two versions (fols 56v–62r and fols 71r–72v). The second of these is in abridged form and follows immediately from John's *De musica*. It is incomplete, ending on fol. 72v with two rubricated headings and blank spaces where the text was to be filled in. The duplication may well have resulted from a misunderstanding between the scribes who collaborated on the production of **V1**. It is possible that the scribe who copied the abridged tonary saw the full version produced by a colleague and – realizing the duplication – abandoned his own effort. **R1** (pp. 143–73) transmits the interpolated version of *Prologus*.[105]

The other manuscripts from the sample contain incomplete or excerpted versions of *Prologus*. Two of these – **M4** (fols 27r–29r) and **R2** (fols 76r–79v) – transmit an identical excerpt (*Prologus* 5–10) that gives the modal ranges and Bern's extensive comments on the peculiarities of certain chants and modes.[106] In **R2**, however, this excerpt is followed immediately by a varied recension of Bern's *Tonarius* (fols 79v–91r), which suggests that these two manuscripts were copied from a common archetype, no longer extant. It was the scribe of that archetype, therefore, who decided to excerpt this portion of *Prologus*. We have already seen that the scribe of **Ka** copied an extensive portion of *Prologus* (Chapters 1–9) in his textbook.[107] Two other codices contain fairly extensive excerpts. The scribe of **M3** copied *Prologus* 1–7 on fols 29v–33v, while the scribe of **V2** copied *Prologus* 1–4 on fols 37v–38v, leaving out Bern's discussion of the species and modes. **M1** contains a portion of *Prologus* on fols 16v–17r. This text is divided in two sections. The first comprises two excerpts (one from *Prologus* 1, the other from *Prologus* 2) that have been combined under the heading 'Orditur proemium subsequentiam tonorum'. (This heading is also found at the beginning of *Prologus* in **D2**, suggesting a link between these two

---

[104] The table and text is given by Schmid, 'Die musiktheoretischen Handschriften der Benediktiner-Abtei Tegernsee', pp. 84–5.
[105] See Chapter 2, pp. 72–80.
[106] Bern, *Prologus* 5–10, pp. 40–62.
[107] See above, p. 195.

manuscripts.) The second section is headed 'Regule cuiusdam sapientis' and comprises *Prologus* 5–7 without any divisions. Finally, fols 39v–41v of L contain material from Bern's *Tonarius* that comments on Aribo's circular diagrams, identical to **Ka**, fol. 33rv.[108]

Herman of Reichenau

On first sight it appears that Herman's *Musica* was not widely disseminated, as only two full recensions survive: **R1** (pp. 91–130) and **V1** (fols 82r–90r). This statistic is misleading. The scribe of **Ka** knew *Musica* well enough to copy an extract on the modes, and Herman's treatise was also known by the Wolf Anonymous, William of Hirsau, Aribo, Theoger of Metz, Frutolf of Michelsberg and the author of *Quaestiones in musica*, all of whom relied upon it in their own work. There must, therefore, have been many more copies than now exist. The textbooks show that Herman's immense reputation as a music theorist was based not only upon his *Musica*, but also upon his three mnemonic verses: *E voces unisonas*, *Ter tria iunctorum* and *Ter terni sunt modi*.[109] Nine of the sample codices contain the mnemonic verses: **Ka**, fols 19r–20r (all three); **L**, fol. 43v (verse 3); **M1**, fol. 20rv (verses 2 and 1 with verse 3 added as a marginal gloss); **M4**, fol. 2r (verse 3); **M6**, fol. 42r (verse 2 with verse 1 in the margin); **M8**, fol. 14rv (verses 3 and 2); **R2**, fols 91v–92v (verses 1 and 3); **V2**, fols 26v, 27v (verses 3 and 2); and **W**, fols 133r–135v (all three). **M5** (fols 21rv, 22r) and **R1** (pp. 178, 180) also transmit the verses, though in both cases this has been as a part of Frutolf's *Breviarium de musica*.

William of Hirsau

William of Hirsau's *Musica* appears in five of the textbooks, three times complete: **B1**, fols 157r–168v; **R1**, pp. 184–230; **V1**, fols 73v–81v. The scribe of **B1** divided William's *Musica* into two books. The first 'book' (fols 157r–163v) ends when the scribe breaks off in the middle of William's twentieth chapter with the words '. . . tertius in F. Quartus in G';[110] the second (fols 163v–168v) is headed 'Incipit liber secundus' and picks up immediately with the words 'Qui primitus musicam artem invenerunt . . .'.[111] This was not the only change made by the scribe: on fol. 169r he added a table showing the gamut, upon which are superimposed the ancient Greek note

---

[108] See below, p. 207.
[109] M. Bernhard, 'Zur Rezeption der musiktheoretischen Werke des Hermannus Contractus', pp. 105–107, 111–14, 115–21.
[110] William, *Musica*, p. 52.
[111] Ibid.

names that had been outlined by Boethius (complete with a Latin translation of their individual meanings) and the tetrachords of the *graves*, *finales*, *superiores* and *excellentes*.[112] (This is yet another example of additions to texts that were frequently made by scribes for didactic purposes.) The division of *Musica* into two books was also made by the scribe of **R1**, but unlike **B1**, it occurs between the thirteenth and fourteenth chapters, ruling out the possibility of an affiliation between the manuscripts.[113]

Two further textbooks contain short excerpts from William's *Musica*. **M4** (fol. 1r) contains a portion of *Musica* 9 on the arithmetical proportions governing the intervals, while **M6** (fols 41r–42r) transmits *Musica* 41 and 40, which give William's monochord measurements in verse and prose (the versified measurements are headed 'Versus Guidonis de mensura monochordi').[114] Like Herman, though to a lesser extent, William's reputation as a theorist was preserved by some short ancillary texts that were ascribed to him by clerks. Aribo mentioned with esteem that William had devised a method for measuring organ pipes, and this section of his *De musica* was copied a number of times by scribes, presumably on account of William's great reputation.[115] In **M1** a set of organ pipe measurements attributed to William has been added as a marginal gloss on fol. 22v.[116]

Theoger of Metz

We have seen how the scribe of the Kassel manuscript (**Ka**) used Theoger of Metz in the production of that textbook. A full recension of Theoger's *Musica* appears in **W**, fols 62v–83r, which was copied at Sts Ulrich and Afra in Augsburg (reformed in 1109 from Theoger's monastery of St Georgen while he was abbot). Another early recension survives in **B2**, fols 170r–178v, which also contains marginal glosses. The scribe of **B2** made a critical decision to move forward the beginning of Chapter 30 to a point midway in Chapter 29. The last three chapters are missing, replaced by a number of *Exempla* from the end of Theoger's treatise and an anonymous *Regula* (fols 177v–178v). Both of these items are copied in another hand, which looks remarkably similar to the neat hand that glossed this copy of Theoger.[117] It seems that it was Theoger's glossator who completed the copy by adding the

---

[112] *RISM B* 3/3, p. 20; William, *Musica*, p. 79.
[113] *RISM B* 3/1, p. 182.
[114] William, *Musica*, pp. 26–7, 70–5. Schmid, 'Die musiktheoretischen Handschriften der Benediktiner-Abtei Tegernsee', p. 14.
[115] Aribo, *De musica*, p. 42.
[116] Pesce (ed. and trans.), *Guido*, p. 122.
[117] Lochner, 'Dietger', p. 145.

Exempla and *Regula*. One further textbook contains excerpts from Theoger: **M1**. Fol. 19r contains a gloss headed 'De synemenon', which is intended as a comment upon part of Guido's *Regule rithmice*. The text of this gloss is an abridgement of Chapter 12 of Theoger's *Musica*. Fol. 39v carries eight diagrams showing the division of each of the eight modes into their constituent *diatessaron* and *diapente*. These diagrams are a combination of the diagrams and text from *Musica* 31-8. They occur in the manuscript just after a tonary (fols 32v-39r), probably on account of their appositeness at this point.

Aribo

That Aribo's *De musica* seems to have found a place more frequently in textbook codices is perhaps because its division into more than a hundred chapters made it a very suitable candidate for excerpting. Extracts appear in seven of the sample textbooks. Only one of these – **R2**, fols 11r-42r – contains the complete text of *De musica*, although the internal order has been mixed up (owing to transcription from a faultily-bound exemplar). Aribo's teaching on the modes appears to have been his most popular legacy. He expressed this concisely with a novel series of intersecting circle diagrams, which will be immediately familiar to anybody today who has studied mathematical set theory: the circles represent the authentic and plagal modes, while their intersection represents the common material. These were the 'modal circles' copied by the Kassel scribe (**Ka**) who accompanied them with passages from Bern's *Tonarius*,[118] as did the scribe of **L**, fols 39v-41r (with *De musica* 37 and 38). They also appear in **M3**, fols 28r-29r (with *De musica* 36-38) and without text in **M4**, fols 7v-8r. The next most popular part of Aribo seems to have been his teaching on the *quadripartita figura* and his own improvement upon it. Extracts on this subject are to be found in **D2**, fols 170v-178v; **M4**, fols 31r-32v; and in **W**, fols 57r-61r, 127v-128v. A number of measurement directions from *De musica* appear in the part of **W** that is devoted to such items. Fols 106r-110v of this codex transmit five chapters dealing with organ-pipe measurements: an 'old' measurement system, a 'new' system attributed to William of Hirsau, Aribo's own measurements, an epigram summarizing them and the chapter entitled 'On how these pipes are suitably made'.[119]

---

[118] See above, pp. 192-3.
[119] Wolfenbüttel, Herzog August Bibliothek, 334 Gud. Lat. 8°, fol. 106r: Antiqua fistularum mensura que inten|ditur |; fol. 107v: Noua fistularum mensura que remittitur; fol. 108r: Aribunculina fistularum mensura nec in toto intensibilis | nec in toto remissibilis sesquitercia et sesqualtera proportione; fol. 109r: Organice dispositionis mensura; fol. 109v: Qualiter ipse congruenter fiant fistule. Cf. *De musica*, pp. 40.43-46.92.

Frutolf of Michelsberg

Frutolf's *Breviarium de musica* and *Tonarius* are transmitted complete only in **M5**, where they occupy fols 3v–72r of the manuscript's seventy-three folios.[120] Nevertheless, this manuscript can still be classified as a textbook, for Frutolf's compendious *Breviarium* – compiled from a variety of sources – covers by itself most of the areas that a scribe would have been interested in. It was in this sense a ready-made textbook. Four of the other sample codices contain extracts: **Ka, M8, R1** and **W**. **R1** devotes pp. 173–183 to a variety of extracts as does **M8**, fols 14v–27r;[121] we have already seen that the scribe of the Kassel manuscript (**Ka**) used Frutolf liberally too. Frutolf's set of verses on the modes – inspired by Herman's examples – proved most popular, as we have seen in the case of **Ka**; it was also copied by the scribes of **R1** and **M8**.[122] Also popular were Frutolf's measurement directions, which are found in all four of these codices. Frutolf, therefore, like Aribo, was found useful in certain respects: it was his verses on the modes and sections on measurements that attracted scholars in particular.

The Wolf Anonymous, Master Henry of Augsburg, John and Quaestiones in musica

The treatise by the Wolf Anonymous is transmitted only in **D2** (fols 182v–189v). Henry of Augsburg's *Musica* also survives in only manuscript: **V1**, fols 90r–91ar. As with Herman of Reichenau, Master Henry's mnemonic verses appear more frequently than his treatise, surviving in three of the sample manuscripts without attribution: **B2**, fol. 182v; **Ka**, fols 18v–19r; and **M1**, fol. 47v (they also appear, as part of Frutolf's *Breviarium de musica* in **M5**, fol. 32v). John's treatise appears in two of the sample codices: **V1**, fols 62v–70v and **V2**, fols 28v–37r. **D1** (fols 110v–143v) is the only source for *Quaestiones in musica* among the sample.

Carolingian works

In contrast to eleventh-century theorists, which make up by far the greater part of the textbooks, Carolingian treatises were copied far less frequently. Four textbooks contain Carolingian material: **Ka, M6, M7** and **V1**. (In the case of **M7**, fol. 278rv, the scribe may not have realized the Carolingian origin of the material from *Musica enchiriadis* that is incorporated into a

---

[120] *RISM B* 3/3, pp. 127–8. See Chapter 2, p. 94.
[121] *RISM B* 3/4, p. 182; Pesce (ed. and trans.), *Guido*, p. 126.
[122] See also A. Rausch, 'Frutolf von Michelsberg', *MGG*. *Personenteil* 7, col. 211.

short text on the modes.) V1 contains an extract from Hucbald of St Amand on fol. 35r.[123] This extract, which gives Hucbald's explanation of the notes of the Greek *systema telion*, follows immediately after Boethius' *De institutione musica* (fols 4r–34v). It serves, therefore, as a glossary for the terminology of Boethius' treatise, in the same way that the Kassel scribe used an extract from Regino of Prüm as a glossary in his textbook.[124] **M6** completes the tally with the anonymous *Musica enchiriadis* and *Scolica enchiriadis*.[125] The amount of Carolingian material in the sample codices contrasts strongly with the amount contained in earlier textbooks. We remember that Hartwic of St Emmeram's textbook (Munich, Bayerische Staatsbibliothek, Clm 14272) contained a good selection of Carolingian material – *Musica enchiriadis* and *Scolica enchiriadis*, *Commemoratio brevis de tonis*, *Alia musica* and Hucbald of St Amand – in proportion to its overall contents. This characteristic is repeated in another compilation made in a Lotharingian centre sometime before or around the middle of the eleventh century: Brussels, Bibliothèque Royale, 10078/95.[126] It contains *Musica enchiriadis* and *Scolica enchiriadis*, Hucbald, *Musica disciplina* by Aurelian of Réôme and extracts from Cassiodorus, in addition to Abbo of Fleury on the abacus, Gerbert on geometry, and numerous short texts on the measurement of bells and organ pipes. Its contents (and absence of *moderni* such as Bern, Herman or Guido) suggest either a deliberate conservatism on the part of the scribe or, more likely, an early date of compilation. Munich, Clm 14272 and Brussels, 10078/95 contain what can be interpreted as up-to-date collections of music-theory sources for their time. The Carolingian authors did not, however, disappear from circulation in subsequent generations: surviving manuscripts and library catalogues show that they were available throughout Germany in our period. The evidence from compilation codices of the late-eleventh and twelfth centuries suggests that clerks were no longer interested in copying the Carolingian authors, favouring the more modern theorists in their place.

---

[123] Hucbald of St Amand, *Musica*, ed. Y. Chartier, *L'Œuvre musicale d'Hucbald de Saint-Amand. Les compositions et le traité de musique* (Montreal, 1995) pp. 198–206.
[124] See above, p. 194.
[125] *RISM B* 3/3, p. 135; Bubnov (ed.), *Gerberti postea Silvestri II papae Opera mathematica*, pp. 302–09; Schmid, 'Die musiktheoretischen Handschriften der Benediktiner-Abtei Tegernsee', pp. 13–15. Schmid points out that the heading 'Musica Adelboldi ad Silvestrum papam', which begins a treatise on fols 30r–31v, is a fifteenth-century addition to a work on finding the density of a sphere.
[126] *RISM B* 3/1, pp. 55–7.

Classical authors

Like the Carolingians, the Classical authors remained largely peripheral to the concerns of the textbook compilers. Boethius' *De institutione musica* appears in three of the codices: **D2**, **Lz**, and **V1**. Only in **D2**, however, has the scribe attempted to integrate Boethius with other texts. Here the opening of Book 2 (Pythagoras' views on 'continuous' and 'discrete' quantities) has been sandwiched between two extracts from Aribo.[127] **V1** transmits *De institutione musica* in full, as did **Lz** at one stage.[128] In the **Lz** and **V1** Boethius appears at the beginning, suggesting that he was viewed as a type of foundation and included for completeness' sake.

Macrobius was of restricted relevance to the textbook compilers: the same single extract from his *Commentarius in Somnium Scipionis* dealing with the numerical proportions that produce harmony was copied in **Ka**, **M4** and **M5**.[129] **L** provides one of only two extracts from Isidore of Seville among our sample codices.[130] A sizeable excerpt from Calcidius' commentary on Plato's *Timaeus* survives on fols 34r–51v of **M3**.[131]

Tonaries

Ten of the textbooks contain tonaries. The tonary in its classic form – a list of chants organized according to mode – is exemplified by Abbot Bern's *Tonarius*, which appears in five of the sample codices: **D2**, fols 157r–167r; **Lz**, fols 53r–60r; **M7**, fols 279r–295r; **R2**, fols 79v–91r; **V1**, fols 56rb–62rb and 71r–72v.[132] Frutolf of Michelsberg's tonary, which was modelled on Bern's exemplar, is transmitted complete only in **M5**, a manuscript virtually devoted to *Breviarium de musica* and *Tonarius*. The scribe of **M8** copied an excerpt containing the chants of the Mass on fols 16v–22v. The tonary found in **R1**, pp. 131–142 has been copied in the same hand as Herman's *Musica*, which immediately precedes it. Both **M1** and **W** contain two tonaries. **M1** has a glossed version of the tonary by Udalschalk of Augsburg (abbot of Sts Ulrich and Afra, 1124–51) on fols 21r–32v, as well as

---

[127] Boethius, *De musica*, pp. 227–9; Pesce (ed. and trans.), *Guido*, p. 63; *RISM B* 3/3, p. 40; *RISM B* 3/6, p. 278.

[128] The Leipzig recension begins mid-sentence on fol. 1r, implying that the present material was once preceded by the beginning of Book 1, which is no longer extant. See Chapter 3, p. 134.

[129] Macrobius, *Commentarius in Somnium Scipionis* 2.1.14–21, pp. 97–8. See Chapter 4, pp. 150–1.

[130] *RISM B* 3/1, p. 137; *GS* 1, pp. 20a–21a.

[131] Pesce (ed. and trans.), *Guido*, p. 163.

[132] On the two versions of Bern's *Tonarius* in **V1** (Vienna, Österreichische Nationalbibliothek, Cod. 51) see above, p. 204.

a tonary comprised of Gradual chants on fols 32v–39r.[133] **W** contains an anonymous tonary on fols 83r–89r and a recension of Udalschalk's tonary on fols 139v–174r.[134]

Notated didactic verses

A number of the manuscripts contain texts that, while being closely related to the tonary, are in fact sets of notated verses designed to provide examples of the different modes (see Plate 10). These texts are misleadingly classified as tonaries by most modern scholars. Delores Pesce, for example, has described fols 2r–7v of **M4** in this way,[135] though the notated verses these folios contain bear far more resemblance to the didactic verses that we have already seen in **Ka**.[136] Similarly, the editors of the *RISM* catalogue have incorrectly described the notated verses on fols 179r–185r of **B** (which are closely related examples in **Ka**) as a tonary.[137]

Verses of this type, on account of their didactic function, were an integral part of the textbooks (they are to be found in all except **Lz** and **M3**). They include the anonymous set beginning 'Primum querite regnum dei', which was copied with notation from one manuscript to another, and Master Henry's set beginning 'Primus ut Exurge'. To these we can add the mnemonics by Herman of Reichenau and the modal verses from Frutolf's *Breviarium de musica* (see Plate 11).[138]

Measurement texts

All of the textbooks being examined here contain measurement texts. These are of three types: monochord measurements, organ-pipe measurements and bell measurements. Each worked on the same principle of dividing materials proportionally to sound the notes of the gamut. They were thus extensions of the theory of the gamut designed more to instruct the student in their working principles than to provide him with practical directions for fashioning them. There were many different and competing measurement systems, some deriving from Boethius and some more

---

[133] On Udalschalk of Augsburg see W. Berschin, 'Odalscalcs *Vita S. Konradi* im hagiographischen Hausbuch der Abtei St. Ulrich und Afra', *Freiburger Diözesan-Archiv* 95 (1975), 82-106.

[134] On the connexion between these sources see Huglo, *Les Tonaries*, pp. 286–93. Udalschalk's tonary is a later addition to **W**.

[135] Pesce (ed. and trans.), *Guido*, p. 137.

[136] See above, pp. 184–5.

[137] *RISM B* 3/3, pp. 20–1; see also Busse-Berger, *Medieval music and the art of memory*, p. 65.

[138] On Frutolf's modal verses see Chapter 2, pp. 107–8.

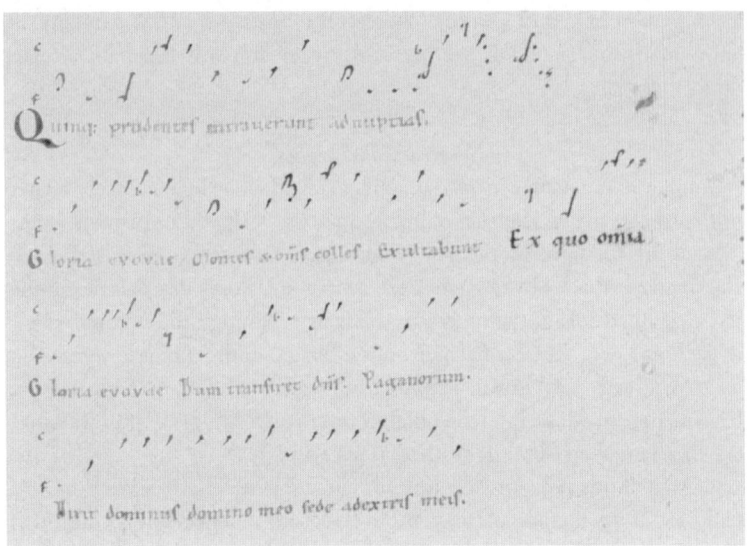

Plate 10   Notated didactic verses on the modes. Munich, Bayerische
Staatsbibliothek, Clm 14965a, fol. 5r

modern. Theorists like Aribo or Frutolf, who gave a number of such directions in their treatises, could provide a scribe with a wide range of alternatives. Other scribes relied on independent sources, choosing what measurements to include in their textbooks. Two codices – **Lz**, fols 60r–61v and **M7**, fols 295v–297r – contain Notker of St Gallen's organ and monochord measurements in Old High German.[139] **W** contains an extensive selection of measurement texts on fols 90v–133r, suggesting that its compilers were particularly interested in this subject. (The popularity of measurement texts in the music manuscripts is paralleled by measurement texts for the abacus, astrolabe and *computus* in contemporary manuscripts containing material on geometry, astronomy and mathematics.[140])

---

[139] See F.-J. Pensel and I. Stahl, *Verzeichnis der deutschen mittelalterlichen Handschriften in der Universitätsbibliothek Leipzig* (Berlin, 1998), p. 191; *RISM B* 3/6, pp. 319–21, *RISM B* 3/3, pp. 139–41.

[140] See Munich, Bayerische Staatsbibliothek, Clm 14836, fols 45r–75v, which contains texts on the different ways of measuring distances using geometry; M. Curze, 'Die Handschrift No. 14836 der Königlichen Hof- und Staatsbibliothek zu München', *Zeitschrift für Mathematik und Physik* 40 (1895), 85–95. See also, Rome, Biblioteca Apostolica Vaticana, Pal. lat. 1356, fols 107v–110r; L. Schuba, *Die Quadriviums-Handschriften der Codices Palatini Latini in der Vatikanischen Bibliothek* (Wiesbaden, 1992), p. 36.

'TEXTBOOK CODICES'

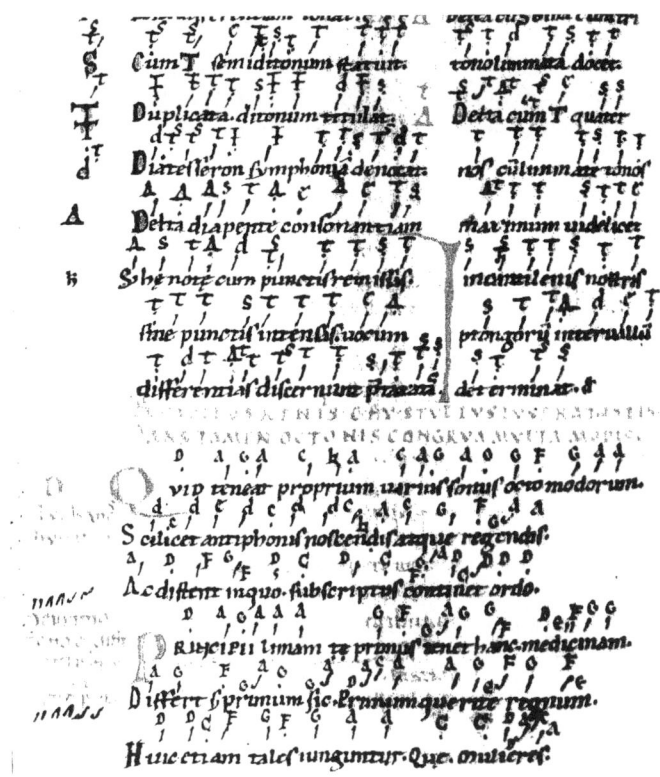

Plate 11 Mnemonic verses from Frutolf of Michelsberg's *Breviarium de musica*. Munich, Bayerische Staatsbibliothek, Clm 14965b, fol. 22v

Other miscellaneous texts

The textbooks also transmit short texts that are often called *florilegia* by historians. It has been suggested that many twelfth-century *florilegia* were compiled in order to instruct students, and the examples in music textbooks confirm this suggestion.[141] The musical *florilegia* are of differing types. Some are straightforward excerpts on various aspects of theory, such as the texts on the range of the modes in **W**, fols 129r–131r,[142] or the short text on transposition in **B2**, fol. 185v.[143] Others are in the form of lists or tables that provide the reader with important information: the fragment listing the names of the Greek Greater Perfect System on fol. 39v

---

[141] Robinson, 'The "Colores rhetorici" in the Investiture Contest', 214.
[142] Pesce (ed. and trans.), *Guido*, pp. 213–14.
[143] *RISM B* 3/3, p. 21.

213

of **M4**, for example.¹⁴⁴ In addition to the notated mnemonic verses discussed above,¹⁴⁵ there are many examples of notated chants cited for didactic purposes: *Virgo Dei genetrix* in **M8**, fol. 28v, or *Mittit ad virginem* in **V2**, fol. 39r, for example.¹⁴⁶ Finally, the scribes who compiled the music textbooks, like their contemporaries in other disciplines, used diagrams to encapsulate and express ideas. Some of these diagrams are types of glosses or commentaries on aspects of the music treatises, while others have a mnemonic function. The 'Guidonian hand', which the scribes believed to have been Guido's invention, is perhaps the most famous example of this.¹⁴⁷

Conclusions

From the study of these codices it is possible to piece together a general format for the music textbooks of the eleventh and twelfth centuries, and thus for the curriculum of music studies in Germany at this time. The scribes were concerned to provide a range of texts that would cover the most important aspects of music theory, those same aspects dwelt upon by the south-German music theorists: the gamut (the rules of proportion governing the intervals), tetrachordal and species theory, the operation of the modes, and the measurement of the monochord, organ-pipes and bells (which are manifestations of the rules of proportion in music). To this end, the scribes favoured modern texts, largely eschewing the Classical and Carolingian authors. In the case of the Classical texts, this was partly owing to their length and the difficulty of working them in with the other materials in the textbooks, and partly because they were already available in the libraries of Germany, should an eager scholar wish to consult them.¹⁴⁸ Carolingian music theory had been neatly encapsulated (and developed) by Bern of Reichenau, rendering these texts redundant to the compilers.

Of the eleventh-century theorists, Guido of Arezzo was by far the most popular: he was to the music theory textbooks what Burchard of Worms was to eleventh-century canonical textbooks. Pseudo-Odo of Cluny was the only other non-German theorist whom the scribes included in their compilations. Of the German treatises that formed the staple of the textbooks, Bern of Reichenau's *Prologus in tonarium* was the most frequently

[144] Ibid., pp. 139–40.
[145] See above, p. 211.
[146] Pesce (ed. and trans.), *Guido*, pp. 143, 127, 204.
[147] See Busse-Berger, *Medieval music and the art of memory*, pp. 85–94.
[148] See Chapter 2, pp. 56–8; Chapter 4, pp. 148–52.

copied. To that the scribes added other German works, doubtless influenced by the suitability of their subject matter. Some of these treatises – those by Herman of Reichenau and William of Hirsau – tended to be copied intact. The authors whose treatises, on account of their structure, were more amenable to excerpting – of which Frutolf and Aribo are the best examples – tended to be copied more frequently, though more rarely in complete versions. This is because the scribes and compilers were able to choose with relative ease and freedom those parts most relevant to their particular concerns.

In most of the textbooks a tonary was a necessary inclusion, because it represented to the scribes the ordered and regular classification of chants according to mode. It was in one sense the culmination of their studies, for it signified that point where the theory of music met the practice of singing. Abbot Bern's *Tonarius* was the most influential, being copied numerous times and inspiring the tonaries of later theorists. To complement the treatises and tonaries, the scribes added numerous didactic and mnemonic verses, which were frequently concerned with the comprehension and understanding of the modes. The textbook then only required the inclusion of passages on measurement and miscellaneous aspects of music theory to be complete. The result was a book telling the teacher or advanced student everything he needed to know about the theory of singing, so that when he sang, he did so correctly. These textbooks are testimony both to the influence of the scholastic practice of compilation upon music, and to the continuing interest of German clerks in music studies during the eleventh and twelfth centuries.

Conclusion

This book has examined what a circle of German scholars thought and wrote about music during the Salian period. The Salian period was one of momentous religious change and intellectual productivity in the western Empire. For many, it is synonymous with the struggle between Empire and Papacy, which dominated the final third of the eleventh century and which focused intellectual attention on canonicial, ecclesiological and doctrinal issues. The results of these studies are expressed most vividly in the polemical literature of the late eleventh century. But the Salian period also saw important intellectual and cultural achievements in the Empire, achievements overlooked by a prevalent historiography that has written the intellectual history of the central Middle Ages with exclusive reference to French sources. The music treatises of the south-German circle – highly sophisticated texts of the *artes* – belie the latent assertion that Salian Germany was intellectually undistinguished and suggest that the so-called 'twelfth-century renaissance' was confined neither to the cathedral schools of northern France nor to the twelfth century.

The south-German circle included some of Germany's leading intellectuals, whose scholarship was not confined to music. Bern of Reichenau was a distinguished liturgist, while his pupil Herman was renowned, even in his own lifetime, as one of the foremost scholars of his age. William of Hirsau obviously possessed a reputation eminent enough to have been suggested to Count Adalbert of Calw as a suitable abbot of Hirsau, a reputation he would subsequently use on behalf of the Gregorian reform, which was characterized by *scientia divinarum litterarum*.[1] Henry of Augsburg and

---

[1] I. S. Robinson, 'The metrical commentary on Genesis of Donizo of Canossa', *Recherches de théologie ancienne et médiévale* 41 (1974), 12–15.

Aribo were cathedral schoolmasters, Theoger of Metz had also spent time in the secular schools, while the learned historian, biblical scholar and liturgist Frutolf was schoolmaster of his monastery at Michelsberg in Bamberg. Yet, all of these scholars wrote at length on music, and it was for this contribution that they were consistently remembered. The reason for their particular interest in music is to be sought in the way it occupied the imagination of their contemporaries: music held for them a position equivalent to that which 'science' holds for us today. It was the primary vehicle for Christian liturgy and, consequently, was encountered a great deal by all clerics. Its importance was further underlined by the Gorze reform, which emphasized the necessity of liturgy and regular communal worship to the vitality of monastic life.

The Gorze reform provided not only the stimulus, but also the initial framework, for the studies of the south-German circle: institutional links arising from the Gorze movement facilitated the transmission of texts and ideas between monasteries. From Reichenau the music theory of Bern and Herman travelled to St Emmeram in Regensburg. Each of these monasteries had been influenced by the Gorze movement: Reichenau from 972 through a succession of reforming abbots and St Emmeram from 975 through the appointment of Ramwold, a monk of St Maximin in Trier, as abbot.[2] Reichenau and St Emmeram were also brought closer by the enthusiasm of Emperor Henry II for monastic reform: it is likely that Henry, who had been educated in Regensburg, encouraged Abbot Bern to move Reichenau closer in line with St Emmeram.[3] The close links between the two monasteries that have been noted by art historians are corroborated by the early appearance of works by Bern and Herman in St Emmeram manuscripts, the appointement of Burchard of Reichenau as abbot of St Emmeram in 1030 and Herman's authorship of a festal office for the canonization of St Wolfgang in 1052.[4]

If St Emmeram was a crucial centre for the dissemination of Reichenau scholarship, then the learned monk William, who would be named abbot of Hirsau in 1069, was the figure who connected many members of the

---

[2] See Chapter 1, pp. 19, 12.

[3] H. Mayr-Harting, *Ottonian book illumination: an historical study* 1 (London, 1991), p. 189.

[4] Ibid.; F. Mütherich, 'Die Regensburger Buchmalerei des 10. und 11. Jahrhunderts', in F. Mütherich and K. Dachs (eds), *Regensburger Buchmalerei: von frühkarolingischer Zeit bis zum Ausgang des Mittelalters. Ausstellung der Bayerischen Staatsbibliothek München und der Museen der Stadt Regensburg* (Munich, 1987), pp. 23–4, 29; A. S. Cohen, *The Uta Codex: art, philosophy and reform in eleventh-century Germany* (University Park, Pa., 2000), pp. 143, 155.

CONCLUSION

south-German circle. Aribo wrote that William loved him 'beyond any worthiness that my poverty may possess', while the close friendship between William and his protégé Theoger of Metz is well attested.[5] The examples of Aribo and Theoger show how institutional links and bonds of personal friendship – often based on the master-pupil relationship – frequently coalesced. Comparable are the examples of Meinzo, *scholasticus* of Constance, who wrote to his former teacher Herman of Reichenau when puzzled by the question of the earth's circumference, or the *scholasticus* of Worms, who sent a copy of Victorinus' *Calculus* to a former pupil and answered questions on Boethius in response to a similar request.[6] There is every reason to assume that Frutolf of Michelsberg, who probably began his monastic career at St Emmeram and consequently must have known William, drew on St Emmeram sources in his *Breviarium de musica* as he had also done in his chronicle and surviving biblical glosses – an assumption warranted by the close links that existed between Michelsberg and St Emmeram in the eleventh century.[7]

The years following William's departure from St Emmeram saw the rise of the Hirsau reform movement in tandem with the intensification of the struggle between the Gregorian papacy and the German king. The Hirsau movement, which largely superseded that of Gorze, also relied on bonds of personal and institutional friendship for its success. Indeed, its more defined structure, coupled with the polarization of ecclesiastical politics in the wake of the Investiture Contest, often strengthened these bonds. As the lines of demarcation between the papal and imperial parties became clearer, many clerics were forced to choose sides: Henry of Augsburg and probably Aribo left their cathedrals for the monastery, just as Bernold of Constance withdrew from his cathedral to enter the reformed monastery of St Blasien in the Black Forest. Bernold's works were circulated to his Gregorian partisans through Hirsau reform networks, networks that also aided the early dissemination of the music treatises of Aribo and Theoger of Metz.[8]

---

[5] Aribo, *De musica*, p. 42.57: Nam meam dilexit parvitatem ultra parvitatis dignitatem, qui est musicus primus modernus videlicet Orpheus et Pithagoras.

[6] E. Dümmler (ed.), 'Ein Schreiben Meinzos von Constanz an Hermann den Lahmen', *NA* 5 (1880), 202–6; *Worms Letter Collection* 32, *MGH Briefe* 4, p. 58.

[7] F.-J. Schmale and I. Schmale-Ott (eds), *Frutolfs und Ekkehards Chroniken und die Anonyme Kaiserchronik* (Darmstadt, 1972), p. 4.

[8] I. S. Robinson, 'Zur Arbeitsweise Bernolds von Konstanz und seines Kreises. Untersuchungen zum Schlettstädter Codex 13', *DA* 34 (1978), 51–122; T. J. H. McCarthy, 'Aribo's *De musica* and Abbot William of Hirsau', *Revue bénédictine* 116 (2006), 80; F. C. Lochner in Theoger of Metz, *Musica*, ed. F. C. Lochner Dietger (Theogerus) of Metz and his "Musica"' (Ph.D. dissertation, University of Notre Dame, 1995), p. 247.

The exploitation of monastic friendship networks by the south-German music theorists enables us to describe them truly as a circle. The contact between members of this circle over the space of some seventy years explains the shared affinity and subject matter of their treatises. The most important and decisive influences upon German music theory were Bern and Herman of Reichenau, who together constituted a *fons formalis* for later members of the circle. Reflecting the practicality of quadrivial studies within the monastic curriculum, Abbot Bern's *Prologus in tonarium* was designed as an instruction manual on the correct singing of plainchant. This 'manual' sought to equip the student with the necessary expertise to understand the theory and rationale behind ecclesiastical song: the gamut of notes, the different musical intervals, the tetrachords and the species of consonance, all of which culminated in the proper understanding and recognition of the eight modes.

The importance of Bern of Reichenau is to be seen in the frequency with which his *Prologus in tonarium* was copied during the eleventh and twelfth centuries. He was used extensively as a source by the Wolf Anonymous and by the author of *Quaestiones in musica*. John regarded him – along with Boethius and Guido – as one of the great authorities on music.[9] Frutolf of Michelsberg also valued him highly, making his own copy of *Prologus in tonarium* in its interpolated version. I have suggested that these interpolations began as glosses on Bern's text that were then copied 'not just in the margins' but continuously in prose 'as expositions are usually written'.[10] They represent the thoughts and efforts of clerks – like Frutolf – to understand and comment upon Bern's text. Some of the additions take the form of short explanatory glosses designed to guide the reader through difficult terms or to clarify involved passages; others are much longer 'extended glosses' that comment upon Bern's teaching in the light of changing trends in music theory or attempt to bring him 'up-to-date' in certain respects.

Abbot Bern's pedagogy was continued and amplified by his pupil Herman of Reichenau for whom only that person who acquired the faculty of 'composing chants correctly, of judging them by rule and of performing them fittingly' could be called a musician.[11] This learned musician Herman

---

[9] John, *De musica*, ed. J. Smits van Waesberghe, *Johannis Afflighemensis De musica cum tonario* (Rome, 1950), p. 44.
[10] See Chapter 2, p. 73.
[11] Herman, *Musica* 15, p. 47: Oportet autem nos scire, quod omnis musicae rationis ad hoc spectat intentio, ut cantilenae rationabiliter componendae, regulariter iudicandae, decenter modulandae scientia comparetur. Quorum trium cui facultas affuerit is demum musicus recte dicendus erit.

contrasted with the 'blind crowd of singers yielding to no reason and acquiescing to no authority'.[12] They 'who confound [music] by permuting one mode for another, who praise only the high notes' should 'justly be judged as inferior and more ignorant than the ass'.[13]

My stress upon the determining influence of Herman of Reichenau is in marked contrast to the frequently made assertion that his music theory did not circulate widely. It is justifiable to say that he – like the other German theorists – was generally unknown outside Germany; but the existence of only two full recensions of *Musica* is not sufficient grounds for concluding that his German reception was similarly limited. His emendation of Abbot Bern's theory was one of the central formative influences upon the south-German circle. By reshaping Bern's three species of *diatessaron* into a system of four species, he created species that retained their characteristic forms of tones and semitones regardless of whether they occurred in the tetrachord of the *graves, finales, superiores* or *excellentes*. More importantly, however, Herman's species of *diatessaron* combined with the species of *diapente* in such a way that the species of *diapason* reflected the patterns of the authentic and plagal modes. Herman thus formulated a codified model for understanding and recognizing the modes 'for which every aim of music strives'.[14] This system of species became the basis of German music theory from the second half of the eleventh century. The utility of Herman's emendations to Bern's species theory ensured its continued popularity.

A consequence of Herman's species theory – resulting in the establishment of a fourth species of *diatessaron* (D E F G) – was the necessity for the conjunction of the tetrachords of the *graves* and *finales* (at D), and the *superiores* and *excellentes* (at d). This conjunction implied that the notes D and d possess a double-function: they are both *tetrardus* (when part of the *graves* and *superiores*) and *protus* (when part of the *finales* and *excellentes*). Here Herman opposed Guido of Arezzo, who allowed them only a *protus* function. It was Guido's immense reputation that made this teaching seem so subversive to the south-German theorists and made it require so thorough a refutation. Herman refuted it forcibly by taking to task the unnamed

---

[12] Ibid.: Porro tercio, hoc est modulandi immo ululandi studio caecum cantorum vulgus occupatur, nullius rationi cedens, nullius sententiae acquiscens . . .

[13] Ibid., pp. 47–8: Sed quo modo sapientur cantant, qui nihil de praedictis sciunt, qui troporum tropo permutantes confundunt, qui solam altisonantiam laudant; in hoc tamen iusto iudicio asino inferiores et imperitiores, qui et multo altius resonat et numquid ruditum mugitu vel alia qualibet voce mutabit?

[14] Ibid.: Maxime tamen troporum tibi curae sit agnitio, propter quos fere omnis musicae laborat intentio.

author who 'failed to notice the oft-mentioned double aspect of D'.[15] His criticism had a lasting effect: its influence is to be seen in William of Hirsau's comment that '[Guido] did not understand the double function of D and d'.[16] Much of William's teaching on this point was repeated by Frutolf of Michelsberg.[17] Aribo too was aware of the centrality of this point for the German theorists: he countered Guido's arguments with the authority of St Gregory who, as 'the author of almost all ecclesiastical chant, recognized its [D] two-fold operation, which in *tetrardus* does not love the authentic and hate the plagal songs'.[18] More importantly than adducing *auctoritas*, however, Aribo employed the powerful tool of dialectic in defence of the south-German position.[19] For this he relied on the textbooks of the *ars logica*: Porphyry's *Isagoge*, Boethius' *Commentarius in Topica Ciceronis* and *De differentiis topicis*.

The impact of dialectic upon the south-German treatises is an example of the interaction between the trivial and quadrivial arts in medieval education. Chapter 3 emphasized the limitations of the older historiography, which regarded the eleventh century as a century hostile to dialectic. The evidence of library catalogues has shown the extensive dialectical holdings of German libraries. These holdings were put to good use by the eleventh-century monks and clerks who produced logical glosses and commentaries. Dialectic also permeated the contemporary mind-set to such an extent that it was discussed in letters and applied to questions of ecclesiology, doctrine and theology, much as Aribo had applied it to music. Even those polemicists who remained wary of dialectical excesses in the hands of the reckless did not deny its value as an intellectual tool when used correctly. The appeal of dialectic to the south-German music theorists stemmed from their delight in definition, distinction and division, which was such a feature of medieval education. Henry of Augsburg's *Musica* is a case in point. From the very beginning of his treatise, Master Henry sought to classify music through a dialectical process of definition, distinction and division, taking his language from the *ars logica* that he taught as '*scholasticus* to the city of Augsburg'. He expressed an interpretation of music that was shared by all German commentators: the elements of music were

---

[15] Herman, *Musica* 19, p. 59; see Chapter 2, p. 83.
[16] William, *Musica* 18, pp. 48–9; see Chapter 2, p. 85.
[17] Frutolf, *Breviarium* 6, pp. 50–1.
[18] Aribo, *De musica*, p. 31.50: Patet admodum, beatum Gregorium totius pene ecclesiastici cantus auctorem duplicem eius cognovisse operationem, qui in tetrardo non potius autenticas, quam plagales diligit odas.
[19] Ibid., pp. 31.52–33.74.

related as a spectrum of genera and species. Similarly, the popularity of Herman of Reichenau's species theory as a way of understanding the working of the modes owed much to its dialectical coherence. Dialectic provided a means of regulating the form and order of music theory. This desire for order in music was a reflexion of the keenly felt medieval preoccupation with regularity. The music theorists believed that ultimate regularity was to be found in the divine, which explains the continuing popularity of works such as John Scottus Eriugena's commentary on pseudo-Dionysius' *Celestial Hierarchy*; Honorius Augustodunensis was minded to write his own *Celestial Hierarchy* in the early twelfth century, for example. As God had created man in His own image so it followed that the universe contained its own hierarchies patterned after the heavenly model. The preoccupation with order in the world is to be seen behind St Anselm's attempts to codify the orders of society. It was also at the heart of the conflict between Empire and Papacy, which has been described by one historian as a 'struggle for the right order in the world'.[20] Eleventh-century conceptions of this universal order, though ultimately rooted in the Bible, were greatly influenced by Plato, whose *Timaeus* was seen primarily as a guide to the order that underpinned creation. Music was but another aspect of this order, a point demonstrated explicitly by the unknown eleventh-century author of a letter on worldly order to Bishop Azecho of Worms, 1025–44. The clerk of Worms reminds his bishop of the relevant authorities (Plato's *Timaeus* and Boethius' *Consolation of Philosophy*) and of the importance of number to God 'who created the universe in number and weight and measure'.[21] He explains how the heavenly hierarchy is replicated in the hierarchy of musical proportions: 'In this way the smaller numbers show the larger proportions, and if one makes an infinite progression . . . no wrong notes will occur'.[22] The importance of order in music was plainly evident to the clerk of Worms, who used the example as a metaphor.

That metaphor was also evident to the members of the south-German circle. They found in *Timaeus* an outline of the plan to which God created the world. That plan relied on number and proportion between the elements of creation. Music, as one aspect of the plan, had its basis in these

---

[20] G. Tellenbach, *Church, state and Christian society at the time of the Investiture Contest*, trans. R. F. Bennett (Oxford, 1940; repr. Toronto, 1991), p. 1.
[21] Wisdom 11.21.
[22] *Worms letter collection* 52, *MGH Briefe* 3, p. 90: Hoc modo in minoribus numeris maiores proportiones demostrantur, et si in infinitum — numerus utique infinitus est — progressio fiat, nulla falsitatis nota occurrerit.

proportions. The south-German theorists and their contemporaries found the emphasis on design and proportion stressed in Calcidius' commentary on *Timaeus*, which was widely available in the eleventh century. Platonic number theory was especially evident in Boethius' *De institutione musica* and *De institutione arithmetica*. Two other texts also played a role in the reception of Platonism: Martianus Capella's *De nuptiis Philologiae et Mercurii* and Macrobius' *Commentarius in Somnium Scipionis*. Of these two Macrobius was by far the more important. In Chapters 5 and 6 of Book 1 and Chapters 1–5 of Book 2 Macrobius spoke in detail about the numerical proportions underlying creation and the way in which *natura* wove these into music.

These passages of Macrobius were of considerable importance to the south-German circle: Bern of Reichenau quoted from them in his *Prologus in tonarium* and this Macrobian emphasis is also apparent in William of Hirsau. The clerks who compiled music theory textbooks during the eleventh and twelfth centuries mirrored this preference, for what little of Macrobius appeared in their codices did so much more frequently than Martianus Capella. This was because the Platonic aspects of Macrobius were more readily apparent than those of Martianus, who dealt extensively with the concrete elements of music theory such as the notes and intervals. Better sources were available for this theory, however, and so Macrobius was of greater interest to the south-German theorists and clerks.

The ultimate expression of Platonism in the south-German treatises is the personification of the natural order as *natura*. Boethius' *Consolation of Philosophy* provided the subconscious model for this with his personification of the goddess *Philosophia*. Her image was adopted by Bern, Herman and the rest of the south-German circle who portrayed *natura* as the embodiment of natural order and harmony. Her proportions governed the art of music and all true music owed her obedience. She was manifested most obviously in the monochord, that instrument so central to the music pedagogy of the eleventh century. Aribo's rejection of the 'quadripartite figure' is in many ways the most explicitly Platonic condemnation of faulty musical reasoning that occurs in the south-German treatises. He denigrates the figure as being 'against the nature of the monochord' and praises his own alternative with Platonic metaphors of generation for being 'within the bosom of nature'.[23]

An important perspective upon the context of the south-German circle is provided by examining the reception of its theory by those scribes and

---

[23] See Chapter 4, pp. 162–8.

CONCLUSION

clerks who compiled music theory textbook codices. The range of texts they copied shows that their preoccupations were similar to those of the south-German circle. They were not generally interested in music as a speculative science. In most cases the portions of Macrobius or Boethius they copied were chosen because they provided an example of the correspondence between melody and the potent (Platonic) symbolism of number theory. The music theorists and clerks, therefore, were interested in the ancient theories – infused as they were with Platonism – because they believed that proper melody was and should be a reflexion of this divine order. Whereas French authors such as William of Conches speculated on the implications of *Timaeus*, the south-German circle applied the details of Platonic number theory to real music.[24]

Use of the Carolingian theorists by eleventh- and twelfth-century clerks was similarly restricted. As the salient points of Carolingian theory had been summarized and assimilated by Bern of Reichenau (and as copies from the ninth and tenth centuries survived in many German libraries) the direct contribution of the Carolingians was necessarily limited. Their main usefulness was as glossaries: the explanations of the Greek note names by Hucbald of St Amand and Regino of Prüm were reiterated by the compilers of manuscripts such as Vienna, Österreichische Nationalbibliothek, Cod. 51 and Kassel, Landesbibliothek, 4° Mss Math. 1 to aid later readers who might have found these names old-fashioned and unfamiliar.

Guido of Arezzo was a *sine qua non* of the music theory textbooks. The fact that most of the textbooks preserve full recensions of his four treatises confirms the testimony of the early twelfth-century historiographer Sigebert of Gembloux who regarded him as above 'nearly all musicians'.[25] In a few codices the order of Guido's treatises is rearranged, or extra material is appended: the compiler of Munich, Bayerische Staatsbibliothek, Clm 14663, for example, inserted the anonymous German treatise *Quomodo de arithmetica procedit musica*, and two excerpts from *Commentarius anonymus in Micrologum Guidonis Aretini* between *Micrologus* and Guido's other treatises. The insertion of commenting texts in this and other manuscripts indicates the concern of these clerks to understand Guido more fully. This concern was a product of the peculiar German response to Guido's teaching that has already been highlighted

---

[24] See William of Conches, *Glosses on Timaeus*, ed. E. Jeauneau, *Glosae super Platonem* (Paris, 1965).
[25] Sigebert of Gembloux, *Liber de illustribus viris* 145, ed. R. Witte, *Catalogus Sigeberti Gemblacensis monachi de viris illustribus. Kritische Ausgabe* (Bern and Frankfurt am Main, 1974), pp. 92–3.

with respect to the south-German circle in Chapter 2. The continuing need of German clerks to interpret Guido with reference to their own position provided the stimulus for works such as *Commentarius anonymus*, which was used to counterbalance Guido by the compiler of Munich, Clm 14463. Though Guido was seminal, he was not the sole sufficient source for German theory. Accordingly, he was supplemented by German theorists in all of the textbooks: whereas he might have sufficed on his own in other areas of Europe, he provided but one part of the German approach to music theory.

The treatises of the south-German circle formed the backbone of the music textbooks, appearing either in full or as excerpts. Bern's *Prologus in tonarium* was the most likely to appear in a full recension, an indication of his formative influence on German music theory. William, Theoger and John were often copied in full, though the twelfth-century scribe of Kassel, Landesbibliothek, 4° Mss Math. 1 rearranged and augmented Theoger to suit his purposes. Aribo was found particularly useful for his diagrams of interlocking circles, which showed the common notes of the authentic and plagal modes, and for his commentaries on Guido's *Micrologus*. Though Herman's *Musica* survives complete in only two manuscripts, its influence was nevertheless extensive: his modal theory was as highly prized by the textbook compilers as it was by the south-German theorists themselves.

The south-German treatises were complemented by a variety of shorter texts with specific uses. Virtually all of the textbooks include mnemonic verses concerned with the intervals and the modes. Here Herman of Reichenau and Henry of Augsburg were especially important. Measurement texts (on monochords, organ pipes and bells) were also a staple, of which the most important examples were those by William of Hirsau, Aribo and Frutolf of Michelsberg. Tonaries, classifying chants according to mode, appeared frequently: the most important was Abbot Bern's *Tonarius*. To this can be added various miscellaneous texts and diagrams, which complete the content of these schoolbooks.

From the evidence of the textbooks it is possible to piece together the curriculum of music studies in Germany during the eleventh and twelfth centuries. It was concerned with the theory of melody and the elements affecting it: the gamut, the species, tetrachords and modes, mnemonics to train the musician in memorization and recognition of the different modal patterns, an understanding of arithmetical proportion, the measurement of the monochord, bells and organ pipes according to these proportions, the importance of these proportions for songs, the careful and correct classification of chants according to mode so as to avoid mistakes. The music theory codices thus reflect the preoccupations of the south-German circle.

The production of textbook codices such as these was a phenomenon common to all of the *artes* at this time and represents but one example of how the study of music proceeded in the same way as the study of other subjects. The importance in the popularization of the textbook genre of subjects like canon law and doctrine – which required the assembling of authorities in convenient handbook form – has been highlighted in Chapter 5. Considerations of space have precluded the examination of a similar textbook movement in the quadrivial arts, though preliminary examination indicates the existence of numerous examples containing collections of arithmetical, geometrical and astronomical texts. A comparative study of these examples would provide a useful means of assessing in greater detail the connexion between music and the other quadrivial arts.

The theorists of the south-German circle are the most prominent representatives of a rich tradition of music-theory studies in Salian Germany. Their treatises are also indications of the advanced state of learning in the German schools when evidence for the subsequently more famous French schools is lacking. This book has attempted to adumbrate the intellectual context of the south-German circle, showing that German monks and clerks regarded music theory not as an abstract study but as a rigorously practical one. Following Cassiodorus' *Institutiones* they believed that whereas 'mathematical science is that science which considers abstract quantity' music is the division of it 'that treats of numbers in relation to those things that are found in sounds'.[26] The study of music theory was for them the study of all the elements that affected the singing, classification, analysis and composition of plainchant. Their preference for practical texts is the most decisive indication of their collective attitude. They approached music theory as early scholastics, copying and adapting texts as necessary, glossing and commenting in their attempts to understand all that lay behind the study of singing. The theorists received and modified each other's ideas; they and a great many nameless scribes and clerks produced music textbooks to guide them and others through the music curriculum. They applied the learning of other *artes* to help them understand singing more fully, and were deeply conscious of the need for order in all that they

---

[26] Cassiodorus, *Institutiones* 2.3.21, ed. R. A. B. Mynors, *Cassiodori senatoris Institutiones* (Oxford, 1937), p. 130: Mathematica, quam Latine possumus dicere doctrinalem, scientia est quae abstractam considerat quantitatem; p. 111: Musica est disciplina quae de numeris loquitur, qui ad aliquid sunt his qui inveniuntur in sonis.

did. But it was the friendship networks and scholarly intercourse that existed between the monasteries and cathedral schools of southern Germany that provided them, like so many other scholars, with the framework for their studies.

BIBLIOGRAPHY

Printed primary sources

Alger of Liège, *De misericordia et iustitia*, ed. R. Kretzschmar, *Alger von Lüttichs Traktat De misericordia et iustitia. Ein kanonistischer Konkordanzversuch aus der Zeit des Investiturstreits. Untersuchungen und Edition* (Sigmaringen, 1985).

Alia musica, ed. E. B. Heard, 'Alia musica: a chapter in the history of medieval music theory' (Ph.D. dissertation, University of Wisconsin, 1966).

——, ed. J. Chailley, *Alia musica (Traité de musique du IXe siècle). Edition critique commentée avec une introduction sur l'origine de la nomenclature modale pseudo-grecque au Moyen-Age* (Publications de l'Institut de Musicologie de l'Université de Paris 6; Paris, 1965).

Annales Augustani, MGH SS 3, pp. 123–36.

Annales sancti Disibodi, MGH SS 17, pp. 4–30.

Annales sancti Georgii in Nigra Silva, MGH SS 17, pp. 295–8.

Aribo, *De musica*, ed. J. Smits van Waesberghe, *Aribonis De musica* (Corpus scriptorum de musica 2; Rome, 1951).

Arnold of Bonneval, *De operibus sex dierum*, PL 189.1515–1570.

Augustine of Hippo, *De musica*, PL 32.1081–1194.

——, De musica, ed. M. Jacobsson, *Aurelius Augustinus De musica liber VI: a critical edition with a translation and an introduction* (Studia Latina Stockholmiensia 47; Stockholm, 2002).

Aurelian of Réôme, *Musica disciplina*, ed. L. Gushee, *Aureliani Reomensis Musica disciplina* (Corpus scriptorum de musica 21; Rome, 1975).

Babb, W. (trans.) and C. V. Palisca (ed.), *Hucbald, Guido and John on music: three medieval treatises* (Music theory translation series 3; New Haven and London, 1978).

Bern of Reichenau, *De quibusdam rebus ad missae officium pertinentibus*, PL 142.1055–1080.

——, *Epistola de tonis, Prologus in tonarium, Tonarius*, ed. A. Rausch, *Die Musiktraktate des Abtes Bern von Reichenau. Edition und Interpretation* (Musica mediaevalis Europae occidentalis 5; Tutzing, 1999).

——, *Letters*, ed. F.-J. Schmale, *Die Briefe des Abtes Bern von Reichenau* (Veröffentlichungen der Kommission für Geschichtliche Landeskunde in Baden-Württemberg. Reihe A, Quellen 6; Stuttgart, 1961).

——, *Qualiter adventus Domini celebretur*, ed. P. Jaffé, *Bibliotheca rerum Germanicarum* 3 (Berlin, 1866), pp. 365–71; ed. F.-J. Schmale, *Die Briefe des Abtes Bern von Reichenau*, pp. 39–46; PL 142.1079–1086.

——, *Qualiter quatuor temporum ieiunia par sua sabbata sint observanda*, PL 142.1085-1088.

——, *Vita sancti Udalrici*, ed. K.-E. Geith, *Das Leben des Heiligen Ulrich* (Quellen und Forschungen zur Sprach- und Kulturgeschichte der germanischen Völker 163 [N.F. 39]; Berlin, 1971); PL 142.1183-1204.

[Bern of Reichenau], *De varia psalmorum atque cantuum modulatione*, GS 2, pp. 91-114; PL 142.1131-1154.

Bernhard, M., *Clavis Gerberti. Eine Revision von Martin Gerberts Scriptores ecclesiastici de musica sacra potissimum (St. Blasien 1784)* (Bayerische Akademie der Wissenschaften. Veröffentlichungen der Musikhistorischen Kommission 7; Munich, 1989).

Bernold of St Blasien (of Constance), *Chronicon*, ed. I. S. Robinson, *Die Chroniken Bertholds von Reichenau und Bernolds von Konstanz, 1054-1100*, MGH SSrG NS 14 (Hanover, 2003).

——, *Chronicon*, ed. and trans. I. S. Robinson and H. Robinson-Hammerstein, *Bertholds und Bernolds Chroniken* (Ausgewählte Quellen zur deutschen Geschichte des Mittelalters 14; Darmstadt, 2002).

——, *Chronicon*, trans. I. S. Robinson, *Eleventh-century: the Swabian Chronicles* (Manchester Medieval Sources Series; Manchester, 2008), pp. 245-337.

——, *De veritate corporis et sanguine Domini*, ed. H. Weisweiler, 'Die vollständige Kampfschrift Bernolds von St. Blasien gegen Berengar', *Scholastik* 12 (1937), 58-93.

Berthold of Reichenau, *Chronicon*, ed. I. S. Robinson, *Die Chroniken Bertholds von Reichenau und Bernolds von Konstanz, 1054-1100*, MGH SSrG NS 14 (Hanover, 2003).

——, *Chronicon*, ed. and trans. I. S. Robinson and H. Robinson-Hammerstein, *Bertholds und Bernolds Chroniken* (Ausgewählte Quellen zur deutschen Geschichte des Mittelalters 14; Darmstadt, 2002).

——, *Chronicon*, trans. I. S. Robinson, *Eleventh-century: the Swabian Chronicles* (Manchester Medieval Sources Series; Manchester, 2008), pp. 99-244.

Bischoff, B. (ed.), 'Glossen Hermanns des Lahmen und Metrische Glossen zu den Paulinischen Briefen (vor 1054)', in B. Bischoff, *Anecdota novissima. Texte des vierten bis sechzehnten Jahrhunderts* (Stuttgart, 1984), pp. 35-48.

Boethius, *Commentarii in librum Aristotelis* περι ἑρμνείας, ed. K. Meiser, 2 vols (Leipzig, 1877-80).

——, *De differentiis topicis*, PL 64.1173-1216.

——, trans. E. Stump, *Boethius's De topicis differentiis* (Ithaca and London, 1978).

——, *De consolatione philosophiae*, ed. L. Bieler, *Anicii Manlii Severini Boethii Philosophiae consolatio* (Corpus Christianorum. Series Latina 94; Turnhout, 1984).

——, *De divisione*, ed. and trans. J. Magee, *Anicii Manlii Severini Boethii De divisione liber: critical edition, translation, prolegomena and commentary* (Philosophia antiqua 77; Leiden, 1998).

——, *De institutione arithmetica, De institutione musica*, ed. G. Friedlein, *Anicii Manlii Torquati Severini Boetii De institutione arithmetica libri duo, De institu-*

tione musica libri quinque. Accedit geometria quae fertur Boetii (Leipzig, 1867; repr. Frankfurt am Main, 1966).

——, *De institutione arithmetica*, ed. and trans. J. Y. Guillaumin, *Boèce Institution Arithmétique* (Paris, 1995).

——, *De syllogismo categorico*, PL 64.0761–0832.

——, *De syllogismo hypothetico*, PL 64.0831–0876.

——, *In Categorias Aristotelis libri quattuor*, PL 64.0159A–0294C.

——, *In Isagogen Porphyrii commenta*, ed. S. Brandt and G. Schepss, *Corpus scriptorum ecclesiasticorum latinorum* 48 (Vienna and Leipzig, 1906).

——, *In Topica Ciceronis commentariorum libri sex*, PL 65.1039D–1174B.

Cassiodorus, *Institutiones*, ed. R. A. B. Mynors, *Cassiodori senatoris Institutiones* (Oxford, 1937); German trans. W. Bürgsens, *Institutiones divinarum et saecularium litterarum. Einführung in die geistlichen und weltlichen Wissenschaften* (Fontes Christiani 39; Freiburg, 2003).

Chronica Monasterii Casinensis. Die Chronik von Montecassino, MGH SS 34 (1980).

Chronica Universalis Mettense, MGH SS 24, pp. 502–26.

Commentarius anonymus in Micrologum Guidonis Aretini, ed. C. Vivell, 'Commentarius anonymus in Micrologum Guidonis Aretini', *Akademie der Wissenschaften in Wien, Philosophische-historische Klasse, Sitzungsberichte* 185/5 (Vienna, 1917).

——, ed. J. Smits van Waesberghe, *Expositiones in Micrologum Guidonis Aretini* (Amsterdam, 1957), pp. 95–172.

Donizo of Canossa, *Vita Mathildis*, MGH SS 12, pp. 348–409.

Dümmler, E. (ed.), 'Das Martyrologium Notkers und seiner Verwandten', *Forschung zur deutschen Geschichte* 25 (1885), 209–12.

—— (ed.), 'Ein Schreiben Meinzos von Constanz an Hermann den Lahmen', *NA* 5 (1880), 202–6.

Engelbert of Admont, *De musica*, ed. P. Ernstbrunner, *Der Musiktraktat des Engelbert von Admont (ca. 1250–1331)* (Musica mediaevalis Europae occidentalis 2; Tutzing, 1998).

Frutolf of Michelsberg, *Breviarium de musica, Tonarius*, ed. C. Vivell, 'Frutolfi Breviarium de musica et Tonarius', *Akademie der Wissenschaften in Wien. Philosophische historische Klasse, Sitzungsberichte* 188/2 (1919).

——, *Chronicon*, MGH SS 6, pp. 33–210.

——, *Chronicon*, ed. F.-J. Schmale and I. Schmale-Ott, *Frutolfs und Ekkehards Chroniken und die Anonyme Kaiserchronik* (Ausgewählte Quellen zur deutschen Geschichte des Mittelalters 15; Darmstadt, 1972).

[Frutolf of Michelsberg], *Rithmomachia*, ed. R. Peiper, 'Fortolfi Rythmimachia', *Zeitschrift für Mathematik und Physik* 25 (1880), 167–97.

Garland [of Besançon], Dialectica, ed. L. M. de Rijk, *Garlandus Compotista Dialectica: first edition of the manuscripts, with an introduction on the life and works of the author and on the contents of the present work* (Assen, 1959).

Gerbert of Aurillac, *Opera*, ed. N. M. Bubnov, *Gerberti postea Silvestri II papae Opera mathematica (972–1003). Accedunt aliorum opera ad Gerberti libellos aestimandos intelligendosque necessaria per septem appendices distributa* (Berlin, 1899; repr. Hildesheim, 1963).

Gerbert, M. (ed.), *Scriptores ecclesiastici de musica sacra potissimum*, 3 vols (St Blasien, 1784; repr. Milan, 1931).

Gerhoh of Reichersberg, *De aedificio Dei*, *PL* 194.1193.

Gesta abbatum Trudonensium (*Continuatio 1*), *MGH SS* 10, pp. 272–317.

Glossa maior in institutionem musicam Boethii, ed. M. Bernhard and C. M. Bower, 3 vols (Bayerische Akademie der Wissenschaften. Veröffentlichungen der Musikhistorischen Kommission 9–11; Munich, 1993, 1994, 1996).

Grecam litteram ideo moderni maluerunt ponere quam latinam, ed. H. Sowa, *Quellen zur Transformation der Antiphonen. Tonar und Rhythmusstudien* (Kassel, 1935), pp. 154–60.

Guido of Arezzo, *Epistola ad Michahelem, Prologus in antiphonarium, Regule rithmice*, ed. and trans. D. Pesce, *Guido d'Arezzo's Regule rithmice, Prologus in antiphonarium and Epistola ad Michahelem: a critical text and translation* (Wissenschaftliche Abhandlungen 73; Ottawa, 1999).

——, *Micrologus*, ed. J. Smits van Waesberghe, *Micrologus Guidonis Aretini* (Corpus scriptorum de musica 4; Rome, 1955).

Haimo of Hirsau, *De corpore et sanguine Domine*, *PL* 118.0815-18.

——, *Vita Willihelmi Abbatis Hirsaugiensis*, *MGH SS* 12, pp. 209–25.

Henry of Augsburg, *Musica*, ed. J. Smits van Waesberghe, *Musica domni Heinrici Augustensis magistri* (Divitae musicae artis collectae A/7; Buren, 1977).

——, *Planctus Evae*, ed. M. L. Colker, 'Heinrici Augustensis *Planctus Evae*', *Traditio* 12 (1956), 149–230.

Herman of Reichenau, *Chronicon*, *MGH SS* 5, pp. 67–133.

——, *De mense lunari*, ed. G. Meier, *Die sieben freien Künste im Mittelalters* (Einsiedeln, 1887), pp. 34–6; ed. A. Borst, 'Ein Forschungsbericht Hermanns des Lahmen', *DA* 40 (1984), 474–7.

——, *De mensura astrolabii*, ed. J. Decker, 'Hermannus Contractus. Über das Astrolab', *Isis* 16 (1931), 200–19.

——, *De octo vitiis principalibus*, ed. E. Dümmler, 'Opusculum Herimanni diverso metro compositum', *Zeitschrift für deutsches Altertum* 13 (1867), 385–431.

——, *De rhythmimachia*, ed. A. Borst, *Das mittelalterliche Zahlenkampfspiel* (Supplemente zu den Sitzungsberichten der Heidelberger Akademie der Wissenschaften, Philosophisch-Historische Klasse 5; Heidelberg, 1986), pp. 335–9.

——, *De utilitatibus astrolabii*, ed. N. Bubnov, *Gerberti postea Silvestri II papae opera mathematica* 2 (Berlin, 1899; repr. Hildesheim, 1963), pp. 109–47.

——, *Historia Sanctae Afrae martyris Augustensis*, ed. D. Hiley and W. Berschin (Musicological studies 65/10; Ottawa, 2004).

——, *Historia sancti Wolfgangi episcopi Ratisbonensis. Einführung und Edition*, ed. D. Hiley, *Historia sancti Wolfgangi episcopi Ratisbonensis. Einführung und Edition* (Musicological Studies 65/7; Ottawa, 2002).

——, *Musica*, ed. and trans. L. Ellinwood, *Musica Hermanni Contracti* (Rochester, NY, 1936).

——, *Regulae qualiter multiplicationes fiant in abaco*, ed. P. Treutlein, 'Intorno ad alcuni scritti inediti relativi al calcolo dell'abaco', *Bullettino di bibliografia e di storia delle scienze matematiche e fisiche* 10 (1877), 643–7; ed. M. Hellmann, 'Der Rechenlehrer Herimannus. Mit Edition der *Regulae, qualiter multiplicationes fiant in abaco* und Abdruck der Bruchtabellen', in W. Berschin and M. Hellmann, *Hermann der Lahme. Gelehrter und Dichter (1013–1054)* (Reichenauer Texte und Bilder 11; Heidelberg, 2005), pp. 33–72.

Hildesheim Letter Collection, ed. C. Erdmann and N. Fickermann, *MGH Briefe* 5 (1950), pp. 15–106.

Honorius Augustodunensis, *De animae exsilio et patri, seu de artibus*, PL 172.1241–6.

——, *Liber XII quaestionibus*, PL 172.1177–1186.

Hucbald of St Amand, *Musica*, ed. M. Gerbert, *De harmonica institutione*, GS 1, pp. 103–25.

——, *Musica*, ed. Y. Chartier, *L'Œuvre musicale d'Hucbald de Saint-Amand. Les compositions et le traité de musique* (Cahiers d'Études Médiévales 5; Montreal, 1995).

Hugh of St Victor, *Commentaria in Hierarchiam coelestem S. Dionysii Areopagitae*, PL 175.0923–1153.

——, *Didascalicon*, PL 176.0739–0838.

Isidore of Seville, *Etymologiae*, ed. W. M. Lindsay, *Isidori Hispalensis episcopi Etymologiarum sive originum libri XX*, 2 vols (Oxford, 1911).

John, *De musica*, *Tonarius*, ed. J. Smits van Waesberghe, *Johannis Afflighemensis De musica cum tonario* (Corpus scriptorum de musica 1; Rome, 1950).

Keil, H. (ed.), *Grammatici latini*, 7 vols (Leipzig, 1857–80).

Mabillon, J., *Annales ordinis S. Benedicti occidentalium monachorum Patriarchae* 5, (Pairs, 1713).

——, *Vetera analecta, sive collectio veterum aliquot operum & opusculorum omnis generis, carminum, episolarum, diiplomatum, epitaphiorum, &c* (Paris, 1723; repr. Farnborough, 1967).

Macrobius, *Commentarius in Somnium Scipionis*, ed. J. Willis, *Ambrosii Theodosii Macrobii Commentarii in Somnium Scipionis* (Bibliotheca scriptorium Graecorum et Romanorum Teubneriana; Leipzig, 1963; 2nd edn 1970; repr. 1994).

Manegold of Lautenbach, *Liber ad Gebehardum*, *MGH Libelli* 1 (1891), pp. 308–430.

——, *Liber contra Wolfelmum*, ed. W. Hartmann, *MGH Quellen* 8 (1972).

Martianus Capella, *De nuptiis Philologiae et Mercurii*, ed. J. Willis, *Martianus Capella opera* (Leipzig, 1983).

Minio-Paluello, L. (ed.), *Categoriae vel predicamenta* (Aristoteles Latinus 1/1–5, Leiden, 1961), pp. xii–xxii.

Musica enchiriadis and *Scolica enchiriadis*, ed. H. Schmid, *Musica et scolica enchiriadis, una cum aliquibus tractatulis adiunctis recensio . . . nova post Gerbertinam altera ad finem omnium codicum manuscriptorum quam edidit Hans Schmid* (Bayerische Akademie der Wissenschaften. Veröffentlichungen der Musikhistorischen Kommission 3; Munich, 1981).

——, trans. R. Erickson, *Musica enchiriadis and Scolica enchiriadis* (New Haven and London, 1995).

Onulf of Speyer, *Colores rhetorici*, ed. W. Wattenbach, 'Magister Onulf von Speyer', *Sitzungsberichte der königlich Preußischen Akademie der Wissenschaften zu Berlin* 1 (1894), 361–86.

Otloh of St Emmeram, *Liber de suis scriptoribus*, PL 146.0027–0059.

——, *Dialogus de tribus quaestionibus*, PL 146.0059–0134.

Otto of Freising, *Chronicon*, MGH SS 20, pp. 83–301.

Paul of Bernried, *Vita Gregorii VII papae*, ed. J. M. Watterich, *Pontificum Romanorum, qui fuerunt inde ab exeunte saeculo IX ad finem saeculi XIII, vitae ab aequalibus conscriptae*, 2 vols (Leipzig, 1862); trans. I. S. Robinson, *The papal reform of the eleventh century: lives of Pope Leo IX and Pope Gregory VII* (Manchester Medieval Sources Series; Manchester, 2004), pp. 262–364.

Peter Abelard, *Dialectica*, ed. L. M. de Rijk, *Dialectica. Petrus Abaelardus: First complete edition of the Parisian manuscript*, 2nd edn (Assen, 1970).

Peter Damian, *Letters*, ed. K. Reindel, *MGH Briefe. Die Briefe des Petrus Damiani*, 3 vols (Munich, 1983, 1988).

Plato, *Timaeus*, ed. J. H. Waszink, *Timaeus a Calcidio translatus commentarioque instructus*, 2nd edn (Plato Latinus 4; London, 1975).

Porphyry, *Isagoge. Translatio Boethii*, ed. L. Minio-Paluello (Aristoteles Latinus 1/6–7. Categoriarum supplementa; Leiden, 1966), pp. 5–31.

——, trans. E. W. Warren, *Porphyry the Phoenician: Isagoge* (Toronto, 1975).

Pseudo-Bernelinus, *Cita et vera divisio monochordi*, GS 1, pp. 312–30.

Pseudo-Odo of Cluny, *Dialogus de musica*, GS 1, pp. 251–64.

Quaestiones in musica, ed. R. Steglich, *Die Quaestiones in Musica. Ein Choraltraktat des zentralen Mittelalters und ihr mutmaßlicher Verfasser Rudolf von St. Trond (1070–1138)* (Leipzig, 1911; repr. 1971).

Quomodo de arithmetica procedit musica, PL 141.0435–0444.

Ratio generalis de initio adventus Domini (PL 142.1088A).

Regensburg Letter Collection, ed. N. Fickermann, *Briefsammlungen der Zeit Heinrichs IV. Die Regensburger rhetorischen Briefe*, MGH Briefe 5 (1950), pp. 259–382.

Regino of Prüm, *Epistola de harmonia institutione*, ed. M. P. le Roux, 'The *De harmonia institutione* and *Tonarius* of Regino of Prüm' (Ph.D. dissertation, Catholic University of America, 1965).

——, *Epistola de harmonica institutione*, ed. M. Bernhard, *Clavis Gerberti. Eine Revision von Martin Gerberts Scriptores ecclesiastici de musica sacra potissimum (St. Blasien 1784)* (Bayerische Akademie der Wissenschaften. Veröffentlichungen der Musikhistorischen Kommission 7; Munich, 1989), pp. 37–73.

Robert of Tomberlaine, *Prologus in Cantica Canticorum*, ed. J. Mabillon, *Vetera analecta . . . &c* (Paris, 1723).

Robinson, I. S., *Eleventh-century Germany: the Swabian Chronicles* (Manchester Medieval Sources Series; Manchester, 2008).

Rudolf of St Trond, *Gesta abbatum Trudonensium. Libri 1–7*, MGH SS 10, pp. 213–72.

Sachs, K.-J. (ed.), *Mensura fistularum. Die Mensurierung der Orgelpfeifen im Mittelalter*, 2 vols (Schriftenreihe der Walcker-Stiftung für Orgelwissenschaftliche Forschung; Stuttgart, 1970, 1980).

Sigebert of Gembloux, *Chronicon* 1028, MGH SS 6, pp. 268–374.

—— *Liber de illustribus viris*, ed. R. Witte, *Catalogus Sigeberti Gemblacensis monachi de viris illustribus*. Kritische Ausgabe (Lateinische Sprache und Literatur des Mittelalters 1; Bern, 1974).

Smits van Waesberghe, J. (ed.), *Cymbala: bells in the Middle Ages* (Musicological studies and documents 1; Rome, 1951).

——, *Bernonis Augiensis Abbatis de arte musica disputationes traditae. Pars A: Bernonis Augiensis De mensurando monochordo* (Divitae musicae artis A/6a; Buren, 1978).

Theoger of Metz, *Musica*, ed. and trans. F. C. Lochner, 'Dietger (Theogerus) of Metz and his "Musica"' (Ph.D. dissertation, University of Notre Dame, 1995).

Tonarius Augiensis, ed. H. Sowa, *Quellen zur Transformation der Antiphonen. Tonar- und Rhythmusstudien* (Kassel, 1935), pp. 81–154.

Vita Meinwerci episcopi Patherbrunnensis, *MGH SS* 11, pp. 106–61.

William of Conches, *Glosses on Timaeus*, ed. E. Jeauneau, *Glosae super Platonem* (Paris, 1965).

William of Hirsau, *Musica*, ed. D. Harbinson, *Wilhelmi Hirsaugiensis Musica* (Corpus scriptorum de musica 23; Rome, 1975).

Wolf, J. (ed.), 'Ein anonymer Musiktraktat des elften bis zwölften Jahrhunderts', *Vierteljahrschrift für Musikwissenschaft* 9 (1893), 186–234.

Wolfger of Prüfening, *De scriptoribus ecclesiasticis*, ed. E. Ettlinger, *Der sogenannte Anonymus Mellicensis De scriptoribus ecclesiasticis* (Straßburg, 1896).

——, *Vita Theogeri Abbatis S. Georgii et episcopi Mettensis*, *MGH SS* 12, pp. 449–79.

Worms Letter Collection, ed. W. Bulst, *Die ältere Wormser Briefsammlung*, *MGH Briefe* 3 (1949).

Secondary sources

Abert, H. J., *Die Musikanschauung des Mittelalters und ihre Grundlagen* (Malle, 1905; repr. Tutzing, 1964).

Adkins, C. D., 'The theory and practice of the monochord' (Ph.D. dissertation, Iowa State University, 1963).

——, 'The technique of the monochord', *Acta musicologica* 34 (1967), 34–43.

Andernacht, D., 'Die Biographen Bischof Ottos von Bamberg' (Doctoral dissertation, Johann Wolfgang Goethe University, Frankfurt am Main, 1950).

Angenendt, A., 'Die Liturgie in der Vita des Johannes von Gorze', in M. Parisse and O. Oexle (eds), *L'Abbaye de Gorze au Xe siècle* (Nancy, 1993), pp. 193–211.

Atkinson, C., '"Harmonia" and the "Modi, quos abusive tonos dicimus"', in A. Pompilio (ed.), *Atti del XIV congresso della Società internazionale di musicologia. Transmissione e recezione delle forme di cultura musicale* (Turin, 1990), pp. 485–500.

Autenrieth, J., 'Bernold von Konstanz und der Codex Sangallensis 676', in *Friedrich Baethgen zu seinem 65. Geburtstag* (Typescript in the library of the MGH; Munich, 1955), pp. 1–17.

——, *Die Domschule von Konstanz zur Zeit des Investiturstreits. Die Wissenschaftliche Arbeitsweise Bernholds von Konstanz und zweier Kleriker dargestellt auf Grund von Handschriftenstudien* (Forschungen zur Kirchen- und Geistesgeschichte 3; Stuttgart, 1956).

——, *Die Handschriften der ehemaligen Hofbibliothek Stuttgart. Codices iuridici et politici (HB VI 1–139), Patres (HB VII 1–71)* (Die Handschriften der Wüttembergischen Landesbibliothek Stuttgart 2/3; Wiesbaden, 1963).

Barker-Benfield, B. C., 'The manuscripts of Macrobius' Commentary on the *Somnium Scipionis*', 2 vols (D.Phil. thesis, University of Oxford, 1975).

Barrow, J., 'Education and the recruitment of cathedral canons in England and Germany 1100–1225', *Viator* 20 (1989), 117–38.

Bauerreiß, R., 'Seeon in Oberbayern. Eine bayerische Malschule des beginnenden XI. Jahrhunderts', *SMGBZ* 50 (1932), 530–55.

——, 'St. Georgen im Schwarzwald. Ein Reformmittelpunkt Südostdeutschlands im beginnenden 12. Jahrhundert', *SMGBZ* 51 (1933), 196–201; 52 (1934), 47–56.

Beach, A. I., *Women as scribes: book production and monastic reform in twelfth-century Bavaria* (Cambridge, 2004).

—— (ed.), *Manuscripts and monastic culture: reform and renewal in twelfth-century Germany* (Medieval Church Studies 13; Turnhout, 2007).

Becker, G. H., *Catalogi bibliothecarum antiqui* (Bonn, 1885).

Berger, K., 'The hand and the art of memory', *Musica disciplina* 35 (1981), 87–120.

——, *Musica ficta: theories of accidental inflections in vocal polyphony from Marchetto da Padova to Gioseffo Zarlino* (Cambridge, 1987).

Bergmann, W., 'Der Traktat "De mensura astrolabii" des Hermann von Reichenau', *Francia* 8 (1980), 65–103.

——, 'Chronographie und Komputistik bei Hermann von Reichenau', in D. Berg and H.-W. Goetz (eds), *Historiographia medievalis. Studien zur Geschichtsschreibung und Quellenkunde des Mittelalters. Festschrift für Franz-Josef Schmale* (Darmstadt, 1988), pp. 103–17.

Bernhard, M., *Studien zur Epistola de armonica institutione des Regino von Prüm* (Bayerische Akademie der Wissenschaften. Veröffentlichungen der Musikhistorischen Kommission 5; Munich, 1979).

——, 'Glosses on Boethius' *De institutione musica*', in A. Barbera (ed.), *Music theory and its sources: antiquity and the Middle Ages* (Notre Dame, Il., 1990), pp. 136–49.

——, 'Überlieferung und Fortleben der antiken lateinischen Musiktheorie im Mittelalter', in F. Zaminer (ed.), *Rezeption des antiken Fachs im Mittelalter* (Geschichte der Musiktheorie 3; Darmstadt, 1990), pp. 7–36.

——, 'Zur Überlieferung des 11. Kapitels in Frutolfs "Breviarium,"' in M. Bernhard (ed.), *Quellen und Studien zur Musiktheorie des Mittelalters* (Bayerische Akademie der Wissenschaften. Veröffentlichungen der Musikhistorischen Kommission 8; Munich, 1990), pp. 37–67.

——, 'Hermannus Contractus', *MGG. Personenteil* 8, cols 1393–5.

——, 'Zur Rezeption der musiktheoretischen Werke des Hermannus Contractus', in W. Pass and A. Rausch (eds), *Beiträge zur Musik, Musiktheorie und Liturgie der Abtei Reichenau. Bericht über die Tagung Heiligenkreuz 6.–8. Dezember 1999* (Musica mediaevalis Europae occidentalis 8; Tutzing, 2001), pp. 99–126.

——, '*The Seligenstadt Tonary*', *Plainsong and medieval music* 13 (2004), 107–25.

Berschin, W., 'Odalscalcs *Vita S. Konradi* im hagiographischen Hausbuch der Abtei St. Ulrich und Afra', *Freiburger Diözesan-Archiv* 95 (1975), 82–106.

——, 'Die Schule der Reichenau (IX.-XI. Jahrhunderts)', in W. Berschin, *Mittellateinischen Studien* (Heidelberg, 2005), pp. 229-36.

——, *Eremus und Insula. St. Gallen und die Reichenau im Mittelalter. Modell einer lateinischen Literaturlandschaft* (Wiesbaden, 2005).

——, 'Hermann der Lahme. Leben und Werk in Übersicht', in W. Berschin and M. Hellmann, *Hermann der Lahme. Gelehrter und Dichter (1013-1054)* (Reichenauer Texte und Bilder 11; Heidelberg, 2005), pp. 15-32.

——, 'Hermann der Lahme als Sequenzendichter. Mit Diskussion der Antiphonen *Salve regina* und *Alma redemptoris mater*', in W. Berschin and M. Hellmann, *Hermann der Lahme. Gelehrter und Dichter (1013-1054)* (Reichenauer Texte und Bilder 11; Heidelberg, 2005), pp. 73-106.

Bischoff, B., 'Wolfger', in K. Langosch (ed.), *Die deutsche Literatur des Mittelalters. Verfasserlexikon* 4 (Berlin, 1953).

——, 'Die europäische Verbreitung der Werke Isidors von Sevilla', in B. Bischoff, *Mittelalterliche Studien. Ausgewählte Aufsätze zur Schriftkunde und Literaturgeschichte* 1 (Stuttgart, 1966), pp. 171-94.

——, *Mittelalterliche Studien. Ausgewählte Aufsätze zur Schriftkunde und Literaturgeschichte*, 3 vols (Stuttgart, 1966-81).

——, 'Literarisches und künstlerisches Leben in St. Emmeram (Regensburg) während des frühen und hohen Mittelalters', *SMGBZ* 51 (1933), 102-42; repr. in B. Bischoff, *Mittelalterliche Studien. Ausgewählte Aufsätze zur Schriftkunde und Literaturgeschichte* 2 (Stuttgart, 1967), pp. 77-115.

Bischoff, B. and W. Stoll, *Mittelalterliche Bibliothekskataloge Deutschlands und der Schweiz* 4/2 (Munich, 1979).

le Boeuf, P., 'La tradition manuscrite du "De musica" de saint Augustin et son influence sur la pensée et l'esthétique médiévales' (Doctoral dissertation, École Nationale de Chartres, Paris, 1986).

——, 'Un commentaire d'inspiration érigénienne du "De musica" de saint Augustin', *Recherches Augustiniennes* 22 (1987), 243-316.

Borst, A., 'Hermann der Lahme und die Geschichte', *Hegau* 32-3 (1975-6), 7-18.

——, *Mönche am Bodensee, 610-1525* (Bodensee-Bibliothek 5; Sigmaringen, 1978).

——, 'Ein Forschungsbericht Hermanns des Lahmen', *DA* 40 (1984), 379-477.

——, *Das mittelalterliche Zahlenkampfspiel. Supplemente zu den Sitzungsberichten der Heidelberger Akademie der Wissenschaften, Philosophisch-Historische Klasse* (Heidelberg, 1986).

——, 'Computus. Zeit und Zahl im Mittelalter', *DA* 44 (1988), 1-81.

Bowen, W., 'St Augustine in medieval and renaissance musical science', in R. R. la Croix (ed.), *Augustine on music: an interdisciplinary collection of essays* (Lewiston and Queenstown, 1988), pp. 29-52.

Bower, C. M., 'The modes of Boethius', *Journal of Musicology* 3 (1984), 252-63.

——, 'Boethius' *De institutione musica*: a handlist of manuscripts', *Scriptorium* 42 (1988), 205-51.'

——, 'The grammatical model of musical understanding in the Middle Ages', in P. Gallacher and H. Damico (eds), *Hermeneutics and medieval culture* (Albany, NY, 1989), pp. 133-45.

——, 'The transmission of ancient music theory in the Middle Ages', in T. Christensen (ed.), *The Cambridge history of western music theory* (Cambridge, 2002), pp. 136–67.

Brambach, W., *Das Tonsystem und die Tonarten des christlichen Abendlandes im Mittelalter, ihre Beziehungen zur griechisch-römischen Musik und ihre Entwicklung bis auf die Schule Guido's von Arezzo. Mit einer Wiederherstellung der Musiktheorie Berno's von der Reichenau nach einer Karlsruher Handschrift* (Leipzig, 1881).

——, *Die Musiklitteratur des Mittelalters bis zur Blüthe der Reichenauer Sängerschule (500–1050 n. Chr.)* (Karlsruhe, 1883).

——, *Theorie und Praxis der Reichenauer Sängerschule* (Karlsruhe, 1888).

le Bras, G., 'Le Liber de misericordia et justitia d'Alger de Liège', *Nouvelle Revue historique de droit français et étranger* 45 (1921), 80–118.

Bresslau, H., 'Bamberger Studien', *NA* 21 (1896), 140–234.

von den Brincken, A.-D., *Studien zur lateinischen Weltchronistik bis in das Zeitalter Ottos von Freising* (Düsseldorf, 1957).

Bucher, T. G., 'Petrus Damiani. Ein Freund der Logik?', *Freiburger Zeitschrift für Philosophie und Theologie* 36 (1989), 267–310.

Bultmann, R., 'Zur Geschichte der Lichtsymbolik im Altertum', *Philologus* 97 (1948), 1–36.

Bultot, R., ' "Quadrivium", "natura" et "ingenium naturale" chez Guillaume d'Hirsau', *Rivista di filosofia neo-scolastico* 70 (1978), 11–27.

Busse-Berger, A. M., *Medieval music and the art of memory* (Berkeley, 2005).

Châtillon, F., 'Recherches critiques sur les différents personnages nommés Manegold', *Revue du moyen âge latin* 9 (1953), 153–70.

Chenu, M. D., *Nature, man and society in the twelfth century: essays on new theological perspectives in the Latin west*, 2nd edn, ed. and trans. J. Taylor and L. K. Little (Toronto, 1997).

Chevalier, U., *Répertoire des Sources Historiques du Moyen Age. Bio-Bibliographie* 1 (Paris, 1905).

Cohen, A. S., *The Uta Codex: art, philosophy and reform in eleventh-century Germany* (University Park, Pa., 2000).

Colker, M. L., 'Heinrici Augustensis *Planctus Evae*', *Traditio* 12 (1956), 149–230.

——, *The reformation of the twelfth century* (Cambridge, 1996).

Cordiolani, A., 'Le computiste Hermann de Reichenau', *Miscellanea di Storia Ligure* 3 (1961), 167–90.

Courcelle, P., *Les lettres grecques en occident de Macrobe à Cassiodore* (Paris, 1948).

Cowdrey, H. E. J., *The Cluniacs and the Gregorian reform* (Oxford, 1970).

——, *Pope Gregory VII: 1073–1085* (Oxford, 1998).

Coxe, H. O. and R. W. Hunt, *Bodleian Library Quarto Catalogues 2: Laudian Manuscripts* (Oxford, 1973).

Crocker, R. L., 'Hermann's major sixth', *Journal of the American Musicological Society* 25 (1972), 19–37.

Curze, M., 'Die Handschrift No. 14836 der Königlichen Hof- und Staatsbibliothek zu München', *Zeitschrift für Mathematik und Physik* 40 (1895), 77–142.

Daniel, N., *Handschriften des zehnten Jahrhunderts aus der Freisinger Dombibliothek. Studien über Schriftcharakter und Herkunft der nachkarolingischen und ottonis-*

chen Handschriften einer bayerischen Bibliothek (Münchener Beiträge zur Mediävistik und Renaissance-Forschung 11; Munich, 1973).

Deason, W. D., 'A taxonomic paradigm from Boethius' *De divisione* applied to the eight modes of music' (Ph.D. dissertation, Ohio State University, 1992).

Dengler-Schreiber, K., *Scriptorium und Bibliothek des Klosters Michelsberg in Bamberg* (Studien zur Bibliotheksgeschichte 2; Graz, 1979).

Desmond, K., 'New light on Jacobus, author of *Speculum musicae*', *Plainsong and medieval music* 9 (2000), 19–40.

Donnat, L., 'Vie et coutume monastique dans la Vita de Jean de Gorze', in M. Parisse and O. Oexle (eds), *L'Abbaye de Gorze au Xe siècle* (Nancy, 1993), pp. 159–82.

Dresser, F., *Petrus Damiani. Leben und Werk* (Studia Anselmiana 34; Rome, 1954).

Dronke, P., *The medieval lyric*, 3rd edn (Cambridge, 1996).

—— (ed.), *A history of twelfth-century western philosophy* (Cambridge, 1988).

Duchez, M.-E., 'Jean Scot Erigène premier lecteur du "De institutione musica" de Boèce?', in W. Beierwaltes (ed.), *Eriugena. Studien zu seinen Quellen* (Heidelberg, 1980), pp. 165–87.

——, 'Description grammaticale et description arithmétique des phénomènes musicaux. Le tournant du IXe siècle', in J. P. Beckmann and W. Kluxen (eds), *Sprache und Erkenntnis im Mittelalter. Akten des VI. Internationalen Kongress für Mittelalterliche Philosophie der Société internationale pour l'étude de la philosophie Médiévale, 29. August–3. September 1977 in Bonn* (Miscellanea mediaevalia. Veröffentlichungen des Thomas-Instituts der Universität Köln 13/2; Berlin and New York, 1981), pp. 561–79.

——, 'Vocabulaire musical et conceptualisation musico-scientifique', *Documents pour l'histoire du vocabulaire scientifique* 2 (1981), 1–18.

——, 'L'émergence acoustico-musicale du terme "sonus" dans les commentaires carolingiens de Martianus Capella', *Documents pour l'histoire du vocabulaire scientifique* 7 (1985), 97–149.

——, 'Le Savoir théorico-musical carolingien dans les commentaires de Martianus Capella. La tradition érigénienne', in *Giovanni Scoto nel suo tempo. L'organizzazione del sapere en età carolingia. Atti del XXIV Convegno storico internazionale Todi, 11–14 ottobre 1987* (Atti del convegni dell'Accademia tudertina e del Centro di studi sulla spiritualità medievale, N.S. 1; Spoleto, 1989), pp. 553–92.

Dümmler, E., 'Cölner Bücherkatalog', *Zeitschrift für deutsches Altertum und deutsche Literatur* 19 (1876), pp. 466–7.

——, 'Über den Mönch Otloh von St. Emmeram', *Sitzungsberichte der königlich Preußischen Akademie der Wissenschaften zu Berlin* 2 (1895), 1071–1102.

Eder, C. E., 'Die Schule des Klosters Tegernsee im frühen Mittelalter im Spiegel der Tegernseer Handschriften', *SMGBZ* 83 (1972), 6–155.

Eggebrecht, H. H. (ed.), *Handwörterbuch der musikalischen Terminologie* (Wiesbaden, 1972–).

Ehlers, J., 'Dom- und Klosterschulen in Deutschland und Frankreich im 10. und 11. Jahrhundert', in M. Kintzinger, S. Lorenz and M. Walter (eds), *Schule und Schüler im Mittelalter* (Cologne, 1996), pp. 29–52.

Eizenhöfer, L. and H. Knaus (eds), *Die liturgischen Handschriften der Hessischen Landes- und Hochschulbibliothek Darmstadt*. *Die Handschriften der Hessischen Landes- und Hochschulbliothek Darmstadt* 2 (Wiesbaden, 1968).

Endres, J. A., 'Lanfranks Verhältnis zur Dialektik', *Der Katholik*, 3rd series, 25 (1902), 215-33.

——, 'Die Dialektiker und ihre Gegner im 11. Jahrhundert', *Philosophisches Jahrbuch* 19 (1906), 20-33.

——, *Petrus Damiani und die weltliche Wissenschaft* (Beiträge zur Geschichte der Philosophie des Mittelalters 8/3; Münster, 1910).

——, 'Studien zur Geschichte der Frühscholastik', *Philosophisches Jahrbuch* 26 (1913), 89-93, 160-9, 349-59.

——, *Forschungen zur Geschichte der frühmittelalterlichen Philosophie* (Beiträge zur Geschichte der Philosophie des Mittelalters 17/2-3; Münster, 1915).

van Engen, J., 'Letters, schools and written culture in the eleventh and twelfth centuries', in J. Fried (ed.), *Dialektik und Rhetorik im früheren und hohen Mittelalter* (Schriften des Historischen Kollegs, Kolloquien 27; Munich, 1997), pp. 97-132.

Englisch, B., *Die Artes liberales im frühen Mittelalter (5.-9. Jh.). Das Quadrivium und der Komputus als Indikatoren für Kontinuität und Erneuerung der exakten Wissenschaften zwischen Antike und Mittelalter* (Stuttgart, 1994).

Erdmann, C., 'Die Bamberger Domschule im Investiturstreit', *Zeitschrift für bayerische Landesgeschichte* 9 (1936), 1-46.

——, 'Bern von Reichenau und Heinrich III.', in C. Erdmann, *Forschungen zur politischen Ideenwelt des Frühmittelalters. Aus dem Nachlass des Verfassers*, ed. F. Baethgen (Berlin, 1951), pp. 112-19.

——, 'Onulf von Speyer und Amarcius', in C. Erdmann, *Forschungen zur politischen Ideenwelt des Frühmittelalters*, pp. 124-34.

Evans, G. R., 'Studium discendi: Otloh of St Emmeram and the seven liberal arts', *Recherches de théologie ancienne et médiévale* 44 (1977), 29-54.

Fellerer, K., 'Die musica in den artes liberales', in J. Koch (ed.), *Artes liberales. Von der antiken Bildung zur Wissenschaft des Mittelalters* (Studien und Texte zur Geistesgeschichte des Mittelalters 5; Leiden and Cologne, 1959), 33-49.

von Fichtenau, H., 'Wolfger von Prüfening', *Mitteilungen des Instituts für österreichische Geschichtsforschung* 51 (1937), 313-57.

Flindell, E. F., 'Joh[ann]is Cottonis', *Musica disciplina* 20 (1966), 11-30.

——, 'Joh[ann]is Cottonis, corrigenda et addenda', *Musica disciplina* 23 (1969), 7-11.

Flint, V. I. J., 'The career of Honorius Augustodunensis: some fresh evidence', *Revue bénédictine* 82 (1972), 63-86.

——, 'The place and purpose of the works of Honorius Augustodunensis', *Revue bénédictine* 87 (1977), 97-127.

——, 'Heinricus of Augsburg and Honorius Augustodunensis: are they the same person?', *Revue bénédictine* 92 (1982), 148-58.

Fournier, P. and G. le Bras, *Histoire des collections canoniques en Occident depuis les Fausses décrétals jusqu'au Décret de Gratien*, 2 vols (Paris, 1931, 1932).

Freise, E., 'Die Äbte und der Konvent von St. Emmeram im Spiegel der Totenbuchführung des 11. und 12. Jahrhunderts', in E. Freise, D. Geuenich and J. Wollasch (eds), *Das Martyrolog-Necrolog von St. Emmeram in Regensburg, MGH Libri memoriales N. S. 3* (Hanover, 1986), pp. 96-106.

Fried, J., 'Die Bamberger Domschule und die Rezeption von Frühscholastik und Rechtswissenschaft in ihrem Umkreis bis zum Ende der Stauferzeit', *Vorträge und Forschungen* 30 (1986), 163-200.

Gams, P. B., *Series episcoporum ecclesiae catholicae* (Regensburg, 1873).

Ganz, D. (ed.), *The role of the book in medieval culture* (Bibliologia: Elementa et librorum studia pertinentia 3-4; Turnhout, 1986).

Gaspari, G., *Catalogo della Biblioteca del Liceo Musicale di Bologna* 1 (Bologna, 1890).

Gibson, M., 'The artes in the eleventh century', in *Arts libéraux et philosophie au Moyen-Age. Actes du Quatrième Congrès international de philosophie médiévale, Université de Montréal, Montréal, Canada, 27 août-septembre 1967* (Montreal and Paris, 1969).

——, 'The study of the *Timaeus* in the eleventh and twelfth centuries', *Pensamiento* 25 (1969), 183-94.

——, 'Lanfranc's "Commentary on the Pauline Epistles"', *Journal of Theological Studies n.s.* 22 (1971), 86-112.

——, 'Latin commentaries on logic before 1200', *Bulletin de philosophie médiévale* 24 (1982), 54-64.

Gibson, M. (ed.), *Boethius: his life, thought and influence* (Oxford, 1981).

Gonsette, J., *Pierre Damien et la culture profane* (Louvain, 1956).

Gottlieb, T., *Über mittelalterliche Bibliotheken* (Leipzig, 1890).

——, *Mittelalterliche Bibliothekskataloge Österreichs* (Vienna, 1915).

Gottwald, C., *Codices musici. Die Handschriften der Württembergischen Landesbibliothek Stuttgart. Die Handschriften der ehemaligen königlichen Hofbibliothek* 6/1 (Wiesbaden, 1965).

——, *Die Musikhandschriften der Universitätsbibliothek München. Die Handschriften der Universitätsbibliothek München* 2 (Wiesbaden, 1968).

——, *Die Musikhandschriften der Staats- und Stadtbibliothek Augsburg. Handschriftenkataloge der Staats und Stadtbibliothek Augsburg* 1 (Wiesbaden, 1974).

Grabmann, M., *Die Geschichte der scholastischen Methode. Nach den gedruckten und ungedruckten Quellen*, 2 vols (Freiburg, 1909-11; repr. Darmstadt, 1956).

Grebe, S., *Martianus Capella 'De nuptiis Philologiae et Mercurii'. Darstellung der Sieben Freien Künste und ihrer Beziehungen zueinander* (Stuttgart and Leipzig, 1999).

Gregory, T., 'Note e testi per la storia del platonismo medioevale', *Giornale critico della filosofia italiana* 34 (1955), 346-84.

——, *Platonismo medievale. Studi e ricerche* (Studi storici [Istituto storico italiano per il Medio Evo] 26-7; Rome, 1958).

——, 'The Platonic inheritance', in P. Dronke (ed.), *A history of twelfth-century western philosophy* (Cambridge, 1988), pp. 54-80.

Gross, J., 'Die Erbsündenlehre Manegolds von Lautenbach nach seinem Psalmen-Kommentar', *Zeitschrift für Kirchengeschichte* 71 (1960), 252-61.

Gümpel, K.-W., 'Pseudo-Odo', *MGG. Personenteil* 13 (2005), cols 1012-15.
Gushee, L. 'Questions of genre in medieval treatises on music', in W. Arlt, E. Lichtenhahn and H. Oesch (eds), *Gattungen der Musik in Einzeldarstellungen. Gedenkschrift Leo Schrade* (Munich, 1973), pp. 365-433.
Gushee, L. and D. Pesce, 'Berno of Reichenau', *NG* 3, p. 442.
Hallinger, K., *Gorze-Kluny. Studien zu den monastischen Lebensformen und Gegensätzen im Hochmittelalter*, 2 vols (Studia Anselmiana philosophica theologica, fasc. 22-25; Rome, 1950, 1951).
Halm, C., F. Keinz, G. Meyer and G. Thomas, *Catalogus codicum latinorum Bibliotheca Regiae Monacensis*, 4 vols (Munich, 1873-94).
Handschin, J., 'Hermannus Contractus-Legende – nur Legende?', *Zeitschrift für deutsches Altertum und deutsche Literatur* 72 (1932), 1-8.
Hankeln, R., 'Sankt Emmeram', *MGG. Sachteil* 8 (1998), cols 940-3.
Hartmann, W., 'Manegold von Lautenbach und die Anfänge der Frühscholastik', *DA* 26 (1970), 47-149.
Haskins, C. H., *The renaissance of the twelfth century* (Cambridge, Mass. and London, 1927).
Hauck, A., *Kirchengeschichte Deutschlands*, 4 vols (Leipzig, 1896, 1900, 1906, 1912; repr. Berlin, 1952-3).
von Heinemann, O., *Die Handschriften der Herzoglichen Bibliothek zu Wolfenbüttel*, 11 vols (Wolfenbüttel, 1884-1913).
Heinzer, F., 'Kodifizierung und Vereinheitlichung liturgischer Traditionen. Historisches Phänomen und Interpretationsschlüssel handschriftlicher Überlieferung', in K. Heller, H. Möller and A. Waczkat (eds), *Musik in Mecklenburg. Beiträge eines Kolloquiums zur mecklenburgischen Musikgeschichte veranstaltet vom Institut für Musikwissenschaft der Universität Rostock, 24.-27. September 1997. Mit einer Zeittafel und einer Auswahlbibliographie zur mecklenburgischen Musikgeschichte* (Studien und Materialien zur Musikwissenschaft 21; Hildesheim, 2000), pp. 85-106.
Helmsdörfer, A., *Forschungen zur Geschichte des Abtes Wilhelm von Hirschau* (Göttingen, 1874).
Hemmerle, J., *Die Benediktinerklöster in Bayern* (Germania benedictina 2; Augsburg, 1971).
Herwegen, I., 'Die hl. Hildegard von Bingen und das Oblateninstitut', *SMGBZ* 33 (1912), 543-52.
Hesslig, R., *Katalog der Handschriften der Universitäts-Bibliothek zu Leipzig* (Leipzig, 1926-35).
Hiley, D., *Western plainchant: a handbook* (Oxford, 1993).
——, 'The Regensburg offices for St Emmeram, St Wolfgang and St Denis', in *Musica antiqua X: Tenth international musicological congress 'Musica antiqua Europae orientalis' Bydgoszcz, September 7th-11th 1994* (Bydgoszcz, 1994), pp. 299-312.
——, 'Das Wolfgang-Offiziums des Hermannus Contractus – Zum Wechselspiel von Modustheorie und Gesangspraxis in der Mitte des XI. Jahrhunderts', in W. Berschin and D. Hiley (eds), *Die Offizien des Mittelalters. Dichtung und Musik* (Regensburger Studien zur Musikgeschichte 1; Tutzing, 1999), 129-42.

——, 'Die Afra-Gesänge des Hermannus Contractus. Liturgische Melodien und die Harmonie des Universums', in M. Weitlauff and M. Thierbach (eds), *Hl. Afra. Eine frühchristliche Märtyrerin in Geschichte, Kunst und Kult* (Augsburg, 2004), pp. 112–19.

Hirschmann, W., 'Aribo', *MGG. Personenteil* 1, cols 905–8.

——, 'Johannes', *MGG. Personenteil* 9, cols 1077–81.

Hochadel, M., 'Zur Stellung des pseudo-bernonischen Traktats De mensurando monochordo und seinem Verhältnis zu Frutolfs Breviarium', in W. Pass and A. Rausch (eds), *Beiträge zur Musik, Musiktheorie und Liturgie der Abtei Reichenau. Bericht über die Tagung Heiligenkreuz 6.–8. Dezember 1999* (Musica mediaevalis Europae occidentalis 8; Tutzing, 2001), pp. 41–68.

Hoffmann, H., *Buchkunst und Königtum in ottonischen und frühsalischen Reich* (Schriften der Monumenta Germaniae Historica 30/1; Stuttgart, 1986).

——, *Bamberger Handschriften des 10. und des 11. Jahrhunderts* (Schriften der Monumenta Germaniae Historica 29; Hanover, 1995).

Hofmeister, P., 'Die Klaustral-Oblaten', *SMGBZ* 72 (1961), 5–45.

Holopainen, T. J., *Dialectic and theology in the eleventh century* (Leiden, 1996).

Hörberg, N., *Libri sanctae Afrae. St. Ulrich und Afra zu Augsburg im 11. und 12. Jahrhundert nach Zeugnissen der Klosterbibliothek* (Veröffentlichungen des Max-Planck-Instituts für Geschichte. Studien zur Germania sacra 15; Göttingen, 1983).

Houben, H., *St. Blasianer Handschriften des 11. und 12. Jahrhunderts. Unter besonderer Berücksichtigung der Ochsenhauser Klosterbibliothek* (Munich, 1979).

Hughes, A., 'Aribo', *NG* 1, p. 579.

Huglo, M., 'Un théoricien du XIe siècle: Henri d'Augsburg', *Revue de musicologie* 53 (1967), 53–9.

——, 'L'Auteur du Dialogue sur la Musique attribuée à Odon', *Revue de musicologie* 55 (1969), 119–71.

——, 'Der Prolog des Odo zugeschriebenen "Dialogus de Musica"', *Archiv für Musikwissenschaft* 28 (1971), 134–46.

——, *Les tonaires. Inventaire, analyse, comparaison* (Publications de la Société française de musicologie 3/2; Paris, 1971).

——, Bulletin Codicologique no. 791, *Scriptorium* 27 (1973), 401–2.

——, 'L'Auteur du traité de musique dédié à Fulgence d'Affligem', *Revue Belge de Musicologie* 31 (1977), 5–17.

——, 'Frutolfus of Michelsberg', *NG* 9, p. 302.

——, 'Tonary', *NG* 25, pp. 594–8.

——, 'Heinrich von Augsburg', *MGG. Personenteil* 8, cols 1212–13.

Huglo, M. and N. Phillips, 'Le *De musica* de saint Augustin et l'organisation de la durée musicale du IXe au XIIe siècles', *Revue des études augustiniennes* 20 (1985), 117–31.

Hüschen, H., 'Bern von Reichenau', *Verfasserlexikon* 1 (1978), cols 737–43.

Hüttig, A., *Macrobius im Mittelalter. Ein Beitrag zur Rezeptionsgeschichte der Commentarii in Somnium Scipionis* (Freiburger Beiträge zur mittelalterlichen Geschichte. Studien und Texte 2; Frankfurt am Main, 1990).

Ilnitchi, G., 'Aribo's *De musica*: music theory in the cross current of medieval learning' (Ph.D. dissertation, New York University, 1997).

——, *The play of meanings: Aribo's De musica and the hermeneutics of musical thought* (Lanham, Md., 2005).

Ineichen-Eder, C. E., *Mittelalterliche Bibliothekskataloge Deutschlands und der Schweiz* 4/1 (Munich, 1977).

Irtenkauf, W., 'Der Computus ecclesiasticus in der Einstimmigkeit des Mittelalters', *Archiv für Musikwissenschaft* 14 (1957), 1-15.

——, 'Zur mittelalterlichen Liturgie- und Musikgeschichte Ottobeurens', in A. Kolb and H. Tüchle (eds), *Ottobeuren. Festschrift zur 1200-Jahrfeier der Abtei* (Augsburg, 1964).

Iwakuma, Y., ' "Vocales", or early nominalists', *Traditio* 47 (1992), 37-111.

Jaeger, C. S., 'Cathedral schools and humanist learning, 950-1150', *Deutsche Vierteljahrschrift* 61 (1987), 596-616; repr. with the same pagination in C. S. Jaeger, *Scholars and courtiers: intellectuals and society in the medieval West* (Variorum collected studies series 733; Aldershot, 2003).

——, *The envy of angles: cathedral schools and social ideas in medieval Europe, 950-1200* (Philadelphia, 1994).

Jaffé, P. and G. Wattenbach, *Ecclesiae metropolitanae Coloniensis codices manuscripti* (Berlin, 1874).

Jakobs, H., *Die Hirsauer. Ihre Ausbreitung und Rechtsstellung im Zeitalter des Investiturstreites* (Kölner historische Abhandlungen 4; Cologne and Graz, 1961).

Jänichen, H., 'Zur Genealogie der älteren Grafen von Veringen', *Zeitschrift für Württembergische Landesgeschichte* 27 (1968), 1-30.

Jeauneau, E., 'L'héritage de la philosophie antique durant le haut moyen âge', in *Settimane di studio del Centro italiano di studi sull'alto medievo, XXII, 1974* (Spoleto, 1975), pp. 17-56.

Jones, L. W., 'The influence of Cassiodorus on mediaeval culture', *Speculum* 20 (1945), 433-42.

——, 'Further notes concerning Cassiodorus' influence on mediaeval culture', *Speculum* 22 (1947), 254-6.

Jørgensen, E., *Catalogus codicum Latinorum medii aevi Bibliothecae regiae Hafniensis* (Copenhagen, 1926).

Joyce, E., 'Speaking of spiritual matters: visions and the rhetoric of reform in the *Liber visionum* of Otloh of St Emmeram', in A. I. Beach (ed.), *Manuscripts and monastic culture: reform and renewal in twelfth-century Germany* (Medieval Church Studies 13; Turnhout, 2007), pp. 69-98.

Keller, A., *Aurelius Augustinus und die Musik. Untersuchungen zu 'De musica' im Kontext seines Schrifttums* (Würzburg, 1993).

Kennedy, V. L., 'The "De officiis divinis" of MS Bamberg Lit. 34', *Ephemerides liturgicae* 52 (1938), 312-26.

Kerkhoff, J., 'Die Grafen von Altshausen-Veringen. Die Ausbildung der Familie zum Adelsgeschlecht und der Aufbau ihrer Herrschaft im 11. und 12. Jahrhundert', *Hohenzollerische Jahreshefte* 24 (1964), 1-132.

Klaper, M., 'Die musikalische Überlieferung aus dem Kloster Reichenau im 11. Jahrhundert und die kompositorische Tätigkeit des Abtes Bern (1008-1048)', in W. Pass and A. Rausch (eds), *Beiträge zur Musik, Musiktheorie und Liturgie der Abtei*

Reichenau. Bericht über die Tagung Heiligenkreuz 6.-8. Dezember 1999 (Musica mediaevalis Europae occidentalis 8; Tutzing, 2001), pp. 1-40.

——, *Die Musikgeschichte der Abtei Reichenau im 10. und 11. Jahrhundert. Ein Versuch* (Beihefte zum Archiv für Musikwissenschaft 52; Stuttgart, 2003).

Klemm, E., *Die romanischen Handschriften der Bayerische Staatsbibliothek. Teil 1: Die Bistümer Regensburg, Passau und Salzburg. Textband. Tafelband* (Wiesbaden, 1980).

Klibansky, R., *The continuity of the Platonic tradition during the Middle Ages: outlines of a corpus platonicum medii aevi* (London, 1939).

Kottje, R., 'Klosterbibliotheken und monastische Kultur in der zweiten Hälfe des 11. Jahrhunderts', *Zeitschrift für Kirchengeschichte* 80 (1969), 145-62.

Krämer, S. and M. Bernhard, *Handschriftenerbe des deutschen Mittelalters*, 3 vols (Munich, 1989, 1990).

Kreps, J., 'Aribon de Liège. Une légende', *Revue belge de musicologie* 2 (1948), 138-43.

Kyle, J. D., 'St Emmeram (Regensburg) as a centre of culture in the late tenth century' (Ph.D. dissertation, Univerity of Pittsburgh, 1976).

Lattin, H. P., 'The eleventh-century MS Munich 14436: its contribution to the history of co-ordinates, of logic, of German studies in France', *Isis* 38 (1948), 205-25.

Lehmann, P., *Mittelalterliche Bibliothekskataloge Deutschlands und der Schweiz*, 2 vols (Munich, 1918, 1928).

Leitschuh, F. and H. Fischer, *Katalog der Handschriften der königlichen Bibliothek zu Bamberg*, 3 vols (Bamberg, 1887-1912).

Leonardi, C., 'Nota introduttiva per un' indagine sulla fortuna di Marziano Capella nel Medioevo', *Bullettino dell' storico italiano per il medio evo e Archivo Muratoriano* 67 (1955), 265-88.

——, 'I codici di Marziano Capella', *Aevum* 34 (1960), 1-99, 411-524.

Linde, J. C., 'Die "Rhetorici colores" des Magister Onulf von Speyer', *Mittellateinisches Jahrbuch* 40 (2005), 333-81.

Lipphardt, W., 'Der Karolingische Tonar von Metz', *Liturgiewissenschaftliche Quellen und Forschungen* 43 (1965), 1-309.

Malcolm, J., 'Epistola Johannis Cottonis ad Fulgentium episcopum', *Musica disciplina* 47 (1993), 159-69.

Maloy, R. 'The roles of notation in Frutolf of Michelsberg's tonary', *Journal of Musicology* 19 (2002), 641-93.

Manitius, M., 'Geschichtliches aus mittelalterlichen Bibliothekskatalogen', *NA* 32 (1906-07), 649-709.

——, *Geschichte der lateinischen Literatur des Mittelalters*, 3 vols (Handbuch der Altertumswissenschaft 9.2/1-3; Munich, 1911-31; repr. 1973-6).

——, *Handschriften antiker Autoren in mittelalterlichen Bibliothekskatalogen*, ed. K. Manitius (Leipzig, 1935).

Marenbon, J., 'Medieval Latin commentaries and glosses on Aristotelian logical texts before *c*. 1150 AD', in C. Burnett (ed.), *Glosses and commentaries on Aristotelian logical texts: the Syriac, Arabic and medieval Latin traditions* (Warburg Institute Surveys and Texts 23; London, 1993), pp. 77-127.

——, 'Platonismus im zwölften Jahrhundert: alte und neue Zugangsweisen', (trans. A. Snell and O. Summerell) in T. Kobusch and B. Mojsisch (eds), *Platon in der abendländischen Geistesgeschichte: neue Forschungen zum Platonsimus* (Darmstadt, 1997), pp. 101-19.

——, 'Supplement to the working catalogue and supplementary bibliography', in J. Marenbon, *Aristotelian logic, Platonism and the context of early medieval philosophy in the West* (Ashgate, 2000), II.

——, 'Twelfth-century Platonisms: old paths and new directions' (English version of 'Platonismus im zwölften Jahrhundert'), in J. Marenbon, *Aristotelian logic, Platonism and the context of early medieval philosophy in the West* (Ashgate, 2000), XV.

——, 'Platonism – a doxographic approach: the early Middle Ages', in S. Gersh and M. J. F. M. Hoenen (eds), *The Platonic tradition in the Middle Ages: a doxographic approach* (Berlin and New York, 2002), pp. 67-89.

Markovits, M., *Das Tonsystem der abendländischen Musik im frühen Mittelalter* (Publikationen der schweizerischen Musikforschenden Gesellschaft 2/30; Bern, 1977).

Märtl, C., 'Die Bamberger Schulen – ein Bildungszentrum des Salierreichs', in S. Weinfurter (ed.), *Die Salier und das Reich 3. Gesellschaftilicher und ideengeschichtlicher Wandel im Reich der Salier* (Sigmaringen, 1991), pp. 327-45.

Masi, M., 'Manuscripts containing the *De musica* of Boethius', *Manuscripta* 15 (1971), 89-95.

Mathiesen, T. J., 'Greece', *NG* 10, pp. 335-48.

Mayr-Harting, H., *Ottonian book illumination: an historical study*, 2 vols (London, 1991).

McCarthy, T. J. H., 'Literary practice in eleventh-century music theory: the *colores rhetorici* and Aribo's *De musica*', *Medium aevum* 71 (2002), 191-208.

——, 'The identity of Master Henry of Augsburg (d. 1083)', *Revue bénédictine* 114 (2004), 140-57.

——, 'Anonymous I and *Prologus in tonarium*: changing interpretations of music theory in eleventh-century Germany', *Journal of the Society for Musicology in Ireland* 1 (2005), 15-29.

——, 'Aribo's *De musica* and Abbot William of Hirsau', *Revue bénédictine* 116 (2006), 62-82.

——, 'Aribo's *De musica, Commentarius anonymus in Micrologum Guidonis Aretini* and Guido of Arezzo: textual correspondence and scholastic method', *Mediaevistik. Internationale Zeitschrift für interdisziplinäre Mittelalterforschung* 20 (2007), 141-61.

——, 'Biblical scholarship in eleventh-century Michelsberg: the *Glosa in vetus et novum testamentum* of MS Karlsruhe, Badische Landesbibliothek, 504', *Scriptorium* 62 (2008), 3-45.

——, 'The origins of *Commentarius anonymus in Micrologum Guidonis Aretini* in the medieval glossing tradition', *Revue d'Histoire des Textes n. s.* 3 (2008), 217-27.

McGuire, B. P., *Friendship and community: the monastic experience, 350-1250* (Cistercian studies series 95; Kalamazoo: Cistercian Publications, 1989).

McKeon, R., 'Rhetoric in the Middle Ages', *Speculum* 17 (1942), 1-32.

McKitterick, R., 'Knowledge of Plato's *Timaeus* in the ninth century and the implications of Valenciennes, Bibliothèque Municipale MS 293', in H. J. Westra (ed.), *From Athens to Chartres: Neoplatonism and medieval thought. Studies in honour of Edouard Jeauneau* (Leiden, 1992), pp. 85-95.

Mews, C. J., 'Monastic educational culture revisited: the witness of Zwiefalten and the Hirsau reform', in G. Ferzoco and C. Muessig (eds), *Medieval monastic education* (London, 2000), pp. 182-97.

Meyer, C., *Mensura monochordi. La division du monochord (IXe–XVe siècles)* (Publications de la Société Française de Musicologie 2/15; Paris, 1996).

——, 'Aus der Werkstatt des Kompilators. Bermerkungen über zwei musiktheoretische Schriften des 11. Jahrhunderts', in M. Bernhard (ed.), *Quellen und Studien zur Musiktheorie des Mittelalters* 2 (Bayerische Akademie der Wissenschaften. Veröffentlichungen der Musikhistorischen Kommission 13; Munich, 1997), pp. 1-12.

——, 'La tradition du "Micrologus" de Guy d'Arezzo. Une contribution à l'histoire de la réception du texte', *Revue de musicologie* 83 (1997), 5-31.

——, 'Organistrum et synemmenon grave. Observations sur l'échelle acoustique dans l'espace germanique (XIe-XIIIe siècle)', in W. Pass and A. Rausch (eds), *Mittelalterliche Musiktheorie in Zentraleuropa* (Tutzing, 1998), pp. 87-106.

Meyer von Knonau, G., *Jahrbücher des deutschen Reiches unter Heinrich IV. und Heinrich V.*, 7 vols (Leipzig, 1890-1909).

Milde, W., *Mittelalterliche Handschriften der Herzog August Bibliothek* (Kataloge der Herzog August Bibliothek Wolfenbüttel 1; Frankfurt am Main, 1972).

Minio-Paluello, L., 'Note sull' Aristotele latino medievale: XV. Dalle Categoriae decem pseudo-agostiniane (temistiane) al testo vulgato aristotelico boeziano', *Revista di filosofia neoscolastico* 54 (1962), 137-47.

Mögle-Hofacker, F. and P. Morsbach, 'Bischoff Gebhard III. von Regensburg' in P. Morsbach (ed.), *Ratisbona sacra: das Bistum Regensburg im Mittelalter. Ausstellung anlässlich des 1250jährigen Jubiläums der kanonischen Errichtung des Bistums Regensburg durch Bonifatius 739-1989. Diözesanmuseum Obermünster Regensburg, 2. Juni bis 1. Oktober 1989* (Munich, 1989), pp. 113-18.

Möller, H., *The Zwiefalten Antiphoner: Karlsruhe, Badische Landesbibliothek, Aug. perg. LX. Printouts from an index in machine readable form: a CANTUS Index* (Ottawa, 1996).

——, 'Reichenau', *MGG. Sachteil* 8 (1998), cols 135-41.

Morin, D. G., 'Le catalogue des manuscrits de l'Abbaye de Gorze au XIe siècle', *Revue bénédictine* 22 (1905), 1-14.

Morris, C., *The papal monarchy: the Western Church from 1050 to 1250* (Oxford, 1989).

Möser-Mersky, G. (ed.), *Mittelalterliche Bibliothekskataloge Österreichs 3* (Vienna, 1961).

Möser-Mersky, G. and M. Mihaliuk (eds), *Mittelalterliche Bibliothekskataloge Österreichs 4* (Vienna, 1966).

Müller, H., *Die Musik Wilhelms von Hirschau. Wiedererstellung, Übersetzung und Erklärung seines musik-theoretischen Werkes* (Frankfurt am Main, 1883).

247

——, *Hucbalds echte und unechte Schriften über Musik* (Leipzig, 1884).
Mütherich, F., 'Die Regensburger Buchmalerei des 10. und 11. Jahrhunderts', in F. Mütherich and K. Dachs (eds), *Regensburger Buchmalerei: von frühkarolingischer Zeit bis zum Ausgang des Mittelalters*. *Ausstellung der Bayerischen Staatsbibliothek München und der Museen der Stadt Regensburg* (Munich, 1987), pp. 23–38.
Mynors, R. A. B., *Catalogue of the manuscripts of Balliol College Oxford* (Oxford, 1963).
Nightingale, J., *Monasteries and patrons in the Gorze reform: Lotharingia c. 850–1000* (Oxford, 2001).
O'Donnell, J. J., *Cassiodorus* (Berkeley, 1979).
Oesch, H., *Guido von Arezzo. Biographisches und Theoretisches unter besonderer Berücksichtigung der sogenannten odonischen Traktate* (Publikationen der schweizerischen Musikforschenden Gesellschaft 4; Bern, 1954).
——, *Berno und Hermann von Reichenau als Musiktheoretiker. Mit einem Überblick über ihr Leben und die handschriftliche Überlieferung ihrer Werke* (Publikationen der Schweizerischen Musikforschenden Gesellschaft 2/9; Bern, 1961).
Packard, S. R., *Twelfth-century Europe: an interpretative essay* (Amherst, 1973).
Parrish, C., *The notation of medieval music* (New York and London, 1957).
Pensel, F.-J. and I. Stahl, *Verzeichnis der deutschen mittelalterlichen Handschriften in der Universitätsbibliothek Leipzig* (Deutschen Texte des Mittelalters 70/3; Berlin, 1998).
Pesce, D., 'B-flat: transposition or transformation?', *Journal of Musicology* 4 (1985), 330–49.
——, *The affinities and medieval transposition* (Bloomington, 1987).
Pez, B., *Bibliotheca Benedictino-Mauriana, seu De ortu, vitis, et scriptis patrum Benedictinorum e celeberrima congregatione s. Mauri in Francia* (Augsburg, 1716).
——, *Thesaurus anecdotorum novissimus. Seu veterum monumentorum praecipue ecclesiasticorum, ex Germanicis potissimum bibliothecis adornata collectio recentissima. Omnia cum praefationibus, observationibus [&c] publici juris facta, a B. Pezio*, 6 vols (Augsburg, 1721–9).
Pfaff, M., 'Abt Wilhelm von Hirsau', *Erbe und Auftrag* 48 (1972), 83–94.
Phillips, N., 'Classical and late Latin sources for ninth-century treatises on music', in A. Barbera (ed.), *Music theory and its sources: antiquity and the Middle Ages* (Notre Dame, Ind., 1990), pp. 120–6.
Pietzsch, G., *Die Klassifikation der Musik von Boethius bis Ugolino von Orvieto* (Studien zur Geschichte der Musiktheorie im Mittelalter; Halle, 1929).
Power, H. S. and F. Wiering, 'Mode', *NG* 16, pp. 777–90.
Préaux, J., 'Les manuscrits principaux du De nuptiis Philologiae et Mercurii de Martianus Capella', in G. Cambier, C. DeRoux and J. Préaux (eds), *Lettres latines du moyen âge et de la Renaissance* (Collection Latomus 158; Brussels, 1978), pp. 76–128.
Rädlinger-Prömper, C., *Sankt Emmeram in Regensburg. Struktur- und Functionswandel eines bayerischen Klosters im frühen Mittelalter* (Thurn und Taxis Studien 16; Kallmünz, 1987).

Rausch, A., 'Der Tonar des Bern von Reichenau und die süddeutsche Tradition', *Musicologica austriaca* 14/15 (1996), 157–66.

——, 'Bern von Reichenau und sein Einfluß auf die Musiktheorie', in W. Pass and A. Rausch (eds), *Mittelalterliche Musiktheorie in Zentraleuropa* (Tutzing, 1998), pp. 133–50.

——, 'Neue Quellen zur Rezeption des "Prologus in tonarium" des Bern von Reichenau', in W. Pass and A. Rausch (eds), *Beiträge zur Musik, Musiktheorie und Liturgie der Abtei Reichenau* (Musica mediaevalis Europae occidentalis 8; Tutzing 2001), pp. 69–98.

——, 'Der Boethius-Kommentar in der Handschrift St. Florian XI 282', *Studien zur Musikwissenschaft* 49 (2002), 7–83.

——, 'Bern', *MGG. Personenteil* 2, cols 1356–9.

——, 'Frutolf von Michelsberg', *MGG. Personenteil* 7, cols 210–12.

Resnick, I. M., *Divine power and possibility in St Peter Damian's De divina omnipotentia* (Leiden, 1992).

Richards, J. C., 'A new manuscript of Heraclius', *Speculum* 15 (1940), 255–71.

Richter, J., *Katalog der Musiksammlung auf der Universitätsbibliothek in Basel* (Leipzig, 1892).

de Rijk, L. M., 'On the curriculum of the arts of the trivium at St Gall from *c*. 850–*c*. 1000', *Vivarium* 1 (1963), 57–64.

Robinson, I. S., 'The metrical commentary on Genesis of Donizo of Canossa', *Recherches de théologie ancienne et médiévale* 41 (1974), 5–37.

——, 'The sources and method of papal and anti-papal polemic: 1073–1112' (D.Phil. thesis, University of Oxford, 1975).

——, 'The "Colores rhetorici" in the Investiture Contest', *Traditio* 32 (1976), 209–38.

——, *Authority and resistance in the Investiture Contest: the polemical literature of the late eleventh century* (Manchester, 1978).

——, 'Bernold von St. Blasien', *Verfasserlexikon* 1 (1978), cols 795–8.

——, 'Zur Arbeitsweise Bernolds von Konstanz und seines Kreises. Untersuchungen zum Schlettstädter Codex 13', *DA* 34 (1978), 51–122.

——, 'The friendship network of Gregory VII', *History* 63 (1978), 1–22.

——, 'Die Chronik Hermanns von Reichenau und die Reichenauer Kaiserchronik', *DA* 36 (1980), 84–136.

——, 'The Bible in the Investiture Contest: the south-German Gregorian circle', in K. Walsh and D. Wood (eds), *The Bible in the medieval world: essays in memory of Beryl Smalley* (Studies in Church history: Subsidia 4; Oxford, 1985), pp. 61–84.

——, 'The friendship circle of Bernold of Constance and the dissemination of Gregorian ideas in late eleventh-century Germany', in J. Haseldine (ed.), *Friendship in medieval Europe* (Stroud, 1999), pp. 185–98.

——, *Henry IV of Germany, 1056–1106* (Cambridge, 1999).

Robinson, P. R., 'The "Booklet": a self-contained unit in composite manuscripts', *Codicologica* 2 (Leiden, 1978), pp. 46–60.

Rose, V. and F. Schillmann, *Verzeichnis der lateinischen Handschriften der königlichen Bibliothek zu Berlin. Die Handschriften-Verzeichnisse der Königlichen Bibliothek zu Berlin 12–14* (Berlin, 1893–1919).

BIBLIOGRAPHY

Ruf, P., *Mittelalterliche Bibliothekskataloge Deutschlands und der Schweiz* 3/3 (Munich, 1931; repr. 1971).

Rusconi, A., Guido d'*Arezzo, monaco pomposiano*. *Atti dei Convegni di studio, Codigoro (Ferrara), Abbazia di Pomposa, 3 ottobre 1997, Arezzo, Biblioteca Città di Arezzo, 29-30 maggio 1998, a curo di Angelo Rusconi* (Quaderni della Rivista italiana di musicologia 34; Florence, 2000).

Sachs, K.-J., 'Tradition und Innovation bei Guido von Arezzo', in W. Erzgräber (ed.), *Kontinuität und Transformation der Antike im Mittelalter. Veröffentlichung der Kongressakten zum Freiburger Symposion des Mediävistenverbandes* (Sigmaringen, 1989), pp. 233-44.

——, 'Musikalische Elementarlehre im Mittelalter', in M. Bernhard and F. Zaminer (eds), *Rezeption des antiken Fachs in Mittelalter* (Geschichte der Musiktheorie 3; Darmstadt, 1990), pp. 105-62.

Sanderus, A., *Bibliotheca Belgica manuscripta, siue, Elenchus vniuersalis codicum mss. in celebrioribus Belgij cœnobijs, ecclesijs, vrbium, ac priuatorum hominum bibliothecis adhuc latentium*, 2 vols (Lille, 1641, 1644; repr. Brussels, 1972).

Schauwecker, H. E., *Otloh von St. Emmeram. Ein Beitrag zur Bildungs- und Frömmigkeitsgeschichte des 11. Jahrhunderts* (Munich, 1964).

Schedler, M., *Die Philosophie des Macrobius und ihr Einfluss auf die Wissenschaft des christlichen Mittelalters* (Münster, 1916).

Schenkl, H., 'Bibliotheca patrum latinorum Britannica 4', *Sitzungsberichte der kais. Akademie der Wissenschaft, Philosophisch-historische Klasse* 126/4 (1892).

Schieffer, T., 'Cluniazensische oder Gorzische Reformbewegung?', *Archiv für mittelrheinische Kirchengeschichte* 4 (1952), 24-44.

Schlecht, R., 'Musica Enchiriadis von Hucbald, übersetzt und mit kritischen Anmerkungen begleitet', *Monatshefte für Musikgeschichte* 6 (1874), 163-91.

——, 'Cluny et la querelle des investitures', *Revue historique* 225 (1961), 47-72.

Schmale, F.-J., 'Zu den Briefen Berns von Reichenau', *Zeitschrift für Kirchengeschichte* 68 (1957), 69-95.

——, 'Zur Abfassungszeit von Frutolfs Weltchronik', *Bericht der historischen Veröffentlichung Bamberg* 102 (1966), 81-7.

——, 'Die Reichenauer Weltchronistik', in H. Maurer (ed.), *Die Abtei Reichenau. Neue Beiträge zur Geschichte und Kultur des Inselklosters* (Bodensee-Bibliothek 20; Sigmaringen: Thorbecke, 1974), pp. 125-58.

——, *Deutschlands Geschichtsquellen im Mittelalter. Vom Tode Kaiser Heinrichs V. bis zum Ende des Interregnum* (Darmstadt: Wissenschaftliche Buchgesellschaft, 1976).

——, 'Bern', *Lexikon des Mittelalters* 1 (1980), cols 1970-1.

——, 'Frutolf von Michelsberg', *Verfasserlexikon* 2 (1980), cols 993-8.

Schmid, A., ' "Auf glühendem Thron in der Hölle." Gebhard III., Otloh von St. Emmeram und die Dionysiusfälschung', in P. Morsbach (ed.), *Ratisbona sacra: das Bistum Regensburg im Mittelalter. Ausstellung anlässlich des 1250jährigen Jubiläums der kanonischen Errichtung des Bistums Regensburg durch Bonifatius 739-1989. Diözesanmuseum Obermünster Regensburg, 2. Juni bis 1. Oktober 1989* (Munich, 1989), pp. 119-21.

Schmid, H., 'Die musiktheoretischen Handschriften der Benediktiner-Abtei Tegernsee. Ein Beitrag zur Erfassung und Sichtung der musiktheoretischen Hinterlassenschaft des Mittelalters' (Doctoral dissertation, Ludwigs-Maximilian Universität, Munich, 1951).

Schmid, K., 'Adel und Reform in Schwaben', in J. Fleckenstein (ed.), *Investiturstreit und Reichsverfassung* (Vorträge und Forschungen 17; Sigmaringen, 1973), pp. 295–319.

Schmitz, H. G., *Kloster Prüfening im 12. Jahrhundert* (Miscellanea Bavarica Monacensia 49; Munich, 1975).

Schrade, L., 'De musica, ed. J. Smits van Waesberghe', *Journal of the American Musicological Society* 9 (1956), 215.

Schreiner, K. (ed.), *Hirsau. St. Peter und Paul 1091–1991*, 2 vols (Forschungen und Berichte der Archäologie des Mittelalters in Baden-Württemberg 10; Stuttgart, 1991).

Schroeder, J., *Bibliothek und Schule der Abtei Echternach um die Jahrtausendwende* (Luxemburg, 1977).

Schuba, L., *Kataloge der Universitätsbibliothek Heidelberg 2. Die Quadriviums-Handschriften der Codices Palatini Latini in der Vatikanischen Bibliothek* (Wiesbaden, 1992).

Schwarmaier, H., 'Reichenauer Gedenkbucheinträge aus der Anfangszeit der Regierung König Konrad II.', *Zeitschrift für Württembergische Landesgeschichte* 22 (1963), 19–28.

Semmler, J., *Die Klosterreform von Siegburg. Ihre Ausbreitung und ihr Reformprogramm im 11. und 12. Jahrhundert* (Veröffentlichungen des Instituts für geschichtliche Landeskunde der Rheinlande an der Universität Bonn 53; Bonn, 1959).

Smalley, B., *The study of the Bible in the Middle Ages*, 2nd edn (Oxford, 1952).

Smits van Waesberghe, J., *Muziekgeschiedenis der Middeleeuwen 1. De Luiksche muziekschool als centrum van het muziektheoretische onderricht in de middeleeuen* (Nederlandsche muziekhistorische en muziekpaedagogische studiën, Series A; Tilburg, 1936).

——, *School en muziek in de middeleeuwen. De muziekdidatiek de vroege middeleeuwen* (Amsterdam, 1949).

——, 'Some music treatises and their interrelation: a school of Liége c. 1050–1200?', *Musica disciplina* 3 (1949), 25–31, 95–118.

——, *De musico-paedagogico et theoretico Guidone Aretino eiusque vita et moribus* (Florence, 1953).

——, *Musikerziehung. Lehre und Theorie der Musik im Mittelalter* (Musikgeschichte in Bildern 3/3; Leipzig, 1969).

——, *Bernonis Augiensis Abbatis de arte musica disputationes traditae. Pars B: Quae ratio est inter tria opera de arte musica Bernonis Augiensis* (Divitiae musicae artis A/6b; Buren, 1979).

Southern, R. W., *Medieval humanism and other studies* (Oxford, 1970).

——, *Scholastic humanism and the unification of Europe*, 2 vols (Oxford, 1995, 2001).

Sowa, H., *Ein anonymer glossierter Mensuraltraktat 1279* (Kassel, 1930).

251

——, 'Zur Handschrift Clm 9921', *Acta musicologica* 5 (1933), 60–5, 107–20.
Stäblein, B., 'Frutolf von Michelsberg als Musiker', *Fränkische Blätter für Geschichtsforschung und Heimatspflege* 5 (1953), 57–60.
Stammler, W. and K. Langosch (eds), *Die deutsche Literatur des Mittelalters: Verfasserlexikon*, 5 vols (Berlin, 1933–55).
Steindorff, E., *Jahrbücher des deutschen Reichs unter Heinrich III.*, 2 vols (Leipzig, 1874, 1881).
Steinmeyer, E. and E. Sievers, *Die althochdeutschen Glossen*, 5 vols (Berlin, 1879–1922).
Switalsky, B. W., *Des Chalcidius Kommentar zu Platos Timaeus* (Beiträge zur Geschichte der Philosophie und Theologie des Mittelalters 3; Münster, 1902).
Tabulae codicum manu scriptorum praetor Graecos et orientales in biblioteca palatine Vindobonensi asservatorum, 10 vols (Vienna, 1864–99).
Teeuwen, M., *Harmony and the music of the spheres: the ars musica in ninth-century commentaries on Martianus Capella* (Leiden, 2002).
Tellenbach, G., *Libertas. Kirche und Weltordnung im Zeitalter des Investiturstreites* (Stuttgart, 1936); trans. R. F. Bennett, *Church, state and Christian society at the time of the Investiture Contest* (Oxford, 1940; repr. Toronto, 1991).
——, 'Zum Wesen der Cluniacenser', *Saeculum* 9 (1958), 370–9.
——, 'Gregorianische Reform: Kritische Besinnungen', in K. Schmid (ed.), *Reich und Kirche vor dem Investiturstreit. Vorträge beim wissenschaftlichen Kolloquium aus Anlass des achtzigsten Geburtstags von Gerd Tellenbach* (Sigmaringen, 1985), pp. 99–113.
——, *The church in western Europe from the tenth to the early twelfth century*, trans. T. Reuter (Cambridge, 1993; repr. 1996).
Thomson, R., 'The place of Germany in the twelfth-century Renaissance', in A. I. Beach (ed.), *Manuscripts and monastic culture: reform and renewal in twelfth-century Germany* (Medieval Church Studies 13; Turnhout, 2007), pp. 19–42.
Thorndike, L., *A history of magic and experimental science*, 8 vols (Publications [History of Science Society], new series 4; New York and London, 1923–58).
Thurn, H., *Bestand bis zur Säkularisierung. Erwerbungen und Zugänge bis 1803* (Die Handschriften der Universitätsbibliothek Würzburg 5; Wiesbaden, 1994).
Toneatto, L., *Codices artis mensoriae. I manoscritto degli antichi opusculi Latini d'agrimensura (v–xix sec.)*, 3 vols (Spoleto, 1994–5).
Trithemius, J., *Chronicon insigne Monasterii Hirsaugiensis* (Basel, 1559).
——, *Annales Hirsaugienses* (St Gallen, 1690).
de Vergille, B., 'Fragment d'un traité de la prière, dédié par Bernon de Reichenau à Henri III, roi de Germanie', *Revue du moyen âge latin* 2 (1946), 261–8.
——, *Dictionnaire d'histoire et de géographie ecclésiastique* 20 (Paris, 1984), pp. 883–7.
Vivell, C., 'Vom uneditierten Tonarius des Mönches Frutolf', *Sammelbände der Internationalen Musik-Gesellschaft* 14 (1912–13), 463–84.
——, 'Die *Quaestiones in musica*, ihre handschriftliche Quelle und ihr mutmaßlicher Verfasser', *Gregoriusblatt* 38 (1913), 51–76.
——, 'Ein anonymer Kommentar zum *Mikrologus* des Guido d'Arezzo', *SMGBZ* 35 (1914), 56–80.
——, 'Nachtrag zu den *Quaestiones in musica*', *Gregoriusblatt* 39 (1914), 51–3.

Vogel, J., 'Rudolf von Rheinfelden, die Fürstenopposition gegen Heinrich IV. im Jahr 1072 und die Reform des Klosters St. Blasien', *Zeitschrift für die Geschichte des Oberrheins* 132 (1984), 1–30.

van der Vyver, A., 'Les premières traductions latines (Xe–XIe siècles) de traités arabes sur l'astrolabe', in *Premier Congrès International de Géographie Historique le haut Patronage de S. M. le Roi des Belges* 2 (Brussels, 1931), pp. 266–90.

Wagner, A., *Gorze au XIe siècle. Contribution à l'histoire du monachisme bénédictine dans l'Empire* (n.p., 1996).

Wappler, E. W., 'Bemerkungen zur Rhythmomachie', *Zeitschrift für Mathematik und Physik* 37 (1892), 1–17.

Warburton, J., 'Questions of attribution and chronology in three medieval texts on species theory', *Music theory spectrum* 22 (2000), 225–35.

Wattenbach, W. and R. Holtzmann, *Deutschlands Geschichtsquellen im Mittelalter. Die Zeit der Sachsen und Salier*, ed. F.-J. Schmale, 3 vols (Cologne and Graz, 1967–71).

Weisheipl, J. A., 'Classification of the sciences in medieval thought', *Medieval Studies* 27 (1965), 54–90.

Werner, K. F., 'Zur Überlieferung der Briefe Gerberts von Aurillac', *DA* 17 (1961), 91–144.

White, A., 'Boethius in the medieval quadrivium', in M. Gibson (ed.), *Boethius: his life, thought and influence* (Oxford, 1981), pp. 162–205.

——, 'Glosses composed before the twelfth century in manuscripts of Macrobius' *Commentary* on Cicero's *Somnium Scipionis*' (D.Phil. thesis, University of Oxford, 1981).

Wiesenbach, J., 'Wilhelm von Hirsau, Astrolab und Astronomie im 11. Jahrhundert', in K. Schreiner (ed.), *Hirsau. St. Peter und Paul 1091–1991* (Stuttgart, 1991), pp. 109–54.

Wolf, J., *Handbuch der Notationskunde 1. Tonschriften des Alterums und des Mittelalters Choral- und Mensuralnotation* (Leipzig, 1913).

Wollasch, H.-J., 'Muri und St. Blasien. Perspektiven schwäbischen Mönchtums in der Reform', *DA* 17 (1961), 420–46.

——, *Die Anfänge des Klosters St. Georgen im Schwarzwald. Zur Ausbildung der geschichtlichen Eigenart eines Klosters innerhalb der Hirsauer Reform* (Forschungen zur oberrheinische Landesgeschichte 14; Freiburg, 1964).

——, 'Das Martyrolog-Necrolog von St. Emmeram als Zeugnis für die Geschichte des Mönchtums im Reich', *MGH Libri memoriales N. S.* 3 (Hanover, 1986), pp. 11–27.

Worstbrock, F.-J., 'Die Anfänge der mittelalterlichen Ars dictandi', *Frühmittelalterliche Studien* 23 (1989), 7–13.

Worstbrock, F.-J., M. Klaes and J. Lütten, *Repertorium der Artes dictandi des Mittelalters* (Münstersche Mittelalter-Schriften 66; Munich, 1992).

Yeldham, F. A., 'Fraction tables of Hermannus Contractus', *Speculum* 3 (1928), 241–5.

INDEX

Note: 'n.' after a page number indicates the number of a note on that page.

Adalbert II, count of Calw 12, 31, 217
Admont, monastery 13, 38, 152, 198
Affligem, monastery 47, 49
Agnes of Poitou, empress 12
Alberic, monk of Monte Cassino 117
Alexander II, pope 15
Alia musica 59, 61, 64, 121, 180, 209
Altmann, bishop of Passau 32
Anno, archbishop of Cologne 12
Anonymous I 43, 44, 52, 77, 80, 93, 99, 100–1, 102, 103, 108, 135–8, 140, 187 n. 55, 203
Anselm II, bishop of Lucca 177, 178
Anselm, archbishop of Canterbury 48, 223
Anselm of Besate 113
Aribo, archbishop of Mainz 19
Aribo, *scholasticus* of Freising 2, 37–40, 43, 49, 47, 50–2, 55, 56, 58, 63, 64, 71, 91–3, 124, 127, 130–2, 218, 219
  De musica, 38–40
    dating 39
    manuscript circulation 39, 149, 150, 190–4, 196, 198, 205–7, 210, 212, 215
    sententiae 40, 53, 89, 90
  dialectic 121, 126–7, 130, 138–45, 222
  Frutolf of Michelsberg and 94, 103–6, 108
  Guido of Arezzo and 87–90, 93, 222, 226
  Herman of Reichenau and 67–8
  Hirsau and 38, 39
  Platonism 147, 157, 162–8, 170, 224

William of Hirsau and 104, 105, 163, 166, 219
Arnold, abbot of Bonneval 171
Arnold, monk of St Emmeram 31
ars dictandi 181 *see also colores rhetorici*; *dictamen*; rhetoric
Augsburg 24, 25, 45–7, 132, 222 *see also* Sts Ulrich and Afra
Augustine of Hippo 55, 110, 111, 148, 170, 177, 178
Azecho, bishop of Worms 16, 119, 223

Benediktbeuren, monastery 13, 152, 162
Bern, abbot of Reichenau 2, 3, 8, 18–23, 24, 26, 28, 29, 36, 39, 40, 42, 43, 44, 45, 46, 51, 53, 82, 87, 90, 93, 94, 99, 100–3, 108, 110, 121, 131, 135, 150, 209, 214, 217, 218, 220, 221, 225
  arrangement of the species 65, 221
  Boethius and 59–60, 62, 74, 152, 159, 169
  Carolingian theory and 60–2
  early life 18–19
  Epistola de tonis 22–3, 29
  Frutolf of Michelsberg and 72, 80, 94–100, 219
  the Gorze reform and 19
  Guido of Arezzo and 8
  musical reputation 21
  Platonism 152–60, 162, 164, 169, 174, 224
  Prologus in tonarium 10, 21, 22, 47, 49, 52
  influence 62–72

255

INDEX

Bern, abbot of Reichenau (*cont.*)
  interpolations 22, 72–80, 99, 187, 219
  manuscript tradition 22, 30, 134, 149, 195, 203–5, 220, 226
  Tonarius 22, 43, 97–9, 108, 134, 192, 193, 198, 203–5, 207, 210, 215
  works 19–20
Bernard, abbot of St Victor in Marseilles 13
Bernard, canon of Constance, *scholasticus* of Hildesheim 15
Bernold, canon of Constance, monk of St Blasien, monk of Schaffhausen 15, 31–2, 33, 39, 108, 116, 176–9, 196, 199, 219
Berthold, monk of Reichenau 24, 32
  biography of Herman of Reichenau 24–6, 27
  continuation of Herman's *Chronicle* 24, 26
Blaubeuren, monastery 13, 173
Boethius 5, 8, 44, 46, 56, 116, 117, 136, 148, 173, 181, 195, 206, 211, 219, 220, 225
  Aribo and 58, 92
  Bern of Reichenau and 59, 62, 74
  Carolingian theorists and 59–60
  Consolation of Philosophy 148, 165 n. 96, 170, 223, 224
  De institutione arithmetica 56–7, 148, 152, 159, 169, 224
  De institutione musica 47, 56, 57–8, 133, 134, 137, 148, 152, 180, 198, 209, 210, 224
  Frutolf of Michelsberg and 43, 95
  Henry of Augsburg and 47
  Herman of Reichenau and 58, 155
  John and 90, 91
  logical works 109, 110, 111, 112, 118, 119, 120, 179 n. 17, 180, 182, 222
    influence on music 122, 128–32, 138, 142, 144, 145
  William of Hirsau and 85, 164
Burchard, bishop of Worms, 176, 177, 214

Burchard, monk of Reichenau, abbot of St Emmeram 23, 29, 30, 218
Burchard, prior of Michelsberg 41, 42

Calcidius 56, 148–50, 153, 161, 168, 173, 210, 224
Cicero 148, 181
  De amicitia 181
  De inventione 46, 198
  Topica 110, 111, 112, 142, 182
Cita et vera divisio monochordi see pseudo-Bernelinus
Cluny, monastery 11, 12, 32, 36
  Cluniac reform 11–13, 19, 32, 35
colores rhetorici 23, 40 n. 158, 89 *see also ars dictandi*; *dictamen*; rhetoric
Commentarius anonymus in Micrologum Guidonis Aretini 53, 90, 93, 201, 225, 226
Commentarius in Somnium Scipionis see Macrobius
Conrad II, emperor 26
Conrad, cardinal bishop of Palestrina 35
Conrad, monk of Hirsau 45

De nuptiis Philologiae et Mercurii see Martianus Capella
De scriptoribus ecclesiasticis, authorship 21 *see also* Wolfger, monk of Prüfening
Dialogus de musica see pseudo-Odo of Cluny
dialectic 4, 5, 8, 9, 10, 40, 47, 109, 146, 181, 182, 222, 223
  attitudes towards 113–20
  dialectical texts 109–13
  influence on music theory 120–45
dictamen 51, 82 *see also ars dictandi*; *colores rhetorici*; rhetoric
Donizo of Canossa, 38

Ellenhard, bishop of Freising 37, 38, 39, 50, 168
Engelbert, abbot of Admont 38
Erbo, abbot of Prüfening 34

256

INDEX

Festal Office *see* Historia
Franco of Liège 51
Frederick, abbot of Hirsau 12, 31
Frutolf, monk and prior of Michelsberg
   2, 29, 40–3, 47, 52, 88, 90, 93,
   124, 184, 196, 205, 208, 212, 215,
   218, 219, 220, 222, 226
   Anonymous I and 99–101
   Aribo and 94, 103–6
   autograph copy of *Prologus in
      tonarium* 42, 72, 219
   Bern of Reichenau and 72, 80, 94,
      95–6, 97–9, 219
   Boethius and 95–9
   Breviarium de musica 10, 58, 94–108,
      213
   dating 94
   manuscript transmission 42 n. 169,
      43, 94, 186, 208
   mnemonic verses 195, 205, 208, 211,
      213
   Chronicle 41, 42
   dialectic and 121
   Guido of Arezzo and 87, 96
   Herman of Reichenau and 94–6,
      101–3, 107–8
   Tonarius 43, 94, 97–9, 208, 210
   William of Hirsau and 94, 101–3, 219
   works 41–3
Fruttuaria, monastery 12
Fulgentius 48, 49, 50

gamut 5, 28, 62, 66, 74, 84, 91, 94, 95,
   104, 105, 121, 122, 128, 130–2, 138,
   145, 155, 160, 171, 180, 194, 195,
   205, 211, 214, 220, 226
Gebhard, archbishop of Salzburg 15
Gebhard, bishop of Regensburg 27, 28
Gorze, monastery 11–12, 13, 15, 19, 23, 28,
   113
   Gorze reform 7, 8, 11–14, 16, 19, 23, 28,
      30, 32, 40, 53, 218, 219
grammar 4, 40, 179, 181
Grecam litteram ideo, anonymous
   treatise 53

Greek note names 44, 65, 186, 187, 188 n.
   55, 194, 204–5, 225
Gregory VII, pope 8, 13, 15, 16, 32, 178,
   179, 196
Guido of Arezzo 2 n. 2, 3, 6–7, 8, 28, 40,
   42, 43, 45, 46, 51, 57, 80, 96, 102,
   131, 139, 149, 150, 164, 183, 198,
   200–3, 209, 214, 220, 221, 222,
   225, 226
   Epistola ad Michahelem 8, 57 n. 11, 80,
      81, 82, 83, 91, 96, 183, 201–3
   German attitudes towards 28, 40,
      80–93, 222, 226
   Micrologus 8, 53, 80, 83–5, 87–92,
      107 n. 192, 183, 200, 201–3, 225,
      226
   Prologus in antiphonarium 8, 80, 81,
      82, 90, 183, 201–3
   Regule rithmice 8, 80, 81, 85, 86, 96,
      183, 200–3, 207
Guidonian hand 195, 214
Gumpold, abbot of Michelsberg 40

Haimo, monk and prior of Hirsau 32, 116
Hartwic of St Emmeram 179–81, 197, 209
Henry II, emperor 18, 19, 23, 218
Henry III, emperor 20, 26, 27
Henry IV, emperor 34, 37, 46, 178
Henry, canon of Augsburg and patriarch
   of Aquileia 45
Henry, monk of Reichenau 16
Henry, *scholasticus* of Augsburg 2, 39,
   43, 45–7, 92, 208, 217–18, 219,
   222
   dialectic and 132–5, 222
   mnemonic verses 47, 184, 208, 211, 226
   Musica, manuscript tradition 46, 208
   works 46–7
Herman, monk of Reichenau 2, 3, 6, 8,
   16, 19, 23–30, 31, 32, 33, 36, 39,
   40, 42–7, 53, 58, 62, 87, 93–6,
   102, 103, 108, 121–4, 134, 138–41,
   150, 163–5, 195, 206, 209, 217,
   219, 220, 221
   Bern of Reichenau and 62–72, 74, 99

257

INDEX

Herman, monk of Reichenau (*cont.*)
   Chronicle 19, 24, 26
   criticism of *Musica enchiriadis* 61
   dialectic and 121
   early life 23–4
   Frutolf of Michelsberg and 96
   Guido of Arezzo and 28, 82–5, 221
   Historia sancti Wolfgangi 24, 27–8, 30, 218
   intervals 96
   mnemonic verses 29, 107–8, 184–5, 185 n. 43, 205, 208, 211, 226
   modal theory 69–72, 80, 82–5, 125, 221
   monochord 101, 162
   Musica 44
      dating 28–9
      manuscript tradition 29–30, 192, 205, 210, 215, 218, 226
      notation system 45, 49, 52
      Platonism 155–7, 160, 169 n. 114, 170, 224
      species theory 65–9, 76, 80, 126, 221, 223
   works 25–30
Hildesheim letter collection 16, 173
Hirsau, monastery 12, 13, 15, 29, 30, 31, 32, 34–6, 38, 39, 45, 116, 138, 162, 173, 196, 217, 218
   Hirsau reform 7, 12–15, 16, 30, 32, 34, 38, 39, 53, 173, 219
Hirsau Anonymous 15
Historia, Festal Office 20, 25, 27, 28, 30
Honorius Augustodunensis 4, 5, 8, 45, 146, 161, 170, 223
Hucbald, monk of St Amand 22, 51, 59, 60, 61, 95, 110, 131, 152, 194, 209, 225
Hugh, bishop of Die, archbishop of Lyons, papal legate 15
Hugh of St Victor 153, 161
Hyginus 46, 198

Immo, abbot of Gorze, abbot of Prüm, abbot of Reichenau 19

intensio 44, 78, 143, 144
intervals 4, 44, 50, 58, 59, 60, 84, 94–6, 98, 101, 103, 107, 123, 125, 126, 130, 134, 151, 153, 159, 168, 174, 184, 185, 186, 189, 192, 194, 195, 206, 214, 220, 224, 226

James of Liège 17, 51
Johannes, Cottonis, John Cotton *see* John
John 2, 10, 46–50, 56, 58, 93, 133
   Bern of Reichenau and 220
   De musica, *Tonarius*, manuscript tradition 49, 50, 196 n. 82, 204, 208, 226
   Guido of Arezzo and 3, 90–3
   identity 47–50
   Platonism 147
John of Affligem *see* John

Leo IX, pope 27
'Liège school of music theory' 17, 37, 44, 49
litterae significativae 49, 88
logic *see* dialectic
Lorsch, monastery 11

Macrobius, *Commentarius in Somnium Scipionis* 44, 56, 133, 148, 150–1, 154–61, 169, 171, 173, 174, 179, 180, 186, 210, 224, 225
Manegold, prior of Lautenbach 15, 34, 35, 57, 108, 161
   views on dialectic 113–16, 171, 173
manuscripts
   Admont, Staftsbibliothek, Cod. 390 152 n. 28
   Austin, Tx., Harry Ransom Humanities Research Center, MS 29 149
   Bamberg, Staatsbibliothek, Msc. Class. 7 152
      Msc. Class. 9 152
      Msc. Class. 18 149 n. 12
      Msc. Lit. 10 47, 47 n. 196

INDEX

Msc. Lit. 134 42
Msc. Patr. 30 179
Basel, Universitätsbibliothek, F. IX. 36 196
Berlin, Staatsbibliothek zu Berlin, Preußischer Kulturbesitz, Lat. oct. 8 149 n. 13
Lat. qu. 106 (**B1/B2**) 197, 198–9, 205, 206, 208, 211, 213
Lat. qu. 202 149 n. 13
Theol. qu. 74 (Cat. 718), 185 n. 43
Bern, Universitätsbibliothek, 681 149 n. 13
Bologna, Civico Museo Bibliografia Musicale, A43 175
Brussels, Bibliothèque Royale, 5266 58 n. 16
1078/95 209
10162/66 50
Cambridge, Corpus Christi College, 111, 24
Cambridge, Trinity College, R. 15.22 (944) 196
Cologne, Dombibliothek, 192 149 n. 12
Copenhagen, Det Kongelige Bibliothek, S. 73 8° 50
Darmstadt, Universitäts- und Hochschulbibliothek, 1988 (**D1/D2**) 44, 50–1, 51 n. 216, 163, 166, 197, 199, 200, 203, 204, 207, 208, 210
3314/3315 189 n. 58
Einsiedeln, Stiftsbibliothek, Cod. 79 181
Cod. 266 152 n. 28
Cod. 611 20 n. 43
Erfurt, Wissenschaftliche Allgemeinbibliothek, Ampl. Oct. 5 116
Heidelberg, Universitätsbibliothek, Cod. IX 20 n. 39
Jena, Universitätsbibliothek, Bos. q. 19 42

Karlsruhe, Badische Landesbibliothek, 504 10, 30 n. 98, 41, 42, 72, 74, 75–80, 196
Kassel, Landesbibliothek und Murhardsche Bibliothek der Stadt Kassel, 4° Mss Math. 1 (**Ka**) 9, 29, 29 n. 93, 151, 151 n. 23, 183–96, 198, 199, 200, 204, 205, 206, 207, 208, 210, 211, 225, 226
Leiden, Bibliotheek der Rijksuniversiteit, BPL 194 (**L**) 197, 198, 199, 200, 202, 203, 205, 207, 210
Leipzig, Universitätsbibliothek, Cod. 1492 52, 53
Cod. 1493 (**Lz**) 109 n. 1, 134, 134 n. 108, 135, 197, 198, 199, 203, 210, 211, 212
London, British Library, Add. 19968 149 n.11
Harl. 2610 149 n.11
Harl. 2652 149 n.11
Melk, Stiftsbibliothek, Cod. 950 72
Metz, Bibliothèque municipale, Cod. 351 78 n. 79
Munich, Bayerische Staatsbibliothek, Clm 514 149 n. 13
Clm 4559 152 n. 28
Clm 4622 162, 162 n. 87, 162 n. 88
Clm 6365 149 n. 12
Clm 9921 (**M1**) 33 n. 117, 109 n. 1, 197, 200, 202, 204, 205, 206, 208, 210
Clm 12205 176
Clm 14271 152 n. 28
Clm 14272 179, 180–1, 197, 209
Clm 14401 152 n. 28
Clm 14436 179–80
Clm 14458 117
Clm 14506 46
Clm 14516 182
Clm 14523 (**M2**) 197, 198, 200, 201–2
Clm 14613 30 n. 99

259

INDEX

manuscripts (cont.)
Clm 14628 175
Clm 14663 (**M3**) 72, 149, 149 n. 13, 197, 200, 200 n. 96, 201, 203, 204, 207, 210, 211, 225
Clm 14689 30 n. 97, 30 n. 99, 33, 149
Clm 14836 212 n. 140
Clm 14965a (**M4**) 150, 197, 200, 203, 204, 205, 206, 207, 210, 211, 212, 214
Clm 14965b (**M5**) 10, 43, 58 n. 16, 94, 95 n. 161, 97–8, 100–3, 104, 104 n. 187, 105–6, 107 n. 193, 151, 151 n. 23, 197, 205, 208, 210, 213
Clm 18541a 182
Clm 18580 46
Clm 18914 (**M6**) 162 n. 88, 197, 200, 202, 205, 206, 208, 209
Clm 18937 (**M7**) 197, 203, 208, 210, 212
Clm 19126 178
Clm 19413 152 n. 28
Clm 19421 (**M8**) 197, 199, 199 n. 98, 200, 203, 205, 208, 210, 214
Clm 19473 181
Oxford, Balliol College, 173A 196
Oxford, Bodleian Library, Laud Lat. 49 182
Laud Lat. 67 117
Oxford, Trinity College, D. 47 57
Paris, Bibliothèque Nationale, Résidu St Germain 215 34 n. 120
Rochester, Eastman School of Music, ML 92/1100 (**R1**) 29, 72, 197, 198, 204, 205, 206
ML 92/1200 (**R2**) 38 n. 144 39 n. 155, 103 n. 186, 105, 197, 198, 200, 203, 204, 205, 207, 208, 210
Rome, Biblioteca Apostolica Vaticana, Pal. lat. 1356 212 n. 140
Reg. lat. 1281 116
St Gallen, Stiftsbibliothek, Cod. 64 27 n. 83
Cod. 381 152 n. 28

Cod. 872 152 n. 28
Cod. 898 22
Salzburg, Stiftsbibliothek St. Peter, a. V. 2 39 n. 155, 103 n. 186
Sélestat, Bibliothèque Municipale, 13 15, 196
Stuttgart, Württembergische Landesbibliothek, HB. VI. 107 177, 199
Trier, Stadtbibliothek, 1897/18 72
Vienna, Österreichische Nationalbibliothek, Cod. 51 (**V1**) 29, 46, 46 n. 192, 163, 194, 197, 198, 199, 200, 203, 204, 205, 208, 209, 210, 210 n. 132, 225
Cod. 176 149 n. 13
Cod. 278 149 n. 13
Cod. 443 149 n.12
Cod. 1050 179
Cod. 2502 (**V2**) 72, 197, 200, 202, 205, 208, 214
Cod. 2376 149 n. 13
Cod. 12600 152 n. 28
Washington, Library of Congress, ML 171 J56 48 n. 203
Wolfenbüttel, Herzog-August Bibliothek, Gud. lat. 334 8º (**W**) 171, 172, 197, 200, 205, 207, 207 n. 119, 210, 211, 212, 213
Gud. lat. 454 176
Worcław, Biblioteka Uniwersytecka, R. 54 42
Würzburg, Universitätsbibliothek, M. p. th. q. 62 179
Martianus Capella, *De nuptiis Philologiae et Mercurii* 4, 44, 56, 110, 111, 148, 151–2, 161, 169, 171, 173, 224
Mathilda, countess of Tuscany 38
measurement texts 3, 46, 95, 104, 162, 181, 185–7, 200, 206–9, 211–12, 214, 215, 226
bells 104, 186, 209
monochord 58, 134, 162, 162 n. 88, 180, 181, 195, 203, 203 n. 100, 206

organ pipe 95 n. 161, 103, 104, 105–6,
    134, 151, 185–6, 206, 207, 209
Meinzo, *scholasticus* of Constance 16, 219
Metz 34, 35, 36, 49
Michelsberg, monastery 15, 30, 40, 42, 43
    n. 174, 112, 113, 218
    library catalogue 41–2, 112, 149
    links with St Emmeram 30, 40, 219
    modes 131, 140, 180, 181, 184, 189, 194,
        195, 204, 209, 210, 211, 212, 213,
        226
    Aribo 90, 91, 141–5, 163, 190–2, 207
    Bern of Reichenau 61, 64, 65, 74, 80,
        153, 155, 157, 158, 159, 195, 204
    Frutolf of Michelsberg 95, 99, 107,
        195, 208
    Guido of Arezzo 90, 131, 202
    Henry of Augsburg 47, 184
    Herman of Reichenau 47, 58, 65,
        68–9, 71, 72, 80, 82–5, 107, 125–6,
        184, 192, 205, 221, 223
    in south-German theory 43, 45, 60,
        94, 125–6, 130, 140, 185, 187, 214,
        215, 216, 226
    interpolations in *Prologus in
        tonarium* 74, 75–8
    nomenclature 6, 59, 71
    Theoger of Metz 71, 87, 187–90, 194,
        207
    William of Hirsau 71, 87, 161
    Wolf Anonymous 44
monochord 3 n. 13, 21, 32, 40, 43, 46, 50,
    51, 58, 62–4, 74, 88, 91, 94, 95,
    101, 104, 122, 123, 124, 134, 139,
    140, 160, 161, 162, 162 n. 88,
    163–7, 170, 171, 172, 180, 181, 186,
    193, 195, 196 n. 82, 203, 206, 211,
    212, 214, 224, 226
Muri, monastery 22, 110
Musica enchiriadis 22, 61, 83, 139, 180,
    204, 209

Niederaltaich, monastery 11
Notker, monk of St Gallen 27, 49, 93, 134,
    212

Odilo, abbot of Cluny 19
Odo, abbot of Cluny 61 *see also* pseudo-
    Odo of Cluny
Onulf, *scholasticus* of Speyer, *Colores
    rhetorici* 4, 23
Otloh, monk of St Emmeram 16, 31, 33,
    40, 113, 115, 139, 147, 169, 173,
    201
Otto, bishop of Freising 26
Ottobeuren, monastery 13, 200

Peter Damian 22–3, 56, 113, 114, 116, 171
Petershausen, monastery 13
Pfäfers, monastery 13, 110
Pilgrim, archbishop of Cologne 21, 62,
    152
Plato 9, 56, 114, 119, 138, 147, 151, 152, 171,
    173, 174
    generation metaphors 158–71
    number theory 152–8, 224, 225
    Timaeus 148–50, 210, 223
    world soul 150, 171, 173
Porphyry, *Isagoge* 109, 110–11, 112, 117,
    120, 148, 179 n. 17, 182, 222
    accidents 131
    genus 123, 128, 132, 134, 138
    property 142–3, 145
    species 124, 132, 138
Prologus in tonarium see Bern, abbot of
    Reichenau
property 5, 59, 70, 142–6
Prüfening, monastery 13, 21, 111, 152
pseudo-Bernelinus, *Cita et vera divisio
    monochordi* 22, 61, 64, 121
pseudo-Berthold of Reichenau,
    'Swabian annalist' 15
pseudo-Cicero, *Rhetorica ad Herennium*
    46, 89, 180, 198
pseudo-Odo of Cluny, *Dialogus de
    musica* 2 n. 2, 46, 51, 61, 85, 85 n.
    112, 110, 139, 149, 150, 198, 203,
    214
Ptolemy 44, 58, 77, 136, 137
Pythagoras 39, 44, 86, 136, 163, 171, 210
Pythagoreans 59, 137, 155

INDEX

quadrivium 4, 30, 31, 32, 33, 36, 42, 115, 134, 150, 180, 198
Quaestiones in musica 2, 10, 29, 50–2, 61, 72, 92, 93, 108, 145, 157–8, 205, 208, 220
   authorship and dating 51–2

Ramwold, abbot of St Emmeram 12, 28, 111, 218
Regensburg letter collection 118–19, 120, 121, 173
Regino, monk of Prüm 22, 60, 83, 176, 177, 194, 209, 225
Reginward, abbot of St Emmeram 27–8
Reichenau, monastery 11, 18, 22, 23, 29, 43, 49, 148, 153, 218
   links with St Emmeram 27–30, 53, 218
remissio 44, 78, 143, 144, 145
rhetoric 4, 23, 40, 50, 77, 90, 112, 114, 134, 151, 169, 180, 181 n. 28, 182
   rhetoric of reform 171
   see also ars dictandi; colores rheotrici; dictamen
Rhetorica ad Herennium see pseudo-Cicero
Rudolf of Rheinfelden, duke of Swabia 12
Rudolf, abbot of St Trond 51, 52, 82
Ruodmann, abbot of Reichenau 19
Ruotpert, abbot of Michelsberg 40

St Blasien, monastery 12, 15, 22, 175, 176, 219
St Emmeram, monastery 11, 12, 15, 16, 23, 27–30, 31, 32, 40, 46, 53, 57, 72, 105, 117, 149, 152, 162, 175, 179, 182, 200, 219
   library 31, 111
   links with Michelsberg 30, 40, 219
   links with Reichenau 27–30, 218
St Gallen, monastery 18, 24, 25, 49–50, 93, 152
St Georgen, monastery 13, 22, 34, 36, 206
St James in Liège, monastery 17, 44, 51, 52, 198, 199

St Laurence in Liège, monastery 17
St Magnus, monastery 45
St Maximin in Trier, monastery 11, 12, 28, 49, 218
St Paul in Lavanttal, monastery 13
St Trond, monastery 51–2, 82
Sts Ulrich and Afra in Augsburg, monastery 13, 149 n. 13, 171, 197, 206, 210
Schaffhausen, monastery 13, 15, 176
Scolica enchiriadis 51, 61, 180, 209
seven liberal arts 4, 35, 55
Siegburg, monastery 12
Siegfried, abbot of Schaffhausen 32
Siegfried, abbot of Tegernsee 115
Siegfried, bishop of Augsburg 46
Sigebert of Gembloux, *Liber de viris illustribus* 21, 81, 82, 225
species of interval 45, 50, 60, 64, 72, 84, 87, 95, 126–30, 135, 136, 137, 155, 184, 204, 214, 220, 223, 226
diapason 5, 43, 44, 65, 66, 94, 121, 125, 127, 129, 158, 193
diapente 4–5, 43, 44, 58, 65, 66, 94, 121, 127–8, 131, 138, 158, 192, 193, 195
diatessaron 5, 43, 44, 56, 65, 66, 94, 121, 126–7, 128, 130, 131, 138, 142, 158, 160, 192, 193, 195, 221
the modes and 59, 65–6, 69–70, 71, 74–80, 99, 103, 125, 192, 195, 221
'Swabian annalist' *see* pseudo-Bernold of Reichenau

Tegernsee, monastery 16, 22, 46, 57, 112, 149, 152, 152 n. 28, 162 n. 88, 176, 178, 181, 182, 199, 202, 203
tetrachords 5, 6, 28, 43, 44, 45, 50, 58, 60, 61, 63, 64, 70, 71, 72, 75, 76, 78, 83, 84, 85, 86, 87, 92, 94, 95, 101, 103, 122–8, 131, 138–42, 145, 153–5, 158, 160, 161, 164, 165–6, 167, 169, 184, 193, 194, 195, 206, 214, 220, 221, 226

262

INDEX

synemmenon 21, 60, 63, 86, 87, 131, 194
Theoger, abbot of St Georgen, bishop of Metz 29, 34–7, 39, 47, 57, 93, 94, 205, 218, 219
Boethius and 58
Guido of Arezzo and 86–8, 90, 93
monochord 63
Musica
  dating 36
  manuscript tradition 175, 187–92, 194, 195, 199, 206–7, 226
  Platonism 157, 160, 161, 162, 168–9
  species 67, 71
  tetrachords 155
Vita 34–6
William of Hirsau and 35, 36, 37, 67, 86, 155, 160–1, 219
Thiemo, monk of Michelsberg 41, 43 n. 174, 58 n. 16, 95 n. 161
Tiemo, abbot of Michelsberg 40
Tonarius see Bern, abbot of Reichenau
Tonarius Augiensis 52
tonary 3 n. 13, 21, 22, 43, 48, 50, 60, 78 n. 79, 94, 95, 97, 100, 102, 107, 180, 181, 189, 195, 196 n. 82, 198, 200, 203, 204, 207, 210–11, 215 *see also* Bern, abbot of Reichenau; Frutolf, monk and prior of Michelsberg; John; *Tonarius Augiensis*
Trithemius, Johannes 24, 31, 34, 35, 36–7, 45 n. 183
tritone 76, 77, 87, 95, 96
trivium 4, 9, 41, 115, 134, 181

Udalschalk, abbot of Sts Ulrich and Afra in Augsburg 200, 210, 211, 211n. 133
Ulrich, abbot of Zell 24 n. 66, 32

Weingarten, monastery 13
Weissenau, monastery 22
Welf IV, duke of Bavaria 46
Wigold, bishop of Augsburg 45, 46

William, monk of St Emmeram, abbot of Hirsau 2, 3, 12, 13, 15, 29, 31–3, 34, 35, 36, 37, 39, 42, 43, 45, 46, 47, 58, 63, 67, 88, 93, 94, 95 n. 161, 108, 150, 155, 157, 164, 196 n. 82, 218, 219
Aribo and 104, 105, 162–4, 166, 219
Bern of Reichenau and 63, 71, 154, 158
dialectic and 121, 124–5, 139
delay in receiving abbatial benediction 31
Frutolf of Michelsberg and 94, 101–3, 104
Gregorian reform and 13, 32
Guido of Arezzo and 85–7, 90, 140, 141, 201, 222
Herman or Reichenau and 63, 71, 85, 124, 139, 140, 185, 205
Musica 33, 71
  manuscript tradition 110, 175, 198, 203 n. 100, 205–6, 215, 226
  organ pipe measurements 104–5, 206, 207
  Platonism 158, 160–2, 169, 170 n. 119, 224
scholarly reputation 32, 115, 206, 217
Vita 31, 32
works 33
Wolf Anonymous 2, 29, 44–5, 49, 52, 72, 92, 93, 108, 135–8, 140, 199, 205, 208, 220
dating and identity 44–5
Wolferad II, count of Altshausen 24
Wolfgang, bishop of Regensburg, saint 25, 27–8, 30, 218
Wolfger, monk of Prüfening 21, 27, 34, 35, 36, 38, 48
De scriptoribus ecclesiasticis 21, 37, 38
Vita Theogeri 34–7
Wolfram I, abbot of Michelsberg 41
Worms letter collection 16, 118, 119, 120, 121, 158, 173, 219, 223

Zwiefalten, monastery 13

263